D1074070

Self-Determination

The Psychology of Personal Freedom

Self-Determination

The Psychology of Personal Freedom

by
Roberto Zavalloni O.F.M.

Translated by
Virgilio Biasiol O.F.M.
and
Carroll Tageson O.F.M.

BF 621 Z313 1962 glas
Zavalloni, Roberto.
Self-determination : the psych

Computer ID: 10102

**FORVM
BOOKS**

Chicago, Illinois

8997

Self-Determination: The Psychology of Personal Freedom, *copyright* 1962
by Forum Books, Library of Congress Catalog Card Number: 62-20201.
*All rights in this book are reserved. No portion of it may be reproduced
in any manner whatever without permission in writing, except for brief
quotations embodied in critical articles and reviews. For information, address*
FORUM BOOKS, 5045 S. Laflin Street, Chicago, Illinois. *Manufactured in the
United States of America. Designed by Publication Associates. Translation
of* La Liberta Personale: nel quadro della psicologia della condotta umana,
*published by Societa Editrice "Vita E. Pensiero" Piazza S. Ambrogio, 9,
Milan, Italy.* NIHIL OBSTAT: Walter L. Farrell, S.J., *Censor Deputatus*
IMPRIMI POTEST: Terence Cronin O.F.M., *Minister Provincial* IMPRIMATUR:
Geo. J. Casey, Vicar General, *Archdiocese of Chicago.* October 11, 1962.

"Les traductions sont comme les femmes: lorsqu'elles sont belles, elles ne sont pas fidèles, et lorsqu'elles sont fidèles, elles ne sont pas belles."
—H. T. Lowe-Porter

Foreword

I am happy to introduce this volume in which Father Zavalloni, my assistant, dear confrere and collaborator, faces the serious problem of human freedom. This he does with courage and solid scholarship. Psychologists have not treated this problem for the last two decades because they have believed the problem of human freedom to be a philosophical one. A few years ago I dealt with it in a small volume on the physiological and psychological foundations of delinquency and in various other articles in which I examined several facets of the delinquent personality.[1] But in these writings I limited myself to the evaluation of the deterministic or positivistic position held by some criminologists in the study of delinquency. So when Father Zavalloni mentioned his intention of treating the problem of freedom I gave him my wholehearted encouragement. Now I am pleased to introduce this work which I consider a striking contribution, one which both psychologists and philosophers will do well to consider.

Man's freedom as confronted by Father Zavalloni is one aspect —perhaps the central one—of human behavior. The term *behavior,* as well as the terms *conduct, action* or *activity,* although used by authors with divergent leanings, have a common character. This could be called "functional," or better, "operational." The notion of function or operation, nevertheless, has different significance according to these various authors.

From a merely external point of view, the activity which results from a group of motor-glandular reactions means that various acts may terminate in the same manner; they have a similar final result, but there is in them no internal unifying principle. An analysis of internal activity shows clearly that it cannot be specified completely from the external point of view, not even on the basis of its results; different actions can have the same final objective and at the same time a very different meaning. What really specifies an action is its meaning.[2] This presupposes, therefore, a reference to subjective tendencies, because the notion of "effect" is implicit in it, as is also that of "intentionality."

Human behavior is a process which presents two aspects: the *external*, manifested in gestures, movements in space or motor modifications; and the *internal*, which is experienced in activities or operations dependent upon the subject as the center of intentionality. If we consider the first, *behavior* is whatever goes under the name of external physical manifestations capable of objective study from without, as any other object of the material world. The second aspect, *human behavior*, is a psychic fact accessible only to the subject of action, which can be studied from within by means of the introspective method. Because of the existence of the latter, man's external behavior also acquires human meaning and exhibits the character of an original unity.

These two facets of human behavior are indissolubly bound together. There is never merely an external aspect without a corresponding internal one, nor vice versa. Human behavior so conceived, while presenting itself as a physical fact, has its source in the inner life. It follows that in order to study it we must use both objective and introspective methods. Clearly, then, psychology understood as the science of man must be a science *sui generis,* having a double object and a double method.[3] Father Zavalloni in this volume proposes a synthesis of this double source of experience. And he is successful. What path does he follow?

There are two methods of considering psychological data: description and interpretation. *Description* can be tackled according to the double object and double method of psychology; it is therefore the result of an analysis which is objective and at the same time subjective. *Interpretation* can be accomplished by two different methods. First, a phenomenon can be interpreted by enumerating the conditions which determine it. In this case the interpretation is formulated by noting a constant and general correlation between the various facts. Second, a phenomenon can be interpreted as a logical consequence of a group of propositions. The interpretation is then formulated in relation to a theory, so that a particular case is part of a general system and becomes one with the whole.

The facts which psychologists of the most disparate schools examine in their treatises are those of experience, the original data of our experience, both objective and introspective, which constitute the basis of our reflection. Psychological data are the phenomena themselves which the individual experiences and manifests. But the psychologist transcends the actual phenomena and recognizes in man certain traits or permanent abilities. Psychology further transcends these multiple "traits" and considers the whole and entire personality of the subject under study, attempting to define the structure of its dimensions. But since psychology is conceived after the model of the natural sciences, it cannot fully understand the meaning of human activity. The human person is related to the universe by a system of values which transcends a mere phenomenal datum.[4]

The *meaningful* character of action is so essential to human behavior that to deny it is equivalent to changing its very nature.[5] For these reasons I have contended that many psychologists give us dehumanized systems. A conception of psychic phenomena which would ignore their meaning or "significance" is partial and incomplete, even from the scientific point of view. As Hadley Cantril justly noted, value-judgments in the experimental research on psychological facts are intimately and essentially bound up with their conclusions. With some reservation we can agree with Cantril that this objectivity, as it is commonly understood, is both illusory and undesirable.[6] Perhaps this can be said also of other sciences that study man. Their data would become useless and meaningless if value-judgments were missing from them. In such cases science is reduced to a mere collection of facts.[7]

Psychologists cannot completely ignore what characterizes in such an evident way the typical manifestations of man. *In the presence of human freedom, psychology has the right and duty to recognize its limits and to declare its incompetence to solve the problem exhaustively. Psychology must admit the existence of this problem, recognizing the reality of the facts which demand its solution.*[8] It would be an absurd position to ignore free human activity as a phenomenal datum; it would be false scientific objectivity to exclude from psychological scrutiny those volitional processes which play such an important part in man's life. "Will" has become an unfashionable topic in modern psychology. Of course, freedom is enumerated in the organization of those elements which Allport calls "factors of personality"; but for the most part psychologists are reluctant to concede reality to freedom as a specific factor of human conduct, and even more so to admit that it is a legitimate object of psychological research. In many studies of personality, authors do not even discuss voluntary activity.[9] Consequently, personal freedom—if not explicitly denied—is completely ignored. Psychologists theoretically abstain from such a problem; in practice, however, abstention amounts to a genuine denial.

If a psychologist conceives his discipline as the investigation of mental life, he must admit that voluntary manifestations are constitutive elements of a specific and primitive aspect of consciousness. In this regard the following affirmation of E. F. Buchner (written more than fifty years ago) is still valid: "To eliminate volition as a scientific datum would constitute a virtual subversion of the science of psychology, since it developed with the intent of representing the nature of mental activity and the course of its development in terms of real and accessible knowledge of facts."[10]

Still it must be recognized, as a correction and completion of what I have just remarked, that whoever follows the most recent psychological literature will notice that the notion of freedom, until a few years ago considered "antiquated and pre-scientic," is again becoming the subject-matter of study. The following statement of Gardner Murphy is very significant on this point. "At present we do not know very much about what, under this process, is called *will;* but it is reasonable to try to make the concept intelligible. Then, at least, most of the facts become less mysterious in seeing that the principal factors of our conduct are not all open to view at the moment of making a decision."[11]

Carl R. Rogers follows the same trend of thought when he writes that, because of the forces liberated by the process of psychotherapy, we must admit "the presence of a spontaneous force within the organism, which has the capacity of integration and re-direction. This capacity of voluntary control is a force or energy we must take into account in every psychological equation."[12] What is the nature of this "force," this "energy," this activity? It is not as important to list the various meanings given to these ideas as to make precise the terms of the problem.

In everyday language many meanings are attributed to the term *liberty*. Even though they are related to one another they are distinguishable among themselves, so that notable difficulties arise in comprehending them. Some imply physical freedom, moral freedom, politico-social freedom, and so on. We pass from one meaning to another without even noticing it. But when such confusion exists in scientific research, serious consequences follow.[13]

All these multiple ways of presenting freedom betray a rather negative attitude, since they exclude the presence of *something* (I use a vague word intentionally) which can induce the individual to follow one course rather than another. The real challenge is to discover whether these various meanings of freedom presuppose a fundamental concept of a psychological nature—one which is characteristic of man's *personal freedom*. A purely phenomenological definition of this concept might be formulated thus: "personal freedom is marked by a psychic process through which a conscious subject, though influenced in his actions by concrete conditions, is capable of self-determination, without being coerced or determined by the impending action of external and internal forces." Of course a phenomenological definition is not exhaustive, as this is not. It is easy to see that many psychologists, when giving us a definition of human freedom, really present a vision of reality in open contrast with the conception men follow in their daily lives. When a student examines the objective data of psychology and psychiatry, he is amazed at the denial (categorical as well as hasty) of human freedom by a number of eminent authors. This position runs counter to man's universal conviction, based on the experience of all who possess normal psychic functions.

In real life, we say that man *can* and *must choose* his own line of conduct. We believe that he can control himself in such a way that he is to be praised or blamed for his actions. That a rational explanation of individual responsibility can be found only in a correct solution of the problem of personal freedom is obvious. Denial of such liberty would amount to the denial of man's real value, and would in the same act abolish the basis of those human relations which rest on the moral and social order. Without personal freedom, politico-social liberties would be meaningless. Man's liberty, "so cherished by those who lose their lives for it," in that case would be only a grand illusion.

Father Zavalloni began to investigate the problem of freedom when he was confronted with this paradox. He proposed to work toward its clarification. As his point of departure he undertook a complete and systematic examination of the multiple *empirical* data, purposing to arrive at a clear synthetic vision. By "experience" one means that proper to psychologists in their laboratory or clinical research, as well as the empirical experience common to every man in the real conditions of life; the latter insofar as it is an object of systematic inquiry.

An integral study of human freedom also includes the "reflective" experience of the philosophers. They believe that we must transcend the study of phenomena to understand their meaning and value. Father Zavalloni, faithful to the duty of a psychologist, rightly upholds the criteria of scientific objectivity, and so excludes data furnished by philosophical reflection. He leaves to the philosopher the duty of examining the conclusive results of his psychological research and of re-elaborating them into a metaphysical view of the problem.[14]

The notion of personal freedom, the heart of this book, refers in the strictest sense to the concept of *personality,* rather than to the concept of *person.* The first term is psychological, the second philosophical. To keep them distinct permits us to distinguish the field of psychology from that of philosophy in the study of man. It is necessary to recall this distinction if we wish to obtain a precise understanding of the thought contained in this book.

The book is divided into two complementary parts. In the first there is an historical survey of the problem and an analysis of the determining factors of human behavior; next the objective studies and research of modern psychology are examined from their double methodological orientation (experimental and clinical). An essential purpose of the psychological analysis is to discover to what extent the influence of unconscious factors is consistent or inconsistent with the doctrine which defends the liberty and responsibility of those actions which are most typically human. In the second part, the data of experience and the consequences deriving from them for ethico-social life and education are interpreted and evaluated from the theoretical point of view. Man's free conduct is considered not as the product of independent faculties but as the expression of his integral and total personality; not as a phenomenon independent of the motives of will but as immersed in and emergent from the complex motivation of the human person in action.

The two complementary parts—psychological analysis and theoretical evaluation—serve to verify the working hypothesis that a normal man is the conscious and responsible creator of his conduct. We can safely say that this book, in the words of an eminent psychologist, aspires to be "the beginning of a bridge between the determinism which is the only assumption upon which science makes sense, and the auto-determination which is the only basis upon which therapy makes sense."[15] Moreover, the present work makes a positive contribution (to my mind an important one) to the objective study of human behavior in a field which is very fundamental and very often poorly understood. This successful task of revision and integration will allow the formulation of a more realistic, and consequently more exact, conception of man's personal freedom and its concrete manifestations. It will contribute towards the realization of a hope enunciated by Gordon W. Allport, one which corresponds to a common aspiration—"the reconciliation of the human nature that psychologists study and the human nature that they serve."[16]

I repeat what I have said: many psychologists have dehumanized human life. The principal merit of this work is to show that one can be a modern psychologist, can use the most modern techniques, and can at the same time embrace the significance of being free. All—we psychologists first of all—must be grateful to the author for this important achievement. A presentation of psychology with a specifically human countenance permits us to investigate further and to examine at its very deepest level our understanding of man.

Fr. Agostino Gemelli O.F.M.
Director of the Laboratory of Experimental Psychology
The Catholic University of the Sacred Heart
Milan, Italy

FOOTNOTES

[1] A. Gemelli, *La Personalità del Delinquente nei suoi Fondamenti Fisiologici e Psicologici* (Milano: Giuffrè, 1948), 2nd Ed. For other articles cf. Bibliography.

[2] G. De Montepellier, "Qu'est-ce que le Comportement?," in *Rev. Philos. Louvain*, 45 (1947), pp. 50 ff.

[3] Concerning the idea of the double object and double method in psychology, I refer the reader to A. Gemelli and G. Zunini's *Introduzione alla Psicologia* (Milano: Vita e Pensiero, 1949), 2nd Ed.

[4] W. Stern, *General Psychology from the Personalistic Standpoint,* trans. D. Spoerl, (New York: Macmillan, 1938), pp. 70-84; J. Nuttin, *Psychoanalyse et Conception Spiritualiste de l'Homme. Une Théorie Dynamique de la Personalité Normale,* Louvain, Publ. Univ. Louvain (Paris: J. Vrin, 1950), p. 288: I. Caruso, *Psicoanalisi e Sintesi del l'Esistenza. Intorno ai Rapporti fra l'Analisi Piscologica e i valori dell 'Esistenza,* Ital. trans. G. M. Merlo, (Torino: Marietti, 1953), pp. 10-13.

[5] H. Baruk, "Experimental Catatonia and the Problem of Will and Personality," in *J. Nerv. Ment. Dis.,* 110 (1949), p. 233. Viktor E. Frankl in his study "Dimensionen des Menschens," published in *Jb. Psychol. Psychother.,* 1 (1953), pp. 186-194, holds that the two dimensions, the "physical" and the "psychic," do not give us a sufficiently complete picture of man. A third dimension, the "spiritual," must be taken into consideration in every attempt to approach human personality. As long as man's experience is analyzed in terms of the first two dimensions only, his value remains uncertain. Man's human portrait will be complete only on the basis of all three dimensions. The same idea is expressed in other works of the same author. Cf. especially: *The Doctor and the Soul,* transl. from the German by Richard and Clara Winston (New York: Alfred A. Knopf, 1955).

[6] H. Cantril, *The 'Why' of Man's Experience* (New York: Macmillan, 1950), pp. 7 ff. Cf. also the following studies by the same author: "An Inquiry concerning the Characteristics of Man," in *J. Abnorm. Psychol.,* 45 (1950), pp. 490-503; "The Qualities of Being Human," in *Amer. Quart.,* 6 (1954), pp. 3-18. In this last study, among other things, he writes: "Since the outstanding quality of human beings appears to be their capacity to participate in the creation of more satisfying value experiences, it is most important to recognize that in the process of choosing, the top criterion for choice is the probability of greater value satisfaction through actions that follow choice" (p. 12).

[7] "All those who cultivate psychology have a special mission. Since this discipline has the particular function of being the link between science and philosophy, or, since it is at least the extreme limit of scientific research, beyond which philosophic investigation begins, all psychologists are called to bind together into an organic view the results of the sciences that study man, then to present them in their totality as aspects of a living being in whom organic and psychic activity manifest themselves in the works which

are the product of the characteristics of human actions." A. Gemelli, "Le Aporie della Moderna Psicologia," in *Riv. Filos. Neo-Scol.*, 46 (1954), p. 115.

8 The following expressions of Eduard Cros can be accepted: "en nous occupant de phénomènes, nous sommes arrivés a la nécessité de less dépasser pour pouvoir les comprendre; et c'est seulement après ce passage sur le terrain metaphysique que nous avons pu comprendre l'homme et ses actions dans leur ensemble." *La Liberté et la Subconscience. Contribution à l'Étude de la Personnalité Humaine* (Lausanne: Imprimeries Réunies, 1917), pp. 134 f.

9 There are many studies on human personality which could be criticized for not taking into consideration volitional activity. I limit myself to the citation of important books which—from other viewpoints—are of very great value: G. W. Allport, *Personality. A Psychological Interpretation* (New York: Henry Holt and Co., 1938). R. B. Cattell, *Personality. A Systematic, Theoretical and Factual Study* (New York: McGraw-Hill, 1950).

10 E. F. Buchner, "Volition as a Scientific Datum," in *Psychol. Rev.*, 7 (1900), p. 507.

11 G. Murphy, *An Introduction to Psychology* (New York: Harper, 1951), p. 132.

12 C. R. Rogers, "Significant Aspects of Client-Centered Therapy," in *American Psychologist*, 1 (1946), pp. 415-422. The necessity of a return to the old concept of "voluntary action" is affirmed by O. Hobart Mowrer in "Motivation and Neurosis," in *Current Theory and Research in Motivation. A Symposium* (Lincoln, Nebraska: Univ. Nebr. Press, 1953), pp. 162-185. "What we commonly call 'habit' should be designated by the older term, 'voluntary action, " p. 174; "I have argued against the idea of 'habit' and have proposed that we replace it with the older notion of voluntary, consciously directed action," p. 175.

13 A. Lalande, *Vocabulaire Technique et Critique de la Philosophie* (Paris: Press Univ. France, 1951), pp. 558-567; L. De Raeymaeker, "Le Problème de la Liberté Personnelle et le Principe de sa Solution," in *Giorn. Metafis.*, 4 (1949), pp. 581-590.

14 R. Zavalloni has completed this present study with an article in which he takes up the problem of freedom from the philosophical viewpoint. Cf.: "Come si pone il problema della Liberta," in *Antonianum*, 35 (1960), pp. 449-502. *Translators.*

15 The quotation is from a letter sent to Father Zavalloni by Prof. Carl Rogers in whose clinic at the University of Chicago Father Zavalloni worked for nearly a year. Prof. Rogers ordinarily uses the term "self-determination." In this letter to Zavalloni, Rogers apparently used the word "auto-determination" because he was making some comments on an article published by Zavalloni in which the word "auto-determination" had been used. *Translators.*

16 G. W. Allport, *The Nature of Personality. Selected Papers* (Cambridge, Mass.: Addison-Wesley Press, 1950), p. 139.

Contents

PART TWO: THEORETICAL EVALUATION

Translators' Preface

The original of this work first appeared in Italy in 1955 as *La Libertá Personale*. Father Zavalloni began his research for it as a postdoctoral Fullbright scholar in the United States, while studying clinical psychology at Fordham University and therapeutic counseling at the University of Chicago Counseling Center under Dr. Carl R. Rogers. It was completed in Italy in the early fifties when the author worked as an assistant to the late Agostino Gemelli O.F.M., at his experimental laboratory, Catholic University of the Sacred Heart, Milan.

Self-Determination: The Psychology of Freedom, because of its thoroughness, its timeliness, and its unquestioned professional competence, should be most welcome to English-speaking readers. It is our hope that this translation will make it clear why the book was so well received in Italy in 1955. (We were heartened to learn from Father Zavalloni recently that a Spanish translation is currently in progress.)

Father Zavalloni makes accessible, for the first time in a single volume, the results and conclusions of the many and varied psychological studies in the field of volition and personal freedom which had been too long scattered among journals and monographs both here and abroad. In view of the renewed interest being shown in this broad area by psychiatrists and psychologists, the work is invaluable in its scope, inclusiveness, and its thorough bibliography.

But its chief merit lies in its thesis. The translators feel that Father Zavalloni has contributed a most penetrating analysis of the data and has formulated a theory which deserves a careful hearing.

The study begins with an exhaustive survey of the psychological literature, European and American, on volition and personal freedom, from the earliest days of scientific psychology to the most recent experimental and clinical findings, including Zavalloni's own provocative research. It then provides a phenomenological analysis of the feeling and experience of freedom, and concludes with a theory of freedom or self-determination along personalistic lines.

Although the problem of personal freedom cannot be solved by psychology alone, Zavalloni maintains that psychologists are not thereby excused from giving it due consideration. Psychology will never adequately be able to explain man to man, as it hopes to do, until it takes into account the universal human experience and conviction of self-initiated behavior, self-determination, or, in a word, personal freedom.

The translators (a philosopher and a psychologist) feel that psychologists will be agreeably surprised at the rich store of data which Father Zavalloni makes available. It has been too long neglected. We hope that philosophers will find in the not insignificant contributions of empirical research new insights and perhaps a new orientation towards the ultimate solution of the vexing problem of human liberty. Freedom emerges from this study as a workable hypothetical construct, linked not to an isolated, abstract "faculty of the will" so much as to the normally-functioning personality as a whole.

A note about our translation. We have tried to adhere faithfully to the author's careful presentation. Except for the usual idiomatic expressions, our policy has been to give English readers the exact equivalent of Father Zavalloni's ideas. At the same time, we have been most cautious to avoid the excess of "professional jargon" to which this kind of writing so often lends itself. The bibliography has been carefully rechecked, and English translations always indicated where these are available.

We are most grateful to the author for his encouragement and constant cooperation in every phase of this task. We must admit that it was of no little benefit that one of us was a former colleague of Father Zavalloni at the Athenaeum Pontificium Antonianum in Rome. Our bibliographical research was most graciously facilitated by Miss Mary Frances Barrett and Mr. Raphael Brown, who opened so many doors for us at the Library of Congress. To them our warmest thanks. To Mr. Eugene Willging, Head Librarian of the Catholic University of America, and Bro. Henry O.F.M., of the Franciscan Monastery Library in Washington, D. C., we are also most grateful. We are especially indebted to our colleague, the Reverend Benedict McCormick O.F.M., Professor of English at San Luis Rey College, for his patient reading of the manuscript and his professional assistance. We wish also to thank our long-suffering students for their help in typing portions of the manuscript, our superiors for encouraging and promoting the completion of this task, and our publishing editor, the Reverend Mark Hegener O.F.M., for his patient understanding of the inevitable delays involved.

Virgilio R. Biasiol O.F.M.
Carroll F. Tageson O.F.M.
San Luis Rey College, California
1962

PART ONE
Psychological Analysis

CHAPTER I

Historical Survey of the Problem

The problem of freedom of the will holds a predominant place in contemporary thought. Science, which has become more and more fertile in new discoveries, has a special fascination for the contemporary mind. It would seem, therefore, that the solution to this problem belongs not to philosophical reflection but to scientific research. Science — and also psychology, insofar as it is a science — has as its object *phenomena,* considered as bound to one another in a causal sequence. Consequently there appears to be no room for free human activity. Confronted by this new type of attack, moralists are alarmed; a new battle of ideas has materialized in which investigators and thinkers of all disciplines are involved. Philosophers, psychologists, mathematicians, biologists and criminologists are in continual dispute about what was once universally accepted, the nature of man's duty and responsibility. The problem of free choice has become the battleground for all who are dissatisfied with either philosophical speculations or the results of scientific observation.

The following historical survey of the problem of freedom will be limited to its development in the 19th century and to the orientation that it took with the birth of psychology as an independent science. We shall take into consideration therefore the immediate antecedents of the problem and its present status in the more representative contemporary schools of psychology.

3

1. The Immediate Antecedents

Early debates on free choice have served to fuse the problem into precise terms. Contemporaries have enlarged and enriched it with new analyses clarifying the relationships which it has with all branches of knowledge. To note the vicissitudes of this problem before the birth of psychology as an independent science, and to search for the partial truth which is hidden in its various solutions should offer a more solid basis for psychological analysis and theoretical evaluation. The determinists hold universal necessity, the moralists universal freedom; but both fall into the trap of seeing everything from their own viewpoint, without being able to find a common ground for "peaceful coexistence." The contrast between science and free human choice cannot fail to be apparent; the problem, then, is to discover a principle of reconciliation.

Following the development that the concept of freedom underwent during the 19th century, three distinct phases can be observed, even though all three overlap.[1] During the first phase, which extends from Maine de Biran to Comte, the problem of freedom is treated according to the *philosophical method*. This method displays a predominantly psychological orientation in France (Maine de Biran, Jouffroy) and a predominantly metaphysical one in Germany (Fichte, Schelling, Hegel). Very soon, however, the tone changes completely. Philosophy is discredited by new scientific discoveries. A new phase then arises, during which the problem of freedom is treated according to the *scientific method*. Consciousness is mentioned only to demonstrate the illusory character of its testimony. This school of thought believes that science, by postulating universal determinism, necessarily implies the denial of freedom. Comte and J. S. Mill, Bain and Ribot, Schopenhauer and Fouillée along with many others arrive at this conclusion, though by different avenues of approach.[2]

Determinism, however, does not perdure; thought cannot be kept a hostage of necessity. Moreover, the idea of duty, which has its roots in human conscience itself, could not be surrendered. A reaction soon appeared. This reaction receives its inspiration from Kant, though it greatly modified his conception. Duty—the essential condition of the individual and social order—must be saved; but duty implies freedom, which affords us the possibility of satisfying and controlling our impulses. The *moral method,* reviving freedom, followed upon the scientific method which destroyed it.

Let us consider briefly the most characteristic points of the three phases just mentioned.

a. Freedom According to the Philosophical Method

Maine de Biran's starting point in establishing freedom was the testimony of our consciousness. In place of a philosophy of passivity, he substituted a philosophy of activity. The primordial fact of the mental process, which is the origin of our conscious life, had been sought only in *sensation.* This, he knew, was wrong. A philosophy of sensation does not explain science, nor the heterogeneity of physical phenomena, nor personality. If we consider the entire problem from all angles, we can see that two elements are required: something which is seen and something which sees, that is, an object and a subject. There is no subject in the sensistic theory (for example, that of Condillac). We cannot therefore stop at sensism. We must study nature, enter more deeply into the mysteries of the soul, in order to discover what is primordial in the nature of man. This is what Maine de Biran attempted.

If I experience pain, if I am in a hot or cold place, I am the subject of a modification wherein I am passive. But if I move a bodily organ, the phenomenon is of a quite different character: I am active. In addition to the external action there is the internal reaction, the movement that the subject produces by himself. In addition to passivity, there is *effort,* which mingles with all the modifications of our human existence as the principle of action. This effort, according to Maine de Biran, constitutes the beginning of muscular movement, the "source" of our entire empirical knowledge, the last reason of all our intellectual discoveries, the condition of every moral progress; effort is the basis of our activity and, as such, is an immediate datum of consciousness.

It is easy to understand the relationship of this concept of effort to man's freedom. Effort and freedom are identical. Freedom reveals itself to us without any doubt: "Considered in its real essence, freedom is the feeling itself of our activity or of this power of acting, of creating the constitutive effort of the ego."[3] "To be" and "to be free" are the same thing for a person. When we act freely, we not only understand the act in itself, but we also feel we have the power of acting otherwise. This feeling of having the power of acting differently is nothing but the memory of a previous act, where our freedom had already manifested itself.

Freedom does not show itself unless it is joined with the intellectual life. Only then can we arrest the impetus of our desires, evaluate motives, give our preference. But ultimately what is freedom?

According to Maine de Biran, freedom does not consist in the preferential choice of an alternative; the choice is *determined* by the motives. Therefore freedom cannot be anything but the act by which the ego opposes the counterweight of the intelligence to *sensible desires*. We have the power of evoking motives and making them disappear and we have the power of making them our own. That is all. When motives have achieved their final goal, the action is determined. So after establishing these bases of a theory of personal freedom, Maine de Biran returns to the determinism of motives.

To Jouffroy, liberty is not the "power of acting" but the "power of willing."[4] He does not distinguish between resolve and deliberation. To his mind every judgment, every act of reflection and attention, is an effect of freedom. Jouffroy returns to the Socratic principle that the only means man has to discover the laws of nature is to inquire into their finality. To those who made causality the whole basis of knowledge, he answers that the point of departure (at least in psychology) is finality. What we must know first of all is our goal, our end. The only way of determining this is to examine our tendencies. But these tendencies are subject to development. They are not present simultaneously, but show themselves little by little. From this observation derives the very penetrating study Jouffroy makes concerning the development of freedom, particularly from the abstract point of view. Freedom, which from the outset enchains the brute activity of the tendencies, finds its first actualization in well-intended self-interest. Then, in the presence of a nobler and more comprehensive ideal, freedom finds its actualization in the good within us and outside us, by respecting the universal order. This is the ideal of duty. Thus freedom and reason work together simultaneously and follow a parallel line in their common development from pleasure to interest, and from interest to duty. The more we depart from the world of instinctive impulses the more we free ourselves from nature; further, the more freedom will tend to identify itself with the universal order and with the good itself.

Maine de Biran and Jouffroy identified consciousness with action, reducing in this manner the constitutive elements of the ego to unity. The German thinkers proceed even farther along this path when they make the external world of objects identical with the interior world of the ego.[5] Fichte holds an absolute ego which, because of its spontaneous self-knowledge, posits the non-ego. Schelling accepts this idea and advances it even farther towards identification. The ego and the non-ego, the subject and the object, are two opposed and irreducible principles. On one side there is free activity of will; on the other there is reason. Only one step is required to arrive at absolute unity. And Hegel takes this step. In his system reason develops because of a principle of immanence, and everything is reduced to intelligibility. Of a sudden, every notion of will, freedom and contingency disappears. With Hegel we enter a world of absolute necessity.

In Hegel's vision of abstract intellectualism, freedom consists in some kind of "power," and therefore in a "possibility."[6] Liberty to do anything we prefer is a false and illusory freedom because it is tied up with the useful and the contingent. The will is really free only when it is identified with the intelligence and when it prefers to arrive at its own formal universality. Liberty, then, is this universality of thought which determines itself; liberty is actually *infinite*—it produces by itself and for itself its own determinations by which it constructs its own existence. Hegel contends that in this universal will all limitations and each particular individuality are annihilated.

b. Freedom According to the Scientific Method

Each of these authors used the same fundamental point of departure as a solution to the problem: internal experience. But experience does not give adequate results unless with patient labor we know how to search out the various elements comprising it. The philosophical method was based on rather vague data of consciousness and exhausted itself in sterile efforts. It was because of this that the scientific method prevailed and became the model of every philosophical system. Now from an insufficient method let us turn to a method which is erroneous in its application. It attempts to solve a philosophical question with the empirical data of science, and nothing else.

The scientific method pits the idea of liberty against the principles of universal causality and conservation of energy. Three types of determinism were bound to follow. First there is *physical determinism,* where induction is used from the laws of matter to laws of spirit. There is *psycho-physiological determinism,* in which the phenomena of thought are conceived as absolutely passive and therefore subject to the laws of the organism. And there is *psychological determinism,* which uses laws of the spirit to deny freedom.

Physical determinism is represented by A. Comte and J. S. Mill, among others. According to Comte, nothing exists but phenomena. This is demonstrated by the development of the human spirit throughout the centuries. These phenomena are nothing but mechanical motion. Psychology is reduced to physiology. Physiology in turn is but a derivative of physics, which is precisely the science of motion. Thus every phenomenon is motion (in the mechanical sense of the term). Every motion results necessarily from an antecedent and determines a consequent. Comte writes: "The explanation of facts, in the last analysis, is merely the explanation of the relationship and unification between particular phenomena and some universal facts, whose number scientific progress increasingly tends to diminish."[7]

Evidently, no philosophical system is further removed from the idea of freedom than Comte's. It not only denies the existence of any metaphysical principle, but sees only a rigorous mechanism in the experimental facts themselves. Notwithstanding this, Comte pretended to save freedom.

John Stuart Mill adopted the fundamental empirical position, according to which only isolated and particular sensations are the basis of knowledge. He does not admit efficient causes, but only physical causes, among which he lists human freedom. His doctrine is that the will is determined like any other physical cause. Our will is the physical cause of our bodily movements and actions;

but the will can cause these movement and actions only in one way, i.e. necessarily and fatalistically. Just as the weather is the physical cause for water becoming ice, or as a spark is the cause for the explosion of gunpowder, so is the will the cause of our bodily movements and actions. He also maintains that from the motives, character and dispositions of a person, we can predict his future behavior with the same certitude with which we can predict a physical event.[8]

Psycho-physiological determinism rests on the idea that consciousness is merely physiological energy in a symbolic—psychic—form, concealed in the organism. It is in virtue of these physiological or mechanical motions and their psychic parallels that images, ideas, volitions, desires, emotions and thoughts manifest themselves within us. This is the doctrine of reflex-ideas, which has two variants in the theories of Alexander Bain and Theodore Ribot.

For Bain, every conscious content is essentially sensory. Ideas are mere "copies" of sensations. Following a method common among associationists, Bain uses the terms *sentiment* or *feeling* to indicate every content of consciousness. Everything he says concerning voluntary action recalls the idea of the prevalence of uniformity or of law. Free choice is also explained according to the doctrine of the uniformity of causality.[9] Actually there is no question at all of free choice, even though the general description of free movement shows how choice becomes an effect. The idea of liberty accompanying such an experience is pure illusion. What happens really is just an impetus or a relaxation of the motive force inherent in ideas.

Polemicizing against Ward, Bain forcefully rejects the method for proving free choice based on mental experience, a method which appeals to the testimony of an "anti-impulsive effort" or of a power of "sub-control." This would imply the negation of uniformity in human activity and consequently cannot be admitted. If in many cases we must grant a margin of uncertainty, we are forced to do so not by the variability of the effects but because of the impossibility of an accurate calculus.[10]

In his study on the pathology of the will, Theodore Ribot rejects without hesitation "the insoluble problem of free choice." He intends to consider volitions as facts, together with their immediate cause, that is to say the motives which produce them, without inquiring "whether these causes suppose causes in *infinitum* or whether there is not some measure of spontaneity added to them."[11] To Ribot the will can be resolved ultimately into volitions, each of which is a fact in itself, an unstable form of activity, an effect varying in accord with the causes producing it.

Voluntary activity appears to resemble for him a phase of progressive development. This development proceeds from simple reflex action, where tendency towards movement is irresistible, towards the abstract idea where tendency to action is almost nonexistent. The primary character of voluntary movements consists in their capacity for adjustment; but they possess this character in common with the majority of physiological movements, there being only a difference in degree. The adjustment itself is a mere effect deriving its cause not from volitive but from intellectual activity. The intelligence acts as a final cause. It generates a continuous adjustment of internal states to external situations. This implies the choice of proper means to reach the goal.

What, then, is "choice" according to Ribot? Free choice considered in itself is only a practical affirmation, a judgment which actualizes itself. Considered extrinsically and physiologically, free choice presents nothing that will distinguish a theoretical affirmation from volition. The only difference is that the latter expresses itself through an act, and is therefore a judgment put into execution. The psycho-physiological task of deliberation results on one side in a state of consciousness, on the other in a group of movements or inhibitions.

Physical determinism uses induction from matter to spirit; psycho-physiological determinism from physical to mental states. In both cases there is a serious methodological deficiency because the phenomenon of volition is either not studied at all or is studied only with the purpose of assimilating it into mechanical movements.

Psychological determinism places the problem in its proper domain, consciousness, and concentrates all its efforts on the nature of our determinations. Here is the core of the problem. Two kinds of psychological determinism can be distinguished. One considers as motives only those states of consciousness which proceed more or less directly from the object. The second adds to these states of consciousness another element proceeding from the subject itself— liberty. The first of these two theories can be called traditional, because it has always held a place in the history of thought; the second is relatively new and was propounded by A. Fouillée.

The representatives of the first type of psychological determinism reason in the following way. Every man has his own manner of thinking, feeling and acting received from nature, called "character." There is a necessary relationship between the character and the destiny of each individual. One acts as he wishes because he wishes as he is: one cannot escape from himself or from what he is. Circumstances can change, character cannot. The more we know of a person's character the better we will be able to predict his inclination in a given circumstance. In organic nature every effect is a necessary product of two factors: first, the natural and primitive force manifested in it; second, the particular cause which provokes such a manifestation. In man, every action is the necessary outcome of his character and of that motive which played the predominant role. Once these two factors are present, the action invariably follows. This position was defended particularly by Schopenhauer.

Schopenhauer believed that our individual acts are not free because they are the outcome of our character, which is "given," and consequently, fixed. A man can do only what he does in every instance. "The entire empirical course of a man's life," he writes, "is consequently in all its events—small and large—as necessarily predetermined as that of a clock."[12] Man's will always acts in accordance with motives, but the *way* in which he reacts to the motives offered by the intellect is determined by his innate and unchangeable character. Motives produce actions which are in accord with the nature of an individual's character. It is true that knowledge varies, and motives change with it; but different motives do not alter the nature of the will.[13]

A. Fouillée's preoccupation was the reconciliation of morality and universal necessity.[14] He attempted to expand determinism and to show that an intelligent being, even though determined, does not wait for things to occur or not occur. His aim was to establish that "true determinism is not realized passively; it forms itself by itself, it modifies itself by itself."[15] Fouillée introduced a new element which lies at the very root of philosophy: freedom. We are not free but we are convinced that we are. This conception alters the whole perspective. It makes the course of our activity as open, as flexible and alive, as variable and progressive as the reality of free choice itself. In every impression found in consciousness there are the two elements of action and reaction. To external action corresponds an internal reaction called "psychic effort." The effort we are conscious of is born in the depths of our being, and it is accompanied by some sort of explosion within our mental activity. Here Fouillée asks the question, "Is this effort really free, as Maine de Biran contended?" He replies that there is no question here of a positive datum. It is possible, in fact, that the consciousness of willing is mere consciousness of moving. But consciousness of acting does not contain freedom.

For Fouillée freedom implies three main elements—the idea of something actual, the idea of an active power, the idea of something which is over and above empirical conditions. These three ideas are offered to us by our consciousness outside the reality of freedom and lead very naturally to the following conclusions. (1) Circumstances have only a secondary influence upon the will. (2) It is up to us to escape the influence of motives. (3) We can perform the entire act by ourselves; we can, that is, posit an absolute principle. From the fact that I discern in myself the possibility of determining myself without motives or even in opposition to motives, I conclude instinctively that I have the faculty of initiating my own modifications. I am a being with freedom. In other words, we are forever ignoring the deepest, most active part of the determining causes, which is the reason why we believe we can determine ourselves.[16]

The idea of freedom, understood as absolute independence from our activity, never shows itself to better advantage than when the ego acts for a universal motive. From this is derived the notion of a superior, or moral, freedom, expressing the ego's independence in relation to the limits of its own limited individuality. However, the idea of human freedom always implies an area of necessity; if we suppress all limitations, we are left with the idea of absolute freedom.[17]

c. Freedom According to the Ethical Method

A determinism opposed to freedom appeared to be the only possible solution to the problem. But there is something stronger than the postulates of positive science—*moral consciousness,* whose data are as old as the world. They cannot be eradicated because they are based on the very existence of human nature. While determinism was enjoying a triumphal ascendancy and was apparently furnishing a new interpretation of moral life, a new reaction appeared which was destined to grow and prosper. Moralists were saying: if science does not give us freedom, morality presupposes it; freedom must exist because morality is necessary. Thus the problem of freedom, which up to that time had been treated scientifically, was thereafter discussed in accordance with the ethical method. This method owes its origins to the critical movement initiated by Kant. During the nineteenth century the neo-critical school developed, of which Secrétan and Renouvier are the most important representatives.

Secrétan, following Kant, begins with the moral law in establishing freedom.[18] But he has his own peculiar way of understanding this method, and arrives at very different conclusions. Secrétan's doctrine could be summarized substantially in this way: one must believe in freedom because, on the one hand, social duty and customs require it as a "temporal agent," and, on the other, because freedom by no means is opposed to science. To Secrétan's mind, consciousness does not demonstrate our belief in freedom. In itself, the instinctive belief in freedom does not prove more trustworthy than sense-perception, which has us seeing the sun circling the earth. But in the case of the moral law, things are different. From whatever point of view we observe this law, which constitutes the ideal of our behavior, we always observe that it implies freedom. Belief in duty is a universal fact, a "characteristic tendency" of humanity which evolutionary explanations cannot obscure. This is an experimental datum, and we must begin with it. It is impossible for a conviction having its roots in the essence of the human spirit to be totally an illusion. It is at least illogical to cast doubt on such a conviction. Man believes in duty from the simple fact that he is a man. The real value of man is his ethical value. Moreover, duty is a practical necessity of human life.

We *must* believe in duty, and consequently in freedom. To prove the existence of duty is to prove the existence of freedom. Our belief in freedom derives logically from our belief in moral law. This does not imply that freedom is demonstrated, because the moral law itself is not demonstrated. Moral law and free choice are indemonstrable, they are objects of faith. The faith is so deeply rooted in human nature that we *must* admit it. Otherwise we should have to doubt everything. To say that duty and freedom are mere illusions is to deny ourselves, to abdicate our own reason. In nature there is a finality which authorizes the conviction that we are not deceived. We have no clear understanding of things, but we have belief, and belief suffices. With Secrétan the dialectic of faith succeeds the dialectic of practical reason.

Moral law demands freedom. It is in the moral law that we must search for that guiding idea which must preside over the interpretation of nature. Therefore freedom need not justify itself before science, but rather science must face the tribunal of freedom. The duties of each must be interchanged, and we shall possess the truth. It suffices to examine science itself to see that we have no right to apply a method intended for the study of matter to the phenomena of thought. It is not science, but abuse of its method, which creates the conflict between science and freedom.[19]

Like Secrétan, Renouvier belongs to the neo-critical school and remains faithful to Kant's idea, that we must save freedom of the will because we must save morality.[20] Where Secrétan falls into Spinoza's pantheism, Renouvier holds that we must avoid this error and establish the radical independence of phenomena. Liberty to him signifies the power of initiating new chains of phenomena, the faculty of intervening in the course of events. Freedom is essentially an empirical energy. We are free every moment of our lives, we are free in the very source of our intelligence. Liberty cannot be rigorously demonstrated. Consciousness does not testify to liberty either in itself or in liberty's manifestation, which is muscular effort. The reasoning process itself cannot give us the reality of free choice. Such a demonstration would be meaningless because, strictly speaking, freedom does not exist; there are only free phenomena whose proper mark is the lack of a determining antecedent. Free phenomena are essentially independent.

Freedom is an immediate corollary of the moral law; there is nothing in it contradictory to human nature. Taken in itself, freedom, like so many other things, is mysterious, but it is not opposed to reason. The determinists must demonstrate that there is a logical contradiction in the doctrine which maintains that a certain being can modify itself and can choose its own means to achieve its goals. Moreover, liberty not only does not imply contradiction, but experience itself furnishes us continuously with indications of its reality. Far from destroying science, freedom constitutes its point of departure. For, if everything were determined, truth and error would be the same thing. Renouvier confronts the partisans of determinism with a dilemma. Either freedom exists, and then error can be understood, or it does not exist, and then error is determined and therefore true. So only one means exists for distinguishing them, only one avenue remains for the establishment of science, the return to freedom.[21]

In formulating a synthesis of the various ways of solving the problem of freedom as they appear in the immediate antecedents of scientific psychology we have two main trends or orientations: the *deterministic* and the *libertarian* theories. They are two extreme positions which exclude one another. Now it is clear that the solution to the problem cannot be reached by adopting one of these positions and rejecting the other. Rather, it must be sought in the possibility of the coexistence of causality and freedom of human action, these apparently contradictory notions.

2. The Present Status of the Problem of Freedom

The problem of freedom is treated in various ways in the schools of contemporary psychology. It is solved according to principles derived from three different approaches, which we can call the *physiological,* the *experimental* and the *personalistic.* The first is represented by "reflexology" and behaviorism, based exclusively upon the data of external behavior. The second is advanced by experimental psychologists who follow both the objective and the introspective methods. The third is the orientation of dynamic psychologists interested in all manifestations of the individual, both conscious and unconscious.

This tentative classification is certainly arbitrary, ignoring the deep interdependence which exists among the various schools of psychology. However, it seems to the present author that this division represents, generally speaking, three widely varying attitudes concerning the issue of freedom. The first position, excluding testimony from consciousness, denies even the possibility of freedom; the second recognizes the existence of the problem but declares its incompetence to solve it; the third, although implicitly and sometimes incoherently, holds that personal freedom is an essential factor in human behavior. The solution to the problem of freedom, therefore, assumes a more and more positive character as research moves gradually from purely physiological to higher psychic phenomena, and from the latter to the specifically human manifestations of personality.

a. The Orientation of Physiological Psychology

At the end of the nineteenth century the study of human behavior changed its object. Where previously psychology was a science of the spirit, now it acquired a tendency to become a natural science. Human behavior had been understood in relation to thought and will; during this period it was considered an objective process of the organism. The revolution was brought about by some very well-known thinkers.

Lloyd Morgan drew attention to the unscientific character of the anthropomorphic method of animal psychology and dictated his famous canon or law:

> "In no case may we interpret an action as the outcome of the exercise of a higher psychical faculty, if it can be interpreted as the outcome of the exercise of one which stands lower in the psychological scale."[22]

The practical implication of this methodological rule is very extensive because it leads indirectly to a position which simply eliminates the intervention of higher psychological faculties from any type of behavior, human included.

The physiological point of view, already applied to the study of human behavior by Lloyd Morgan and developed by Edward L. Thorndike and Petrovitch Pavlov, was systematized by John B. Watson. Common sense as well as traditional introspective psychology hold that human behavior is an intentional and "free" activity. But common sense holds above all that human behavior is an emanation of personality, a spontaneous activity in which, certainly, exterior data play their part, but in which ideas and personal self-determination are essential factors. It is actually in opposition to these factors, conceived as "intangibles," that the behaviorist attempts to define every type of behavior as a "response" to an external "stimulus."[23] Positive science attempts to explain the relationship between two phenomena as a natural event independent of "intangible" factors, such as the contents of consciousness and free choice. The link between stimulus and response is a mechanism of the physiological order, *the nerve reflex.* The palpable reality of the nervous system takes the place of the mental processes of pre-scientific psychology.

It is evident that there is no room for freedom in such a strict behaviorism.[24] When we fail to recognize a clear distinction between voluntary activity and involuntary responses we deny implicitly the *possibility* of human freedom. If reflex and voluntary behavior were simply identical (as H. Peak endeavored to show), or if human action could be reduced to stimuli and responses alone,[25] then the essential conditions of free activity would no longer exist.

In a recent study, which treats of the relationship between science and human behavior in a strictly behavioristic manner, B. F. Skinner asserts clearly that a truly scientific approach to human behavior is incompatible with the notion of personal freedom. Without hesitation he chooses a positivistic orientation and inclines towards a truly environmental determinism. He proposes the thesis that the principles of "operant conditioning" derived from the observation of animal behavior can explain every aspect of human activity in scientifically acceptable terms, without any reference whatever to such notions as consciousness, volition, introspection, images, feelings or any other psychic entity or function. He writes:

> "The behavior of the individual organism is our 'dependent variable'—the effect for which we are to find the cause. Our 'independent variables'—the causes of behavior—are the external conditions of which external behavior is a function."

The laws which express the relations between the dependent and independent variables—"the cause-and-effect relationships in behavior—are the laws of science. A synthesis of these laws expressed in quantitative terms yields a comprehensive picture of the organism as a behaving system."[26]

Through "operant conditioning," the environment builds all our basic behavioral repertoire. There is no aspect of human activity which cannot be reduced to physical dimensions. A need or desire is a mere condition which results from deprivation and is characterized by a special probability of response. Emotions are not causes, but mere fictitious entities. The only valid cause is the external stimulus. Self-control, the pondering of a solution to a problem, self-consciousness, are all reduced to mere external behavior. Man controls himself exactly as he would control the behavior of another—by manipulating the external variables. In this manner emphasis passes from individual control to the authoritarian control of social behavior.

The theory of reflex reactions is based on the principle of determinism, which, as is commonly known, rejects psychological freedom. Pavlov did not make any scientific attempt to show experimentally how voluntary control develops, but he maintained that every action is inevitably determined by a complex of external and internal stimuli. Olof Kinberg, who defines voluntary actions as "the most complex chain of reflexes," thinks that he has discovered the neurological reason for the conflict of motives postulated by the old psychology. For him,

> "Motives are subjectively nothing but forms of behavior considered possible and experienced as at least somewhat desirable. Thus choice between different motives in the meaning given to the word in everyday psychological language is nothing but an illusionary belief that a person is capable of deciding which of different kinds of behavior experienced as possible and desirable he is going to execute. When the amount of facilitation and inhibition are nearly equal, and the possibilities of the different modes of behavior are experienced as of about the same magnitude, the subject has the feeling of being able to choose anyone of them. This is an illusion."[27]

An attempt to reconcile determinism and freedom was undertaken later by the founder of reflexology. Pavlov writes:

> "We have before us living organisms, man included, producing

a series of activities, manifestations of force. And there is an immediate impression, hard to surmount, of some spontaneity. In the case of man, as an organism, this impression appeals to almost every one as obvious, and an assertion to the contrary seems absurd."[28]

Evidently, there is deeply rooted in the minds of men the conviction that we possess something which is not subject to physical determinism. Pavlov thinks that this question, whose practical importance he cannot ignore, can be discussed scientifically and at the same time in a manner consistent with the common feeling of all men.

Here is Pavlov's tentative solution to the problem. Man is a system which is subject like other systems to the inevitable and uniform laws of nature. But the human system is unique from the viewpoint of contemporary science—it is the highest self-regulating system. From this vantage point the method for investigation of the human is precisely the same as of any other system. The basic difference is that our system is self-regulating in the highest degree. It maintains itself, it repairs itself, readjusts itself by itself. Therefore, Pavlov concludes, "there still remains in life all that is also embraced in the idea of freedom of will with its personal, social and civic responsibility."[29] So for Pavlov the possibility of freedom still exists. But is such a conclusion harmonious with his theory of reflexes? An affirmative answer seems most difficult.

b. The Orientation of Experimental Psychology

The method of analyzing freedom was fervently discussed during the first days of scientific psychology, and it is still being tossed about even now, though generally with negative results. Let us see what view psychologists have taken towards this problem during the last fifty years.

William James upholds the position which was most common among the first psychologists. He says that psychology, if it wishes to become a science, "must, like any other science, postulate a complete determinism . . . and, thus, abstract from free will, without necessarily denying its existence." James is fully aware that such an approach to the problem of free will does not determine whether free choice exists or not, and therefore does not give us the final word on the problem of freedom. Even though it is necessary "to let psychology frankly admit that *for her scientific purposes* determinism may be 'claimed,' " James thinks that "the readjustment can be made. This claim on the part of psychology for determinism has only a relative goal, and it may be crossed by counter-claims on the part of ethics." For James, "the deterministic assumption of psychology is merely provisional and methodological."[30] He simply sidesteps the issue and makes no serious effort to solve it. Recourse to ethics does not enable us to find such a solution. If psychological conditions force us to deny the possibility of acting freely, such freedom cannot be reestablished in another way.

The theory of Edward B. Titchener, propounded shortly after William James, represents the most common orientation of psychologists concerning freedom. With many other well-known psychologists, Titchener relegates the task of solving the conflict between determinism and indeterminism to philosophy. As a psychologist, he believes that "Voluntary and involuntary actions differ not as causeless and caused, but rather in the character of the causality to which they are subject."[31] As we shall see later, this last assertion of Titchener is doubtlessly correct. It also evidences a very common misunderstanding: that to affirm freedom is to deny all causality, whereas in reality we simply have another kind of causality.

Oswald Külpe and his school clearly depart from the evasive answers most experimental psychologists usually present. He introduced volitional activity and particularly the process of free choice as subjects for laboratory experimentation.[32]

Külpe's ideas were followed by very well-known writers of theoretical psychology. Stout, for instance, maintains that a full discussion of freedom involves an examination of the relationship between intelligence and will, between the individual will and the reality of the universe. We must decide whether, psychologically speaking, it is possible for a person to think and to understand consciously and freely. He concludes that

"truth and freedom are ultimately topics for the metaphysicians. As psychologists, we deal not with the ultimate possibility of will and thought, but only with their mode of occurrence as time-processes taking place in the individual mind."[33]

Thus Stout makes it clear that the psychologist, even though he lacks the competence to provide the ultimate reason for freedom, cannot ignore the fact of its concrete manifestation.

Similar to Stout's doctrine is that of John Dewey, the psychologist-educator. He considers the discussion of free will a typical expression of the consequences deriving from the separation of morality and human nature. He believes that men are weary of this futile questioning and are anxious to dismiss it as a metaphysical subtlety. Nevertheless this problem contains within itself the most practical of all moral questions, the nature of freedom and the means of achieving it. According to Dewey, "the significance of the traditional discussion of free will is that it reflects precisely a separation of moral activity from nature and the public life of men. One has to turn from moral theories to the general human struggle for political, economic and religious liberty, for freedom of thought, speech, assemblage and creed, to find the significant reality in the conception of freedom of will." [34]

Confronted with these various positions, we cannot help but observe the truth of William James' statement: "the problem of free will is insoluble on strictly psychological grounds." [35] But this does not mean that we can ignore the issue of freedom as a psychological experience. One can say that ignoring the problem does not necessarily involve the denial of the existence of free will. Practically speaking, however, there is little distinction between ignoring a problem and its actual denial. Consequently, psychology would be blind if it fails to recognize the existence of a problem so vital to human behavior; at the same time, however, psychology recognizes its own incapacity of resolving it completely on a scientific level.

Let us look now at the problem of freedom as it is treated in modern experimental research. It attempts to answer the question: "Is a science of man's free behavior possible?" [36]

The object of psychology is the study of behavior. With regard to man, philosophical experiences attest that behavior is free. Psychology does not intend to limit itself to a sociological description alone, or even to a statistical study of the *modus agendi* men follow in various life-situations. Psychology aims to establish laws of behavior in order to be able to predict—so psychologists affirm—

human progress and development. The question proposed can be formulated thus: Does the psychology of behavior presuppose the denial of our freedom? Again (if the answer is negative), what precise significance can be given to the investigation of those laws of a specific type of behavior considered free under another aspect?

Nuttin rejects as insufficient the solution which presents freedom as a characteristic of only *some* important actions of life, while the quasi-totality of our ordinary behavior would be determined by the internal and external factors of the life-situation. This answer is too vague, and moreover cannot withstand a profound analysis of human activity. As a matter of fact, activity cannot be divided simply into free actions and actions of instinctive or automatic behavior. Rather, analysis shows that freedom is like a fluctuating level, which the spiritual components of our personality establish in the performance of each of our actions.

Psychology of behavior does only this: it isolates certain controllable factors. Our problem, then, can be formulated in precise terms: Is it possible or not scientifically to determine the influence exercised by any particular factor on man's free behavior? This is, in effect, the study of "motivation." To illustrate, let us consider the case of an accidental interruption of an activity. The formal purpose of such an investigation is not to establish whether the activity will inevitably be taken up again; rather the purpose is merely to discover if such an interruption gives rise in the subject to a tendency to take up again and complete the action.

It is very clear that the influence of one factor—in this case, the interruption—upon the repetition of an activity cannot be determined unless we examine whether the subject actually initiates the action again. And here the subject's free decision can play a very important part. This decision will be taken on the basis of tendencies and motives evaluated by the subject. The experimentalist cannot exceed the limits of this statistical outcome. It must be noted that even here the object of research belongs to a field in which the experimentalist does not encounter the free intervention of the subject; in fact, one may or may not repeat the activity in question. But the art of research consists in showing through a detailed control of other factors whether the interruption is of such a nature as to provoke the tendency to complete the action in the consciousness of the individual. This tendency is the effect of a psychological process which, as such, precedes the subject's free decision, and hence cannot be controlled by it. This tendency created in us by the interruption (in the hypothesis that other factors do not impede its actualization) will be precisely one of the motives considered by the subject in his free decision whether or not to begin the action anew. With Nuttin we can conclude that "the experimental research concerning man's free behavior is a formal research into the factors which influence this behavior, and not into the process of deliberation. Thus there is no real opposition between experimental research and the free intervention of the subject." [37]

c. The Orientation of Personalistic Psychology

Common sense as well as the speculative "sciences of the spirit" have always considered man's behavior as the expression of what he is thinking and willing in a specific life-situation. What a man does is explained as a function of the content of his inner life. This is one of the essential forms of man's endeavor to understand what is happening around him. Such endeavor consists in giving "meaning" to single activities and phenomena and in relating them to a specific subjective intention. It is precisely as a function of this type of comprehension that man understands spontaneously the conduct of his fellow men and regulates his educational activity and his social organization.

From the viewpoint of rational motivation—the intention or conscious content of the psychic life—a very penetrating psychological analysis of human behavior has been developed through the centuries. Sociologists, men of letters and moralists, as well as important authors of descriptive psychology (men like Dilthey, Spranger and others), successfully utilized this type of explanation. The "understanding" approach to human behavior is also applied to the scientific study of man. This interpretation, linked with an experimental approach, is used by Kurt Lewin, an objective and influential psychologist. He began his scientific career as an associationist with, however, particular interest in the motives of action and in the modalities of willing.

Lewin's point of departure in volitive and affective psychology is an investigation of the part and weight that the *will* has in human actions and in the fundamental law of association. His original aim was to verify and make more precise the work of Narciss Ach.[38] He dedicated himself vigorously to what can be called in a broad sense the motivation of human behavior. His writings show a steadily growing interest in the problem of the relationship between the will and the functions of memory. His theoretical position did not reach completion until his remarkable publication in 1926 on *Vorsatz, Wille und Bedürfniss,* which indicated clearly the affinities of his thought with Gestalt psychology.[39] One notes in his work an analysis of the intentional behavior of man very similar to the solutions of the traditional psychologists.

When Lewin presents his dynamic theory of personality he re-examines the study of the problem of training from a strictly psychological viewpoint, with special insistence on the problem of freedom.[40] He gives the example of a person who oscillates between various possibilities and desires, and who is incapable at the proper moment of actualizing what seems to him to be the more suitable solution. Schools should teach each individual pupil precisely this: to decide and to choose freely among the various possibilities presented to him. The pupil must form a realistic vision of life, taking responsibility for his actions by exercising his freedom. Only in a life-space which is sufficiently free can the pupil form a clear idea of reality, in a life-space where he has the possibility of choosing his goals according to his needs, and at the same time the possibility of experiencing fully the objective difficulties in his way. Only thus can his capacity to actualize a responsible decision be developed.

"Understanding" psychology, which with Lewin assumed an experimental character, developed in a very peculiar way towards a phenomenological approach. Today, not only philosophical psychology but even clinical psychology and psychiatry accept this approach in various ways. *Daseinsanalyse,* better known as existential psychology, together with similar forms of existential analysis, shows particular interest in the study of human freedom.

Another trend in personalistic psychology made a timely appearance to complete, rather than to contradict, the approach which we have just delineated: depth-psychology. The emphasis which depth-psychology puts on human behavior is that of understanding the whole human person. In its attempt to explain human behavior as a function of motivation and the conscious contents of thought, the earlier psychological approach had succeeded in offering an explanation for a very large area of human activities. But another field of behavior (mainly what is called more or less pathological, irrational and purely affective) was not studied fully. It was considered unimportant in the sense that it did not affect the normal behavior of a rational man. The merit of throwing new light upon this little-explored sector belongs, as is well known, to physicians like Charcot, Janet, Breuer, Freud and others. Depth-psychology discovered the meaning and explanation of unconscious forms of conduct, revealing their origin and their hidden motivation. It extended the domain of knowledge to one of the sectors of human conduct which seemed to be absent as long as conscious motivation alone was being considered. Because of this new inquiry into the deepest, unconscious motivation of human actions, clinical psychology offers particular points of interest in relation to the problem which is the subject of this study.

As a movement within pathology and psychiatry, clinical psychology is a revolt against the dominant somatic tendencies of associationism and reflexology, a revolt against the intellectual emphasis of many psychologists. A clinical psychologist seeks in the personality of his subjects their emotional tone, suggestibility, irrational habits, and weakness of will. The problem of free choice is crucial in psychotherapy, whose aim is to free the patient from that psychopathological state which forced him to seek treatment. (We shall see later whether such an aim can be achieved without the power of volition in the human person; whether the process of liberation presupposes the existence of an initial freedom in man.) The essential point is to determine in what measure the influence of unconscious factors upon human conduct is consistent with the doctrine of man's free and responsible self-determination. Clinical experience will thus throw new light on the problem of personal freedom.

FOOTNOTES

[1] An interesting treatment of the problem of freedom during this period, though marked by a great diversity of interpretation, is offered by the following authors: G. L. Fonsegrive, *Essai sur le Libre Arbitre. Sa Théorie et*

son Histoire (Paris: Alcan, 1896); C. Piat, *La Liberté. I. Historique du Problème au XIX Siècle, II. Le Problème* (Paris: Lethielleux, 1894-1895); G. Calò, *Il Problema della Liberta nel Pensiero Contemporaneo* (Palermo: Sandron, 1907); K. Joel, *Der Freie Wille. Eine Entwicklung in Gesprachen* (Münche: Bruckmann, 1908); G. C. Bussey, *Typical Recent Conceptions of Freedom* (Greenfield, Mass.: 1917). For a bibliography on this problem cf.: J. Fellin, *Die Willensfreiheit. Zur Bibliographie des Problem* (Graz: Leuschner und Lubensky, 1928). A deeper analysis of the classical doctrines on freedom is given by Henry Daudin, *La Liberté de la Volonté. Signification des Doctrines Classiques* (Paris: Press Univ. France, 1950).

[2] E. Tegen, *Moderne Willenstheorien, I. Spencer, Bain, Ribot, Lotze, Sigwart, Wundt; II. Munsterberg, James, Ziehm, Selz* (Uppsala, Ludequist, 1924-1928).

[3] Maine De Biran, *Essais sur Les Fondements* (1859), II, p. 287.

[4] T. Jouffroy, *Le Système de la Nécessité*, IV Leçon.

[5] C. Piat, *op. cit.*, I, pp. 73-96; L. Müffelmann, *Das Problem der Willensfreiheit in der Neusten Deutschen Philosophie* (Leipzig: Barth, 1902); A. Messer, *Das Problem der Willensfreiheit*, 3 Aufl., (Gottingen: Vandenhoek and Ruprecht, 1922); T. Steinbuechel, "Die Philosophische Grundlegung der Katholischen Sittenlehre" in F. Tillmann, *Handbuch der Katholischen Sittenlehre*, Band I, (Düsseldorf: L. Schwann, 1938), pp. 370-382.

[6] C. Fabro, "La Dialettica della Libertà e l'Assoluto" (Per un Confronto fra Hegel e Kierkegaard), in "Kierkegaard e Nietzsche," *Archivio di Filosofia* (Milano-Roma: Bocca, 1953), pp. 45 ff.

[7] A Comte, *Cours de Philosophie Positive* (1830), IV Leçon.

[8] J. Stuart Mill, *A System of Logic* (1851). Cf. Book 6, Chapter II, where Mill treats of freedom and necessity. Cf. J. Rickaby, *Free Will and Four English Philosophers, Hobbes, Locke, Hume and Mill* (London: Burns & Oates, 1906).

[9] A. Bain, *The Emotions and the Will* (New York: Appleton, 1888), pp. 479 ff.; M. Davidson, *The Free Will Controversy* (London: Watts, 1942), pp. 68-75; M. Pradines, *Traité de Psychologie Générale. III, Le Genie Humain: Ses Instruments* (Logos) (Paris: Univ. France, 1948) 2nd ed., pp. 356 ff.

[10] A. Bain, "Dr. Ward on Free Will," in *Mind*, 5 (1880), pp. 116-124.

[11] T. Ribot, *The Diseases of the Will*, trans. J. Fitzgerald, (New York: Humboldt, 1884), pp. 2 ff.

[12] A. Schopenhauer, *Parerga und Paralipomena*, t. VI, pp. 242 ff.

[13] For a critical analysis of Schopenhauer's thought on "character-determinism" cf. Frederick Copleston, *Arthur Schopenhauer, Philosopher of Pessimism* (Andover: Burns Oates & Washbourne, 1946), pp. 142-159.

[14] A. Fouillée, "Les Nouveux Expédiants en Faveur du Libre Arbitre," in *Rev. Philos.*, 14 (1882), pp. 585-617; "L'Homme Automate," in *Rev. Deux Mondes*, 76 (1886), pp. 548 ff.; *La Psychologie des Idées-Forces* (Paris: Alcan: 1893).

15 A. Fouillée, *La Liberté et le Déterminisme* (Paris: Alcan, 1895), II, c. 1.

16 A. Fouillée, "Existence et Dévelopment de la Volonté," in *Rev. Philos.,* Juin 1892.

17 A. Fouillée, *La Liberté et le Déterminisme* (Paris: Alcan, 1895), pp. 11, 90, 223.

18 C. Secrétan, *La Civilisation et la Croyance* (Paris: Alcan, 1887), p. 170: "Le liberté donne un prix à la vie et constitue proprement l'humanité." Cf. A Virieux-Reymond, "La Philosophie de la Liberté de Charles Secrétan et le Portique," in *La Liberté. Actes du IV Congrès des Sociétes de Philosophie de Langue Française,* Neuchâtel, 13-16 Septembre 1949, (Neuchâtel: Baconnière, 1949), pp. 408-411.

19 C. Secrétan, "Evolution et Liberté," in *Rev. Philos.* Aout 1885. Emile Bréhier, commenting on the relationship between freedom and metaphysics, indicates to which trend of thought Secrétan's doctrine is linked: "A la fin du XVIIIe siecle, le problème renaît: la liberté de l'agent, son autonomie est une exigence de la morale; chez Kant déjà la liberté est posée comme une sorte d'absolu qui commande la notion que l'on doit se faire de la structure de l'être; le déterminisme, parce qu'il ne s'applique qu'à des phénomènes, ne contredit pas la liberté. De là, on vient vite a faire de la liberté le caractère foncier de l'être; la liberté humaine, au lieu d'apparaître, ainsi qu'au temps des lumières, comme un résultat de la civilisation propre à l'humanité, est saisie comme un aspect de la liberté universelle. Alors naissent, sous des formes certes très diversesmais jallies d'une même inspiration, des métaphysiques de la liberté, celles de Fichte, de Schelling, de Schopenhauer, de Secrétan. Elles se rattachent toutes à la doctrine de Plotin." Emile Brehier, "Liberté et Métaphysique," in *Rev. Intern. Philos.,* n. 6 (1948), p. 2.

20 C. Renouvier, *Essais de Critique Générale,* t. II: Traité de Psychologie Rationelle. Cf. V. Hansen, "L'Idée de la Liberté chez Kierkegaard et Renouvier," in *Proceedings of the Tenth International Congress of Philosophy* (Amsterdam: North Holland 1949), pp. 1191-1194.

21 This concept was taken into consideration recently by F. Gonseth, *Déterminisme et Libre Arbitre. Entretiens: Les Problèmes de la philosophie des Sciences,* (Neuchâtel: Editions du Griffon, 1947): "Si l'erreur et la vérité de nos jugements étaient également necessaires, il n'y aurait plus d' autonomie de l'ésprit et partant il n'y aurait plus ni vrai ni faux. . . Parmi les conditions nécessaires pour que le vrai soit concevable, il y a l'existence de la liberté, d'une certaine liberté de juger" (p. 111).

22 L. Morgan, *An Introduction to Comparative Psychology* (New York: Scribner's 1901), p. 53. Cf. J. Nuttin, *Tâche, Réussite, et Échec: Théorie de la Conduite Humaine,* Studia Psychologica, (Louvain: Publ. Univ. Louvain, 1953), pp. 11 ff.

23 Cf. for example the following assertions of B. F. Skinner in *The Behavior of Organisms. An Experimental Analysis* (New York: Appleton-

Century, 1938): "The inner organism may in resignation be called free, as in the case of 'free will,' when no further investigation is held to be possible" (p. 3); "Most of the pressure behind the search for eliciting stimuli has been derived from a fear of 'spontaneity' and its implication of freedom. When spontaneity cannot be avoided, the attempt is made to define it in terms of unknown stimuli" (p. 20).

24 J. Maritain, in his article "The Conquest of Freedom," which appeared in R. N. Anshen, *Freedom. Its Meanings* (New York: Harcourt, Brace, 1940), writes on this subject: "Pure empiricists likewise cannot understand the existence of free will, because recognizing only sensory sequences, the idea of causality upon a spirit by itself has no meaning for them . . . To the extent that science reveals dynamic elements working in our physical activity, they see in the mere existence of these elements the proof that the same operate in a necessarily determining fashion which is precisely what remains to be proved" (p. 632).

25 H. Peak, "An Evaluation of the Concepts of Reflex and Voluntary Action," in *Psychol. Rev.*, 40 (1933), p. 87. Cf. E. R. Hilgard, D. G. Marquis, *Conditioning and Learning* (New York: Appleton-Century, 1940), p. 258; F. Irwin, "The Concept of Volition in Experimental Psychology," in F. P. Clarke and M. F. Nahm, *Philosophical Essays in Honor of Edgar Arthur Singer Jr.*, (Philadelphia: University of Philadelphia Press, 1942), pp. 115-137; "Motivation," in H. Helson, *Theoretical Foundations of Psychology* (New York: Van Nostrand, 1951), pp. 201 ff. The distinction between voluntary and involuntary behavior is practically eliminated by B. F. Skinner in *Science and Human Behavior* (New York: Macmillan, 1953), pp. 110-116. He writes: "In the present analysis we cannot distinguish between involuntary and voluntary behavior by raising the issue of who is in control. It does not matter whether behavior is due to a willing individual or a psychic usurper if we dismiss all inner agents of whatever sort." *Ibid.*, p. 111.

26 B. F. Skinner, *op. cit.*, pp. 35, 62-69, 149, 237, 317. Skinner decidedly rejects every internal causal agent and thinks that, if we recognize the existence of "inexorable variables" as the entire basis of human behavior, "we are likely to drop the notion of responsibility altogether and with it the doctrine of free will as an inner causal agent. This may make a great difference in our practices. The doctrine of personal responsibility is associated with certain techniques of controlling responsibility — techniques which generate a sense of responsibility or point out an obligation to society. These techniques are relatively ill-adapted to their purpose." *Ibid.* p. 116.

27 O. Kinberg, "Motive, Choice, Will," in *Theoria*, 14 (1948), pp. 230-231.

28 I. P. Pavlov, "The Reply of a Physiologist to Psychologists," in *Psychol. Rev.*, 39 (1932), p. 102.

29 I. P. Pavlov, *loc. cit.*, p. 127.

30 W. James, *Psychology*, (Cleveland-New York: World Publishing,

1948), p. 461.

31 E. B. Titchener, *An Outline of Psychology* (New York: Macmillan, 1923), pp. 359 ff. Cf. *A Primer of Psychology* (New York: Macmillan, 1925), Rev. Ed., pp. 254 ff.

32 An interesting, though very succinct, historical account of this trend of the Würzburg school and of the men who studied volitional activity—an account which is not easily found in other books—is offered by Henryk Misiak and Virginia H. Staudt in their recent study: *Catholics in Psychology. A Historical Survey.* (New York: McGraw-Hill, 1954), Cf. especially pp. 111-120, 276-278.

33 G. F. Stout, *A Manual of Psychology*, 4th Ed. revised in collaboration with the author by C. A. Mcae (London: University Tutorial Series, 1932), p. 654.

34 J. Dewey, *Human Nature and Conduct. An Introduction to Social Psychology* (New York: Modern Library, 1930), p. 9.

35 W. James, *op. cit.*, p. 455.

36 On this point, cf. the short but penetrating analysis of Joseph Nuttin: "Liberté et Psychologie du Comportement," in *Proceedings of the Tenth International Congress of Philosophy* (Amsterdam: North Holland, 1949), pp. 915-917.

37 *Ibid.*, p. 917. Concerning the experimental study of the possibility of predicting man's free behavior, cf. the following work by the same author: *Tâche, Réussite et Échec: Théorie de la Conduite Humaine.* Studia Psychologica, (Louvain: Publ. Univ. Louvain, 1953), pp. 432 ff.

38 K. Lewin, "Das Problem der Willensmessung und das Grundgesetz der Association," in *Psychol. Forsch.*, 1 (1922), pp. 191-302; 2 (1922), pp. 65-140. Cf. also the important studies published by Lewin's disciples in *Psychologische Forschung,* under the general title, "Untersuchunger zur Handlungs — und Affektpsychologie," from 1926 to 1937.

39 K. Lewin, *Vorsatz, Wille, und Bedfürfnis. Mit Vorbemerkungen über die Psychischen Kräfte und Energien und die Struktur der Seele* (Berlin: Springer, 126), p. 43. With regard to the concept of "total action" in Lewin's thought and his relationship with Gestalt psychology, cf. G. W. Hartmann, *Gestalt Psychology. A Survey of Facts and Principles* (New York: Ronald Press, 1935), pp. 202-240; W. D. Ellis, *A Sourcebook of Gestalt Psychology,* with an Introduction by K. Koffka (London: Routledge & Kegan, 1938), pp. 283-299.

40 K. Lewin, *A Dynamic Theory of Personality. Selected Papers,* trans. D. K. Adams and K. E. Zener, (New York: McGraw-Hill, 1935). Cf. also "Education for Reality," pp. 171-175. Lewin, without holding Montessori's method in its orthodox form, says that this much is certain: "The child in the Montessori school learns precisely and primarily this: to decide himself, and to choose freely between possibilities which are given him. This is doubtless one of the most positive aspects of Montessori education." *Ibid.*, p. 171.

CHAPTER II

The Determinants of Human Behavior

If we are to understand how human behavior actualizes itself, we must uncover and explain the interplay of a whole complex of forces in action. We must unravel the total genetic picture of the functional organization of those energies which intervene therein. These can be classified into two fundamental groups, energies of the physical order and energies of the psychic order. The first constitute the *physiological determinants* of human behavior, reducible to stimuli or conditioned reflexes. The second constitute the *psychological determinants* of behavior, of either conscious or unconscious origin, of individual or social character. *Voluntary self-determination,* even though essentially belonging to psychic determinants, must be considered as a factor specific to human activity, to be classified separately. It can be defined as the power an individual has of acting with conscious intentionality, of producing a true voluntary act, of actualizing a volition in the true meaning of the term.

Voluntary self-determination in this last sense is vastly different from that type of voluntary control which is simply identified with conditioning or its process. Most conditioned responses, established by reinforcement of an already existing neural connection, differ in a significant manner from voluntary behavior. In common language, the "voluntary" character of an action refers to acts which are preceded by an idea or intention, to those acts whose consequences man foresees. These, then, are acts over which the individual has the highest degree of control, acts not determined by a particular environmental situation.

The experimental study of certain elementary forms of action has brought into focus the automatic and direct influence which the "effect" exercises over the development of behavior. The effect previously obtained influences the future conduct of an individual.[1] Thus the question of the effect is linked to the general problem of behavior. This problem is related to the essentially historical character of man's existence, and therefore of human behavior as it develops in "time" as a function of what is produced in the individual himself. The temporal dimension of behavior has two directions, or rather, two phases. It is set in the perspective of the "future" as well as in the perspective of the "past." The future perspective, which introduces into behavior a constructive element, constitutes a line of development which is specifically human.

The development of behavior in relation to the environment is another dimension of behavior, inseparable from the historical one. These two dimensions—*the temporal and the environmental*—together characterize the existential situation of man and synthesize all the determinants of human behavior.

1. Physiological Determinants

The physical world around us and, more directly, our own corporeal world, constitute the sum total of the external and internal stimuli which give rise to the physico-environmental determining factors of human behavior. These "determinants" are as varied as the stimuli themselves. But they can be reduced in the last analysis to a more or less complicated form of the S-R (stimulus-response) relationship through which all human behavior can be explained on the level of physiological reactions.

Psychologists who study the response of the subject in relation to external environmental "stimuli" place emphasis upon the changes that occur progressively in the subject's organism (changes which are due to the repetition of the act and its effect). According to behavioristic theories the future contains nothing creative; it is completely explained as a function of the past. One's preceding behavior and its repercussions upon the organism determine future forms of conduct. The examination of some representative experimental studies which can be considered as characteristic of an entire series will enable us to clarify the problem. The present analysis does not pretend to be exhaustive; it intends only to depict the salient features of the problem.

a. Experimental Research on Conditioning

Among the various experiments dealing with this topic, we must mention first the classical study of C. V. Hudgins. To explain the acquisition of voluntary control, he posits conditioning. In a work published in collaboration with W. S. Hunter, he maintains that what has been called "will" can be conceived, at least partially, in terms of conditioning.[2] The elements of the experiment are as follows. A bright light is thrown upon the eye of the subject; the experimenter measures the contraction of the pupil. The operation is repeated about a hundred times through a mechanism operated by the subject himself. He presses a dynamometer and pronounces the word "contract" when the lamp throws light into his eyes. After this prolonged reinforcement the subject must press the dynamometer and say the word "contract" without the light-stimulus. The pupil contracts just the same. In a second phase the sole pronunciation of the word "contract" makes the pupil contract; whispering of the word or an internal pronunciation of it have a similar effect. The interior world becomes for Hudgins and Hunter the world of muscular activity in the form of conditioned stimuli.

A valid experimental demonstration of the acquisition of voluntary control seems impossible, since the most relevant events are buried deep in the complexity of the nervous system. By reason of their nature they cannot be expressed only in terms of external stimuli and muscular reactions. We must recognize, according to the two above-mentioned authors, that considerable progress must be made before faith in the solution of the venerable problem of volition ceases to be merely an unjustified pretension.[3]

B. F. Skinner has clarified the correspondence that exists to some extent between his own concept of "operant" behavior and what traditionally is considered "voluntary" behavior.[4] It should be pointed out that even though some similarity between the types of behavior can be admitted, the profound differences that exist cannot be ignored. Recently Juliette Boutonier demonstrated with convincing evidence the failure of the "reflexological" attempt to reduce the acquisition of habits and spontaneous behavior to a simple process of conditioning.[5]

Reflexes have received considerable attention from psychologists because the experiments of Pavlov, his school, and his followers in many countries have hinted at the possibility of explaining through conditioned reflexes at least the majority (if not all) of human actions. The conditioned reflex would be not merely one important element of man's activity, but this selfsame activity—the will included—would be reduced in the last analysis to reflexes of greater or less complexity. The *reflex act* thus becomes the universal *model* of every type of activity, from which the voluntary act is distinguished only by virtue of its greater complexity.

Can the idea of the reflex act really explain the voluntary activity of man satisfactorily? This opinion, theoretically justifiable, does not stand up when confronted with factual evidence. Many experienced clinicians and keen observers are struck by the fact that the type of volition which is similar to reflex activity is abnormal volition, and not the normal variety. In the present stage of experimentation, consciousness, reflection, judgment and voluntary determination must be considered as superior psychic attributes, which are not only alien, but also functionally opposed to the reflex properly so-called.

No experiments on conditioned reflexes have considered human behavior as it manifests itself in actual daily life. All explanations of voluntary control based upon conditioned reflexes are inadequate. Let us see now whether we can take a step forward by considering the experimental work of Alexander R. Luria, who maintains that we can control our behavior, and teaches us how we can best obtain, in his opinion, a result.[6]

b. Voluntary Control as Motor-Adjustment

The psychological theories concerning the problem of the control of behavior may be divided into two groups. While a first group of psychologists considers will as a momentous factor in human behavior and the study of it as a problem of psychological science, a second group takes the opposite position. The psychologists who consider themselves positivists, or even materialists, insist that "will-force" should not be a decisive object of psychological investigation. They hold that "will-power" is unable to produce the acts which are attributed to it, and are convinced that behind the subjective process there must flow some definite stimuli impelling the person to this or that reaction, giving only the appearance of spontaneity. The first group of psychologists made the problem one of "will-power," the second, a problem of stimuli. The first group worked with a freely acting subject, the second, with the problem of automata directed by physiological tension.

According to Luria's opinion, the cause of the disagreement is to be sought not only in the difference in the viewpoints and backgrounds of the various authors, but in their extreme oversimplification of the problem. They try to envisage a unified and single process where there exist many intricate mechanisms of the organic apparatus. Luria asserts that:

> "that which had always been counted as will *par excellence* was shown to have nothing to do with will, and the realization of the intention or purpose of the preliminary choice or postuulated problem, approximated so closely in its structure the reflex act that in a detailed analysis they practically merged."[7]

If it is true, as Luria maintains, that the structure of the "willed process" cannot be considered a simple one, we still cannot validly conclude that "its essential part—the existence of the willed act—could not be reckoned as spontaneous, but on the contrary it manifests all the characteristics of an involuntary, automatic mechanism." Luria is wrong in identifying the "willed act" with a pure "spontaneous" act, and in confusing the characteristics of motivation with those of an automatic mechanism. Similarly, if it is true that we often perform automatic acts which are preceded by deliberation and decision, this does not mean that the "willed act is involuntary," nor that the "problem of the will simply consists in the problem of connections."[8] In reality, it is not at all evident that all human activity may be explainable in terms of connections, and neither is it demonstrated that these same connections are, besides being means of expression, also immediate and real causes of all such activity.

Kurt Lewin's research on the mechanisms of the "quasi necessities" (*Quasi Bedürfnisse*) capable of creating artificial tension cannot, according to Luria, explain the process of voluntary action in all its specificity.[9] Notwithstanding this criticism, Luria maintains that Lewin's study puts us on the right path to the solution of the problem. To Luria, the problem of behavior is that of the origin of artificially created stimuli.

In order to explain the nature of the specific stimuli of "willed acts," Luria attempts to follow the investigation along the path of genetic development. The question which arises is this: what is the origin of the establishment of such artificial necessities and of the subsidiary internal stimuli which distinguish human behavior from animal behavior? Luria answers that since man is able to control not only the external world, but his own behavior indirectly by the creation of artificial necessities and stimuli produced artificially especially for the purpose, we have evidence of a cardinal factor in the development of behavior. But is there not good reason to believe that such behavior is a compound product of psychological growth, in the process of which the primitive, natural forms of behavior are complicated by new, acquired forms? This development includes the dynamic mechanism which allows man to master his behavior and automatically to bring about the corresponding reactions.

In Luria's opinion, the voluntary act, as accomplished by the will, is a myth. A normal adult is unable to control his behavior by means of a direct application of his own will-power. Self-control is always the effect of auxiliary artificial stimuli. "Voluntary behavior," Luria asserts, "is the ability to create stimuli and to subordinate them."[10] The control of behavior comes from without. In the first stages of control man creates certain external stimuli, which produce within him definite forms of motor behavior. The primordial voluntary mechanism evidently consists in the external setting, that is, in the production of artificial stimuli which mobilize and direct the natural forces of behavior.

To make concrete his study of the problem of voluntary control of behavior, Luria attempts to demonstrate "how the indirect forms of behavior can attain the same end as was reached through will-power."[11] Now we must ask whether Luria really succeeded in his goal. In his experimental research he deals with abnormal persons, whose behavior could hardly qualify as real, voluntary activity. It follows that his supposed scientific investigations and experiments on voluntary control of behavior are actually an approach to mere automatic processes. Luria himself had to confess that "it is difficult and without avail to use normal human adults whose psychological processes attain a considerable degree of complexity."[12] To explain such complexity is the very problem to be solved, but Luria has simply avoided it. It would be of greater interest to be able to obtain the control of behavior in the case of normal human adults. Until this is done, it will remain to be demonstrated whether the indirect forms of behavior can obtain the same goal which is achieved by the power of will.

In agreement with Luria is Paul T. Young, who is also convinced that the stimulus-response relationship is valid for voluntary as well as for reflex phenomena. An action considered impossible by direct application of will-power is realizable when formulated in words, or when a "motor-set" has been established. The term "set" is used by Young to designate a temporary preparation of the organism. This is established either by verbal instructions or by nonverbal environmental conditions which determine the pattern of activity as well as the configuration of individual conscious experience. The preparatory adjustment exists in the nervous system and sometimes in the muscles as well; for this reason it is called "organic set."[13]

According to Young, the will is the "postural set" or "adjustment" of the individual towards his task. The problem of will is centered around the conditions which lead to the existence of a determining postural set or adjustment. This problem comes up in connection with voluntary attention. It is a common belief that voluntary concentration of attention is capable of increasing the efficiency of school work. The suggestion or command of the teacher to give attention to some particular point or subject may be temporarily effective, but all too often this command merely induces a temporary shift of "bodily adjustment." The phrase "concentrated attention," if it means anything psychologically, signifies a motor-set or adjustment relative to a particular task. The attentive individual is definitely predisposed towards some activity, whereas the inattentive individual for the moment lacks a fixed goal-orientation. The essential factor in voluntary attention is postural set or adjustment.

Once the attentive set has become established, the individual continues along some fixed line of activity, but every now and then there are competing determinations and distracting stimuli which partially obstruct the activity in progress. This inhibition builds up tension which the individual feels as muscular effort; it gives him a sense of exerting will-power, of acting under difficulties. Consequently, we speak of voluntary attention, of deliberation and decision. In this sense the problem of will centers around the mechanism of determining set and postural adjustment.[14]

Faithful to the hypothesis that mind and brain are one and the same, Young identifies the conscious goal or purpose of a human action with the postural set or adjustment of an individual. To clarify the intentional character of behavior, psychologists presupposed the existence of certain determining factors, to which they gave various names. According to Young, to assume a "mental determinant" on the basis of individual conscious experience is just as valid as to assume inner "neural determination" on the basis of objectively observed behavior. It follows that mental and bodily determinants of behavior are identical, both being assumed to explain certain facts of experience. A purpose which persists and a neural or neuromuscular set are one and the same thing.[15]

The identification of "purpose" and "neural set" (as proposed by Young) completely destroys the characteristics proper to free human activity. And what is the basis of this presupposed identity? It is an extremely illogical assumption. Two different types of "determination" of behavior are considered identical because they are believed to be the basis of the explanation of certain facts of experience. Evidently, this is not by any means demonstrated.

c. The Role of the "Confirming Reaction" in Man

The position of Edward L. Thorndike, who prefers to classify himself as an associationist or "connectionist,"[16] is in harmony with the preceding ones. He presents his theory in a form much more elaborate and complicated, and claims to explain even the highest manifestations of human behavior. Thorndike turns to the currents of thought which made of the "law of effect" a "connectionist" theory of behavior, human activity included.

Thorndike's central idea is that mental life can be studied perfectly from without. In this he is the precursor of Watsonian behaviorism, which has as its characteristic the elimination of the cognitive factor from behavior in general. Thorndike is convinced he has found the universal law of all behavior. He is aware that we must elevate the "law of effect" to a scientific level and tie it definitively to the explanation of behavior in terms of stimulus and response. The link which joins "response" to "stimulus" is a mechanism of the physiological order—the *"neurone connection."* The tangible reality of the nervous system substitutes for the mental processes of all previous psychology. The satisfying effect acts not upon a past connection, but on the organism of the subject in such a way that it provokes a certain change by which the organism itself will henceforth react in a determined, preferred manner.

In studying animal behavior, Thorndike really intended from the outset to study human behavior. In an article published in 1908 in honor of William James, Thorndike explains the philosophical implications of his scientific research.[17] In this essay he treats of the "law of effect" in a general way for the first time, applying it also to the understanding of human behavior, hence introducing the latter into the domain of positive science. His theory is distinct from the philosophical materialism of the nineteenth century, because it does not treat of a philosophical system but of an experimental study of behavior and of a positive law. This law, according to Thorndike, would explain man's rational and free behavior in the same manner that physical science explains a natural phenomenon.

In his 1908 article, Thorndike expressly treats the problem of freedom and of free behavior. The problem consists in explaining the tendency toward the satisfying and the "better" effect manifested in human activity. This tendency is conceived in a pragmatic manner according to William James' viewpoint. Freedom of human behavior is merely the possibility of a development towards the satisfying and the better. Thorndike is aware that this tendency in the development of behavior is conceived by the philosophers as linked with indeterminism as far as human behavior is concerned. It is precisely this point that he intends to refute, by demonstrating that this tendency towards the better can be explained perfectly within the framework of the laws of nature governing behavior. It is here that his "law of effect" intervenes. And it is by means of this that the study of man's free behavior can be inserted into the science of natural phenomena, which is regulated by a rigorous determinism.

The author demonstrates his thesis in the following way. One must explain how the tendency toward the better can be understood without presupposing that an effect of some condition in nature be undetermined. To obtain this, Thorndike must apply and generalize his law of effect in such a way that human activity is also included. Because of this law, the satisfying effect strengthens the connection between the preceding situation and the manner of acting which produces this effect, and consequently eliminates the inappropriate response. So the direction and development of behavior toward what gives more satisfaction — the satisfying effect — is explained as a function of this strengthening of the connection. Thorndike says also that the direction and the tendency of man towards a goal are ultimately the mere reinforced physiological connection existing between a given situation and the satisfying effect obtained from past experience. To his way of thinking, psychology in the past was not aware that this direct influence of the effect could be applied to the reasoning process as well as to motor-responses, to thought as well as to behavior.[18]

In later works, published between 1930 and 1940, Thorndike strove to give experimental proof to his theory that human behavior is directed by the automatic influence of the satisfying effect upon the *stimulus-response* bond. His proof consists in demonstrating that behavior develops automatically, that is, without the intervention of cognitive factors, in the direction determined by the satisfying effect already experienced. The examples which he furnishes as proof of his theory are based mainly on unconscious learning. Thorndike deduces from them, prescinding from any intervention of memories and other cognitive representations, that the satisfying effect automatically reinforces the connections between a given event and a specific behavior. Ultimately, these reinforced bonds direct and rule human behavior. Phenomena such as the definition of a goal, or the choice of an alternative, are mere expressions on a conscious level of what is simply a more or less reinforced bond which, as such, rules behavior.

Thorndike speaks also of "spiritual and mental attitudes," "tendencies," "goals," and "free choice." These terms, according to Nuttin, who has made a profound study of Thorndike's theory, signify the mere external connections or bonds between a particular stimulus and a corresponding response.[19] Thorndike himself is particularly careful to explain this clearly in several passages. But at times he seems to overlook it, and uses common terms. For this reason his position at times appears ambiguous. The choice of such and such a goal to be reached, of such and such an object to be used, is merely the effect of a reinforcement of bonds or connections between an actual event and the response which must be achieved. That the subject "tends toward" such and such an object and "chooses" it, is required by the existence of a reinforced bond. Man tends towards the satisfying as towards a goal. This anticipated good is merely the effect of a previous satisfying experience. After all this, it surprises Nuttin that Thorndike should propose in one of his last books that the "confirming reaction," which reinforces the connections, "may be in some cases the act of a free agent, a free will." To that extent a man modifies himself to suit himself and is thus an *"imperium in imperio naturae."*[20] "We have the impression," Nuttin writes, "that here Thorndike, by his willingness to retain all the factors that common sense applies to human behavior, formally contradicts himself." Nuttin finds strange this pretense of Thorndike in opposing man to nature by distinguishing the influence of environment from the action that man exercises upon himself. This action emanates from the satisfying effect, and the fact that an effect satisfies him depends, among other things, on the goals he has in mind. It is in this that liberty consists. "Since Thorndike himself tells us that these goals are as mechanistic in their nature and action as any other thing, we cannot understand how he could call them the effect of a free activity."[21]

Nuttin's observations are undoubtedly logical, if we presuppose that Thorndike's system is so much a finished product and so well defined that it does not admit of the least possibility of further development. Actually, I do not understand how we can accuse Thorndike of a formal contradiction, as Nuttin would like to do; I would prefer to call it an evolution and clarification of one's ideas.

In fact, to prove that Thorndike describes as mechanical the goals that intervene in human behavior, Nuttin quotes some passages that were written in 1931, which is about twelve years before his *William James Lectures*.[22] It is possible that Thorndike, applying himself to studies in social psychology, began to understand that some of his explanations of human behavior were inadequate; it is possible that he conceived the specific determinants of human behavior differently, even though he upheld his general method of explaining behavior. It seems to me that we can find in the latest assertions of Thorndike the introduction of a specifically human factor, which provides the basis for an explanation of free activity. This new factor would be expressly that segment of psychic causality which he defines as "teleological." For Thorndike the "confirming reaction" resolves the conflict between *common-sense teleology* and *mechanistic science*: the first affirms that we do what we do mainly because we actualize our purposes or acquire what we want; the second says that mind is a part of nature really determined by natural forces, like a motor or a radio. Our purposes (albeit teleological) are part of nature; they exist as part of the control previously mentioned or of the regulating apparatus of the mind. They act by means of a natural force exerted by the "confirming reaction."[23] This confirming reaction is proper to animals as well as to man. But there is a type of "confirming reaction" which is specific to man, which, Thorndike writes,

"may be in some cases the act of a free agent, a free will, in the most useful sense of those words. Science hitherto has denied this or seemed to deny it. Science commonly thinks of the modifications in human beings as caused by the environment."

And he adds that environment

"in this very broad sense of the world with all its persons, customs, arts, religions, and sciences, undoubtedly determines most of what occurs in a man and most of what is rewarded. Most, but not all. To some extent a man modifies himself. . . Each person is a center of a creative force, modifying himself more or less to suit himself. A fraction of mental causation is thus teleological."[24]

Man's purposes for the most part determine what satisfies him.

The "confirming reaction" has the property of reinforcing every modifiable connection upon which it acts. It generally reinforces those tendencies which harmonize with man's purposes. The goals of an individual can thus exercise control over human behavior not only in the principal cases of deliberate choice, but also over what he thinks and does at every single moment. The events that human purposes can control directly are the modifiable connections in the brain which the "confirming reaction" can reach and reinforce. Indirectly they determine the ideas man thinks and retains, the acts he repeats, the habits he acquires. Consequently they influence man and his environment very extensively. Thorndike maintains that

> "science as the destroyer of freedom, origination and purposes is a bogey-man imagined by a superficial philosophy. What science does to freedom of the will, the creative elements in human life, and the control of events by human purposes is not to deny them, or even limit them, but to show how they exist and operate in the natural world of reality."[25]

Thorndike's assertion seems to me substantially true if correctly understood; and it is the more interesting since it comes from an experimental psychologist.

At the same time, Thorndike rejects the exaggerations of philosophers who ignore the real conditions of the human person and the unjustifiable position of those psychologists who attempt to deny all the data of human experience not objectively observable. While Thorndike's doctrine strictly speaking is culturally derived from associationist psychology, still it seems to transcend its mechanistic models, insofar as it introduces a "teleological notion" and a "confirming reaction" in specifically human behavior. Thus it leaves the door open for man's personal and social values.

The psychologists whose thought we have just examined explicitly deny man's freedom or refuse to consider it a real factor in human behavior. But the conclusion of this brief survey of the physiological determinants of human behavior leaves the possibility of a positive analysis of the problem unsolved.

2. The Psychological Determinants

The psychic "determinants" which are the subject-matter of our study throughout the following pages can be of conscious and unconscious origin, of an individual or a social character. The empirical data here examined are related to post-hypnotic suggestion and auto-suggestion, psychic determinism in the Freudian system, finalistic determination in the Adlerian system, the cultural determinism of the social psychologists, and finally, the perceptual determinants of behavior.

a. Post-Hypnotic Suggestions and Auto-Suggestion

It is commonly accepted by psychologists that post-hypnotic suggestion can be efficacious over a long period of time. The unanimous results of experimental studies seem to indicate that some post-hypnotic suggestions, such as those described by Bernheim, can remain a hundred per cent effective for a period of at least three months.[26] It is a well-established fact that a hypnotized person, after being awakened from the hypnotic trance and recovering his normal state of consciousness, can perform acts commanded of him during the hypnotic state without being conscious of the command. We must therefore presuppose that the command exists unconsciously in the subject. The representation of the command and the need of performing it arise in consciousness at a certain moment; but the source of the representation continues to be unconscious. The action is carried out as a spontaneous manifestation of personality itself. This seems to have serious consequences for the problem of man's free activity. The real question, then, is this: can such an act, arising as it does from the unconscious, be considered free? Some authors hold that post-hypnotic suggestions are performed irresistibly and necessarily. Beaunis, among others, thinks post-hypnotic suggestion is irresistible; he points out the following characteristic of acts which are performed in a moment far removed from the suggestion. The subject has the impression that the initiative for performing these acts "derives from his own depths; in reality he executes them not under the controlled and reflexive effort which is the source of all our rational actions, but under the influence of the suggestion he received; and this he does with the same necessity as a falling rock." In short, he considers himself free while he is not. According to Beaunis "this is a decisive blow inflicted upon the argument derived from common sense to prove free choice."[27] It is evident that under these circumstances post-hypnotic suggestion deprives man of his responsibility. It is certain that an individual in an hypnotic state who is prodded to commit a crime and really performs it is not responsible.

It seems exact to say that in the case of an abnormal person such as an hysteric or an abulic, hypnotic suggestion produces its effect irresistibly, even though such persons maintain an appearance and feeling of spontaneity and freedom. Beaunis himself posits a condition for the infallible execution of the suggestion. The subject must have been hypnotized often by the same person, which implies a weakening of the power of resistance. In other cases, especially with normal persons, the subject resists the execution of the act since it is opposed by stronger tendencies. Bernheim tells us: "the effect of suggestion in post-hypnotic actions is not absolutely fatalistic; some subjects resist it."[28]

In a recent study on the experimental foundations of hypnotism, Andre M. Weitzenhoffer points out that in the past no aspect of the problem of freedom was more controversial than that of the relationship between volitional activity and hypnosis.[29] A superficial examination of hypnotic phenomena would tend to make us believe that a subject can be induced by the hypnotist to do anything. For many years this was actually a common opinion; it was thought then that the will of the subject in the hypnotic state was entirely under the control of the hypnotist.

There is a point here which is particularly interesting in relation to our present study. Can a person be induced under hypnotic influence to do something contrary to his will? In considering the capacity of the subject to resist hypnotic suggestion we must distinguish clearly between innocuous and harmful suggestions. In the latter case the subject's reaction can be very different. The majority of the investigations concerning the problem of human freedom and hypnosis have taken into consideration situations which imply harmful stimuli. Rowland, Wells, Brenman, Schneck, Watkins,[30] and older experimenters like Bernheim all agree that the subjects in an hypnotic state can be induced to commit crimes and other anti-social acts. On the other side, Bramwell, Schilder and Kauder, Hollander, Hull and Erickson[31] do not agree with their conclusion, since in their experimental studies they found some support for the opposite opinion.

Weitzenhoffer, in his analysis of experimental studies on the potential anti-social use of hypnotism, points out the importance of making a distinction between a *normal situation,* the situation of "being awake," and the *hypnotic situation;* a distinction between what is determined by the hypnotist and what is determined by the subject himself. The behavior of the hypnotized person can be called a function of the stimulus-model as perceived by him in the hypnotic state. If the situation appears acceptable to the subject, socially or in any other way, he can probably be induced to perform anti-social acts. But if the subject perceives the situation as contrary to his own ethical system, it is very improbable that he can be induced to commit criminal acts.[32]

Relying upon an analysis and an evaluation of the experimental data, it seems that we can arrive at these conclusions: (1) whatever the intrinsic compulsive urge of the hypnotic suggestion might be, it cannot of itself induce subjects to commit anti-social acts; (2) subjects can be induced to act criminally if a distortion in the perception of their actions is produced, if the suggestion causes the subjects to perceive their actions as if they were happening in a non-criminal context. From the objective study of suggestibility we can deduce this general picture: hypnosis does not abolish or alter in any way the subject's will in any essential manner; the subject himself behaves in the way most suitable to the total situation defined by a suggested action.

Suggestion exercises over human behavior an influence which is broader, surely, but weaker than that of post-hypnotic effects. The truth of this statement will be clarified if we consider the exact meaning of "suggestion." Charcot found that a person in an hysterical state could also be put into a deep hypnotic trance. He applied this finding to the treatment of hysteria as well as to the interpretation of hypnosis, believing that hypnosis is a peculiar pathological state of the organism. The Nancy school vigorously opposed this point of view, since in their opinion a mitigated form of hypnosis could be induced in almost every normal person; hypnosis is merely a passive and receptive state produced by suggestion. The phrase "there is no hypnosis, but only suggestion" sums up the point of view of this school.

To Bernheim the word "suggestion" has such a broad meaning

that it includes persuasion as well as advice and teaching. In general it signifies any influence of one psyche upon another. "Suggestion" refers to any idea accepted by the intellect through hearing, reading or sight, whether it comes to existence spontaneously, or is awakened by an internal impression, or evoked by circumstances from the outside. Whatever the source of this idea, it constitutes a suggestion. Considered from this point of view, the doctrine of suggestion embraces vast boundaries; it includes all human experience. Suggestion is present in every event; all men act under its influence and differ among themselves only because of different degrees of susceptibility. Bernheim writes:

> "Everything that makes its way into the mind through the senses, everything that happens in consciousness because of the association of ideas through reading and education, everything that is developed by the subject himself, all actions, all convictions of every origin: these constitute suggestion." [33]

Bernheim's thought on suggestion is given fresh attention by the leader of the Nancy School, Emile Coué, and developed further in its teaching on "auto-suggestion." Coué's principal merit, prescribing from his practical work, is that he stresses once again the role of suggestion in man's life. Emphasis is put upon the assimilation of an idea in an unconscious mind. If, for instance, I happen to mention casually to a friend that a book is very interesting, it could be that the idea I caused in the mind of my friend is assimilated by him in a completely unconscious manner, with the result that he buys the book and reads it. This is a typical example of suggestion in the strict sense of the word. Certainly, the idea comes from me, but it makes its way into the mind of my friend, it becomes part of him, is assimilated as his own. Suggestion consists precisely in this influence which leads to action; and it is always *auto-suggestion*. Coué writes: "Suggestion does not indeed exist by itself. It does not and cannot exist, except on the *sine qua non* condition of transforming itself into auto-suggestion in the subject." [34]

Auto-suggestion so understood is essentially a kind of hypnotism directed against ourselves, and is defined as "the influence of the imagination upon the moral and physical being of mankind." The psychological theory upon which auto-suggestion is based is formulated as follows. Our mind determines not only our mental states, our feelings and our emotions, but also the very delicate adjustments and actions of our body. There are many examples of the influence of the mind upon the organism wherein suggestion plays an evident role. Fascination, obsession, and infatuation in its psychological sense are common phenomena. Efforts directed by the will are useless; they serve only to intensify the attention given to the thing we have in mind and reinforce the impossibility of doing what we should do. Only indirect means are successful against obsession and infatuation. To Coué's mind, when imagination and will are in conflict, imagination invariably wins; nothing could be more false than to define the will as "the faculty of freely determining certain acts." [35] Before affirmations of this kind, it is impossible to agree with E. B. Barrett when he writes that "in theory Coué's position is perfectly sound." [36]

Coue thinks that in order to understand the role of auto-suggestion in human life, it is sufficient to realize that "the unconscious self is the grand director of all our functions." Elsewhere he says:

"We possess within us a force of incalculable power, which, when we handle it unconsciously, is often prejudicial to us. If on the contrary we direct it in a conscious and wise manner, it gives us the mastery of ourselves." [37]

We have the right to ask how we can do this, if the unconscious self is the director of all our functions; how can we regulate our activities without presupposing the existence of a will power which is totally independent of the imagination? If we suppose that Coué's absolute law is true (that the will which we so gloriously affirm succumbs always to the imagination), then it is difficult to see how man can derive positive results from this therapeutic method. If Coué's law were true, all human activities could be reduced to mere automatism.

b. Psychic Determinism in the Freudian System

Our entire psychic activity, at least according to the most frequent and explicit assertions of Freud, is determined, unfree. The majority of our psychic acts are unconscious. This unconscious activity determines our conscious life. The end-result of the conflict of instincts within man does not derive from a decision or choice but from a simple difference of intensity. A valid analogy, therefore, that better represents this concept is the parallelogram of forces which is described in treatises of physics. In this way we understand how students of Freudian thought, like Rudolph Allers, can say that "Free-will is indeed a notion which cannot find its place within the system of psycho-analysis."[38]

Freud categorically denies the existence of human freedom. About this there is no doubt. We quote two random passages: "You have an illusion of a psychic freedom within you which you do not want to give up. I regret to say that on this point I find myself in sharpest opposition to your views."[39] In another place Freud speaks of "our suppressed acts of volition which nourish in us the illusion of Free Will."[40] These passages from Freud's works establishing the explicit denial of man's free activity could be multiplied.

It must be pointed out, however, that in Freud's works we can find some concessions, more or less explicit, in favor of freedom, such as the following: "After all, analysis does not set out to abolish the possibility of morbid reactions, but to give the patient's ego *freedom* to choose one way or the other."[41] These affirmations reveal the clear contrast between the theoretical notions of Freud and the practical demands of his therapeutic method. Let us see, as Roland Dalbiez suggests, whether or not Freud brought forth new arguments in favor of psychic determinism against the concept of man's personal freedom.[42]

A fundamental principle of the Freudian system is that certain inadequacies of our psychic functions and certain actions which seemingly are unintentional show themselves to be very well motivated when they undergo psychoanalytic investigation. They appear to be determined by the action of unconscious motives.[43] When we assert that a certain portion of our psychic functioning is inexplicable through intentional ideas, we manifest our ignorance of the determinism in our mental life determinism goes further than we are aware of, Freud believes.

While Freud was preparing a protocol of one of his patients for publication, he paused to consider the fictitious name he should give her in his article. There seemed to be a wide choice, but only one name came to his mind, Dora. He concluded that the exclusiveness in this case was based on strong internal associations. After this example of interpretation of the apparent choice of a name, a similar experiment was repeated with the same result. A man who did not know how to determine a number found the solution readily when his wife named a number which was apparently abitrarily chosen. As a matter of fact, the woman understood very well from which complex her husband's number originated, and chose her own number from the same complex, which was surely common to both, as it dealt in this case with their relative ages. The number that occurred to the man expressed a repressed wish which, fully enunciated, would read: "for a man of thirty-four years of age as I am, only a woman of seventeen would be suitable."

Freud finds that not only names and numbers, but also mental occurrences of different kinds of words, regularly prove on analytical investigation to be very definitely determined.[44] An experience which is typical of the proof offered for this presupposition was told to Freud by one of his patients. One day he was crossing the frontier between France and Spain. While he was on the train, on the railroad-bridge over the Bidasso (the boundary between the two countries), the following words came to him suddenly: "But the soul is already free, floating on a sea of light." Judging by the rhythm, the words must have been a part of some poem, but what it was had escaped his memory entirely. A month or so later, he chanced to find Uhland's poems. He opened the volume and his glance fell on the verse: "but the soul is already free, floating on a sea of light." These were the concluding lines of "The Pilgrim." He read the poem and recalled dimly that he had known it many years before. The setting is Spain, and this seemed to him to be the only relation between the remembered verse and the locale of the railroad journey. But he was only half satisfied with his discovery and so continued to turn the pages of the book mechanically. His eye soon lighted on a poem which bore the title, "Bidassao Bridge."

I have reported these facts concerning the unconscious motivation of names, numbers and words to indicate the type of incidents upon which Freud depends to establish his denial of freedom. These apparently arbitrary selections prove for Freud the hypothesis of an absolute psychic determinism. True, man has a profound conviction of free choice, but this conviction is incompatible with belief in determinism. As far as he can observe, the conviction of freedom does not reveal itself in serious and important decisions; in these we have rather an impression of psychic compulsion. Freud writes:

> "It is in trivial and indifferent decisions that one feels sure that he could just as easily have acted differently, that he acted of his own free will and without any motives."[45]

It is difficult to understand how Freud can deny a universal experience which testifies precisely the opposite of what he says, that is, that freedom actually would appear only in serious and important decisions, while trivial and indifferent decisions become almost automatic. The reason for this fallacy can be found perhaps in the erroneous presupposition that freedom implies the exclusion of all motivation (as appears in the passage just quoted). In the last analysis, when the Freudian school rejects freedom, it bases itself entirely upon the success of psychoanalysis, which attempted to establish the existence and nature of determinism in many cases until then inexplicable. There is no doubt that psychoanalysis can claim real successes. But wherein do these successes lead us to modify the essential position of the problem of free will? What psychoanalysis has contrived to explain is such phenomena as the lapsus, dreams, mental disturbances, and neurotic symptoms. But what sensible person has ever dreamed of denying that the facts in question were determined? It is astonishing, Dalbiez points out, that Freud imagines that his opponents could regard the lapsus as a free act.[46] Let us say once and for all that the problem of free will need not be discussed in a field where it does not arise.

The question becomes more interesting when the psychoanalysts apply the analytical method to the study of the normal psyche, and attempt to show that its functioning excludes freedom no less than that of the morbid psyche. Horace W. Frink tells us that on a certain day he was in a state of perplexity about his private affairs. He soon realized that he would not be able to solve his difficulties without having recourse to a friend. The choice lay among three men with whom he was very close. But his choice fell on a fourth individual, a certain X, with whom he was but slightly acquainted. In seeking for the causes of such a strange decision, it came to him that on the night before his visit to X, he had had a dream in which he experienced certain difficulties that represented his present dilemma. To solve it he had invoked the aid of a certain T, who had been a member of his household when Frink was a boy and in whom he had placed great confidence. Frink at once understood why he had had recourse to X in the present situation. He now noticed for the first time that there was a great physical resemblance between X and T, although they were of very different ages. This had led Frink unconsciously to identify X with T, and to feel towards the former the confidence which his childhood experience had legitimately caused him to feel towards the latter.[47]

This story, though told by Frink to explain the phenomenon of "transference" and not to discredit free will, can be used here legitimately as an illustration of how the Freudian school attempts to prove its point: that a choice carried out by a healthy-minded individual is not free, but results from many influences arising from the unconscious. Let us grant that Frink interpreted the unconscious determinants of his attitude towards X correctly. Do facts of this kind adduce anything at all novel against the belief in man's free will? Certainly our past, our stock of previous experiences, our present unconscious world exert—without any need to reappear in the field of consciousness—a great influence on our decisions. The merit of psychoanalysis is that it contributed to the possibility of ascertaining which elements of the past are active in any given case. But this in no way justifies the Freudian denial of freedom. Psychoanalysis contributes only—and this is without doubt a splendid scientific achievement—to the ascertaining of the limits of freedom in concrete situations of human life.

The examples cited can be viewed as cases of "unconscious motivation"—a phenomenon that happens very frequently and, one might even say, in a rather predominant way in daily life. Such examples offer to the majority of psychoanalysts an argument in favor of psychic determinism. As a matter of fact, the general attitude of Horace W. Frink just quoted is strictly deterministic.[48] Similarly deterministic is the position of all those who consider themselves faithful disciples of Freud. A. A. Brill writes:

> "It was not, however, until after I read Freud's 'Psychopathology of Everyday Life' and after analyzing my own faulty acts and dreams, that psychic determinism became clear to me.

For Freud demonstrates clinically what Spinoza formulated in his system of thought."[49]

According to Eric G. Howe, Freud ended, from the psychological point of view, the interminable controversy between liberty and determinism, declaring conclusively that "freedom is an illusion" and that our behavior is determined by forces and experiences of which we are for the most part unconscious.[50] Much of what we consider free seems, after psychoanalytic investigation, merely the last link of a chain whose origin must be sought in the unconscious sources of human action. We are the victims not of an eternal fate, but of an "eternal compulsion," whose origin lies outside our own experience and probably even outside our consciousness.[51]

c. Finalistic Determinism in the Adlerian System

It seems that the emphasis Sigmund Freud put on causality has its counterpart in the emphasis Alfred Adler put on finality. In considering the psychic symptoms of a person, Freud, who interests himself above all in the genesis of these symptoms, stresses the development which failed, the goal which was not reached. But Adler immediately seeks to discover from analysis of the same psychic symptoms the benefits and compensations that accrue to a subject. In this way the Freudian defense-mechanism appears to be integrated almost unconsciously into an efficient teleological system.[52]

If it is true that the Adlerian system has a finalistic tendency which is in opposition to the causal tendency of Freud, it is also true that this does not fully characterize the difference between the two schools. This difference is actually so great that according to Rudolf Allers it is very difficult to call Adler's individual psychology a form of psychoanalysis.[53] Psychoanalysis attempts to interpret human action according to a biological-process model. It considers conscious and voluntary activity a special type of conditioned reflex. Individual psychology, on the other hand, is inclined to explain even reflex actions—certainly those known as instinctive or impulsive—according to a voluntary-set model. The use of the term "will" in individual psychology, insofar as it concerns the fundamental processes of human nature, is the main characteristic differentiating the two systems.

According to Adler's individual psychology, the understanding of human personality consists in detecting the concrete aim that a person pursues in everything that betrays himself. In man finality shows itself under three forms: *biological finality, rational finality* and the so-called *personal finality*. Man is a psycho-physiological being; in him therefore we find finality at the biological as well as at the psychic level. But finality of the psyche is not located only at the conscious level where it constitutes "rational" finality. It is also at a deeper level, the unconscious, where it constitutes "personal" finality. In Adler's system, personal finality dominates and directs, in the last analysis, everything that happens in man, and it is in this perspective that we must understand the meaning of human behavior.

To Adler, the knowledge of reality and personal values is an essential element in the normal and satisfactory development of character. Since this point differs greatly from psychoanalysis, individual psychology affirms in its own way the freedom of the human will. It must be pointed out, however, that this theory is consistent only when there is freedom of choosing among various possibilities. If the cognition of the postulates of reality and the positive values that depend upon these postulates is sufficient to make a person change the course of his life, we can say then that a man is forced to act according to the order of values. Thus the psychic determinism of psychoanalysis apparently is replaced in Adler's individual psychology by some type of intellectual and moral determinism.

A problem arises. How do we reconcile an adequate knowledge of values with freedom of choice? Adler's emphasis upon human responsibility would provide, according to some authors, the key to its solution. I refer here to some recent studies by Oliver and Brackfield. For them, "moral responsibility and Adler's psychology are consubstantial in their essence."[54] Brackfield is surprised that Adler could admit in the human person the existence of something autonomous and imponderable, completely incalculable and unforseeable, which he calls the "response" to all external and internal influences.[55] The Adlerian doctrine emphasizes the autonomous and indeterminate character of man; every individual is responsible before his conscience. Whatever the factors of his psychological, physiological, biological, hereditary, environmental or educational circumstances might be, he is responsible for the use he makes of them and for the way he lives. Heredity, environment, and education are factors which *condition*, but do not *determine* human conduct. Using a classic illustration, we might say that the body is the thesis, the environment is the antithesis, and the unforseeable "response" is the synthesis, an autonomous and creative synthesis.

Adler departed from a strictly organic point of view and arrived at conclusions entirely opposed to his first insight. He soon understood that it is not the organic structure in itself that determines the compensation or the passive adjustment of the individual, but rather the psychic structure. Physical determinism was displaced at first by psychological determinism. But experience showed later that the individual is master of his reactions, that all subjects give autonomous responses, and that such responses, though very strongly conditioned, are never previously determined. Consequently, Adler was persuaded that "conditionism" and not "determinism" characterizes human activity. The individual becomes a person; freedom and moral responsibility reappear.[56]

This is the interpretation of Brackfield. But do this freedom and responsibility really follow from an act of true conscious self-determination? I think not, because of the distinction Adler makes between "rational" finality and "personal" finality.

Adler's position is open undoubtedly to equivocal and even opposite interpretations. His theory of psychic phenomena is not expressed very clearly; in fact, individual psychology claims to give not causal but teleological explanations. The "secret aim" of life, however, is also a type of tropism, a continuous compensation for inferiority complexes. The purpose of education or of psychotherapy would be then to harmonize the individual tendency with that of the community.[57]

Recently, H. L. Ansbacher attempted to demonstrate that Alfred Adler's views on causality and indeterminism agree with some present orientations in personality theory, such as those of Kurt Lewin and Gordon W. Allport.[58] Ansbacher posits as his premise the distinction between *efficient* and *final* causes. The first pertains to the objective, behavioristic trend; the second to the subjective, phenomenological trend. The main difference between these two types of causes resides in the temporal dimension. The efficient cause looks to the past, the final cause towards the future.

In Adler's theory "the objective determinants are mere probabilities, not direct causes."[59] He fully recognizes the efficient causes as sources of probabilities, but is not satisfied with them. He wants to arrive at a psychological theory adequate for each individual case. The understanding and the prediction of a man's behavior are helped greatly when we know his interests, aims and ideals— the final causes that guide him. "Only after we are acquainted with the impelling goal and with a knowledge of its direction, can we attempt to understand its various movements."[60] "The psychic life of man is determined by his goal."[61]

The real problem is to know where and how this last end (which may be totally obscure and generally unconscious) originates. If it is produced by environmental influences we fall into a mechanistic psychology. Even the idea that it could have been produced by hereditary and indigenous causes, such as instincts, is decidedly rejected by Adler. As Neuer points out, Adlerian teleology is not transcendent, introduced into the finalized structure from without; it is an immanent teleology which puts the origin of finality in the finalized structure itself.[62] An immanent teleology implies an extreme indeterminism. "A boy," writes Adler, "works in a realm of freedom with his own creative power."[63]

Ansbacher interprets in an Adlerian sense even the ideas of Allport and Murphy; he identifies indeterminism with final causes, and final causes with the so-called "self-determinism."[64] A viewpoint similar to that of Adler is expressed in a recent study by Cameron. He adopts the principle of final autonomy or as he defines it, "the concept of autonomous reaction."[65] But all this, it seems to me, fails to prove indeterminism, and least of all man's personal freedom. Furthermore, invoking the progress of physical and biological science to affirm the reality of Adlerian indeterminism and finalism is an evident sign of a serious confusion of ideas.[66]

d. Cultural Determinism of the Social Psychologists

Properly speaking, cultural determinants are the social factors of psychic determinism. And socio-cultural determinants must in fact become psychic phenomena in order to exercise some kind of influence on human behavior. What distinguishes these determinants from the psychic factors discussed in the preceding pages is a difference of origin.[67] While Freud, for example, stressed the influence of the internal constitution of the individual, the representatives of the so-called sociological orientation in psychoanalysis stress rather the social and cultural influences; such is the case, for example, with Karen Horney.

Karen Horney represents a new orientation in analytical theory. Her critical re-evaluation of psychoanalytic theories finds its origin in a dissatisfaction with therapeutic results. She found that almost every patient presents problems for which psychoanalysis as commonly accepted does not offer any solution. Her conviction is that psychoanalysis must rid itself of these limitations of its apparatus which derive from the fact that it is an instinctive and genetic psychology. When character traits cannot be explained as the result of instinctive needs, the whole emphasis falls upon the life circumstances that forge one's character. Consequently, the disturbances of every kind which can be noted in human relations become the crucial factor which serves to uncover the genesis of neurotic conflicts. A basically sociological orientation replaces the anatomico-physiological trend of the orthodox psychoanalysts.

What implications do these fundamental changes have for psychoanalysis? When the ego is considered no longer as a simple organ of execution and control of instinctive needs, certain human functions like will power, judgment, and decision-making are reintegrated in their former dignity; moral problems also gain in importance. In such a perspective, the essential aim of the psychoanalytic method is to help the patient to face frankly those moral problems still unsolved in all types of neurosis, and to take the proper attitude toward them.

The position taken by Karen Horney towards psychoanalysis seems to lead her to a revision of Freudian determinism. She writes:

> "The denial that mental faculties may exist in their own right fosters insecurity of judgment."[68]

This would seem to imply the refusal to accept determinism—at least for some of man's faculties. There is no question, however, of denying every kind of determinism inherent in Freud's system. Actually, new determinants of human behavior are brought to light; the psychic processes remain unchanged. Horney regards

"as the most fundamental and most significant of Freud's findings his doctrines that psychic processes are strictly determined, that actions and feelings may be determined by unconscious motivations and that the motivations driving us are emotional forces." [69]

To Karen Horney's mind the hypothesis that psychic processes are as strictly determined as physical processes is a conviction Freud was able to arrive at only after he recognized unconscious processes and their effects. Such a hypothesis proved to be the most constructive, and had to be considered as one of the premises without which analysis could not take a single step in its daily work. Robert P. Knight points out rightly—that Horney "has repudiated the determinism inherent in genetic psychology in favor of the determinism of cultural influences." [70]

The predominant role of culture in determining human behavior was stressed emphatically by the anthropologist Leslie A. White. Many examples are proffered by him to demonstrate how we are culturally determined, even in the most insignificant aspects of our activity. His assumption is that culture forms man totally. [71] He fought vigorously to make an independent science of culture. [72] For this purpose he examined the historical development of the various sciences and applied the results of this research to his own field. His theory of the history of science is that scientific investigation passed, in every case in its history, on one side through animistic, anthropocentric, voluntaristic interpretations, and on the other side, through naturalistic, materialistic and deterministic interpretations. Science emerges, according to White, when naturalism triumphs over animism. From all this it follows that the science of culture must be totally deterministic.

White applies this conclusion rigorously. He opposes strongly those scientists (mainly sociologists) who hold that we could increase our control over civilization if we could increase our knowledge of social phenomena. For example, after making some comments on Gordon W. Allport's suggestions for a research project on international cooperation, White calls the lack of understanding and realism shown by Allport in this case pathetic. And he adds:

> "No amount of development of the social sciences would increase or perfect man's control over civilization by one iota. In the man-culture system, man is the dependent, culture the independent, variable. What man thinks, feels, and does is determined by his culture."[73]

The social psychologist recognizes the existence of forces that function as determinants of behavior. These forces can be "physiological" such as hunger and sex, or "sociological" such as approval and reward. They can be present at birth, or appear when the organism is mature; but in any case they are not the only forces that determine man's behavior. Experience leads the psychologist to recognize other factors at the roots of human activity. C. Kluckhohn, in his *Mirror for Man,* develops this idea: there are periods in the life of nations during which, as in the life of the individual, the external opposing forces are almost equally balanced; it is then that such intangible forces [as 'will" or "belief"] enter into the picture and tip the scale to one side or another.[74]

b. Perceptual Determinants of Behavior

Factors of prime importance in determining man's concrete modes of behavior are his vision and understanding of the "world" in which he lives, his actual situation and position in this world, and the content and the object of his aspirations. It is necessary to keep in mind man's concrete situation in the study of human behavior, because specifically human factors without doubt play a major role in it. Man creates his world and lives in it. His existence consists in being "situated" among things and other men who live for themselves. The term *world* signifies man's psychological and behavioral field, the world of phenomena or the world as he understands it and as it appears to him. The realization that man's existence is "situated" in the world is stressed and put in the first place by psychologists who receive their inspiration from clinical psychology and psychotherapy.[75]

If today personal factors of perception are emphasized so much, it is because a new psychological orientation tends more and more to study man in his unity and in his indivisible totality. Perceptual organization of the outside world is mainly accomplished by means of various environmental and subjective factors. Perception is the result of a "perceptual synthesis" elaborated by the subject. As a matter of fact, the essential factor of perception is that selective process by which we isolate from the formless sum-total of sensory data the representative configurations to which we attribute a personal meaning.[76] Our manner of perceiving is subject to an evolution parallel to the development of personality. The adult's perceptual differentiation seems to be dependent upon a welter of preceding experiences. It is important, therefore, to know what the perceptual determinants of each individual are.

The way a man sees reality is subordinate not only to the ability of his physical equipment to discover stimulating configurations, but also to the modifications which derive from the impact of experience. The characteristics of the physical structure of the perceptual system have the function of "structural determinants"; the modifications in the practical use of this structure have the function of "experiential determinants." These two types of determinants are indissolubly bound together. Every experience modifies the possibility of reaction in the structure; the modified structure then defines specifically the resultant perceptual configuration.

Man's primordial psychic activity consists in building a "world," starting from stimuli which act upon the organism. This is a world which is perceived and known, and as such is an object of meaning. The behavior of man who exists in a world which is known by him in his own way is a response to a situation significative of this world. Thus in studying human behavior we come to emphasize (1) the development of our cognition of the "world," (2) the development of motivation which produces profound modifications of behavior in relation to prior experience and to many other factors. Man everywhere shows essential ways of relating himself to the world, ways necessary to him which can be called his fundamental needs. These fundamental needs are not only "situated" at the level of his physiological relationships, but, on the contrary, specific needs are also manifested in him at the level of his social and spiritual contact with the world.

3. The Volitional Factor as a Determinant

We have seen that the innumerable forces which play a part in man's behavior and determine him to perform a specific act can be grouped into three different categories: (1) physiological forces in relation to the physico-environmental situation; (2) psychological forces realized by subconscious or unconscious subjective dynamisms; (3) conscious forces called by psychologists "voluntary control," "conscious control," or "normal component" in opposition to possible psychopathological components of the individual. We have yet to examine how forces of the third type, the conscious and volitional components, enter into the general picture of the determinants of human behavior.

Man's fate is determined in a notable way by the *genetic constitution* each receives from his parents which is actualized at the very moment of conception. We are what our hereditary patrimony permits us to be. But our constitution represents only a group of possibilities which express themselves during the formation of the individual in his morphological and physiological traits: man's "phenotype." There are traits which have a strictly genetic determination and materialize no matter what the circumstances might be. There are other traits more or less modifiable by the conditions of development and of the environment in which the human being grows. Since heredity gives us only general tendencies, it may well happen that some small differences in the functioning of the psyche (often acquired from earliest infancy) can actualize in the psychic life of an individual certain irreversible habits, ways of looking at the world, and ideas which give to each individual his originality.

It follows that individual psychic development can be understood only in the framework of the psyche itself. "In addition to heredity and environment," writes Emile Guyenot, "it is necessary to introduce a third main factor: the human soul which perceives, elaborates, demonstrates and judges."[77] We cannot ignore the existence of this specifically human force in the normal person, which is confirmed by a profound introspective conviction. Its characteristics are, according to this author, "more certain than any external phenomenon, which we know only by means of our poor sensory impressions and our conceptual elaboration."[78]

The problem of the existence and the efficacy of conscious volitive control is one of the most frequently discussed questions in all psychological literature. In the first part of this chapter we have considered the problem of volitive control at the level of physiological experience. The experimental research there analyzed attempted to substitute the phenomenon of "conditioning" for that of will-power.[79] Let us see now how this problem is faced by some of the foremost authors in psychology; how it is treated in the face of the results of the most typical experimental investigations.

a. Theories of Speculative Psychologists

An examination of the criteria indicated by William McDougall as characteristic of human behavior reveals that these imply a certain degree of freedom. It is this element of free self-determination that McDougall wishes to preserve as the distinctive trait of man's mind. The concept that "will is character in action" and that "conscience is moral character" is fundamental to McDougall's thought.[80] Human behavior, therefore, is essentially *moral* behavior. It is generally admitted that this implies volition in its true sense. In the most complete acts of the will that follow upon an act of deliberation, the intellect cooperates fully with the character of the individual. Volition, then, becomes the expression of the entire personality. It is in this context that McDougall posits the question of freedom. Do we have to accept determinism and deny every freedom, every power of voluntary decision to the will, or can we believe that the course of human events is not strictly determined and forseeable; that human decisions are truly new beginnings from which new lines of determination will derive in the future? McDougall holds the second alternative.

That the human mind, in its more noble efforts, can create new things and think new forms of thought never brought to light before, seems undeniable in view of any great work of genius. Now if the human mind is so highly creative in its more noble forms and efforts, how could we deny its creativity in the moral struggles of the common man? According to McDougall, "the belief in a certain creative power of original determination is a necessity of our moral nature"; on the contrary, "the belief in strict determinism on the part of a man who actively pursues his goals and puts forth strenuous effort is, then, merely a symptom of mental disorder of so mild a nature that there may be good hope of his recovery."[81]

In agreement with McDougall are Sully and Ward, at least concerning the problem of freedom. James Sully writes: "The culminating phase of volitional development is action accompanied by the consciousness of freedom."[82] The process of deliberation gives origin to a particularly vital feeling of "self-determination" in acting; and it is in this act of self-determination that the understanding of the role of consciousness in its more complex and impressive manifestations is developed. The feeling of being able to determine oneself produces a particularly clear understanding of ourselves not only as agents or causes, but also as selectors and determiners of the results of deliberation. It produces, in other words, the *consciousness of freedom* in its most distinctive form. On the other hand, it is evident that psychology cannot "directly settle the point whether the consciousness of freedom, which undoubtedly exists as a psychical fact, guarantees the objective existence of any such thing as a self determining principle. So far the psychological and the philosophical problems are distinct."[83]

When he examines the problem of whether we are free internally, James Ward feels that, when such freedom is held to imply a certain sovereignty or autonomy of self over and against bodily appetites or blind desires, there can obviously be no question of its existence until the level of self-consciousness is reached and maxims or principles of action are possible. The young child, the brute and the imbecile, even when they do as they like, have not this freedom; though they may be said to act *spontaneously,* that is without constraint, they cannot be said to act *voluntarily* in the proper sense of the term. They are "externally free" in the absence of "external constraint," but they are not "internally free."[84]

This internal, positive, creative freedom means the power of self-determination. Man is not completely determined by circumstances; on the contrary, the circumstances themselves receive their specific character from man. Man has in his consciousness a standard of values by which he can estimate the motivating circumstances, and even himself. He can add something to his mental, and even more to his moral stature; he may have an ideal and he can determine *"proprio motu"* to strive to realize it. So in the opinion of Ward, "we may claim on empirical ground to have found that psychological freedom is not only negative, but positive, not mere freedom from constraint but freedom to initiate, to turn circumstances to account, even so to deal with ourselves."[85]

b. Results of Specific Psychological Research

Among the many psychological studies which might be cited as showing the presence of a power of organization and control is an interesting piece of research by Edward Abramowski.[86] In his experimental studies, Abramowski found one subject who manifested very marked psychogalvanometric reactions but was able to inhibit them at will. He determined to make the matter a problem of special investigation, to determine whether or not the ordinary emotional reaction measured by the galvanometer could be inhibited by volitional effort. The sum of the swings of the galvanometer in a series of experiments, in which the subject made no effort to control his emotional reactions, was compared with the swings of a series in which he tried to use all his force of will to remain absolutely calm and indifferent to everything that might happen. The results of Abramowski's investigation demonstrated that some subjects definitely manifested this power of volitional control over their emotional manifestations. And though all did not manifest it at first, there was a definite improvement in this power with practice. This depends on a central power of control which prepares the subject to receive stimuli of any kind with indifference and a resultant lowering of emotivity. Abramowski's experiments point clearly to a power of the human mind to exert some kind of an influence which controls mental life more or less successfully and can even affect the organic reactions to emotional experience. Consequently, these experiments favor a positive solution of the problem of human freedom, insofar as they show the presence of a factor truly essential for man's free activity. But these experiments do not resolve the issue of whether such a power, whose existence was experimentally demonstrated, is really free to exert or not exert the influence of which it is apparently capable.

A further proof of the existence of a controlling factor in mental life was presented by C. A. Richardson. His purpose was to differentiate such control from scholastic achievement and intellectual ability.[87] He utilized a modified form of the "Downey Will-Temperament Tests" into which he introduced such factors as the ability to switch readily from one train of activity to another, the ability to work near the level of maximum capacity, and the power to concentrate on a task until satisfied that it is accomplished. His battery of tests has a low correlation with both intelligence and educational achievement, whereas intelligence and educational achievement are highly correlated.

Let us approach voluntary activity from the viewpoint of factor analysis. This method, by utilizing what Charles E. Spearman defines as "the new incomparably more powerful technique than available previously," introduces once more the volitional factor, which all modern psychologists had abandoned as an entity which escapes experience. And with the volitional factor, impulses, inclinations, instincts and the like return once more as subject-matter for psychological research. With factor analysis, to quote Spearman again:

> "over and above all the impulses, inclinations, instincts, etc., struggling with one another there re-emerges an all-controlling 'will.'A will, too, as Webb shows, the strength of which has high correlations with the representative 'good' qualities." [88]

The technique of factor analysis has been applied to a series of tests which imply volition, with the definite appearance of another general factor, presumably corresponding to the will.

An investigation by Edward Webb on the relationship between intelligence and character based on the factor analysis of mental life led to the discovery of a voluntary factor.[89] This new factor underlies various personality traits which demand from the individual an active control of his behavior. Charles E. Spearman considers this finding of Webb his most important discovery. Together with the general intelligence factor "G" (Spearman's "G" factor) a second factor of wide generality exists: factor "W" (Webb's will factor). Factor "W" is prominent on the character side of mental activity; it may be taken as "consistency of action resulting from deliberate volition or will." [90]

An attempt to make a factor analysis of character was carried out by Rose McDonough through the study and observation of a number of character traits.[91] Fifty students in the seventh and eighth grades served as subjects and, unknown to themselves, were studied as to various traits by three teachers, who then rated the extent to which their behavior was more or less strongly characterized by each of these traits. Thirty-four personality traits were studied. The co-efficients of correlation of these traits were then compared. This study showed that the group of traits centering around the will give rise to a worthwhile, strong, capable personality. If we observe these traits, we see that they suggest that those individuals who possess them have good control over their behavior, whereas in the emotional, unsatisfactory, inadequate type of personality this control seems to be lacking.

Voluntary control appears from this study to be a real factor in mental life. Rose McDonough's "will factor" is evidently the same as that found by Edward Webb. Thus we find evidence for a general factor underlying the following series of traits and functions of the mind: attention, truthfulness, self-control, will, reliability, stability, refinement, religion, response to reproof, attitude towards work, and generosity. The W-factor technique shows that inter-correlations of all these personality traits are accounted for by one and the same thing. It is evident that this is something that has to do with the control of the mind and the behavior of the individual. This can be understood if there is a real ability in the mind of man, a specific faculty, whose function it is to control the flow of thought and behavior.

Spearman emphasizes that Webb's results were followed and illustrated by F. Aveling's no less important discovery ten years later. Aveling established that a voluntary decision, far from being the effect of the conflict of one conation with another, does not contain any feeling of *effort*. This shows that we are dealing with a *sui generis* act which is neither cognitive nor conative. The will-act has its own specific qualities, its *voluntary* character, something that does not belong to any other conscious experience.[92] Spearman's thought could not be better summed up than in the following statement, whose importance cannot be overemphasized:

> "Aveling's decision together with Webb's 'W' would appear to restore to us at last some solid foundation for the ethical distinction between right and wrong. A distinction which, perhaps fortunately, the usual modern writers on character have not seen that they have eliminated."[93]

FOOTNOTES

[1] J. Nuttin, *Tâche, Réussite et Échec: Théorie de la Conduite Humaine, Studia Psychologica.* (Louvain: Publ. Univ. Louvain, 1953), pp. 5 ff.

[2] C. V. Hudgins, "Conditioning and the Voluntary Control of the Pupillary Light Reflex," *J. Gen. Psychol.* (1933), 8, 3-51. W. S. Hunter and C. V. Hudgins, "Voluntary Activity from the Standpoint of Behavior," *J. Gen. Psychol.* (1934), 10, 198-204. The acquisition of voluntary control over the motor-processes was studied experimentally by J. H. Bair in his "Development of Voluntary Control," *Psychol. Rev.* (1901), 8, 474-510, even before the phenomenon of conditioned responses was discovered.

[3] E. R. Hilgard, D. G. Marquis, *Conditioning and Learning* (New York: Appleton-Century, 1940), pp. 276 ff.

[4] B. F. Skinner, *The Behavior of Organisms. An Experimental Analysis* (New York: Appleton-Century, 1938), pp. 112 ff. From a more recent work that was analyzed briefly in the preceding chapter, *Science and Human Behavior* (New York: Macmillan, 1953), it appears evident that there is a deep and irreducible distinction between Skinner's concept of "operant" behavior and the traditional concept of "voluntary" behavior.

[5] J. Boutonier, *Les Défaillances de la Volonté,* 2nd Ed. (Paris: Press Univ. France, 1951), pp. 10-23.

[6] A. R. Luria, *The Nature of Human Conflicts, or Emotion, Conflict, and Will. An Objective Study of Disorganization and Control of Human Behavior,* trans. from Russian by H. Horsley Gantt, (New York: Liveright, 1932), pp. 397-428.

[7] *Ibid.,* pp. 398-399.

[8] *Ibid.,* 399.

[9] K. Lewin, *Vorsatz, Wille and Bedurfnis. Mit Vorbemerkunger uber die Psychischen Krafte und Energien und die Struktur der Seele* (Berlin: Springer, 1926).

[10] A. Luria, *op. cit.,* p. 401.

[11] *Ibid.,* p. 402.

[12] *Ibid.,* p. 403.

[13] P. T. Young, *Motivation of Behavior. The Fundamental Determinants of Human and Animal Activity,* (New York: John Wiley, 1948), p. 195.

[14] *Ibid.,* pp. 213 ff.

[15] *Ibid.,* pp. 185 ff.

[16] R. S. Woodworth, *Contemporary Schools of Psychology,* (New York: Ronald Press Co., 1948), p. 56.

[17] E. L. Thorndike, "A Pragmatic Substitute for Free Will," *Essays Philosophical and Psychological in Honor of William James* (New York-London, Longman's, Green, 1908), pp. 587-610. Cf. J. Nuttin, *Tâche, Réussite et Échec* (1953), pp. 287-295.

[18] E. L. Thorndike, *Ibid.,* p. 608. Cf. also the following assertions: "There is a superstition among philosophers that human thinking is less a part of nature than human action, that independence, creativeness, and trans-

cendency fit mental better than muscular behavior" (*Ibid.*, p. 608). "The modifications in human behavior thus belong to science as truly as the repetitions" (*Ibid.*, p. 610).

19 J. Nuttin, *op. cit.*, p. 291.

20 E. L. Thorndike, *Man and His Works: The William James Lectures 1942-1943* (Cambridge, Mass.: Harvard Univ. Press, 1943), pp. 39 ff.

21 J. Nuttin, *op. cit.*, pp. 293 ff.

22 E. L. Thorndike, *Human Learning* (New York: Appleton-Century, 1931). "Purposes are as mechanical in their nature and action as anything else." P. 122.

23 E. L. Thorndike, *An Experimental Study of Rewards* (New York: Columbia University Press, 1933), p. 67; *Human Nature and the Social Order* (New York: Macmillan, 1940); *Selected Writings* (1949), pp. 16 ff.

24 E. L. Thorndike, *Man and His Works*, pp. 39 ff.

25 E. L. Thorndike, *Human Nature and the Social Order*, pp. 394-395.

26 H. Bernheim, *De La Suggestion*, 2nd Ed. (Paris: Doin, 1888), p. 45 and p. 47. Cf. W. Bergmann, "Hypnose and Willensfreiheit im Lichte der Neureen Forschung," *Frankfurter Zeitgemüsse Broschüre*, Bd. 31 (1912), pp. 129-156; J. Nuttin, *Psychoanalyse et Conception Spiritualiste de l'Homme. Une Théorie Dynamique de la Personalité Normale* (Louvain: Publ. Univ. Louvain; Paris: J. Vrin, 1950), pp. 175 ff.; A. M. Weitzenhoffer, "A Note on the Persistence of Hypnotic Suggestion," *J. Abnorm. Psychol.* (1950), 45, 162; *Hypnotism: An Objective Study in Suggestibility, Mental Health Sciences* (New York: John Wiley, 1953), pp. 101-107.

27 J. S. Morand, *Hypnotisme et Suggestion* (Paris: Garner, 1889), pp. 322 ff.

28 H. Bernheim, *De la Suggestion*, 2nd Ed. (Paris: Doin, 1888), p. 52. Bernheim quotes some interesting cases which show the internal conflict produced in the subject by a suggestion and prove how the subject can evoke sufficient strength to act as he wishes.

29 A. M. Weitzenhoffer, *Hypnotism: An Objective Study in Suggestibility, Mental Health Sciences*, (New York: John Wiley, 1953), pp. 196-206.

30 L. W. Rowland, "Will Hypnotized Persons Try to Harm Themselves or Others?" *J. Abnorm. Soc. Psychol.*, (1939), 34, 114-117; W. R. Wells, "Experiments in the Hypnotic Production of Crimes," *J. Psychol.*, (1941), 11, 63-102; N. Brenman, "Experiments in the Hypnotic Production of Antisocial and Self-injurious Behavior," *Psychiatry* (1942), 5, 49-61; J. M. Schneck, "A Military Offense induced by Hypnosis," *J. Nerv. Ment. Dis.*, (1947), 106, 186-189; J. C. Watkins, "Anti-social Compulsions induced under Hypnotic Trance," *J. Abnorm. Soc. Psychol.* (1947), 42, 256-259.

31 M. J. Bramwel, *Hypnotism: Its History, Practice, and Theory* (Philadelphia; Lippincott, 1930); R. Schilder and O. Kauder, "Hypnosis," *Nerv. Ment. Dis. Monogr. Ser.* (1927), n. 46; B. Hollander, *Methods and Uses of Hypnosis and Self-Hypnosis*, (New York: Macmillan, 1928); C. L. Hull, *Hypnosis and Suggestibility: An Experimental Approach* (New York: Ap-

pleton-Century-Crofts, 1933); M. H. Erickson, "An Experimental Investigation of the Possible Anti-Social Uses of Hypnosis," *Psychiatry* (1939), 2, 391-414.

32 A. M. Weitzenhoffer, "The Production of Anti-Social Acts under Hypnosis," *J. Abnorm. Soc. Psychol.* (1949), 44, 388-397. *Hypnotism: An Objective Study in Suggestibility, Mental Health Sciences* (New York: John Wiley, 1953), pp. 203 ff.

33 H. Bernheim, "De la Peur en Thérapeutique," *Bull. Gen. Ther. Med. Chirur.* (Sept. 30, 1886).

34 E. Coué, *Self Mastery through Conscious Autosuggestion* (New York, American Library Service, 1922), p. 11.

35 *Ibid.*, p. 7.

36 E. B. Barrett, "Couéism in Theory and Practice," *Cath. Mind* (1923), 21, p. 33.

37 E. Coué, *op. cit.*, pp. 25, 34.

38 R. Allers, *The Successful Error: A Critical Study of Freudian Psychoanalysis* (New York: Sheed & Ward, 1940), p. 78.

39 S. Freud, *Introductory Lectures on Psychoanalysis*, trans. Riviere (London: Allen and Unwin, 1921), p. 38.

40 S. Freud, *Collected Papers*, Volumes I-IV, authorized translation under the supervision of Rivière, Vol. V edited by J. Strachey (London: Hogarth Press, 1950), Vol. IV, p. 388.

41 S. Freud, *The Ego and the Id* (London: Hogarth Press, 1927), p. 72. Similar expressions in favor of freedom can be found in the same book by Freud, pp. 75, 79, 80, 82. *Translators.*

42 R. Dalbiez, *Psychoanalytical Methods and the Doctrine of Freud,* trans. F. T. Lindsay, (New York: Longmans, Green, 1941), Vol. II, pp. 295 ff.

43 S. Freud, *The Basic Writings of Sigmund Freud,* trans. A. A. Brill (New York: Modern Libr. 1938), p. 150.

44 Sidney J. Baker's recent study, "The Mathematics of the Unconscious," *J. Clin. Psychopathol.,* (1951), 12, 192-212, starts from Freud's viewpoint on the coincidence of numbers. He analyzes a series of cases taken from Freud, psychoanalytic literature and from his personal experience in order to establish a certain mental ability, unconscious or pre-conscious, to perform mathematical operations in a manner different from the conventional one. These operations imply essentially the selection of a series of numbers, whose sum total is constant and significant in the subject's associative framework. Baker's intricate study raises the problem whether certain actions, insufficiently examined, can reveal something of their mechanical character.

45 S. Freud, *The Basic Writings,* trans. A. A. Brill (New York: Modern Library, 1938), p. 162.

46 S. Freud, *Introductory Lectures on Psychoanalysis,* pp. 37 ff. Cf. R. Dalbiez, *Psychoanalytical Methods and the Doctrine of Freud,* p. 296.

[47] H. W. Frink, *Morbid Fears and Compulsions: Their Psychology and their Psychoanalytic Treatment* (New York: Moffatt, Yard, 1918), pp. 117-119.

[48] *Ibid.*, pp. 19-29.

[49] A. A. Brill, "Determinism in Psychiatry and Psychoanalysis," *Amer. J. Psychiat.* (1938), 95, p. 600.

[50] E. G. Howe, *Motives and Mechanism of the Mind: An Introduction to Psychopathology and Applied Psychology* (London: Lancet, 1931), pp. 59 ff.

[51] For a more positive interpretation of Freudian thought, cf. infra, Chapter Seven of this study.

[52] M. Choisy, "Psychoanalysis and Catholicism," *Cross Currents* (1951), 3, 84.

[53] R. Allers, *The New Psychologies* (New York: Sheed and Ward, 1938), pp. 31 ff.

[54] O. Brackfield, "La Responsabilité Morale dans la Psychologie Individuelle d'Adler," *Psyché* (1951), 59, 554.

[55] O. Brackfield, "El Libre Albedrío como Problema Sociologico," *Rev. Intern. Soc.* (1948), 21, 15. A very positive notion of freedom appears in the following text of Alfred Adler: "The psychotherapeutic treatment has for its object, consequently, to show the patient how in his preparations while awake and occasionally in his dreams, he is always attempting in an habitual manner to fall into the ideal situation of his main path; to show him that first, through negativism and later on his own free will, he can change his life-plan and with it his system and so gain a contest with human society and its logical demands." *The Practice and Theory of Individual Psychology* (New York: Harcourt, Brace, repr. 1946), p. 50.

[56] O. Brackfield, "La Responsabilite dans La Psychologie Individuelle d'Adler," *Loc. cit.*, 556.

[57] I. A. Caruso, *Psicoanalisi e Sintesi dell'Esistenza: Intorno ai Rapporti fra l'Analisi Psicologica e i Valori dell'Esistenza*, Italian trans. G. M. Merlo (Torino: Marietti, 1953), pp. 19 ff. The relationship between the individual and the community in the theory of Adler has been put into focus by Leonard Deutsch in his article, "Von Kausalitat zu Schopferischer Freiheit," *Int. Z. Indiv.-Psychol.*, (1951), 20, 165-174. This article also appeared in English in somewhat modified form, "From Causality to Creative Freedom," *Indian Psychol. Bull.* (1951), 9, 132-142. The various manifestations of nature are examined in the categories of inorganic matter, microorganisms and plants, animals and man, in regard to the direction of their behavior in line with the laws that govern their development. Man shows himself to be capable of elevating himself over natural laws more than any other category, by choosing his own goals and developing creative activity. Beyond that point where human conduct is determined by psychological laws, the science of man loses the power of prediction and becomes a normative discipline. The individual psychology of Adler is the first system of this type. Its ideal

goal is man's internal freedom, his independence from the natural laws that rule his manner of acting. Nature pursues in its creatures, and also in man, egotistical goals; man cannot make his freedom triumph except by developing altruism.

58 H. L. Ansbacher, "Causality and Indeterminism according to Alfred Adler and Some Current American Personality Theories," *Ind. Psychol. Bull.* (1951), 9, 96-107. An issue of the *Indiv. Psychol. Bull.* Vol. 9, fasc. 3-4, (1951) was devoted almost exclusively to the study of the relationship between determinism and indeterminism according to Alfred Adler.

59 A. Adler, "Religion und Individual psychologie," in E. Jahn & A. Adler, *Religion und Individualpsychologie. Eine Prinzipielle Auseinandersetzung über Menschenfuhrung* (Wien, Rolf Passer, 1933), p. 74.

60 A. Adler, *The Practice and Theory of Individual Psychology* (New York: Harcourt, Brace, repr. 1946), p. 244.

61 A. Adler, *Understanding Human Nature* (New York: Permabooks, 1949), p. 19.

62 A. Neurer, "Courage and Discouragement," *Int. J. Indiv. Psychol.* (1936), 2, p. 35.

63 A. Adler, *What Life Should Mean to You* (Boston: Little & Brown, 1931). A thorough treatment of the problem can be found in H. W. Von Sassen, "Causality versus Indeterminism," *Individ. Psych. Bull.* (1951), 9, 125-126. He maintains that the "negative and vague term *indeterminism* is not sufficient." (p. 123.) A brief communication from Mrs. G. Von Sassen, under the same title, states clearly that the solution of the problem of freedom cannot be found in the antimony "causality versus indeterminism," but in the two terms "causality and indeterminism." In this sense we must also understand Paul Fischl's position in "Das Problem der Willensfreiheit in Individualpsychologischer Beleuchtung," *Int. Z. Indiv.-Psychol.* (1951), 20, 175-182.

64 H. L. Ansbacher, "Causality and Indeterminism according to A. Adler," *Loc. Cit.*, p. 105; G. W. Allport, *The Nature of Personality: Selected Papers* (Cambridge, Mass.: Addison-Wesley Press, 1950), p. 108 and p. 163; G. Murphy, *Personality: A Biosocial Approach to Origins and Structure* (New York: Harper, 1947), p. 645.

65 D. E. Cameron, "The Current Transition in the Conception of Science," *Science* (1948), 107, 555.

66 In order to uphold the theory of their master, many followers of Alfred Adler have recourse to the principle of indeterminacy of contemporary science. Cf. in particular I. Neufelf, "Psychological Implications of the Causality-Finality Scheme," *Ind. Psychol. Bull.* (1951), 9, 127-132; R. Dreikurs, "Causality versus Indeterminism," *Indiv. Psychol. Bull.* (1951), 9, 108-117. But Dreikurs falls into the fallacy of believing that man's essential freedom, i.e., his self-determination, implies the *absence* of causality. Doubtless his advice is very sound when he warns us to be wary of falling into the temptation (into which many scientists finalistically oriented do fall) of

making the goals of a person the *determinant causes* of his behavior, while the individual himself is the one who elaborates his own goals and can at the same time change them. (*Ibid.*, p. 116.) But this does not mean that free behavior is absolutely uncaused. Therefore the following conclusion of Dreikurs seems to be very inexact: "The concept of man must remain inadequate as long as we have not shed the concept of a determining causality." (*Ibid.*, p. 117.)

[67] On the various forms of social determinism and their relative influence, cf. Georges Gurvitch, *Déterminismes Sociaux et Liberté Humaine: Vers l'Étude sociologique des Cheminements de la Liberté, Bibliothèque de Sociologie Contemporaine* (Paris: Press Univ. France, 1955). He describes the contribution of the human factor to social structures, but does not tell us very much about the way in which true human freedom (that is, psychological freedom) produces its effects.

[68] K. Horney, *New Ways in Psychoanalysis* (New York: Norton, 1939), p. 187.

[69] *Ibid.*, p. 18.

[70] R. P. Knight, "Determinism, Freedom, and Psychotherapy," *Psychiatry*, (1946), 9, 254.

[71] L. A. White, "Man's Control over Civilization," *Sci. Mo.* (1948), n. 3; B. Stewart, "Some Determinants of Social Change," *J. Soc. Psychol.* (1951), 33, 33-49; E. T. Prothro, "Cultural Determinism: A Challenge to Action Research," *J. Soc. Psychol.* (1952), 35, 205-215.

[72] L. A. White, *The Science of Culture* (New York: Farrar, Straus, 1949). For the cultural and social factor of psychological determinism cf. L. Stengel, "Die Frage der Willensfreiheit von Standpunkt der Kulturbiologie," *Biologie* (1940), 9, 213-221; P. Salzi, "Liberté Psychologique et Vie Collective," *Psyché* (1947), 2, 1414-1422. Cf. also the discussion presided over by Jacques Madule on the topic, "Pression sociologique et Liberté Personelle," in *L'Humanisme et La Grace* (1950), pp. 79-90.

[73] L. A. White, *The Science of Culture* (New York: Farrar, Straus, 1949), pp. 330 ff. G. Allport, "Guide Lines for Research in International Cooperation," *J. Soc. Issues* (1947), 3, 21-37.

[74] C. Kluckholm, *Mirror of Man* (New York: Whittlesey, 1949). According to some authors, truth alone will be able to free man from a dangerous type of cultural slavery. The psychiatrist K. Menninger sums up one of his books in this way. Freud said that the voice of the intelligence is weak but added that it is persistent and, hence, may be expected to assume a larger control over the instincts if it be granted time, encouragement and assistance. His theme is that the recognition of the forces within us constitutes the first step in their control, and that our intelligence should be applied to forestalling or repairing damage rather than to devising more ingenious forms of retaliatory destructiveness. *Love against Hate* (New York: Harcourt, Brace, 1942).

[75] G. S. Klein, "The Personal World Through Perception," in R. R.

Blake and G. V. Ramsey, *Perception: An Approach to Personality* (New York: Ronald Press, 1951), pp. 66-88; C. R. Rogers, "Perceptual Reorganization in Client-Centered Therapy," in Blake and Ramsey, *op. cit.,* pp. 307-327; C. R. Rogers, *Client-Centered Therapy: Its Current Practice, Implications and Theory* (Boston: Houghton Mifflin, 1951), p. 483.

76 A. Gemelli, *Percezione e Personalitá* (1951); R. Zavalloni, "Novi Aspectus Phaenomenologiae Perceptionis," *Antonianum* (1954), 29, 63-88.

77 E. Guyenot, "Hérédité et Liberté," *L'Homme devant la Science* (Neuchâtel: Baconnière, 1952), p. 9.

78 *Ibid.,* p. 97. Cf. Henri Baruk, "Le Problème de la Volonté: Nouvelles données psychophysiologiques," *J. Psychol. Norm. Path.* (1939), 36: "Nous avons vu plus haut combien ce sentiment de liberté peut être fragile, et comment il peut être suspendu par certaines causes somatiques et toxiques. Mais ces causes somatiques ne sont pas les seules à agi. Le fonctionnement de notre esprit, surtout dans le domaine moral, est extremement sensible à l'atmosphere générale qui l'entoure, à l'éducation reçue, aux conceptions et aux croyances qu'il adoptées, au milieu psychologique et social, en un mot est une foule de facteurs spirituels qui jouent un role considérable dans l'evolution de la personalité" (p. 422).

79 Cf. Juliette Boutonier on the characteristics of voluntary activity, *Les Défaillances de la Volonté,* 2nd Ed. (Paris: Press Univ. France, 1951), pp. 3-10.

80 W. McDougall, *An Outline of Psychology* (New York: Scribner's Sons, 1923), p. 442.

81 *Ibid.,* p. 448.

82 J. Sully, *The Human Mind: A Text-Book of Psychology* (New York, Appleton, 1892), Vol. 2, p. 292.

83 *Ibid.,* p. 364.

84 J. Ward, *Psychological Principles,* 2nd Ed. (Cambridge: Cambridge Univ. Press, 1920), p. 404.

85 *Ibid.,* p. 407.

86 E. Abramowski, "Recherches Experimentales sur la Volonté," *J.Psychol. Norm. Path.* (1913-1915), 10, 491-508.

87 C. A. Richardson, "The Measurement of Conative Factors in Children and their Influence," *Brit. J. Psychol.* (1928-1929), 19, 405-412.

88 C. E. Spearman, "A New Method for Investigating the Springs of Action" in M. L. Reymert, *Feelings and Emotions: Wittemberg Symposium* (New York, McGraw-Hill, 1928), p. 48; cf. also *The Abilities of Man* (London, Macmillan, 1927).

89 E. Webb, "Character and Intelligence," *Brit. Psychol. Monogr. Suppl.,* (1915), 1, 53 ff.

90 C. E. Spearman, *op. cit.,* pp. 47 ff. *"G and After: A School to End Schools,"* in C. Murchison, *Psychologies of 1930* (Worcester, Mass.: Clark Univ. Press, 1930), p. 359.

91 R. McDonough, "The Empirical Study of Character," *Stud. Psychol.*

Psychiat. vol. 2, n. 4 (Washington, D.C.: Catholic Univ. Press, 1929). Cf. T. V. Moore, *The Driving Forces of Human Nature and their Adjustment* (New York: Grune & Stratton, 1950), pp. 164 ff., 325 ff.

92 F. Aveling, *Personality and Will* (Cambridge, Cambridge Univ. Press, 1931), pp. 91 ff.

93 C. E. Spearman, *op. cit.,* p. 48. Roback has authored a thorough study on the psychology of character. He represents the trend mentioned by Charles E. Spearman. Cf. A. A. Roback, *The Psychology of Character* (1952), p. 675.

CHAPTER III

Factors in the Selective Process

This present analysis is based on observations of authoritative psychologists who have treated the problem of motivation systematically. More particularly, it is based on the observations of leading experimenters who have bequeathed to us the results of their experimental research concerning the selective process. Some of these experimenters are very familiar to students of psychology; they have been examined and summarized many times. But the author of this study believes that, for completeness of treatment, these experiments must be examined once more; and he will add some observations of his own. These experiments on the topic of motivation are so vital to the broader problem of freedom of will that they cannot be ignored. We must first point out that these experiments have been strongly criticized because too often the experimenters have been guilty of an excessive oversimplification in their descriptions of volitional acts. It has been pointed out and rightly so, that the circumstances of real life are hardly found in these experiments whose extreme technical precision seems superfluous and even harmful. In fact, during these experiments man's spontaneous and complex activity is often restricted to an almost fixed model or pattern.[1] Despite these limitations, these experimental studies are of great importance for an adequate understanding of the phenomenology of voluntary activity.

The results obtained by Ach, Michotte, Prüm, Barrett, Martin,

Wells and others allow us to formulate a detailed analysis of the process of voluntary choice. This process entails a fourfold series of factors which can be indicated by the following terms: *motivation, deliberation, decision,* and *execution* or *actualization.*

Motivation indicates the reasons or the factors which influence the process of choice. It concerns the presence of the alternatives from which the individual will choose. *Deliberation* reveals a discussion on the part of the subject, perhaps verbalized, perhaps not, and an evaluation of the possibility of choice. The subject experiences a state of doubt or hesitation, a state of expectancy and indecision accompanied by muscular tension and respiratory disturbance. *Decision* (sometimes also called *resolution*) is the true choice in its real sense. It indicates the act with which the subject *decides* (or resolves) in favor of one of the possible alternatives. With this act, the subject commits himself with a definite solution to the problem of choice. *Execution* (*actualization*) indicates the actual "carrying out" of the decision already taken, or, inversely, the lack of the "carrying out" of what has been decided. Execution constitutes, in the opinion of the author of this study, a logical but not essential factor of the selective process.

It does not seem superfluous to call attention to the fact that the process of choice is a continuous phenomenon; in other words, it is a phenomenon which, psychologically speaking, does not allow distinct parts which are present *in actu* (i.e. psychologically, the parts are not distinct). The above-mentioned four factors may appear at times as *different modes* of one and the same continuous act, i.e. as *successive* phases of the selective process; however, they must be conceived rather as four complementary factors which can also occur *simultaneously,* especially *motivation* and *deliberation* on the one hand, and *decision* and *execution* (*actualization*) on the other. In order that these factors of the selective process be understood in their true light, it is necessary to picture them in a general theory of action. It seems useful, therefore, to begin with a short analysis of the relationship between *motivation* and *human behavior.* The intent of all this is to give some general idea of the various theoretical positions on the problem and to point out what is specific in human behavior.

1. Motivation and Human Behavior

The concept of motivation, in one guise or another, has played a major explanatory role. But it is not safe to assert that students of behavior have reached appreciable agreement as to how drives and motives can be most meaningfully defined, what mechanisms are involved in each case, how many drives function as behavior determinants. In the preceding chapter, when we examined these same determinants, we saw which role that desires, needs, and drives (of which man is not even aware) play in man's behavior. The voluntary act establishes order between instincts and our spontaneous responses. But if the will organizes man's instinctive life, we must remember that it is this same inferior sphere which furnishes the most demanding, if not always the most decisive, motives to voluntary activity. James R. Angell observes "that all the great persistent types of human purpose have their roots in instinct and the appetites of man." [2]

Many modern theorists and researchers on motivation maintain that the most significant drives of human behavior are not the biogenetic and instinctive drives, but the *"learned"* drives which are "acquired" during the normal course of socialization and cultural development. Very significant on this point is Theodore M. Newcomb's opinion that a general theory of motivation will be adequate and satisfactory only if it will take into consideration the full social context. [3] Against this new trend, which minimizes vociferously the importance of the biogenetic and instinctive drives and overemphasizes the social and acquired drives, Judson S. Brown and Harry F. Harlow have recently raised their voices in criticism. [4] The fundamental reason for the existence of these different viewpoints in contemporary theories of human behavior revolves around this problem: whether or not the *cognitive power* is also involved in the explanation of human behavior. One's position on this point determines his viewpoint on the entire mechanism of human behavior.

a. Contemporary Motivational Theories

The common assumption running through most contemporary theories is that motives are "deficit tensional states" which energize organisms until relief is obtained or "equilibrium" restored. Broadly conceived, this "tensional theory of motivation" has received its support from such widely different sources as Freud, Hull, Miller and Dollard, and Mowrer.[5] But this theory seems inadequate. Various objections, which have not received the attention they merited, have been raised against it by Young and Hebb.[6]

The idea that motives are essentially "tensional" in nature and energize organisms presents serious difficulties. First of all, the notion of a motive as an *"energizer"*—as a concept which is needed in order to explain the activity of the organism—is untenable. In fact the organism is already active. Besides, the motive concept is needed to explain *"directedness"* of activities rather than their overall intensity level. Another difficulty with the tension notion arises when motive is conceived essentially as a negative affective state derived primarily from painful experiences.[7] We can rather say on phenomenological and experimental grounds that any theory of motivation must take into account the active (or positive) comforts and pleasures of life, as well as discomforts, tensions, and their relief.

All authors agree that there are certain special types of conditions which give rise to motives, and nearly all agree that "motivated behavior" is in some way distinguishable from "unmotivated behavior."

One of the earliest and certainly one of the most influential ways of thinking about motivation was to start with the notion of *survival* of the species or of an individual member of the species. This idea, which was central to the doctrine of evolution, has had an extremely powerful influence on psychologists as widely different in other respects as Freud and Hull. Psychoanalysis and behavior theory could unite in the belief that life is a struggle for survival and that nature must have provided organisms with some innate signals which would warn of approaching threats to survival.[8] This theory also presents serious difficulties. In the first place, some survival needs produce a motive and some do not. In the second place, it is often hard to determine just what the organism's survival needs are. A third difficulty with the assumption that all motives are ultimately derived from or dependent on primary biological needs is that biological needs provide only a very partial basis for explaining how behavior is guided and controlled. We should not conclude from this, however, that biological needs have no connection with motivation.

Implicit in Hull's system is another idea about motivation, which has been developed most fully by Miller and Dollard. This idea is that a drive is a strong stimulus which impels action. Any stimulus can become a drive if it is made strong enough. The stronger the stimulus, the more drive function it has. In reality, it often happens that decreases in stimulation appear to cause an increase in motivation (e.g., a dark night), whereas an increase in stimulation may cause a decrease in motivation (e.g., a light in a dark night).

Hebb has perhaps provided the most pertinent criticism of the motivational models so far discussed. The new theory he presents replaces the notion of "stimulus intensity" with the notion of *"variations in neural patterning."* Hebb begins by defining motivation as a hypothetical construct with certain *neural* attributes. The term motivation, then, refers (1) to the existence of an organized phase sequence; (2) to its direction or content, and (3) to its persistence in a given direction or stability of content.[9] The crucial factor here is that whatever succeeds in this respect in the organism can be called a motive. In Hebb's opinion, it is the organization of behavior rather than its intensity which requires the motive concept. A live organism is an active organism, and no strong stimuli are needed to get it moving. While the preceding theories were too simple to account for all the facts, this one is too general; the experimenter in fact can know only with difficulty whether something is a motive or its effects in a particular instance.

In a recent book, McClelland and others define motive as "the redintegration by a cue of a change in an affective situation." [10] The word "redintegration" in this definition is meant to imply previous learning. In this system all motives are learned. The basic idea is simply this: certain stimuli or situations involving discrepancies between expectation (adaptation level) and perception are sources of primary, unlearned affect, either positive or negative in nature. McClelland and others declare they have based their theory of motivation upon "redintegrating affect" because they wanted to give a more limited base to motives. Another reason for their theory is the overwhelming evidence of the importance of selective sensibility in guiding and directing animal behavior. They are forced, therefore, to apply the same criteria to human behavior, because, in this regard, in their opinion there is no clear distinction between man and other animals. The advantage of Hebb over McClelland and others — an advantage more of degree than of kind — consists only in the wider series of situations which cause *affective responses*. Man's fantasy-life is a "free-response situation" if it is presupposed that the background is not too "structured." It is "free," because the testing conditions do not place any external constraints on the responses which are possible. Man holds an advantage in relationship to animals because of his freedom of fantasy-life, but the problem is identical in both cases, according to McClelland and others: to minimize or know the situational and habit determinants of behavior.

The theories that we have delineated above reduce all forms of external and internal behavior to different types of bonds. These theories are opposed by theories of behavior which attribute in one form or another an essential role to *cognitive activity and to conscious motivation*. We can recognize in this style of thinking elements of various theories such as those of Köhler, Lewin, Tolman and Krech. Their differences aside, all these authors conceive the relationship among situation, response and its effect on the level of perceptual and cognitive functions. In these theories, behavior is not actualized as a function of "reinforcement" automatically produced upon a fortuitous S-R bond by a previous effect.[11] What distinguishes them is the presence in the organism of a *psychic factor,* i.e. of a cognitive function.

The cognitive theory of behavior implies a consequence which is essential for the development of behavior. It introduces an intermediate phase between stimulus and behavioral response, in which the motivation of the organism is manifested. This intermediate phase, created by the cognitive factor, implies a more or less endless number of possibilities of behavior, i.e. a variety of means more or less capable of leading to a particular effect. This intermediate phase constitutes a reserve of possible ways of behavior by which man's creative power can produce new actualizations. It permits two kinds of learning: (1) learning under the form of acquisition of habits and reflexes; (2) learning under the form of acquisition of cognitive dispositions.[12] Only when motivation materializes in a behavioral form which is cognitively possible is an actualization effected.

Having considered these two groups of theories, one can say that we are dealing not only with two incompatible theories of behavior in general, but rather with *two levels of behavior*. In other words, one can say that we have to deal with two components of a complex mechanism, two processes which can intervene in variable proportions in most of the behavioral forms. Certain types of behavior are located either at one or the other of these two poles, the automatic and the cognitive, while other types of behavior occupy intermediary positions. There are, in fact, behavioral forms in which the cognitive element is practically absent; and there are others in which the progressive reinforcement of bonds seems to play a very secondary role. At the level of human behavior, especially of that characterized as *free,* it seems that no substitution can be found for the active intervention of the cognitive function.

b. Constructive Development of Human Behavior

One of the most essential characteristics of behavior is "directedness." This "directedness" shows itself objectively in behavior itself. Animal behavior is oriented towards "specific and privileged goals" which can be considered as the "purpose" of their action. Behavior, since it is oriented towards a specific goal, arrives at an effect which can be qualified in terms of value, satisfactory or unsatisfactory, according to whether or not the intended objective is obtained. In man this privileged goal most often is not of a purely physiological character; it is rather a task or a duty which man imposes on himself. Success or failure are defined as a function of the subject's "directedness" towards a determinate goal which man intends to attain. The rewarding effect of an action serves as a means to achieve another goal or another satisfactory effect.

One of the essential traits of the development of certain forms of human behavior is this series of goals which man himself proposes to himself.[13] Man constructs a system of coordinated media in order to attain a further goal. The most characteristic trait of human dynamism is not man's attempt to solve the tension created in him by the distance between the proposed goal and the present situation. It is rather the constructive manner in which he elaborates new projects once this tension is reduced. There is in man an impulse which tends toward new realizations and so breaks the state of rest and equilibrium as soon as it is attained. In this case we are dealing with new anticipations and new projects, elaborated by a dynamism which is essentially constructive.

The salient fact in the development of human behavior consists in its *progressive and constructive nature*. This shows that there is motivation and therefore a goal yet to be attained at the beginning of every behavioral manifestation. In man this motivation does not consist merely in a repetition of satisfactory behaviors performed in the past in order to arrive once more at the rewarding effect previously obtained. Rather, this motivation always assigns to man new goals in such a way that behavior follows a line of constructive development. A change is produced in man from the rule of responses to that of motivation and understanding of the "world" in which he is situated.

Man behaves in a world which exists for him insofar as it is perceived and known in a specific way. His behavior is an answer to a meaningful situation in this world. Since man is always in contact with his world in specifically human ways, some specific needs appear in him on the plane of his social and spiritual contact with this world. The biological needs themselves have, in man, a cognitive form. This knowledge of biological needs has this effect, that their influence on behavior is not manifested under the form of periodic compulsions, but rather under the form of activities and goal orientations more or less stable and continuous. Man develops in himself dynamic orientations which continue to interest him even after a momentary satisfaction of need. This is applied in particular to needs which are specifically human. These needs exist and grow in a characteristic and personal manner under the form of comparatively durable spheres of interest, varying in strength, which constitute the basic motives of human activity.

Human needs must not be studied as the extension of infantile or physiological forms of motivation, but in the framework of exchanges and differentiated relationships comprising man's complex life in the world. The state of need constitutes in an adult a situation integrated with the totality of his life. The link which joins behavior to a need, or to the state of tension created by a need, is neither a simple nor a uniform link in all cases. In certain situations, the accumulated tension explodes into behavioral forms which lack any efficacious directedness towards a goal to be attained; such is the case in many emotional responses. In other situations a less strong or less explosive tension results in instinctive responses or a variety of behavior increasingly systematic; such is the case with most animal and infantile behavioral patterns. Finally, in other circumstances, need shows up as an activity of the cognitive function. Such is the case with manifestations of specifically human behavior.

These two aspects of man's psychic activity, *motivation* and *cognition,* cannot be conceived separately in their concrete functioning. "Need" expresses itself in the form of a cognitive activity under tension, that is, directed towards goal attainment. Need acts in man as a conscious and experienced situation under the form of an elementary necessity of the "human condition." "Need," then, becomes "value." To the extent that need associates and identifies itself with cognitive activity, behavior assumes a constructive character.

c. Motivation and Personality

The effect of an activity which is elaborated according to the process described above cannot be identified with the response which leads to the satisfaction of an organic need. Man's constructive activity must be considered in relation to the structure of his personality. The goal man proposes for himself or the project he conceives is, to a certain extent, an activity in which his personality shows forth and in which his "ego" is more or less involved. Man's behavior, in fact, is nothing other than his *personality in action,* that is, man as he exists and acts in the world.

The personal factor plays an enormous role in human behavior; it defines the content of man's psychic life, his cognitive activity and motivation. The content of psychic life is in reality essentially *personal.* Physical and cultural factors influence man's behavior only in the measure that they are incorporated into his personal life. In this case, therefore, we are dealing with the problem of determining what personality factors intervene in the concrete instance, in other words, of determining why certain behavioral forms and certain contents of consciousness are incorporated into ulterior behavior. Therefore, on the one hand, we must keep in mind the strict relationship which exists between cognition and behavioral forms, and, on the other hand, the link that joins these behavioral and cognitive forms to motivation. A present state of need, of task, or of affectivity implies the actualization of the behavioral and cognitive models which are incorporated into the system of a previous experience.

The system into which a response or a datum is incorporated frequently must be considered an orientation of interests or needs elaborated in a cognitive way. For this reason the incorporated data are easily evoked on the cognitive level, without reviving the need itself. Because of this process of incorporation, certain behavioral responses and certain ideas of the world are integrated into the subject's dynamic system. They are, so to speak, "prefigured" to a variable degree in a state of need in a personality that pursues a goal. Projects, goals and actual needs are equally prefigured in some way in man's behavior and previous motivations.

Psychoanalysis inaugurated in psychology the tendency to look for "motives" of an act in the dynamic contents of the *past* of the individual. It opened the path to a genetic orientation in the study of motivation. There are psychologists who protest against this historical orientation and prefer to explain behavior in terms of the framework of present dynamic factors, i.e. as a function of what is given and lived in the "field" of the present situation.[14] This reaction against genetic theories and against reduction of every present motive to instincts which are considered more fundamental, is at least partially justified. Consequently, McLeod is right when he says that often, following this method, psychoanalysts attempt to explain a present situation through forces that were once active but now are not. He is right especially when he emphasizes that continuity in the dynamic process does not necessarily imply identity with the essential elements which make up the motive or drive of the two different phases of this development.[15] But there is danger of exaggeration when we attempt to separate completely present motives from every fundamental need. The return to more universal needs cannot always be called a return to a past phase of dynamic development. In reality there are cases in which a present motive is nothing but a concrete form which is assumed in certain circumstances by a more general need which continues to exist as such.

In a study of the psychology of motivation elaborated by *methodic introspection* (a study under many aspects open to criticism, but which reveals a deep human sensibility), Paul Diel calls us back to fundamental needs, whether biological or spiritual, to their development, and also to their deformation in relationship to man's personality. All psychic reactions observable exteriorly, he maintains, have internal causes, i.e. the motives. Responses can be observed, measured, interpreted statistically. But the sum total of these reactions, that is, the psychic life, cannot be understood unless we understand first of all their internal causes, i.e. motives. To understand psychic life fully it is absolutely necessary to understand intra-psychic reactivity.

Man can evaluate his desires, which become in this way the constant driving forces of his responses. The evaluation can be correct or false. But often man does not want to acknowledge his false evaluation and represses it into the subconscious. And thus it becomes a "false motivation." [16] This false motivation is found more or less in every human psyche; it represents an "impotence" of the spiritual function, a deformation of the spirit. Man can find a remedy for it only in himself, by observing his psychic functioning, by re-examining his right or wrong evaluation. He cannot find the truth of his internal life except by combating false motivation. This he does by dissipating the affective and subconscious darkness.

False motivation has various forms and masks. To unmask these forms is to perform a "methodic introspection." But no matter how methodic this introspection might be, there is always something that it will never find: the multitude of psychopathological manifestations, their physiological co-determination, their description and their "nosological" classification. There is also something that external observation, no matter how experimental it might be, can never uncover: the "lived" determination, the "lived" motivation, the profound understanding. The psychology of motivation must therefore necessarily complement experimental psychology.

2. Analysis and Evaluation of Motives

Examination of some concrete cases from daily life will permit us to see how acts of the will can be differentiated according to the external circumstances and, even more, according to the attitude of each individual. When, for instance, we want to mention a book whose title has slipped our memory, this thought impels us to get up from the desk, go to the bookshelf and note down the title. This is a simple "act of the will." But presupposing that we do not want to interrupt the train of thought, we then deliberate whether to leave the desk or not, and finally we decide to get the book and do so. This is an "act of choice." Of course, no act of the will appears from nowhere; it always has a preparatory period which runs its course within the person before it breaks forth in overt action.

a. Characteristics of Motivation

It is by means of motives that a particular act is attached to the totality of the person. It is therefore evident that the problem of motives is of great significance, not only for psychology, but for ethics, criminology, and one's whole outlook on life as well. In addition to the conscious incentives of will, there may be others which, proceeding from the larger depths of the psyche, carry the true forces that nurture the act of will. William Stern distinguishes between two kinds of motives of action: the pheno-motive and the geno-motive. He points out that motives must not be given the independent status of "forces" that can struggle with one another. When we speak of "conflict" of motives, the expression must be taken metaphorically only: "It does not fit the actual causation of the willing." [17]

"Pheno-motives" derive their strength from the "geno-motives," which have their roots in the complexity of personality. The immediate geno-motive is always a need. This reduction of the geno-motives to needs does not signify a sinking of will to the lower level of vital drives, but the reversal: an elevating of needs to the plane of intellect. Of course, there are many human needs which do not generally take the channel of the will for their fulfillment, such as sleep. Other vital needs can be satisfied with extremely simple acts of will, e.g. nutrition. In contrast to these, there are other needs whose goals are too remote and too complex to be attained directly. They can be fulfilled only because man is capable of willing. According to William Stern, "The variety of genuine geno-motives in human action is infinitely greater than the oversimplified theories of the depth psychologists will admit, for new geno-motives are continually arising from pheno-motives." [18]

In experimental research a "motive" is the reason or justification for the decision; motivation is the relationship existing between the motives and the act of choice.[19] The perception of an alternative is sometimes accompanied by an impression of its value. This "valuing" can also take the form of a value judgment. Motivation therefore implies consciousness and the weighing of values.[20] According to M. Simoneit, motivation expresses the action of a subject who compares the value of two concepts, one of which is kept in consciousness longer than the other.[21] It is only natural that motives present themselves to consciousness in different degrees of attractiveness. The personal factor plays an important role because the strength of motives depends not only on the quality of the alternatives but also on the tendencies of the subject. Motives therefore must not be considered outside their natural role in the motivation of the voluntary act, because they are not separate entities or independent forces. They are integral parts of motivation; they depend upon it both for their form and their strength.

Some experimenters—especially Michotte, Prüm and Barrett—have classified motives from the point of view of *form* and *content*.[22] From the viewpoint of form, motives might appear as judgments, representations or impressions of value, etc. From the viewpoint of content, the reason for decision depends on the value proper to the motive, whatever its origin.

The reasons for acting can also be classified into *objective* and *subjective* motives. The "objective" motives derive their value from the very action to be executed; they are called "intrinsic" when their basis rests on some quality of the object, such as the facility and representability of the operation. They are called "extrinsic" when the basis is founded upon external accidental circumstances, such as rarity and duration. "Subjective" motives are found under the form of an active tendency: wish, desire or repulsion; they may appear as a "sudden" impulse to follow an alternative rather casually, or as a capricious tendency to change an habitual trend. Lindworsky characterized as "inferior" or "elementary" those motives whose value depends on the pleasant feeling evoked by them, and as "superior" those whose value is known by the grasping of a relationship.[23]

All of this shows that a variety of terms has been used to differentiate the motives of the will. But a close examination of the factors embraced by these terms reveals less of a variety than first appears. The most pertinent distinction between various reasons for action can be found in the writings of N. Ach. Motives in a *strict* sense are only *conscious facts,* like feelings of pleasure, appreciation, etc.; motives in a *broad* sense are *unconscious* processes, insofar as they function in a particular case as determinants of action.[24]

Motives, then, can appear under different forms, and these forms can be assumed, one after the other, by the same motive. But among the various forms there exists a *genetic dependence;* they do not happen by chance, but follow definite laws of development. A motive can present itself in a given case under a form completely different from its original content. Two important factors concur in this transformation of the form of a motive: automatism and various inhibitory mechanisms in the determining tendencies. The inhibition of the determining tendency acts in an opposite way to that of its exercise; actually, it initiates a regressive development, a return to primitive forms of motivation, while exercise leads to a progressive development. Evidence for such development can be found in the experiments of Boyd Barrett. The motives that appeared initially in a purely hedonistic form ("this is pleasing") developed more and more into a deontological type, and in the succession of experiments they were replaced by judgments ("this can be taken" or "this must be chosen").[25]

The same phenomenon was noticed by Michotte and Prüm in their experiments on voluntary choice, even though their intention was not to study the general development of motives from the "hedonistic" viewpoint to the "deontological." They were interested particularly in the development of the "rarity" motive, which seemed from the start to have a deontological character. The development of this motive, however, clarifies the point in discussion. The characteristic of "rarity" is not due to the alternative itself, but rather to its position in the series of experiments. The rarity of an alternative does not necessarily constitute a value in itself, because in different circumstances this characteristic can have an absolutely opposite value. The rarity motive appears in the process of choice under the form of an imperative judgment which passes through successive phases, until the judgment becomes increasingly less conscious.[26]

The simple presence of a determined value or motive does not lead necessarily to the volitive act. The motive must first reach an appropriate strength. The motives can be varied according to the contrasts found among values or according to the different degrees of awareness. Often the subjects are conscious of an increase or a decrease in strength of a particular motive. In order that the choice be made in favor of a determined motive, it is necessary that it reach a certain degree of strength. There are various ways to reinforce motives: education, contrast, certain personal factors and other accidental causes. The process of reinforcement of motives can be of long or short duration according to the time which is required for a motive to assume a degree of sufficient value to cause the subject's response.[27]

b. *Evaluation of the Alternatives*

The second factor in the selective process is *deliberation,* which appears as a phase of variable duration and provides a definition of the relative value of the motives for action. When two or more types of behavior are considered, each of them must be put in relationship to the concept that the subject has of himself, and they must be compared among themselves from this point of view. Desires and aversions which arise during deliberation are not mere impulses. They present themselves to consciousness as the reasons why one should act in one way or another. While the deliberative process is developing, the reasons in favor of one or other alternatives become motives for choice. When a decision is made, the reasons which prevail become motives of action.

William James describes most vividly what happens in the deliberative process when the mind has many objects before it, related to each other in antagonistic or in favorable ways.[28] The mind would like to suggest to itself an action, but while some additional objects or considerations block the motor discharge, others solicit it to act. The result of such a mental state is that peculiar feeling of inward unrest known as *"indecision."* As long as it lasts, with various objects before one's attention, we are said to deliberate. The process of deliberation contains an endless degree of complication. At every moment of the deliberative process our consciousness is of an extremely complex thing, namely, the whole set of motives and their conflict. Deliberation may last for weeks and months, occupying the mind continuously or at intervals; but at the end the problem is solved. Voluntary actions differ from impulsive actions because the deliberative process precedes the execution of the act. This deliberation is accomplished on the basis of the individual's past experience and of his personal evaluation of the alternatives.

James' way of thinking, the fruit of profound psychological intuition, was confirmed and partially clarified by the results of some psychological experiments deserving of analysis. In an experimental process like that of Michotte and Prüm, deliberation contains these elements: (1) the perception of the stimulus; (2) discussion of motives; (3) immediate preparation of the choice or intermediate phase (a state of indecision which precedes the act itself of the final decision). The perception of the stimulus demands on the part of the subject a concentrated attention upon the stimulus itself. It is accompanied by a state of consciousness which refers both to past experiences and to the instructions given by the experimenter. The discussion of motives involves the establishment of the alternatives and their evaluation. The alternatives are constructed from responses arising at the beginning of the experiment, under the influence of associative factors. The value judgment in choosing one of the alternatives does not necessarily occur as a result of an intellectual process. The actual affective factors that intervene in the formation and reinforcement of motives do play an important part, but the determining weight is given by the practical judgment of value which the subject makes both in an imperative way ("I must do this") and in a comparative way ("this is more worthwhile than that").

The end of the deliberative process is generally realized when the subject has found, after a more or less complete analysis, a dominant positive value for one of the alternatives. When the motives that are applied to one or another alternative are absolutely positive or negative, and when the two alternatives have been evaluated in the same manner, the subject becomes aware of the necessity to decide. But between the end of the discussion of motives and the moment in which the decision becomes concrete, a relatively long interval of time ordinarily intervenes. Within this time the individual finds himself in a characteristically subjective state. A threefold series of phenomena then is observed: (1) an awareness of doubt, hesitation, oscillation; (2) a consciousness of waiting, suspension; (3) general muscular tension. These phenomena which constitute the intermediate phase of the process of choice are intermingled in such a way that they produce, as an accumulative result, a typically subjective state.

In an experimental study on acts of choice, Honoria M. Wells used the introspective method which was also used by Ach, Michotte and Prüm, but with some modifications. She based her experiments on the procedures which Michotte himself had developed for his pupil, Boyd Barrett.[29] The alternatives of choice were not as trifling as those of Michotte and Prüm. In Wells' experiments the subjects were requested to choose between two liquids of different tastes and to drink the chosen liquid immediately. In a series of preliminary experiments the taste of each liquid became firmly associated with a definite nonsense syllabile. Thus each of eight nonsense syllables was gradually transformed into a "name" by which a liquid of a definite well-known taste was designated. In each experiment two of these nonsense syllables were presented to the subject and two glasses containing the corresponding liquids were placed on the table just beneath the spot where the nonsense syllables appeared. The instruction was: "You are to choose, for a serious motive, between these two tastes and drink the one you have chosen. React as quickly as possible."

In Wells' research, the evaluation of the alternatives was more or less established during the taste trial. After these trials the subjects were asked to write their preferences in a graded sentence. The stimulus-words immediately presented to the subject two alternatives, which normally would have a meaning and a clearly defined value.

The importance of establishing the true value of the alternatives was seen clearly by Michotte, and there is no doubt that this is the real reason which induced him to develop the experimental procedure followed by Boyd Barrett.[30] In addition to this, it was Michotte's opinion that for progress in the study of motivation it was indispensable to know *how* to evaluate the alternatives present during the discussion of the motives, and to be able to have prior knowledge of the particular meaning of each. Such knowledge is necessary for weighing the influence which a value exercises upon the discussion of motives, its duration, and its complexity, as well as the modification of a value following its opposition to another value.

In an experimental study of the factors and types of voluntary choice made under the direction of R. S. Woodworth, Alfred H. Martin attempted to cross-validate the previous experiments in this field and to investigate further the nature of the mental phenomenon implied therein.[31] This important study contains two series of experiments.

In the first series the subject was asked, during the initial phase, to imagine a certain situation. Then, during the principal phase, he was asked to consider various alternatives, in order to lead to a choice between them. In a variation of the experiment the subject was asked to reconsider this decision, keeping in view the opposite alternatives. A complete introspective protocol was written on the various phases of this process. In the second series of experiments the subject was asked to make a choice between two kinds of odors by sniffing the given odor for two seconds, and then putting into effect the decision made. The procedure followed in this second series of experiments was similar to that of the first.

A synthesis of the results of these experiments shows that the deliberative process of choice begins with the acceptance of the task and develops during the orientation of the various alternatives. During the principal phase of the research there is a more detailed process of exploration, where the subject experiences momentarily first one and then the other alternative. All these taste experiments were accompanied by kinesthetic and organic phenomena. These latter tend to be suspended at the moment of assent and to cease finally with the actual decision which is realized through fixation of one of the alternatives in the focus of attention.

3. Decision and Execution of Choice

In order to have a clear understanding of the problem it will be useful to recall the terminology of Wilhelm Wundt on this point.[32] When a clearly perceptible conflict among antagonistic motives precedes the realization of an act, volition is then called a "selective act," and the process from which it results is called "choice." The prevalence of a motive over other simultaneous ones can be understood only if we presuppose such a conflict in every case (although we sometimes perceive it clearly, sometimes obscurely, and sometimes not at all). Only in the case in which the conflict is clearly perceived can we speak of a "selective act" in the proper sense.

According to Wundt's terminology, the phase which immediately precedes the realization of the act is called "resolution" in the case of common voluntary acts, and in the case of selective acts, "decision." The first term indicates simply that the action must be carried out in agreement with some motive which is consciously adopted; the second term indicates that various courses of action are presented to the subject as possible and that a choice is then actualized.

In the present study the terms "resolution" and "decision" are taken as synonyms because there seems to be no essential difference between them. Even in the first case we are in the presence of a conscious act of evaluation in favor of a motive and an act of fixation on one alternative in preference to others.[33]

But how does the actualization of the decision come about? It is precisely at this point that the crucial question of human freedom arises. According to those who hold the absolute freedom of man, decision implies, at least in certain cases, the intervention of a factor which was not present at all in the process of deliberation. The opponents of liberty maintain that decision is the natural result of conditions which are at work in the deliberative process itself. Before these two opposed positions, we must recognize, as the distinguished G. F. Stout has rightly affirmed, that:

"Now it must be admitted that the transition from the state of indecision to that of decision is often obscure and that it frequently appears to be unaccountably abrupt. This makes it difficult or impossible to give a definite disproof of the libertarian hypothesis on psychological grounds." [34]

a. Determination of the Selective Act

When in the process of deliberation the original suggestion prevails or is finally extinguished by alternatives antagonistic to it we then arrive at the moment of decision, or, in William James' expression, at the point of "pronouncing our voluntary fiat" in favor of one possibility of choice. Following the lead of James, let us review the most characteristic types of decision and the complexity of symptoms and phenomena which distinguish them.

The *first type* of decision can be called "rational." This takes place when pro and con arguments in relation to an action are generally and almost insensibly fixed in the mind, and then terminate with the determination of a clear inclination in favor of an alternative. It is then adopted without effort or coercion. In this smooth transition from doubt to certitude we seem to be *passive,* but we have a perfect awareness of being free.

In the *second type* of decision our feeling is mostly one of letting ourselves be pulled with a certain indifferent acquiescence in one direction accidentally determined from without. In this case we are convinced that we could follow one way or the other after all.

In the *third type,* determination seems also to be accidental, but it comes from within, not without. It often happens, when the absence of a directive principle leaves us perplexed, that we begin to act almost automatically; the intolerable state of suspense is so vivid in us that we cast ourselves furiously into action.

In the *fourth type* of decision, deliberation is often concluded as suddenly as in the third type. This follows on some external experience or some unexpected internal change, when we pass very suddenly from a casual and negligent state of mind to a state of readiness and composure.

There is a *fifth type* of decision in which we feel as though we ourselves, with a certain obstinacy, have pushed the balance of the alternatives in one way rather than in another. The feeling of effort, absent in the preceding forms of decision, is subjectively and phenomenologically present in this last type.

An accurate examination of these various modalities of decision permits us to point out the main difference between the first four types and the fifth one in a specific way. In the last case both alternatives are kept firmly in mind, while in the other cases — at the moment of decision in favor of an alternative — the mind abandons the other completely. The feeling of "internal effort" which accompanies the act is an element which places the fifth type of decision in stark contrast to the preceding ones and makes of it a mental phenomenon of a singularly specific character. The existence of effort in the consciousness of each individual is a datum of common experience. With regard to its meaning, however, the most serious differences of opinion exist.

William James points out:

"Questions as momentous as that of the very existence of spiritual causality, as vast as that of universal predestination or freewill, depend on its interpretation." [35]

In the experience of effort we feel we can realize what we really *do* each moment. The effort seems to be, in other words, not like a fixed reaction, but rather like an independent variable. If it is really so—that is, if the quantity of our effort is not a function determined by other data (motives, character, etc.)—then according to common language our will is free. James concludes in this way:

"The question of fact in the free-will controversy is thus extremely simple. It relates solely to the amount of effort of attention which we can at any time put forth." [36]

Let us move now from this introspective description to the data of experimental research. Michotte and Prüm have pointed out in their previously mentioned experimental study that only the specific phenomenon of voluntary decision—in the measure that it exists outside the actuality of what is willed—was a matter of general experience. It was never studied according to the method of systematic experimental introspection. In the experiments which preceded their own, the problem of decision had been studied either *before* the observable phase, or it was obscured by the presence of other processes which made the analysis impossible. To analyze decision, the experimentalists were forced always to have recourse to occasional observations. Michotte and Prüm tried to study the same phenomenon of decision independently of its actualization or execution. At the moment when the decision—voluntary choice in its proper sense—is made, the presence of extremely complex phenomena in the subject is always noted. There are certain observable conscious modifications: (1) the characteristic subjective state of the intermediary period evolves and resolves itself; (2) one of the alternatives is fixed in the mind with an act of preference; (3) voluntary choice is materialized at last into specific forms.[37]

We have seen that the subjective state which precedes decision has in it a consciousness of doubt, a state of anticipation and the presence of accentuated muscular reactions. At the moment of choice a radical transformation is determined in the subject. Doubt gives way to certainty, waiting resolves itself, and, in general, muscular tension relaxes. These conditions must be considered as the profound causes that determine the character of decision. The decision is a "vivid" one when it is accompanied by a strong transformation of muscular tension; it is "weak" (*"fredda"*) when muscular tension is weak or absent. This "feeling of activity"—the expression the subjects use to indicate such an experience—which corresponds to the resolution of the tension does not always coincide with voluntary decision. Hence it cannot give to decision its specific character. On the contrary, this phenomenon is not noticed at all in some of the cases of voluntary intervention. In addition, it can be clearly *consecutive* to decision itself.[38]

When the decision is made, the preferred alternative is present to consciousness. It is reduced to a mere "intention," to something "determinable" which is related to choice. The object of volition is not simply the alternative which is present to the subject but the "designation" of this alternative. Michotte points out that it is *the fact of designation* of the alternative which is voluntary; it is not the alternative, as such, which is willed.[39] Because of preferential designation the alternative is fixed in the subject's mind. Fixation consists in a "consciousness of direction," "direction towards," a "mental gesture" which sometimes appears under the form of a true judgment, even though it is not always expressly formulated.

The appearance of voluntary choice can occur under two distinct forms: *decision* properly so called, and simple *consent*. What distinguishes these two processes is, first of all, a difference in the way in which they make their appearance in consciousness. Choice is always considered as a true "decision" when it appears immediately after the discussion of the motives, or during the pause when there is either doubt or the consciousness of waiting. Choice is considered "consent" when, at the moment which immediately precedes it, the most favored alternative is conscious in a special way and its value clearly present to the subject's mind. The character of choice, therefore, is deeply related to motivation. Consent is produced only in very well defined conditions when the subjects are in the presence of alternatives of more or less equal value. Michotte and Prüm hold that this equivalence of the alternatives must be considered a remote cause of the consent.[40] When the most attractive alternative is before the consciousness, the phenomenon of "designation" and the "consciousness of direction" that are so characteristic of true decision need intervene no further. Then a simple "let it pass," a mere "adhesion" suffices to determine the volitive act.

In an experimental study on the various types of decision, J. W. Bridges attempted to investigate the correlation among constancy, time and accuracy of decision. The same experiments were repeated after a determined period of time to establish the reliability of the results.[41] The term "decision" does not seem quite proper in this context because the process which is designated in this way is habitually related to volition, while in Bridges' study the act is executed for esthetic motives rather than for purposes of future activity. It belongs to the category of mental judgments.

The aforementioned work of Alfred H. Martin was intended primarily to reduce the emphasis generally placed on primary motives and to heighten instead the "actual moment" of decision. This he calls the *self assertive tendency*.[42] In view of this principle, it is possible — even when two favorable alternatives are considered — to choose one and to exclude the other completely. According to Martin, three different types of decision clearly result from his investigation: preference-decision, conflict-decision, indifference-decision. The first of these (the only one accompanied in great measure by the self-assertive tendency) is the most characteristic and most common. If the process of choice were merely a process of competition among alternatives, then conflict-decision would be more predominant than preference-decision, since the subject is inclined at the outset toward *both*. But this is not the case. In reality the predominant type is the preference-decision, by which only one of the alternatives remains clear and distinct to the mind, while the others are removed from the central field of attention. It follows that decision is related not to native tendencies, but rather to their direction through the work of the self-assertive tendency.

b. Execution of the Preferential Choice

The conclusive "fiat" of decision accomplishes and completes voluntary action. The external execution of the decision does not have any importance from the phenomenological point of view of the will; it can be effected without a true voluntary decision. Again, there can be a true voluntary decision without its actualization for reasons independent of us. In the first case the action cannot be attributed to the man who performed it; in the second, it belongs to him at least intentionally.[43] But let us consider the definition of the role of "actualization" of voluntary choice in some experimental studies.

In Ach's experimental research the method of procedure consisted in executing a voluntary decision made prior to the period of observation in the experiment. A notable modification was introduced by Michotte and Prüm. Their method of experimentation was developed so as to favor the act of choice during the main period of the experiment. This procedure shortened the period of response considerably and allowed introspection to follow choice at once, since on principle the execution of a preferred alternative was omitted. But this raises a fundamental objection to the procedure itself. Is it possible to provoke a voluntary act by excluding *a priori* every possibility of execution in a subject already informed of this exclusion?

In the great majority of cases, the idea of "actualization" was absent both during deliberation and at the moment of decision. The choice of one of the alternatives is not an act that "must be performed," but the "act in itself," prescinding of course from its actual execution or absence of its future execution. The idea of non-actualization intervened by way of exception. Where the idea of actualization was present, it was considered in itself and not insofar as it had to be executed in a given moment. The conditions of execution can then become an object of discussion without implying the idea of its effective actualization. This is most important when we consider it in terms of daily life. Here it seems that ordinary decisions are based habitually on the actual conditions of execution. Michotte and Prüm demonstrated in their experiments that actualization, as such, is not an essential condition of the process of choice. What is discussed during deliberation is not "the act which will be carried out after choice," but the "act realized under such conditions." The fact of the ultimate execution could not be taken into consideration at all. "The idea of concrete actualization can intervene; it need not necessarily." [44]

Michotte answers the objections that Ach made against the theoretical considerations mentioned above. He clarifies his ideas by saying that it is really the phenomenon of choice which is voluntary. And this voluntary choice of "fixating" one of the alternatives does not tend in any way towards actualization. From the phenomenological viewpoint, the voluntary act of choice leads towards the alternative considered in itself, not towards future actualization. It is evident therefore that actualization of preferential choice depends on an act of the will distinct from that which constitutes decision or choice properly so called. [45]

Michotte's doctrine, if reduced to its simplest form, is this. In cases of choice such as those he investigated, there is a coordination between two voluntary acts: an act of the will which determines choice and another act of the will in the eventual execution of the potential alternative. These two acts are coordinated between themselves, but this coordination does not make the voluntary character of the first dependent on the efficacy of the second; under this aspect, the two acts are independent. It follows that an essential difference exists between the "decisions" of Ach and the "voluntary choices" of Michotte. [46] In the first case there is question of "doing," of an actual "acting," complete in itself—a total voluntary act, a "will" accompanied by execution. In the second, it is a question of a mere *"pure velle"* separated from its actualization—a volitive act, an activity lived at the moment of decision, which tends to an actualization distinct from this prior activity.

The subsequent execution of a voluntary act is conditioned by the preceding volition, by the act of decision, and is under the influence of what Ach has called the "determining tendency." This means that the will, after resolving to perform an action, continues its activity, though unconsciously perhaps, in order to reach its goal. Robert E. Brennan defines the determining tendency as the "persistent effort of the will to reach its goal." [47] By virtue of the "determining tendency," even when the original resolution leaves the mind completely, the instruction can be carried out to completion. [43]

To Ach's mind, determination, conceived as a complex of determining tendencies, is one of the psychological factors unconsciously at work in the psyche of an individual. Its characteristic aspect is that of evolving itself according to the knowledge of the task which is to be executed. The volitive act, implied in accepting a task, produces a "determining tendency" which favors the execution of the task. [49] The "determining tendency" can therefore be considered as a particular *after-effect* which emanates, in the main, from the knowledge of the action to be performed, and induces its realization. Such a tendency carries with it an ordered development of psychic phenomena.

FOOTNOTES

[1] H. Gruender, *Experimental Psychology* (Milwaukee: Bruce, 1932), p. 413, pp. 417 ff.; C. Blondel, "Les Volitions," in G. Dumas *Nouveau Traité de Psychologie,* t. VI (1939), pp. 334 ff.

[2] G. R. Angell, *An Introduction to Psychology* (New York: Henry Holt, 1918), p. 238.

[3] T. M. Newcomb, "Motivation in Social Behavior," in *Current Theory and Research in Motivation: A Symposium.* (Lincoln, Nebraska: Univ. of Nebraska Press, 1953) writes: "Theorists from McDougall and Freud to Murphy and Rogers have properly accorded to the self a central place; though not always, in my judgment, have all of them seen that place in its full social context. Not only are self-orientations part and parcel of other-orientations, I would insist; they are inextricable from the eternal triangle of self, other persons, and the common environment. A general theory of motivation, when it is mature enough to include these interdependent orientations, will have borrowed from a theory of motivation in social behavior, as well as helping to establish it" (p. 159). Ernest R. Hilgard writes: "The important human motives are inter-personal both in origin and in expression." "Human Motives and the Concept of the Self," *American Psychologist* (1949), 4, p. 379.

[4] J. S. Brown, "Problems Presented by the Concept of Acquired Drives," in *Current Theory and Research in Motivation: A Symposium* (Lincoln, Nebraska, Univ. Nebr. Press, 1953), pp. 1-21, writes: "Many contemporary students of motivation hold to the view that the most significant of the human drives are not biological; rather, they are learned during the normal course of socialization and development. Unfortunately, the ardor with

which this view is defended and the degree of confidence placed in its sound-ness far exceed the precision with which the details of the underlying mech-anisms have been specified" (p. 18). H. F. Harlow, "Motivation as a Factor in New Responses," *Ibid.*, writes: "I am convinced, however, that compari-tive and physiological psychology have much to offer and that limited con-tributions which have been made to date stem in large part from misdirec-tion and unfortunate channelization of effort and from limitations imposed by errors of conceptualization" (p. 24).

5 C. H. Hull, *Principles of Behavior* (New York: Appleton-Century-Crofts, 1943); N. E. Miller and J. Dollard, *Social Learning and Imitation* (New Haven: Yale Univ. Press, 1941); O. H. Mowrer, *Learning Theory and Personality Dynamics* (New York: Ronald Press, 1950).

6 P. T. Young, "Food-Seeking Drive, Affective Process and Learning," *Psychol. Rev.* (1949), 56, 98-121; D. O. Hebb, *The Organization of Be-havior: A Neuropsychological Theory,* (New York: Wiley, 1949).

7 Such is the theory of O. Hobart Mowrer, who holds that the motive is a state of anxiety because of the possibility of painful sensations. But he himself suggests that the notion of discomfort is not adequate in all cases. *Op cit.*, p. 725.

8 C. H. Hull, *op. cit.*, p. 17.

9 D. O. Hebb, *op. cit.*, p. 181. On the physiological aspects of motiva-tion cf. the recent study of Eliot Stellar, "The Physiology of Motivation," *Psychol. Rev.* (1954), 61, 5-22.

10 D. C. McClelland et al., *The Achievement Motive* (New York: Ap-pleton-Century-Crofts, 1953). For a synthesis of the various theories on motivation and a detailed exposition of the thought of McClelland and his collaborators, cf. the entire chapter, "Toward a Theory of Motivation," *op. cit.*, pp. 6-96.

11 Cf. Leo Postman, "The Experimental Analysis of Motivational Fac-tors in Perception," *Current Theory and Research in Motivation: A Sym-posium* (Lincoln, Nebraska: Univ. Nebr. Press, 1953), pp. 59-108. Says Postman: "We assume that motivational consequences serve as emphasizers and that their effectiveness is not to be ascribed to a process of need reduc-tion" (p. 86). With regard to the relationship between "connection" and "cognitive functions," cf. J. Nuttin, *Tâche, Réussite et Échec: Theorie de la Conduite Humaine,* Studia Psychologica, (Louvain, Publ. Univ. Louvain, 1953), pp. 32-45.

12 Learning becomes a fundamental factor in the theory of motivation. A new element which is learned brings some changes both in man's cogni-tive structure and in his system of needs-tensions. A pleasant effect often produces a change in the interests or values of the subject, namely a change in the relation between one goal and another. Learning and motivation are two factors which influence one another. "If there is any teaching which has come from Freudian psychology," says Ernest R. Hilgard, "it is that motives are organized in some sort of hierarchy within the individual, resulting in a

value-system expressed in behavior. This system may go by such names as *character-structure* or *ego*, but whatever it is called, it becomes very important for the learning of that individual." E. R. Hilgard, *Theories of Learning* (1948), p. 348.

[13] It was noted, for example, that the reaching of a goal often produces a reinforcement of efforts toward other goals in the same line of behavior. Cf. J. L. Child and W. M. Whiting, "Effects of Goal Attainment: Relaxation versus Renewed Striving," *J. Abnorm. Soc. Psychol.*, (1950), 45, 667-681. On the constructive development of human behavior, cf. J. Nuttin, *Psychoanalyse et Conception Spiritualiste de l'Homme: Une Théorie Dynamique de la Personalité Normale* (Louvain: Publ. Univ. Louvain; Paris, J. Vrin, 1950), pp. 233-260, 340-341; *Tâche, Réussite et Échec* (1953), pp. 46-52; 456-465.

[14] As a protest against the genetic trend, we can quote the "field-theory" of Kurt Lewin and the "theory of functional autonomy of motives" of Gordon W. Allport. Cf. K. Lewin, *A Dynamic Theory of Personality: Selected Papers*, trans. D. K. Adams and K. E. Zener (New York: McGraw-Hill, 1935); *Principles of Topological Psychology* (1936); G. W. Allport, *The Nature of Personality: Selected Papers* (Cambridge, Mass.: Addison Wesley Press, 1950), pp. 76-113.

[15] R. B. MacLeod, "The Phenomenological Approach to Social Psychology," *Psychol. Rev.* (1947), 54, 193-210.

[16] P. Diel, *Psychologie de la Motivation: Théorie et Application Thérapeutique* (Paris: Press Univ. France, 1948). Paul Diel elaborated his theory of motivation as a function of the therapeutic method. According to him, a disturbed imagination is the origin of the false motivation of personality. The duty of a psychotherapist is to cure the individual from every form of open or hidden false motivation. Cf. especially pp. 86-106.

[17] W. Stern, *General Psychology from the Personalistic Standpoint*, trans. D. Spoerl (New York: Macmillan, 1938), p .408.

[18] *Ibid.*, p. 418.

[19] A. Michotte and E. Prüm, "Etude Experimentale sur le choix volontaire et ses antecedentes immediates," *Arch. Psychol.* (1910), 10, 209.

[20] E. B. Barrett, *Motive Force and Motivation-Tracks* (London, Longmans, Green, 1911), p. 51.

[21] M. Simoneit, "Die mit Bewusstsein der Freiheit Erfolgende Einstellung und Beeinflussung des Bewusstseins als Kern ds Willenserlenisss: Sine Phenomenalen Merkmade," *Arch. Ges. Psychol.* (1937), 98, 286 ff.

[22] A. Michotte and E. Prüm, *op. cit.*, pp. 210-236; E. B. Barrett, *op cit.*, pp. 66.67.

[23] J. Lindworsky, *Experimental Psychology*, trans. H. R. De Silva (New York: Macmillan, 1931), pp. 304 ff.

[24] N. Ach, *Analyse des Willens* (Berlin: Urban und Schwarzenberg, 1935), p. 342.

[25] E. B. Barrett, *Motive-Force and Motivation-Tracks* (London: Long-

mans, Green, 1911), pp. 105-141.

26 A. Michotte and E. Prüm, *op. cit.*, pp. 213-236.

27 On the problem of the reinforcement of motives, cf. especially E. B. Barrett, *op. cit.*, pp. 83-92; J. Lindworsky, *op. cit.*, p. 307. Barrett holds that reinforcement must not be understood in terms of addition or subtraction because the will is moved only by that motive which is assimilated by the individual. A motive can be reinforced by other motives, but this does not mean that the will acts for more than one motive. Lindworsky more accurately specifies the problem of the plurality of motives. He maintains that the union of various weak motives can produce a total value and thus give rise to a volitional act.

28 W. James, *Psychology*, (Cleveland-New York: World Publishing, 1948), pp. 428 ff.

29 H. M. Wells, "The Phenomenology of Acts of Choice," *Brit. Psychol. of Monogr. Suppl.* (1927), 11, 1-155. E. B. Barrett, *op. cit.*

30 A. Michotte, "Note à propos des Contributions Récentes a la Psychologie de la Volonté," *Ann. Inst. Sup. Philos.* (1912), 1, 666.

31 A. H. Martin, "An Experimental Study of the Factors and Types of Voluntary Choice," *Arch. Psychol.* (1922) N. 51, 105.

32 W. Wundt, *Outlines of Psychology*, trans. Charles H. Judd, 2nd Rev. Ed. (Leipzig, 1902), pp. 206 ff.

33 Decision or resolution implying a deliberative process is always in relation to the conscious state of the individual; but this does not mean that every choice is conscious. To avoid the frequent errors on this point, it seems opportune to introduce the distinction between *conscious choice* and *unconscious choice*. Conscious choice is decision or choice in its proper meaning; unconscious choice indicates both an organismic discrimination and an unconscious psychic selection. Cf. R. Zavalloni, "The Process of Choice in Therapeutic Counseling," *Antonianum*, 29 (1954), 313 ff.

34 G. F. Stout, *A Manual of Psychology*, 4th Rev. Ed. in collaboration with the author by C. A. Mace (London: Univ. Tutorial Series, 1932), p. 634.

35 W. James, *op. cit.*, p. 434.

36 *Ibid.*, p. 456. This thesis of William James will be evaluated more carefully *infra* in Chapter VII.

37 A. Michotte and E. Prüm, *Étude Experimentale*, pp. 182-192.

38 Many authors drew attention to the role of muscular sensations and of the sensations of motion in voluntary phenomena. But their importance was highly exaggerated when the attempt was made to find in the "feeling of effort" or in the "feeling of activity" the characteristic phenomenon of the will. The frequent concomitance of the two phenomena does not justify their identification.

39 A. Michotte, *Note à propos des contributions, op. cit.*, p. 700, note 3.

40 A. Michotte and E. Prüm, *Étude Experimentale, op. cit.*, pp. 190 ff. The research of Honoria M. Wells confirmed substantially the classification

by Michotte and Prüm of the types of voluntary choice. She was able to demonstrate the existence of both the decision-type and consent-type, but she does not believe that they are so clearly distinct as the other two authors presuppose. Many responses of her subjects could not be classified according to one type or the other. In her opinion, "decision" is a quick and energetic orientation of the activity of the subject at the moment of the choice; "consent," on the other hand, even though it is also a true choice, is less vigorous and does not show a sudden "actualization" of the subject's activity. Cf. H. M. Wells, "Phenomenology of Acts of Choice," *Brit. Psychol. Monogr. Suppl.* 11, 1927, 106-113.

41 J. W. Bridges, "An Experimental Study of Decision Types and Their Mental Correlates," *Psychol. Monogr.* (1914-1917), n. 72, 1-72.

42 A. H. Martin, "An Experimental Study of the Factors and Types of Voluntary Choice," *Arch. Psychol.* (1922), n. 51, 1-115.

43 A. Gemelli, *La Responsabilità nelle Azioni Umane dal Punto di Vista della Psicologia e Psichiatria, Contributo del Laboratorio de Psicologia,* Serie XII, (Milano: Vita e Pensiero, 1944), p. 219. The idea that the "actualization" of the decision is not essential to voluntary choice has important moral and juridic consequences. According to Gemelli, it is not necessary, in order to judge human responsibility, to determine how the "actualization" or external execution of deliberation happened. What is important is to study what happens in man's conscience in all those cases in which man has consciousness of his own responsibility, that is, when he believes that the action is his own. A. Gemelli, *La Personalità del Delinquente nei suoi Fondamenti Biologici e Psicologici,* 2nd Ed., rev. (Milano: Giuffré, 1948), p. 237.

44 A. Michotte and E. Prüm, "Étude Experimentale," *loc. cit.,* p. 136.

45 A. Michotte, "Note à propos des Contributions," *loc cit.,* pp. 697 ff. N. Ach, *Ueber den Willensakt: Eine Replik* (Leipzig: Quelle und Meyer, 1911), pp. 31-36.

46 N. Ach, *op. cit.,* p. 315 and and p. 320.

47 R. E. Brennan, *General Psychology: An Interpretation of the Science of Mind Based on Thomas Aquinas* (New York: Macmillan, 1937), p. 359.

48 F. Aveling, *Personality and Will* (Cambridge: Cambridge Univ. Press, 1931), pp. 83 ff.

49 N. Ach, *Analyse des Willens* (Berlin: Urban und Schwarzenberg, 1935), pp. 143 ff., 166 ff.

CHAPTER FOUR

Scientific Studies of Voluntary Choice

Among all the problems to which psychologists have addressed themselves, the phenomenon of volitional activity is without doubt the one that leaves them most perplexed. Investigations in this field are scarce, the results generally inconclusive. In fact, any attempt to schematize and to express in quantitative terms the complex phenomenon of voluntary action seems destined to fail when we are confronted with the eminently dynamic character of this activity. Such attempts simply have the effect of demonstrating that the higher functions of man, by the very fact that they involve in an eminent way his whole personality, cannot be expressed by numerical formulas without severe loss to their complexity and depth. Statistical data tend to be too abstract, and they fail to reflect many of the interesting features presented by actual instances of voluntary action. It is evident that the force of a motive, the importance of an alternative, the firmness of a decision escape strict numerical control.

In spite of these deficiencies and limitations, it does seem reasonable to assert that the scientific study of voluntary choice is a legitimate and promising endeavor in view of a certain number of particularly interesting and experimental investigations and of a growing volume of scientific research on material of a clinical nature. A new contribution, and one of decisive importance in the phenomenological analysis of voluntary choice, has arisen from the recent

104

development of new recording techniques for use in psychotherapy. The exactness with which therapeutic interviews can now be recorded and transcribed has resulted in psychological materials of extraordinary value, permitting one to conduct an objective analysis of the personal qualities of an individual.

The body of knowledge concerning voluntary choice which will be analyzed in the present chapter is derived from the results of *experimental research,* from the data of *clinical experience* and, as a particular aspect of the latter, from the experimental data of *psychotherapy.* Finally, the freedom of man will be examined according to the principles of that new orientation in psychiatry called *existential analysis,* which is an attempt to grasp the significance of human activity in relation to the existential mode of the subject.

1. Results of Experimental Research

Many prominent psychologists have succeeded in obtaining by means of experimental studies an empirical description of strong volitional acts under controlled conditions. The introspective protocols of the subjects demonstrate that the internal act of willing is clearly distinct from other cognitive processes which are equally present. As a result of his investigations, Narciss Ach concluded that all attempts to identify the act of willing with cognitive, sensory or intellectual processes, or to reduce the will-act to a combination of such processes, are utterly impossible. The act of willing is an experience totally different from other cognitive processes.[1]

Ach uncovered four factors which were present in the consciousness of his subjects during the experiment: 1) *a feeling of muscular tension,* which arises from various parts of the body, especially from the region of the head, as an effect of attention; 2) *a consciousness of effort,* i.e. the consciousness of having to overcome obstacles by executing some action; 3) *an objective element,* considered as a representation of the goal, i.e. ideas and thoughts regarding the task which is to be accomplished; 4) *a subjective element,* i.e. an act in which the subject is conscious of himself under the form of a decision: "I will," "I can." The subject's consciousness of acting is the pre-eminent characteristic of the volitional act and is absent in other conscious processes.

In their experimental study of voluntary choice, Michotte and Prüm observed the same mental activity that Ach had encountered.[2] Their subjects clearly perceived the presence of a special factor in volitional processes. They report that this fact differentiates the manner of appearance of volitional phenomena from the mechanism of association and induces the subject to interject the ego itself into the description of his experiences. This factor is none other than the "consciousness of acting" and it is absolutely distinct from the feeling of "muscular activity." The latter manifests itself as a simple accompaniment of certain phenomena, i.e. as a characteristic which does not stand of itself as a content of consciousness, but which has need of a substrate to qualify it.

a. The Phenomenon of "Consciousness of Acting"

What seems to be characteristic of the intervention of the volitional factor and gives it the character of an action is the consciousness of "doing," of "acting," of "choosing," of "directing oneself towards," of "saying," of "ceasing to proceed," etc. The consciousness of acting must therefore be considered as a form of intervention of the phenomenological ego in psychic life. It must be added that subjects accurately distinguish this consciousness of acting from the phenomena associated with mere feelings. The consciousness of acting is the characteristic which distinguishes voluntary action from all other activities. The decisions in which this factor is encountered are not only spontaneously attributed to the ego, but are considered by all the subjects to be voluntary. All the other elements can be disposed of without this feature losing the characteristic by which it is considered voluntary.

Michotte and Prüm assert clearly that the consciousness of acting does not appear in itself to be an exclusive attribute of those phenomena which are commonly termed voluntary. Nevertheless its presence always conditions the characteristic of voluntariness of the phenomena which it accompanies.[3] According to these authors, strict agreement exists between the phenomena which they have observed and those reported by Ach concerning the subjective experience of voluntary action. They submit that the "present factor" of Ach (*das aktuelle Moment*) is undoubtedly the one they have termed "consciousness of acting." This "present factor" occurs during the act which accompanies the conscious content "I will," but is completely distinct from it, because the latter can exist without the phenomenon having the character of a voluntary act. Michotte claims that Ach understands the role of the consciousness of acting in a manner absolutely analogous to his own: one is dealing always with an "activity directly lived."[4]

The data obtained by Ach, Michotte and Prüm have caused a great deal of discussion. R. H. Wheeler undertook to verify these data for himself and arrived at entirely different conclusions. "In a voluntary choice," he argues, "there is no consciousness of activity as such, no awareness of an immediate and unanalyzable self and no conscious conative striving process." He maintains that all his subjects were of one accord in admitting that "in their most genuine and difficult acts of choosing such experiences as might be termed 'feelings of mental activity,' 'immediate consciousness of the self,' 'consciousness of effort, of willing,' etc. could be analyzed as organic and kinesthetic processes, with occasional visual, auditory or verbal accompaniments."[5] In determining the objective validity of Wheeler's experiments, it must be borne in mind that all his subjects had well-defined theoretical convictions concerning the very facts they observed.

One of the reasons which induced Honoria M. Wells to undertake her own experiments in the phenomenology of acts of choice was that of verifying the phenomenon of "consciousness of acting," affirmed particularly by Michotte and denied by Wheeler. Wells found that between the motivation in the flow of consciousness, one is dealing with two phenomena which are strictly correlated, and which she describes as "consciousness of acting" and "consciousness of self." The first of these two phenomena depends on the second, because the individual is conscious of himself as the one experiencing, the doer, the subject of the act, and simply cannot become conscious of acting in an abstract way, detached from reality

As for the change which is observed in the consciousness of a subject during the volitional process, Wells believes she can "identify the dynamic experience which appears in consciousness at that moment with the 'consciousness of self-activity' reported by Michotte and Prüm and the 'actuelle Betatigung' of Ach."[6] Wells found no justification for Wheeler's statement that consciousness of self-activity can be reduced to kinesthetic and organic sensations as its fundamental elements. She found evidence on the contrary that consciousness of self-activity is absolutely distinct and different from kinesthetic and organic phenomena. These may accompany it, but they are not necessary to it.[7]

Alfred M. Martin's experimental study, which we have frequently quoted, verifies and confirms Michotte and Prüm's results, and also those of Wells, since the factors which are found in the psychic processes by these experimenters are substantially identical.[8] The results of Martin's study, however, differ from the results of Wheeler's "experimental investigation of the process of choosing." The point of difference concerns the *cause* of the voluntary-motor-process and final result, choice. According to Wheeler, the ultimate *cause* and the ultimate *reason* of the process of choosing would be, in the last analysis, only *associative* (the ego is but a bundle of sensations), and would act by means of mechanical forms of relaxation and reinforcement of the sensory bond (sensations are the constitutive elements of all our conscious processes). But Martin attributes choice, the final result, to a *directive cause* which is called, after McDougall's terminology, a "self-assertive tendency." This tendency gives to Ach's phrase, "I really want," its true meaning. Thus we can say that the final result of voluntary choice assumes, in the last analysis, the significance of a "self-assertive tendency." On the other hand, the "consciousness of acting," demonstrated by Michotte and Prüm, is reinforced both in its function and its content. This consciousness of acting can be conceived as a directive tendency, which manifests itself as a special determination. In opposition to Wheeler's assertion, the result of Martin's experiments demonstrates that no type of analysis can reduce the voluntary process to a group of elementary and marginal experiences.

b. The Experience of the Self-in-Action

In the acts of voluntary choice, the consciousness of acting is intimately connected with the consciousness of self, so that it is impossible to formulate it without this latter concept. The subjects of the aforementioned experiments could not otherwise describe their experiences.

According to Lindworsky it is worth noting that, in all the experiments on the will which had some success, the subjects always expressed the *ego-in-action* when they attempted to describe the act of willing.[9] These expressions certainly indicate vividly the subjective experience of the act of willing.

The various emotional experiences which were described by Ach's subjects took place without any activity of the ego, and so spontaneously that not one of the subjects mistook these emotional experiences for the act of the will itself. Ach inferred from the objective data obtained from his subjects that the emotional theory of the will is untenable. None of the experiences could be reported without the interposition of the ego as the subject of the action. The act of willing differs from all the other acts and processes precisely because the ego is experienced as the originator of the experience. The ego-in-action which is observed in the volitional act is not a matter of inference but an "immediate datum of experience." [10] In Ach's experiments, so vigorous was the active interposition of the ego that it was accompanied by characteristic bodily attitudes such as energetic gestures and imperative verbal expressions, etc. These bodily attitudes were but the *outward sign* of the conscious attitude of the ego-in-action.

Michotte and Prüm in their study found that the conscious experience of the ego in voluntary acts was an experience of a special character, which should not and could not be confused with other conscious experiences. It was a consciousness involving the subjet's own personal activity, which is so vividly present in the voluntary choice. A subject asserts: "It is I who have chosen; it is I who have designated, who have determined," and adds, "Any other way of expressing it would be false. I cannot say, 'That was brought about in me'; no, it is I who did it."

This consciousness of the ego, these two authors point out, seems to be one of the primary criteria of the phenomenon of volition.[11] At a certain point in the experiment, the subjects experience the intimate link which joins the "fiat" of the decision to the concept of the causality of the ego. Of course this concept is not present at the moment of the act of willing, but only when the subject has to describe exactly what went through his mind during the act of will-

ing. On the one hand, this phenomenon is in opposition to the mechanical course of the psychic life which is absolutely neutral in
this regard, and, on the other hand, to the consciousness of being
acted upon, of being influenced, of feeling passive in any way.[12]

The fact that the subject experiences the will to actualize that
which he himself decides and determines to do is a discovery of the
greatest importance for the phenomenology of the act of willing.
This same experience was the goal of a more recent group of experimental studies supervised by Gustav Störring.

Sophie Trouet studied the motives which lead to the act of
choice.[13] She distinguished various groups of motives. Particularly
significant is the "affective" motivation which may appear under
various forms: feelings which are caused by the circumstances
leading to decision (for example, hesitation produced by the feeling of perplexity); mental or subjective feelings which determine
the decision (e.g. a state of fatigue). What deserves to be pointed
out in Trouet's experiments is precisely this distinction between the
objective and subjective motives which lead to decision.

Paul Skawran improved Trouet's method and was more successful in determining the conditions of voluntary choice.[14] He demonstrated that an affective state in which pleasant feelings are predominant constitutes a tendency towards a stronger action, while a
passive state of the same type tends towards a minimum of activity.
The choice appears as the effect of different elements. The direction
of voluntary activity is given by the goals which one wants to reach.
Motives lead to decision according to their own laws; but the person as such, because of the powerful number of feelings it can
mobilize, is able to arrest at any moment the role of these laws and
to permit the preferred action to triumph.

Hubert Rohracher concluded from his experimental studies that
"the essence of will is an activity of the personality." [15] In a situation which postulates an act of choice, the person as such orients
itself towards a concrete goal. Since a general tendency is now present in the person, that procedure then follows which appears the
most suitable for attaining the chosen goal. It was this influence of
the personality—i.e., the intervention of the ego in voluntary activity—which induced some psychologists to attempt new experimental
studies.

c. The Consciousness of Freedom in the Process of Willing

The limitation of the selective process in the experiments of Sophie Trouet and Paul Skawran were noted by Käthe Gies, who therefore attempted to observe the phenomenon of voluntary choice in the real circumstances of daily life. She did not try merely to discover what happens to the subject during the experiment, but also to understand the causal dependence of the acts which appeared during the experimental situation from the conditions in the subject which preceded them. In other words, her point of view is that of understanding in what way a present voluntary action can be determined by previous acts of the will.[16] The choice had to be made by the subjects for the same motives which seem to prevail in their real life. The subjects were asked to pay particular attention to those cases where they had a clear feeling of acting with full freedom, and had to give an account of the causes and conditions of this feeling.

This method of research allowed the experimenter to clarify what she calls "the experience of the consciousness of freedom in the process of willing." [17] It must be pointed out that most of the subjects speak in their protocols of "a consciousness of freedom," or of "a feeling of freedom," according to whether the intellectual or emotional factor seems clearer. The characteristics of the experience of freedom are as follows. The subjects faced two alternatives whose motives for action seemed of equal force. "I can freely propose to myself," a subject writes, "the reasons why I chose one alternative rather than the other. No objective compulsion exists." "Objective compulsion" is conceived as the effect of the motives which originate from the alternatives to be chosen. Thus a relationship between the "alternatives of choice" and the presence of "the ego-who-chooses" is established. The subject recognizes in this case that the motives are not unconditionally determining him, and says: "Certainly I can, if I want to, provide a stronger motive to each of my inclinations." But in another case the subject feels that it is "difficult to arrive at a decision because no reason is given to him why he should choose one alternative rather than the other." But when this subject perceives the situation clearly and understands the relationship between the alternatives and the person who must choose, he asserts: "I am free to decide in favor of one alternative; I am not determined by definite motives which are forcing me."

The following protocols show how the subjects of the experiment feel the autonomy of the ego in the act of deciding: "I can make this choice, but only if I want to"; "I must choose between two alternatives . . . ; to arrive at a conclusion I do whatever I want. This depends only on my personality. My experience tells me that I am such that I can act freely. . . In this way I decided freely." It must be pointed out that the conviction, "I could also make the opposite choice," is present not only before the resolution or after the decision has been taken, but also *at the very moment* of the voluntary determination. The active intervention of the ego, since only the ego can decide, gives a further experience of freedom. "I decide for the first alternative"; "I experience a direct feeling of freedom when I am ready to accept this motive, because I am clearly and fully conscious that I could decide also in favor of other alternatives." The activity of the ego is clear in this assertion: "I am ready to submit myself to the motive; I feel that I made an internal choice absolutely of my own free will, without any coercion from without." According to the observations of the subjects, the decision is taken only by the activity of the conscious ego, and it appears to them as "a choice completely free." [18]

From the results of Gies' study, we can characterize the experience of freedom as a complex one whose elements can be synthesized as (1) a clear understanding of the situation or of the objects of choice: the alternatives are present with this or that value; (2) the establishment of a connection between the possibilities of choice and the subject who chooses; (3) the active intervention of the ego as a source of energy and the consciousness that the decision is autonomous; (4) a pleasant feeling linked with the consciousness of not being determined, but of taking a decision freely, as the following assertion illustrates: "I feel perfectly free."

To summarize the fundamental ideas of Gies' experimental study: there is an experience of freedom when the motives for the opposing alternatives are equal. But the same experience can also be found in the case of motives of differing value, because the ego can make its own decision even against a predominant motive. *The feeling and the consciousness of freedom are fundamentally reducible to the self-determining action of the subject.* It is clear that this does not exclude the influence and the conditioning effect of the motives which exist in the subject who is responsible for the action.

Gustav Störring has examined the consciousness of freedom in several experimental studies made under his direction, particularly with an eye to the findings of Käthe Gies.[19] In a great number of cases, Störring points out, the consciousness of the freedom of the will manifests itself by means of the awareness and the active intervention of the ego. Obviously there can be an act of determination and choice without the consciousness of the ego playing any role in it. This takes place when the "impulses" of the will, which by the majority of the subjects are called "motives," do not have sufficient efficacy.

According to Störring, the consciousness of freedom can occur in various ways and circumstances. It can be produced, after the establishment of alternatives of equal value, in the form of *addition*: something is added to one of the alternatives. It can be produced, after the establishment of a strong tendency towards the actualization of one of the alternatives, in the form of *resistance* of the ego to this tendency. And after the establishment of a difference of energy between the motives for action and the active intervention of the ego, it can be produced in the form of a *surrender* to one of the impulses or motives for acting.

In Käthe Gies' study the initial portions of the protocols give the impression of a deterministic concept of voluntary activity. Later sections, however, stress so clearly the consciousness of freedom that the reader cannot understand the first statements in a deterministic way. Störring's own experiments likewise show the non-deterministic character of this consciousness of freedom, because the subjects openly declare they are free to make or not to make their preferential choice.

d. Prediction of Choices and Responsibility

By studying the introspective protocols of his subjects, Narciss Ach was able to predict—even in rather complicated multiple-choice problems—the selections of the subjects with one hundred per cent accuracy. Ach concludes from his experiments that the behavior of a man in various situations is essentially determined by his character.[20]

At the International Congress of Psychology held at Groninck in 1926, Ach described an experiment which he felt to be decisive in demonstrating the possibility of predicting voluntary choices. He experimented with some subjects in a very limited field, studied their character in its relationship to the activity in question, and could predict how his subjects would act in a given situation. The author calls attention to the following proposition as the main conclusion of his experiments: "Even in so-called free choice, the sequence of mental phenomena is uniquely determined." [21] The argument leading to this conclusion might be formulated: If by an experimental study of a subject's mind I can arrange for him a choice of activities of such a character that I can always predict the selection he will make, then the selection made is not a genuine free choice but one that is uniquely determined.

It is evident that in Ach's opinion the determining factor is man's psychological structure. Joseph Froebes answers that it is illogical to conclude "that actions are uniquely determined only because they can be in some manner predicted." [22] Froebes has therefore rejected the conclusion which argues from a correct prediction to a correspondingly necessary determination. But Ach seems never to have realized the force of this objection, which is of maximum importance.

Working from the presupposition that this method of prediction proves determinism of human actions, Ach attempted to explain the feeling of freedom by means of a distinction between two types of consciousness: "dynamic consciousness" and "indeterministic consciousness." Dynamic consciousness can be expressed by the phrase, "I want to carry out what I will to do"; indeterministic consciousness can be expressed in the following way: "I need not execute what I will do." When one refers these states of consciousness to the same action — which represents the indeterministic aspect of the feeling of freedom—then, because of an abstraction which transcends the facts, the positive and negative forms are applied to one and the same act: "I can do, and I need not do what I will." Ach asks himself at this point: What is the root of this feeling? It is the intervention of the ego which, needing to maintain its superiority, tends towards complete freedom. This need in practice is never reached effectively in our consciousness, but it presents itself as an ideal towards which we unconsciously tend.

At the congress of Psychology held in Bayreuth in 1938, Ach maintained that the idea of being free in our actions leads man to the feeling of *responsibility,* and the reality of this feeling exercises of itself a motivating causality. In this way the consciousness of being responsible for one's actions takes over the instinctive and habitual forces of our behavior. Consequently the feeling of freedom, even though an illusion, exercises a real force upon human behavior.[23] Ach does not seem aware of the contradiction which is implied in his method of reasoning. If man is determined in his actions, if freedom is merely an illusion, how can he say that the feeling of freedom exerices some influence on human behavior? Ach's attempt to reconcile determinism, as he understands it, with human responsibility is a failure. This problem will be the subject-matter of a more thorough examination in the second part of this study.

e. Psychological Characteristics of Hesitancy

Recently Jósef Reutt attempted to develop an experimental method which would be sufficiently complete, varied and precise, and would at the same time remedy certain deficiencies in the preceding studies.[24] Those which Reutt sums up and criticizes at the beginning of his book are the studies of Michotte and Prüm in Belgium, of Lüderitz in Germany, of Chojecki and Dybowski in Poland. The main objection that Reutt raises against their findings is the artificial and fragmentary character of the experiments. The phenomenon of hesitancy, he says, was not studied as it should have been in its total development, under the various psychological aspects that occur in real life. The imperfections of the above-mentioned experiments demonstrate the difference which exists between a fictitious or meaningless hesitancy and a real and important one; in other words, between an apparent choice in a laboratory and an effective and responsible choice in real life.

In order to avoid as carefully as possible the deficiencies of other experiments, the author developed an experimental plan, broad and varying, which comprises various stages. Reutt's experiments include, in the first place, a true experimental study of those phenomena of hesitancy which are directly observable. Secondly, his research presents accounts of hesitancy as experienced by various persons on the occasion of some important event in their lives.

The experiment comprises four different situations, each one of them with a different kind of choice proposed to the subject.

First situation: the investigator offers the subject the possibility of making a real choice between two packages.

Second situation: the investigator reads a letter to the subject which he received from a college girl who is facing the following problem: either to continue her studies with excellent prospects or abandon her studies in order to help her brother, who is seriously ill in a concentration camp. The investigator asks what he should write to this girl.

Third situation: the investigator offers two free passes to a movie; the subject can accept or reject the offer.

Fourth situation: the investigator asks the subject to find other persons who would be willing to undergo his experiments; the subject is free to accept or reject this proposal.

The experimental study of these four cases of hesitancy and choice was undertaken from two different but complementary points of view: (1) from the objective viewpoint, careful observation of the behavior of the subject and its variations in the successive situations; (2) from the subjective viewpoint, a personal account of the subject of what he feels during the state of hesitancy; the effort of the subject himself to describe his psychological state.

The second part of Reutt's research entails retrospective accounts of hesitations as they were experienced by the subjects in different circumstances of life. This part is of considerable interest because it refers not to events of little importance, as generally happens in the laboratory experiments, but to serious situations where hesitancy and decision have a particular importance for the subject. As examples of these various alternatives characterized by hesitancy, the following cases can be given: indecision whether or not to plunge into the water and save a person who is drowning; the hesitancy of a person who is in danger—whether or not to call for help; a situation created by war—whether to take part in the resistance movement or to subscribe to a declaration imposed by the Germans; hesitancy with regard to the choice of a profession, of courses of study, etc. This part of Reutt's research happily completed, from the psychological viewpoint, whatever of the superficial or fictitious there is in a laboratory experiment.

The results of Reutt's study can be summarized briefly. Hesitancy is defined as a complex psychic phenomenon, *sui generis*. The phenomenon is characterized intellectually by a state of uncertainty, and affectively by a rather unpleasant state of anxiety, of indecision and uneasiness; this state presents itself to the subject's consciousness under the aspect of a problem to be solved. The psychological characteristics of the phenomenon are outlined by the author in the following way. The phenomenon varies in its duration, intensity and modality of occurrence in relation to individual differences, to the object of hesitancy, and to the conditions which accompany it. The same phenomenon is then analyzed from the viewpoint of its psychological structure, of its form and its dynamism, with its discontinuities, irregular oscillations, intervals of interruption and recurrence, and particular modalities of development.

The main qualities of this study are its method, the ingenious organization of the experimental research, and the choice of subjects (one hundred and six, almost all university students). Reutt's method allowed him to observe the phenomenon of hesitancy under various aspects in a more complete manner than in the preceding experimental studies. Hesitancy was studied under the form of the actual phenomenon as it was happening, as well as under the form of memory; it was examined under the objective and controllable aspect, and under the subjective and introspective aspect; as an intellectual phenomenon and as an affective phenomenon. One objection which could be raised against this method is that it does not offer an objective measure of the duration of hesitancy, nor does it allow us to capture the moment at which hesitancy begins. Another reservation: since the experiment utilized only intellectuals as subjects, this might have influenced the predominantly intellectual character of hesitancy, a facet particularly stressed by the author. Nevertheless, Reutt's work is certainly a positive contribution to the phenomenology of voluntary choice.

2. Factors Derived from Clinical Experience

The clinical method permits investigation of the depth of motivation in human action. Thanks to this method, the true motives of the will have been so thoroughly investigated that this approach can compare with the best laboratory analyses, while behaviorism had previously reduced to a minimum the intervention of dynamic factors in the stimulus-response relationship.[25]

Clinical psychologists have written extensively of the relationship that obtains between integration of personality and the ability to resolve a problem. Their experience with mental disorders and with psychic disturbances had induced the belief that a deficiency in this field constitutes, properly speaking, the fundamental difficulty in functional illnesses. Often a nervous disorder has its cause in a selective process which has not been resolved. A series of difficult decisions can terminate in failure because the negative effects of the psychic disturbances accumulate. The patient cannot stop worrying about the simple decisions of daily life. Nervous exhaustion caused by his main problem makes everything a problem. This indecision can be extended very broadly into the past and the future.

a. Automatism and Voluntary Decision

Pierre Janet offers a clear proof that the inability to make decisions is the main characteristic of neurotic patients. He does not explain this inability in terms of excitement or muscular tension, but in terms of energy or "mental force."

According to Edwin R. Guthrie: "Janet's *force mentale* is closely related to the muscular excitement which serves for the reinforcement of action. The depressed person is a person in whom the somatic conditions for vigorous action are not present. It is common knowledge that decisions are much more difficult to make when we are fatigued or weak from illness. In a normal person the very occurrence of a conflict serves to produce the excitement which makes the situation unstable, introduces new elements into it and so resolves the conflict. In fatigue or illness or in the neuroses the excitement fails to reach the point necessary for overcoming the block."[26] Doubtless this is true. But there does not seem to be any reason to diminish and almost deny the difference which exists between muscular and mental effort. Guthrie's conviction does not seems to be in accordance with the general doctrine developed by Janet in his main works. The following passage shows clearly that Janet's distinction, challenged by Guthrie, is more profound and substantial than Guthrie implies: "In spontaneous illness, as in experience, we notice the lack of a voluntary and conscious function, but the continuation of an involuntary and subconscious function. This is a curious verification of our hypothesis concerning one of the first and most important degrees of cerebral and mental dissociation."[27]

In a revised edition of his study on automatism, Janet specifies the characteristics of the will, pointing out that "in various studies on abulia we have demonstrated how the novelty of the acts and the conscious and personal character of the action should have been considered as essential elements of the will."[28] It is evident that these essential elements, which are attributed by Janet to the will, cannot in any way be ascribed to muscular tension. Therefore a real distinction between muscular and mental effort or tension is at least implicit in Janet's doctrine.

Janet conducted many experiments on automatic writing, on unconscious acts, and similar dissociations. As a conclusion to these studies, he thinks that it would be profitable to examine under what aspect and to what degree the free and normal act differs, at least apparently, from this mechanical and strictly determined activity, which is *automatism*. His studies resulted in the reduction of the varying phenomena of automatism to their essential factors. The majority of them depend on a state of anesthesia or dissociation. This state is due essentially to the narrowing of the field of consciousness; and this in turn to the weakness of the power of synthesis and to the dissociation of the mental factors into different groups which are more restricted than usual. Such dissociation does not result in an excited state, but in depression or weakness. This effect permits us also to conclude that there is a particular moral weakness consisting in the inability of the subject to unify and condense psychological phenomena and to assimilate them into an efficient synthesis. Janet writes: "Just as physiological difficulty to assimilate has been called *physiological misery,* so we propose to call this moral disturbance by the name of *psychological misery.*"[29]

After having defined automatic phenomena as characteristic of abnormal persons, Janet proceeds to consider the lower forms of normal activity. He begins with this presupposition: if automatic phenomena are due only to weakness, then they must exist in the normal as well as in the abnormal person, the only difference being that in the normal man they are masked and superseded by other more complex phenomena. The rich man already has the bread and water that the poor man has, but he has many other things that the poor do not have; the healthy person possesses the automatisms of the sick person, even though the healthy person has in addition other higher faculties. Distraction, instinct, habit and passion—these are phenomena that the personal consciousness leaves to automatic development. What separates a normal from an abnormal person is this: the normal person possesses an activity superadded to the automatic activity which he has in common with the abnormal person. Automatism constitutes the entire life of persons in the state of "psychological misery," while in sane persons automatism is found only in certain inferior, habitual and emotional acts because this state is completed and superseded by the will.

When he analyzes the nature of the superior voluntary activity, Janet returns to the theory of volitional effort of William James in order to show how voluntary activity is distinguished from inferior activity. He stresses one important factor, *the judgment of the will*.[30] In his opinion voluntary acts are determined by judgment or ideas of relation; when judgments do not intervene, there is no voluntary action. Volitional effort consists precisely in the systematization of images and memories which then express themselves automatically. "The psychological misery" found in sick persons does not allow them to actualize even the elementary syntheses which constitute one's functional perceptions; *a maiori,* it does not allow them the syntheses necessary to voluntary activity. It is the intervention of judgment which characterizes true voluntary attention.

This voluntary activity determined by judgment has its own characteristics. It presents, first of all, a unity and harmony which are much more perfect than automatic activity. The latter in fact has its origin in a very weak synthesis which involves only a small number of images; it does not persist long in the same direction, and on the whole it appears very incoherent and changeable. While automatic activity leads man through various psychological states, voluntary activity tends towards a unity of the psychological life.

It must be pointed out finally that the automatic act is rigorously determined, because it is the brutal, unmodified expression of the phenomena which actually exist in the subject. The automatic act can depend on only one isolated image, or it can be the effect of a great number of phenomena or of an entire psychological state. In other words, the automatic act can have degrees of complexity, but it is always determined and can also be easily predicted. But when the automatic act is the effect of a judgment or of an idea in general, it acquires a real independence. Doubtless this act is always the expression of a psychic phenomenon not contained in the preceding images or in the psychological situation given. We have to deal then with a new and unexpected phenomenon, such as consciousness itself, which appears at the center of mechanical phenomena in the organic movement and represents, in relation to them, something undetermined and free. There is nothing freer, according to Pierre Janet, than that which cannot be predicted. Is not the act of a man of genius the freest act in the world? The more man is capable of thinking a personal idea of his own, without the help of external sensations or preceding associations, the more he approaches genius and freedom.[31]

Automatism depends in all its manifestations, as we have seen, on a deficiency in the capacity of synthesis, namely on a debility or psychological "weakness." The genius, on the other hand, has the power of forming completely new ideas that nobody would be able to know or predict. He possesses the highest degree of moral power. Ordinary men oscillate between these two extremes: the weaker the moral power, the more determined and automatic they are; the more their moral power increases, the freer and more ethical they are.

The judgment considered by Janet as the essential element of voluntary activity in many cases manifests the characteristic of "reflexive assent." [32] The presentation of alternatives and their evaluation must be considered imaginative attempts at action in the form of a dialogue or debate in the mind. Such mental debate gives rise to social responses within ourselves. In these internal dialogues we recall moral laws, we praise or blame the various protagonists and even ourselves, and we relive the memory of similar actions and their favorable or unfavorable consequences. After a notable intermediary period, which takes the form of a relative delay (quite long in certain subjects), one makes a decision and arrives at a conclusion.

The result on the part of the subject is either a positive or a negative assent. The idea is definitely rejected or is transformed into a voluntary act or reflexive conviction. We are dealing then not with simple voluntary actions, but with *decisions* in which there is an adjustment to the action on the part of the entire personality. The action becomes personal much in the same way the conviction became real. Of course this task of "reflexive assent" is prolonged and difficult, but it can be actualized in normal persons. If it is true that the most common psychic disorder consists precisely in the inability to carry reflection to its completion, to make a decision, to arrive at a conclusion different from the premises, then we have an indirect but nevertheless real demonstration of the freedom of the will in the activity of a man who is unaffected by psychological weakness.

b. The Will as a Therapeutic Factor

To search for the concept of freedom of the will in the framework of the psyche as described by Freud is useless. We could object, Dalbiez observes, that Freud treats the abnormal and not the normal psyche, and that an appeal to freedom of the will is not a therapeutic method.[33] Actually, both psychic and somatic sicknesses are defined in relation to health. The goal of treatment represents, then, a return to normality, to the possibility of reassuming our own freedom. Freud should have preserved the role of freedom in the economy of the human psyche. He did not do so because his empirical orientation led him necessarily to ignore the spontaneity of the will.

Otto Rank, who represents a deviation from the orthodox psychoanalytic trend, used the term "will" with full awareness that the will has its place in modern psychology as it has in popular belief. The latter associates will-power with the possibility of being healed.[34] Rank, of course, did not think that the neurotic could be liberated from his symptoms by means of volitional effort according to the popular concept. But he did grasp a fundamental truth which psychology up to that time had ignored, and he utilized it in a doctrine of the will as it appears in human relationships, particularly in therapeutic relationships.

Rank's starting point is the concept of "will-power," on which therapeutic success, in the last analysis, depends. A demonstration for the existence of such a factor is found in the so-called process of "transference," which for Freud represents a repetition of a childhood experience, and which for Rank becomes a creative expression of the growth and development of the personality in the therapeutic experience. What is really effective in Rank's doctrine of "transference" is that same factor which appears strongly in every relationship between two human beings—the will. When two wills clash, either the one overthrows the other, or both struggle with and against one another for supremacy. According to Rank, Adler intuited the importance of this battle for supremacy—"the will to be on top"—as he calls it, but he is wrong in considering this type of "will to superiority" as the ultimate psychological fact without offering a psychology of will in general, which alone would make these phenomena intelligible.

Rank's aim is to show how rehabilitation of the will can resolve many problems in one stroke. Although the will always played an important role in clinical experience, it never enjoyed a psychology of its own which would have made of it a scientifically acceptable therapeutic factor.

Our problem can be considered under a twofold aspect: (1) to note how therapy of the will is denied in the analytical approach, and (2) how voluntary power is expressed in a therapeutic experience. In Freud's psychoanalysis, the will evidently plays no role or function; but the exclusion of the will is possible only to a limited degree. Even though it would seem paradoxical, we could say with Rank that "Psychoanalysis, in its therapeutic consequences, is an involuntary proof of the existence and strength of the will, and this was and also is its only therapeutic value." [35] Actually, the analytic situation shows not merely that the exclusion of will is impossible, but that every attempt to exclude it only strengthens the will-reactions. The goal of Freudian psychoanalysis is to free the subject from tension or to overcome repression. But the goal of Rank's "constructive or positive therapy" is the transformation of the negative expression of the will into a positive or creative expression.

The "causal principle" of the psychoanalytic theory implies denial of the "volitional principle"; in fact, this "causal principle" makes an individual's thinking, feeling, and acting something based on forces independent of the individual, and thus it frees him from responsibility and guilt. The supposed opposition between the two principles — causal and volitional — derives, according to Rank, from a misconception of the causal principle. Psychic causality differs from physical causality because in physical causality there is an endless chain of causes which cannot be closed unless we postulate a first psychological cause. Rank writes:

> "Only in the individual act of will do we have the unique phenomenon of spontaneity, the establishing of a new primary cause. In this case, not only the will but the individual as bearer of it, represents a psychologically new fact, which does not arbitrarily interrupt the causal chain with any kind of final assumption of free will, but actually sets in motion a new causal chain." [36]

In this way the idea of will is correlative with the idea of man as the initiator of a new series of causes.

Rank compares his doctrine to Freud's and opposes it. He points out that psychoanalysis gives the individual merely a new kind of excuse for his inability to will and a release from the responsibility of consciousness. The task of "constructive or positive therapy," on the contrary, is to lead the individual to accept himself and his own responsibility voluntarily. The therapeutic factor has the effect of seeking and creating for him that psychic state which eliminates fate in him and gives him the self-determination he deserves. Fate and self-determination psychologically correspond to two different attitudes of the individual facing the problem of the will: fate is the "causal force," self-determination is ethical freedom of the will. This means that man is not only a psychological personality but also a moral personality. The principle of causality applied to the psyche of man leads necessarily to the recognition of a force, but "the only force which rules in psychic life is the force of will which is the psychic representative of causality." [37]

In his *Truth and Reality* Rank stresses his conviction that the reintegration of the concept of the will in psychology resolves a whole series of problems in a very simple and satisfactory way. This seems so evident to him that he does not understand how psychologists can still oppose "the complete recognition and valuation of will as a great psychic power." If we restore to the will its own psychological rights, the whole of the psychology of man becomes of necessity a psychology of "consciousness." And the psychology of the "unconscious" "unveils itself to us as one of the numerous attempts of mankind to deny the will in order to evade the conscious responsibility following of necessity therefrom.'" According to Rank, "free will belongs to the idea of guilt or sin as inevitably as day to night." [38]

Even though there were no other proofs in favor of man's freedom, the consciousness of guilt or culpability would be sufficient to prove that freedom of the will is an actual fact.

c. The Creative and Integrating Power of Man

Rank traced the development of the will-conflict of an individual and discovered a negative and a positive aspect of the conflict. The negative aspect leads the individual to the admission of the consciousness of guilt; the positive leads him to the performance of his duty. This "duty," in the event that the will is capable of asserting itself and its own activity at the ethical level, can lead finally to "creativity," which alters, reforms, and builds anew the internal and external environment of the individual. From a purely psychological analysis of the act of the will, Rank arrived at a critical evaluation of its content.

This same concept can be found in the system of Carl G. Jung. In order to understand correctly the doctrine of this psychologist concerning the problem of man's free activity, we must first of all take his point of view and recognize with him the *full reality of the psyche*.[39] To Jung the psychic world is no less real than the physical world. Even though the psychic world is not immediately tangible and visible, it is fully and clearly a matter of experience. All our knowledge comes to us by the mediation of the psyche, which is therefore one of the most important aspects and one of the most essential conditions of experience.

By psyche Jung understands the totality of all psychological processes, both conscious and unconscious. And by totality he understands something more than unity as it is understood, for example, by Gestalt psychology. His concept of totality implies a kind of integration, a unification of parts, a "creative synthesis" which includes an active and directive power of the psyche. Even though we might have a full knowledge of everything that the present contains, the future would be very uncertain and unforeseeable; this is because, in addition to mechanical laws, there exists in nature a creative principle of life which is free to choose and create new forms. In psychology this would mean that the human being can have a real, though not unconditioned, freedom of choice, and thus can exercise a decisive influence on mental or psychic development.[40]

In agreement with Jung, Kurt Goldstein holds that every study of human behavior which does not take into consideration the "creative power of man" is absolutely inadequate. This introduction into the human psyche of a positive force in order to correct the deficiencies of Freudian pessimism and neo-behavioristic relativism is of maximum importance for motivation and for the theory of values. In Goldstein's system, *"man is free to make his own decisions: the capacity to bear anxiety is a proof of it."* Such a capacity, the manifestation of a genuine courage, is nothing else than an affirmative response to the difficulties of existence. The phenomenon of anxiety requires the ability to see a particular experience in the framework of a broad context, that is, the ability to "take an attitude towards the possible" and "to maintain freedom of decision in regard to various possibilities." This ability is peculiar to man. The proof of it is that persons who are affected by brain injuries have lost it, and have suffered such a consequent impairment of freedom that they are completely helpless when facing an anxiety situation.[41]

The manner in which creatures in general, and human beings in particular, cope with anxiety provides insight into their nature. According to Goldstein, there is nothing that shows us more clearly the connection between freedom and the capacity for sustaining anxiety (and which makes it so evident that freedom is inherent in human nature), than the difference between the behavior of a person with a brain injury and a normal person. This difference, then, shows clearly that freedom is a faculty which belongs to the essence of human nature. The more a normal person is able to bear pain and grief, sorrows and anxiety, the more he preserves his freedom. Goldstein maintains that man must seek harmony in an active way, in a way which is proper to him because "he is free to make his own decisions. One might evaluate this freedom as essentially positive or essentially negative; certainly it remains a basic characteristic of human nature." [42]

The creative and integrating power of a normal person—and, conversely, the lack of such a power in a physically and psychically disturbed person—has been particularly emphasized by Henry Baruk. This psychiatrist, whose stress on the "synthetic power" of the human person calls to mind Pierre Janet's doctrine, studied the functioning of voluntary activity by using mechanical means, through which he obtained psycho-physiological reactions from his subjects. [43] Consciousness remains, but will-power is suspended in "cataleptic" sleep. Voluntary initiative can be abolished by a peculiar sort of torpor which seizes the patient and renders him incapable of acting, even though he remains conscious. Certain intoxicating agents can bring about a special torpor which "freezes" not only the body but the psyche as well, and impedes the free exercise of the will. The main consequence of every mechanical disturbance of the normal functioning of the will is more or less to deprive the subject of his freedom, of his psychological independence. This privation of freedom is felt not only on the physical level, e.g. privation of bodily movements, but it also affects the entire psychological and ethical life. The sick person notices the diminishing or the disappearance of the feeling of freedom.

Baruk points out also that if we remain in the field of impartial clinical observation, we should recognize that one of the psychological differences between healthy and sick persons is this: healthy persons have the feeling of acting freely, while sick persons find themselves under the influence of a morbid state which ultimately takes on the character of a more or less impelling determinism. The feeling of freedom is very weak, and can be suspended by certain somatic and intoxicating agents. But such agents are not the only ones that act upon human behavior. The functioning of the psyche is extremely sensitive to the general surrounding environment, to the education a person has received, to the ideas and beliefs which he has adopted, and to his psychological and social makeup. In short, a person's psyche can be influenced by a multitude of spiritual and environmental factors which play a very considerable role in the development of his personality.

At the conclusion of another study Baruk observes that the results of psychophysiological research demonstrate that the *functions* which are called *voluntary* constitute the *greatest synthetic power* that a psychophysical personality can have.[44] It is this synthetic power which enables us to control ourselves and to act at the same time. When this synthetic power is weakened under the influence, for example, of an intoxicating agent, the personality becomes disturbed in its psychic functions; as a result of this disturbance, a tendency towards more accentuated automatisms is noticed. These automatisms at first continue to wear the mask of voluntary acts, but actually they have already lost the fundamental character of voluntary acts and their freedom. A gradual descent occurs from the free act towards a determined act, then towards compulsion, and finally towards psychic and neurological automatisms.

3. Voluntary Choice in Psychotherapy

The kind of experience to be considered in the following pages refers both to the dynamic principle of self-actualization and to the "holistic" orientation found in modern-day biology and psychology.

The fact that one of the most fundamental characteristics of organic life is its tendency towards total, organized, purposeful responses is becoming more clearly recognized by all. The explanation of behavior based solely on the "stimulus-response" relationship is becoming inadequate and unacceptable in psychology. A remarkable fact which must definitely be taken into consideration is that the organism is at every moment a totally organized system. Its characteristic orientation is in the direction of an ever greater independence and autonomy.

The ideas of "mental effort" and of "constructive therapy," which were met respectively in the systems of Janet and Rank, still remain fundamental concepts; but the stress is placed on man's whole personality rather than on his will-power alone.

In the following pages we shall attempt a sufficiently thorough if not exhaustive account of man's free activity as it is presented in contemporary psychotherapy, mainly on the basis of the principles of non-directive psychotherapy or of client-centered therapy. This trend stresses more strongly than any other the value and the constructive power of human personality.

a. Insight and Constructive Choice

In the system of Carl R. Rogers the point of departure is the idea of "reality." Leaving aside any attempt to solve the problem of its constitutive elements, reality can be defined for practical purposes as "the private world of individual perceptions." The perceptual field is therefore the reality to which the individual reacts. Strictly associated with this is the idea of "self-perception" or *insight*. Various formulations have been used to define this term, but all of them emphasize the fact that insight is essentially a new way of perceiving oneself and, as such, it implies the factor of choice, i.e., the perception of various alternatives. Rogers writes: "Genuine insight includes the positive choice of more satisfying goals." [45]

This act of choice has been called "creative will." This term does not imply the idea of a new, mysterious force which suddenly enters the picture. Rather it signifies that power of choice which is manifested when the individual is confronted by two or more alternatives for the satisfaction of his needs. In psychotherapy, insight generally implies a choice between alternatives which give immediate and temporary satisfaction and others which offer delayed but permanent ones. In this respect man chooses the course of action which gives him the maximum satisfaction even though that satisfaction is delayed. This permits us to conclude that insight must be reached and won by the subject himself, because there are some choices that perhaps nobody can make in his place. If the therapist fully recognizes this limitation, the possibility that the choices will be constructive and can be actualized greatly increases.

The decisions which have been taken tend to be completed by actions which move the subject in the direction of new goals. Such actions are proof that the insight which has been reached is genuine. The progress that the subject makes towards a positive orientation of his behavior is almost always, in effective psychotherapy, an invariable concomitant of insight. From an objective point of view, the progress might be very insignificant, but it is its direction which is important. An interesting example of this way of proceeding can be found in the case of Barbara, which is cited by Rogers.[46]

Feeling unable to assume the responsibility of making a decision, Barbara wishes at first that the therapist decide for her. But in a subsequent interview she resolves to try to explore this responsibility herself, even though she is not yet sure of herself. Later, between the third and the fourth interviews, Barbara tries to carry out this decision, but it is so difficult for her that her old neurotic symptoms return in full force. By the time of the fifth interview, the client has assimilated this decision and feels comfortable with it. In the following interview the client shows that she has taken the decisive step and knows how to exploit fully the positive meaning that such decision has for her. It cannot be doubted that the satisfactions accompanying this action — the increased confidence in her ability to direct herself toward positive goals — constitute a significant force which is capable of carrying the client forward in other areas demanding new decisions. The various steps that Barbara took in order to arrive at her final decision have a symbolic value which transcends their objective importance.

Associated with the development of insight is the process of "clarification" of the various possibilities of action. This process is often characterized by an attitude which does not seem to be too hopeful. The client seems to say, "This is what I am! I see it more clearly, but how can I reorganize myself in a different way?" Rogers thinks that the proper function of the therapist is to help the client as he attempts to clarify his various possibilities of choice and to understand the feeling of fear and the lack of courage that he experiences.

The case of Herbert Bryan illustrates this point clearly. During the fourth interview the client makes this assertion: "As I lost a belief in a personalized sort of deity I sought signs from nature and other things like that. But I must learn to assume my values without the justification of the outside." [47] It is interesting to see how Mr. Bryan reacts to this new insight: he begins to understand what insight implies in terms of behavior. Then, after a significant pause, there follows the recognition that the forces which are in conflict within himself are fully balanced. The therapist does not try to alter the balance, but simply communicates to the client that he (the client) is faced with a difficult decision. The therapist is actually in the presence of the most crucial decision of the entire therapeutic experience. Will the client be able to actualize his fundamental insight? During the fifth interview the therapist recognizes that the client has taken some courageous steps towards this goal and that he looks at himself with much more confidence. During the sixth interview, Mr. Bryan has decided definitely to follow the difficult path of psychic maturity, rather than the easy road of neurotic evasion. After a frank examination, during the psychotherapeutic treatment of all the difficult and dangerous aspects of the road ahead, Mr. Bryan made his preferential choice. Delayed satisfactions took precedence over the immediate satisfactions of neurosis.

b. Responsibility and Control of Behavior

In addition to the concepts of insight and constructive choice mentioned in the preceding pages, some other factors are accentuated in therapeutic experience. Chief among these are the concepts of *responsibility* and *control of behavior*. Both are of great importance in relation to the problem of voluntary activity.

In many cases of "psychological maladjustment" one of the causes for concern on the part of the individual is that certain types of behavior continue beyond his control. "I do not know why I do it. I do not want to do it, yet I do it," is a statement encountered often in clinical cases. "I am just not myself when I do those things," "I have no control over those reactions," and the like are also frequent. In each case the reference is to behavior which, to use the exact expression of Rogers, "is organically determined on the basis of experiences denied accurate symbolization."[48]

Conscious control becomes more difficult when the organism strives to satisfy needs which are not admitted by the conscious ego. Tension is then produced and, if the individual becomes to any degree aware of it, he feels anxious, because he feels himself to be psychologically maladjusted, unsure of his direction. Such statements as "I do not know what I want," "I cannot decide on anything," "I do not have any real goal," are also frequent in therapeutic counseling. All of these indicate a lack of any integrated purposeful direction on the part of the individual, and, in the last analysis, a lack of self-control.

This illustration of psychic maladjustment leads, inversely, to the characterization of psychological adjustment as a liberation from internal tension, as integration of the personality and its consequent self-control. When the individual is able to bring his organic experiences to the level of consciousness, then a sure-footed psychic integration and a tranquillizing feeling of orientation are actualized within him. He feels that his energies can be and actually are directed towards a well-defined goal of self-actualization. The conscious acceptance of impulses and perceptions strongly increases the possibility of self-control. A person who succeeds in accepting his own experiences acquires a feeling of being able to direct himself. Consequently, it seems that the concept of "conscious awareness" can be used almost interchangeably with that of "conscious control." [49]

Conscious control is a process by which the individual makes use of his potentialities and contains his impulsive motivation within the limits of an adjustment which is morally and socially acceptable. Acquiring control is a process of maturity; it implies the conscious ability to initiate, sustain, suppress, repress or terminate human behavior, especially in relation to its affective expression. Even though the existence and the intensity of feelings, emotions, and impulses of an individual can be determined unconsciously, and thus remain outside conscious control, it is equally true that there are well defined methods to harness and direct these psychic phenomena.

Clinical psychology and psychiatry, in their theoretical models of diagnosis and therapy, paid little attention in the past to the problem of self-control. The reason for this must be sought in the almost universal conviction that human behavior is subject to a form of psychic determinism, represented by a series of factors — instincts, childhood conditioning, constitutional traits, unconscious complexes and other processes — over which a person can exercise very little conscious control. But it is important, and we could say even consoling, to point out that the reaction to this trend seems to be assuming ever increasing proportions and considerable vigor.

The position of a clinical psychologist as important as Frederick C. Thorne deserves to be pointed out in this respect. Repeatedly he has emphasized the importance of a re-examination of the entire problem of voluntary control to facilitate a return to a more rational position, one which recognizes the existence of personal factors in favor of self-control, and develops diagnostic techniques and treatments of those psychic disturbances which are characterized by a deficiency in the control of behavior.[50] Thorne maintains that it is illogical even to consider the possibility of developing methods for improving voluntary control unless the theory of psychic determinism can be modified. It must recognize the existence of phenomena which indicate that the organically-intact personality is capable of evaluating and modifying its own behavior in adaptive self-regulation. The deterministic theory *"disregards this most patent fact that people do possess enormous resources for intelligent adaptation and self-regulation of conduct."* [51]

Thorne's own opinion is that well-integrated behavior can occur within the organism at different levels of complexity; the highest levels are characterized by an integration which is purposeful, voluntary and conscious.[52] This conception admits the existence of various degrees of psychic determinism at the lower levels of personality, but presupposes that men become free at the higher levels of integrated behavior. The existence in the personality of psychic processes designated by terms such as "self-control," "conation," "volition" or "volitive power" is difficult to demonstrate; but it can be inferred by objective and subjective observations of behavior where a person manifests some ability to suppress or inhibit his affective expressions with selective criteria and to initiate voluntary action by appropriate means. One of the most evident manifestations of introspection is that a normal person is fully aware of his capacity to reflect upon problematic situations, weighing the various possibilities of action, and then choosing that solution which best fits his actual needs.

Discussing the significance of the self-control which is developed during the psychoanalytic process, Izette DeForest clearly points out that rational control is impossible without self-consciousness.[53] Control does not imply a rigorous repression or inhibition of the feelings, but rather an intelligent choice of the emotions to be shown and of the manner of showing them. Man recognizes that these emotions need not be expressed necessarily in behavior and that it is his privilege to decide in this regard. As a result of this experience, he acquires a conscious understanding of himself which permits him to choose his own lines of behavior. This exercise of choice increases man's directive strength so that he is capable of ruling his own destiny.

All those who have had some clinical experience with client-centered therapy are very much aware that the phenomenon of the reorganization and direction of behavior on the part of the individual assumes an ever-increasing importance. The nature of this phenomenon is such that it seems to defy an adequate explanation — according to Carl R. Rogers — on the basis of determinism, which is the predominant philosophical assumption in the majority of psychological works. The capacity of the individual to reorganize his attitudes and his behavior is a surprising power; it involves a fundamental spontaneity which cannot be ignored when one studies human psychology. To illustrate a particularly important aspect of this problem, a very significant passage from Carl R. Rogers deserves to be cited in full:

"The clinical experience could be summarized by saying that the behavior of the human organism may be determined by the influences to which it has been exposed, *but it may be also determined by the creative and integrative insight of the organism itself.* This ability of the person to discover new meaning in the forces which impinge upon him and in the past experiences which have been controlling him, and the ability to alter consciously his behavior in the light of this new meaning, has a profound significance for our thinking which has not been fully realized. We need to revise the philosophical basis of our work to a point where it can admit that forces exist within the individual which can exercise a spontaneous and significant influence upon behavior which is not predictable through knowledge of prior influences and conditionings. The forces released through a catalytic process of therapy are not adequately accounted for by a knowledge of the individual's previous conditionings, but only if we grant the presence of a spontaneous force within the organism which has the capacity of integration and redirection. *This capac-*

ity for volitional control is a force which we must take into ac-
count in any psychological equation." [54] (The last sentence of this
quotation has been italicized by Zavalloni. *Translators.*)

Such factors as "the perception of various alternatives," "constructive choice," "clarification of possible decisions," "responsibility for our own actions," "conscious and voluntary control,"
which we have encountered at various steps of major or minor development in the psychotherapeutic process, would be absolutely
without value if they were founded on a deterministic hypothesis
conceived in the fashion of physical causality. Certainly, man
would not be able, under an hypothesis of this kind, to evaluate
and to choose the goals of his own activity.

c. The Power of Choice: A Function of Personality

According to a report by S. Lipkin, a subject describes his psychotherapeutic experience in this way: "The impression I received
was of being left alone, all on my own with my problem. . . But I
soon discovered that by talking of my indecision and problem I
was able to see clearly that my problem was being solved of my
own initiative rather than the counseling of my interviewer." [55]

On the basis of his broad clinical experience, Rogers can make
this affirmation safely: "One of the elements which appears to
stand out prominently in the initial reaction of the client is the
discovery that he is responsible for himself in this relationship." [56]
The acceptance on the part of the subject of his own responsibil-
ities, the reorganization of his own attitudes, and the new orientation of his entire behavior assume an ever-increasing importance.

In his introduction to the study of Charles A. Curran on personality factors in the therapeutic process, Rogers points out that the
author "places great weight upon the fact that it is by independent,
conscious choice of values that the person gradually becomes himself, as differentiated from other individuals, and that this choice
of personal values is the basic aspect of personality reorienta-
tion." [57]

A careful analysis of psychotherapeutic interviews reveals that
the basic functions of personality are "insight" and "free choice."
In fact, if psychotherapy is successful, the subject acquires keener
self-perception and becomes capable of making new and more

satisfying choices. A demonstration of this progress towards self-actualization can be deduced from the case of Alfred, which was studied by Curran.[58] The author stresses the fact that the individual, on his own responsibility and of his own independent choice, is capable of actualizing a normal adjustment. This had been affirmed previously by Frederick H. Allen in the conclusion of his outstanding study on the psychotherapy of children. Allen writes: "The therapeutic point of view, of which I have written in this book, has its roots deep in a concept of individual responsibility. Its recurrent theme is that individuals can be helped to help themselves. At a time when the world needs new orientation to the essential place of the individual, we need to emphasize the strengths of human nature and its capacity for self-responsibility."[59]

When we compare the fundamental points of agreement between the studies of Rogers and Curran and those of Royer, Raimy, Snyder and Lewis, we see clearly that, at the end of the therapeutic process, the subject begins to seek independent solutions of his problems and manifests a greater capacity to carry out his decisions.[60] The power of voluntary choice seems to spring directly from the insights which were recently acquired and from a consequent new scale of values.

This problem was recently considered by the author of the present study, and conclusions were arrived at which confirm and give a greater precision to the conclusions of the above authors.[61] The results obtained demonstrate that man's ability to make voluntary choice must be considered as a function of the integration and adjustment of his personality. This power of choosing increases or decreases according to the general development of the therapeutic process. The more the individual builds up an adjusted and integrated personality, the more he becomes capable of facing situations and solving the problems of life.

In the clinical cases that form the basis of our study, the changes which can be noticed in the subjects are truly amazing. Particularly interesting are the profound changes concerning the insight the subjects gain into themselves and their reacquired ability to make rational decisions. These subjects end with a feeling of confidence: they are much more capable of deciding on the basis of personal judgments and of standing on their own feet. This new condition makes it far easier for them to adopt their preferential choices and to make those decisions in the face of situations which previously caused them to be perplexed and disturbed.

In the last analysis, the most significant effect of psychotherapy is the reacquired capacity of acting freely once again, i.e. of acting with conscious self-determination, without tension, without being almost dragged along by impulsive emotions or by forces which are outside their control. The power to make conscious decisions is the most characteristic factor of a well-integrated personality. The highest dignity of man, in fact, is actually that of knowing how to assume full responsibility for his own actions.

The problem of how to make rational choices without being determined by impulsive forces is not merely an aspect of the organization and integration of personality; it is the central problem to which all others can somehow be reduced. The ability to make our own preferential choices on the basis of moral principles of conscience is the highest expression of voluntary control. When this ability is exercised in a stable and permanent manner, then it appears as self-discipline in practice, and it truly characterizes man's rational behavior.

4. Human Freedom and Existential Analysis

A new trend has recently developed which is introducing far-reaching innovations into the field of classical psychoanalysis. This new orientation has adopted a language which seems more adequate for our times and more suitable for expressing the anguish of a changing epoch such as ours: the language of *Existentialism*. The problems of classical psychology are studied from a different viewpoint and with a broader perspective. One of the most avid exponents of this new trend is Ludwig Binswanger, whose existential analysis is intended to be a phenomenological clarification of the various modalities by which the existence of the particular individual expresses itself.[62]

Martin Heidegger is the thinker who has most influenced Binswanger. It must be pointed out, however, that if the doctrine of Binswanger appears similar to Heidegger's in some basic formulations and in the use of the same terminology, it does not follow that the doctrines of the two men are similarly philosophical. Danilo

Cargnello writes: "We would make a mistake from the very start if we confused Heidegger's philosophy with Binswanger's existential analysis." [63] Heidegger's work is phenomenological, but the aspects of human existence and reality are viewed and considered with a declared and explicit *ontological* concern or preoccupation. Binswanger, on the other hand, is essentially concerned with the investigation of the human phenomena by themselves. He appears to be always a *psychologist,* or better, an *existential analyst* first, and only secondarily a philosopher.

An objection which has been raised against existential analysis is that it is a "science of man" which is based upon too many philosophical premises.[64] Binswanger, on his part, continues to insist that he is an existential analyst and not an ontologist or a metaphysician. His existential analysis is a science and, like any other science, it pursues the ideal of the exact sciences and uses their methods. Substantially, his science is pure phenomenology.[65] Existential analysis moves on a plane which is neither philosophical in the strict sense, nor naturalistic. It moves on the phenomenological plane, where the phenomena of existence are considered in themselves without any reference to the problem of ontological reality. It moves on the plane of that *sui generis* science of man which is psychology.[66]

This new phenomenological trend has put us in contact with an important body of facts heretofore neglected. It implies, principally, the introduction of the soul into the study of psychology. Psychopathology has undergone an important change. Henri Baruk of France and Viktor E. Frankl in Austria have contributed notably to this change. These two authors have written with particular acumen and convincing force on the treatment of mental disturbances. Their attempt to break through the barrier of biologism and psychologism and to build a psychotherapy based on ethical values seems to be successful. Igor A. Caruso writes: "We cannot sufficiently appreciate the fact that today there is a psychotherapy, nay, even a psychiatry which without any hesitation recognizes spiritual values; this is a therapy which both starts from the 'spiritual,' and 'directs itself towards the spiritual.' "[67] The spiritualistic orientation which is evident in all the works of Baruk and Frankl is intended as a call to an existential analysis which takes into consideration *all* the dimensions of human personality.

a. Responsibility and "Existential Psychology"

There is an indefinite number of "ways" or "modes" by which a being can make its existence felt. Of particular interest for this study on personal freedom are those modes of existence where *human aggressiveness* is asserted. There are two modes of existence which without doubt distinguish men from animals, and which therefore are proper to man only. These two modes, where human aggressiveness is clearly asserted, are: (1) "keeping of one's word," or the mode of responsibility; (2) "good reputation," or the mode of human historicity.[68] The principle of *existential responsibility* is related to the first of these two modes of aggressiveness. It is under this aspect that the principle is of interest to the existential analyst.

When we take one at his word, we mean to bind him to his word as a member of a society which is ruled by determined, juridical and ethical laws and by accepted customs. The factor by which and from which this person allows himself to be bound is, in this case, a well-defined and identifiable action, which expresses the actualization or non-actualization of a certain public or private duty. In short, in the mode of responsibility a person is bound from the viewpoint of his moral obligations.[69]

To let oneself be held on one's responsibility is doubtless to bind oneself. But he who determines himself in this case is no longer the man of biological determination, the man of instincts or passions. On the contrary, he is a man who, in this particular situation at least, is able and wishes (he could also not wish just as well) to determine himself to a certain way of acting, to bind himself to a particular task or duty. In fact, *he who binds himself on his own word to perform an act of responsibility becomes a possession, a chattel, a slave of another*. This happens at the very moment in which he gives his consent to the person who requires this consent from him and proposes to him the performance of this particular task or duty. The person to whom he is bound is always a member or a symbolic expression of a social institution. Therefore a private duty is somehow always a public duty.

The self, in binding itself to a responsibility, binds an authentic aspect of itself, its own *moral ipseity*; this is an authentic aspect of itself because it is put freely at the mercy of another.[70] When the self is bound in this way, it does not feel itself to be determined in its actualization as a person while it remains faithful to the ethical obligation. On the contrary, when the self is forced to assume a responsibility by another person, the situation changes, and the human person is in another modality of existence. In such cases the ego does not perform its duty freely, but under the influence of pressures, suggestions and threats. The ego or the self does not bind itself freely, but is bound or forced by another against its own will.

The mode of responsibility which is freely accepted, as well as the modalities of friendship and love (of which Binswanger has given an original interpretation), escape every causal determinism and every kind of conditionism, and are, therefore, a supreme testimony that existence cannot be reduced to "naturalism." Man is never reducible to a mere manifestation of biological life because he can always make use of his inalienable freedom, be it great or small. This can be done even at the moment when the instincts and exigencies of our nature seem most demanding.

This property of man appears to be more evident yet from some comparisons we can make between Binswanger and Freud, between existential analysis and psychoanalysis.[71] It has been demonstrated that Freud attempted to reduce the study of man's psyche to the same level as the study of any other object of nature. It is clear, on the other hand, that Binswanger recognized that psychology does not belong to the category of the physical sciences, that psychology cannot be an experimental science in the same sense that the natural sciences are, but that psychology is first of all a science of human experience. The antimony that today divides Binswanger from Freud is, in the last analysis, the same antimony that divided Dilthey from Spencer in the past. This antinomy consists in Dilthey's denial of the thesis of Spencer, who held that the methods used by the biological sciences are valid even for the study of man as man. The man of Freud is the *"homo naturalis,"* the man of Binswanger is the *"homo existentialis."* The basic principle for Freud is *man's nature;* the basic principle for Binswanger is *man's existence,* his own being-in-the world.

Just as any other natural science, psychoanalysis also deprives

phenomena of their qualitative aspects and of the modal significance they have in man's life, taken in its broad and universal
sense. In contrast, existential analysis makes clear that it is really
the modal significance of these phenomena which expresses man
as such. The psychoanalysts say that the life (and not the existence) of an individual develops as an expression of the species
within the limits of the constancy of its naturalistic manifestations.
The existential analysts retort: well and good, but all this has nothing to do with the interpretation, the meaning, the significance of
the phenomena of life and existence. Psychoanalysis uses as its
clinico-experimental basis the life-history of the individual; but because of the presupposition from which psychoanalysis begins,
this life-history is nothing but a type of physiological-naturalistic
history of the individual. Since psychoanalysis attempts to derive
the superior phenomena from the inferior, it cannot understand
the meaning of values at all. Existential analysis also stresses the
life-history of the individual. But existential analysis does not call
attention alone to the contents which are enclosed in the life-history of the individual, and does not insist alone on the mass of
biological functions; it calls attention also to the contents which are
expressed by language. Existential analysis does this in order to be
able to understand not only the life-history of the individual, but
also the Weltanschauung the individual has and the fact that he is
a being-in-the-world.

These differences concerning the concept of man and the method
of understanding human phenomena contain, as a logical consequence, a fundamental difference in the idea of freedom. The existential responsibility of Binswanger is opposed to the psychic determinism of Freud. Writes Cargnello: "I who am talking to you
am forced to feed myself with bread in order to live (I am determined by my nature); I who talk to you am permitted to do so, I
am permitted to address you as a lecturer (i.e., I am in a psychological relationship with you); however, notwithstanding every
psychological pressure and against practical reason and common
sense, I could, merely if I wanted to, stop talking and leave (that
is, I could show you that I am free from every determinism, both
physical and psychological). It is really because of this possibility
of acting in an indefinite number of ways and modes, and, mainly,

because I am a free being, that I am designated as man." [72]

b. Human Freedom and Logotherapy

Depending on the emphasis we put on one or the other aspect of the doctrine of Viktor E. Frankl, we can speak of logotherapy, existential analysis, or medical care of the soul.[73] To Frankl, the central problem is that of consciousness understood as perennial intentionality towards values, in the sense of "being responsible." The conscious being is therefore to be identified with the responsible being. Logotherapy attempts to make the subject aware, by means of a profound dialectical contact, of all his human potentialities; to make him understand that life always has a meaning; that he is supposed to actualize some values; that he, even though not free from the coercions of his own nature, is always free to face these coercions or determinations in one way rather than in another; to assume, in other words, his own responsibility.[74]

Frankl criticizes both psychoanalysis and individual psychology for the narrowness of their views concerning the concept of consciousness. Psychoanalysis considers consciousness as awareness or knowledge of the self; individual psychology identifies consciousness with responsibility. Neurosis is, for psychoanalysis, a limitation of the ego qua consciousness; for individual psychology, neurosis is a limitation of the ego qua sense of responsibility. But what is the meaning of being human except this: being conscious and responsible at the same time? [75] There is a need of "a psychotherapy which begins from the soul" in order to capture an adequate image of the real human being, in his physical, psychic and spiritual completeness.

Contemporary psychotherapy, rooted in the fallacy of psychologism, is absolutely incapable of penetrating the depth of human values. If psychotherapy wishes to be effective, it must reaffirm that human freedom which has been completely overlooked.[76] Along with the psychologism of the last century we have had biologism and sociologism during the same epoch, all of which have helped to set up a caricature of man. No wonder that a reaction to this naturalistic view was forthcoming. This counter-view calls attention to the fundamental notions of being human and being free. The primordial fact of being responsible has at last been restored to the center of our field of vision. Frankl returns insistently to this fundamental point of his doctrine: "If it is true, as it is true, that human responsibility is the essential foundation of being human, then the foundation of this logotherapy, whose need we insist upon, must be the analysis of existence, understood as analysis of *being-human*, that is, of *being-responsible*." [77]

The doctrine of Viktor E. Frankl holds that man cannot be responsible unless he is free. Man therefore is free. This does not mean that he oscillates freely and is suspended in empty space. He is coerced by many bonds; but these bonds are supporting pillars on which his own freedom is erected. The soul is bound to matter, to existence in the world. But in his development man transcends the world in which he lives. Man can be defined as a being who knows how to free himself even from what determines him. The table before me is and remains what it is, at least for its part—that is to say, unless a human being puts his hands to it and changes it. But the human being who sits opposite me at this table decides in every case what he is to be during the next second, what he will say to me or conceal from me. "The freedom of decision, so-called freedom of the will, is for the unbiased person a matter of course; *he has a direct experience of himself as free*." [78]

Freedom of the will is opposed by three forces of destiny: man's biological, psychological and sociological destiny. By destiny Frankl means that which is essentially exempt from human freedom, that which lies neither within the scope of man's power nor his responsibility. These three forces weigh heavily on human freedom. The dialectic between freedom and destiny reveals to us the spiritual drama in which man is engaged.

Considering first those cases and situations in which man is in contact with his own "biological destiny," Frankl realizes how much man's own physiology can limit his freedom, and how much, on the other hand, freedom can influence his own physiology. Frankl holds that, in the face of the so-called fatalism of biological determination, man can always oppose the "forces of the soul" against the "forces of nature." Biological destiny is the material which must be shaped by the free human spirit. From the point of view of man, this is what it exists for. Man is called to incorporate his biological destiny into the structure of his life in a meaningful way, to make it uniquely his own. We are always encountering persons who have succeeded admirably in overcoming the original handicaps and barriers to freedom that biological factors have imposed, who have surmounted brilliantly all the initial obstacles to their spiritual development.

"Psychological destiny" seems equally to stand in the way of human freedom. Psychoanalysis has stressed that we should see in every spiritual event nothing else but the unconscious mechanism which sustains it. The psychoanalysts depict man as a being dominated by instincts, which with their dynamic forces drive him irresistibly where they wish. But any unbiased observer, Frankl points out, must recognize the obvious fact that the instincts merely make proposals, so to speak, while the ego decides what to do about these proposals. The ego can decide, resolve, conclude, choose freely; the ego wills. Certainly the ego, qua expression of the will which freely decides, needs the dynamism of the instincts; but the ego is never exclusively determined and driven by them. The danger of the psychoanalytic concept of man, who is reduced by it to an expression of the dynamics of instinctuality, is that it culminates in fatalism. It is a conception which, in the last analysis, can be identified with the fatalism of the neurotic.

Man is also influenced by "social destiny." Every individual is surrounded by a net of interpersonal relationships. The social organism on the whole conditions man. But Frankl maintains that the so-called social laws never determine the individual completely; that is, they never deprive him of his freedom of will. Such laws cannot affect him without first passing through a zone of individual freedom where they leave their mark upon the individual's behavior. It is because of this that man conserves, even in respect to his social destiny, an area within which free decision is possible.

His terrible experiences in a concentration camp brought Frankl to the realization that, even though personal freedom is greatly limited, there still remains to man a last type of freedom: that which gives man the possibility of forming his own existence in his own way. Man can in every case and under any circumstance conserve his freedom to decide in favor or against the influence of his environment. From this it is clear that Frankl has accentuated the role of human freedom so strongly that he exaggerates it.[79]

c. Moral Conscience in Psychiatry

Perhaps no one in our time has studied and illumined this problem more thoroughly than Henri Baruk. His studies, all based on solid experimental foundations, deserve particular consideration.[80] Baruk starts from the fact that modern psychiatry, dominated largely by Freud, is for the most part oriented towards the study of the instincts. These instincts doubtless constitute an important part in the motivation of human conduct. But Baruk's personal researches in human psychology and psychiatry have convinced him that the instincts, no matter how important they are, are not the principal motives of human activity.

Man is immersed in his social environment, and all his actions are dominated largely by his psychological relationships with other individuals. The behavior and freedom of each person are limited by the obligation of not doing evil to others. Man therefore in his social behavior is subjected to an interior judgment. This judgment cannot be put aside or evaded because man cannot remain content even when he tries to save external appearances. This tremendously powerful motive which regulates the life of the individual is "moral conscience."

In a recent study in experimental psychiatry, Baruk investigated at length the role of moral conscience in both healthy and sick persons. He found that in human personality, over and above such factors as the neurological apparatus, the psycho-motor mechanisms, and the instincts, there is a factor of formidable power which dominates and unifies them, a factor specific to human nature: moral conscience. Baruk writes: "It is strange to observe that modern psychology, in its progression toward the discovery of the various elements of human personality, has deified alternately the elementary reflex mechanisms (behaviorism of Watson), and the diverse and multiple instincts and their mutual struggles (Freud), but that now it finds itself placed before the sole true force which commands all the preceding elements and gives to the personality its sense, its purpose." [81] In mental illnesses, moral conscience constitutes the most resistant force. It sometimes survives even the deterioration of intelligence and suddenly reappears after having been apparently extinguished.

In this way Baruk was led to rediscover on scientific, critical, and experimental grounds the capital role of moral conscience. While for Freud moral conscience is an artificial censor derived from social customs, for Baruk it seems to be "the most profound element of human nature, the element which cannot possibly be ignored and which has the role of bestowing peace and tranquillity, if it is followed. . ." [82]

Conscience is linked to freedom. To be conscientious, to judge the value of one's actions and their consequences, to know how to choose, all presuppose human acts made without pressure, with full freedom. It suffices to mention what the experimental observations brought to light: that the main effect of illness is to diminish or to suppress freedom. The comparison between the actions of a sick person, deprived of his freedom, and of a healthy person is the best argument for the assertion that *we cannot prescind from the notion of freedom*. But freedom is weak, and menaced constantly by both external and internal causes. These threats are the illnesses which dissociate the human personality, and various social factors. All these tend to suppress freedom and consequently, moral conscience.

The data of moral conscience must be able to direct the instrument of execution which resides in the voluntary mechanisms. Between the judgment of good and evil and man's behavior a deep chasm may often exist. Because of this the moral problem is inseparable from the problems of freedom. It will not suffice to conceive the judgment of good and evil; it is also necessary to be able to apply it in practice and to follow the orientation which is chosen. In this way the intimate relationship between the problem of conscience and that of freedom, as well as between instincts and feelings, becomes clear. Baruk tells us that "we forget too often that instinct in man is transformed into a tremendous force, because of its intimate union with the entire person." [83]

From the division of human nature into elementary factors we pass to discovery of its unity. But this unity cannot be actualized without a complex synthesis, in which moral conscience must be in harmony with other forces without splitting them. In its guidance of behavior, moral conscience must utilize the mechanisms and the instruments of execution, among which the most complicated and the highest are the voluntary processes. An essential and indispensable task, therefore, belongs to moral conscience. Says Baruk: ". . . although granting to these mechanisms all the importance which they merit, one must recognize that they are nothing without the general direction, and this is why the moral problem dominates the entire problem of human personality." [84]

FOOTNOTES

[1] N. Ach, *Ueber den Willensakt und das Temperament* (Leipzig: Quelle und Meyer, 1910), pp. 241, 247 ff. For a synthesis of Ach's doctrine, based on experimental investigations, especially concerning the problem of the volitional act, cf. Franz Hofmann, *Beitrage zum Problem der Freiheit des Willens unter Berüucksichtigung von Erfahrungen mit dem Rorschachchen Psychodiagnostischen Formdeuteversuch* (Zurich: Neue Zürcher Zeitung, 1950), pp. 40-45.

[2] A. Michotte and E. Prüm, "Étude Expérimentale sur le Choix Volontaire et ses Antécédentes immédiates," *Arch. Psychol.*, (1910), 10, 193 ff.

[3] Ach objected to Michotte that he was wrong to consider the phenomenon of the "consciousness of the act" as the exclusive characteristic of the voluntary phenomenon. Cf. *Ueber den Willensakt: Eine Replik* (Leipzig: Quelle und Meyer, 1911), pp. 3 ff. Michotte counters this objection, saying it does not represent his thought: "We have never considered the 'consciousness of the act' as the exclusive characteristic of the will." However, "all other factors remaining identical, the voluntary character disappears with it." Note "A Propos des Contributions Recentes a la Psychologie de la Volonté," *Ann Inst. Sup. Philos.*, (191), 1, 699 ff.

[4] N. Ach, *Ueber den Willensakt und das Temperament, op. cit.*, pp. 240 ff.; A. Michotte and E. Prüm, *op. cit.*, 310 ff; A. Michotte, *op. cit.*, pp. 699 ff.

[5] R. H. Wheeler, *An Experimental Investigation of the Process of Choosing* (Oregon: Univ. Oregon Publ., 1, 1920, n. 2), p. 51.

[6] H. M. Wells, "The Phenomenology of Acts of Choice," *Brit. Psychol. Monogr. Supl.* (1927), 11, 121.

[7] H. M. Wells, *op. cit.*, 147.

[8] A. H. Martin, "An Experimental Study of the Factors and Types of Voluntary Choice," *Arch. Psychol.*, (1922), n. 51, 106 ff.

[9] J. Lindworsky, "Zur Jungsten Experimentellen Willensuntersuchung," *Arch. Ges. Psychol.*, (1932), 86, 536.

[10] N. Ach, *Ueber den Willensakt und das Temperament, op. cit.*, pp. 307 ff. The protocols of other experimental investigations confirm the experiment of Narciss Ach. Among the many examples which could be quoted, I limit myself to this passage of Honoria M. Wells: "The 'Self' makes one of the motives its own, and in the process of tending one end in preference to another we shall show, by quotations from our protocols, that we have a direct lived and cognized experience of the 'Self-in-action'," *op. cit.*, p. 78.

[11] A. Michotte and E. Prüm, *op. cit.*, 133. Cf. H. Gruender, *Experimental Psychology* (Milwaukee: Bruce, 1932), pp. 409 ff.

[12] A. Michotte and E. Prüm, *op. cit.*, 192.

[13] S. Trouet, "Der Willensakt bei Wahlhandlungen: Eine Experimentelle Untersuchung," *Arch. Ges. Psychol.*, (1923), 45, 157-202.

[14] P. Skawran, "Experimentelle Untersuchunge über den Willen bei Wahlhandlungen," *Arch. Ges. Psychol.* (1927), 58, 95-162.

[15] H. Rohracher, *Theories des Willens auf Experimenteller Grundlage* (Leipzig: Barth, 1938), p. 188. For an analysis and an evaluation of Hubert Rohracher's thought, cf. Franz Hofmann, *op. cit.*, pp. 45-64.

[16] K. Geis, "Experimentelle Untersuchunger über den Willen mit Berücksicktigung der Entstehung des Bewusstseins der Willensfreiheit," *Arch. Ges. Psychol.*, (1930), 74, 4.

[17] K. Gies, *op. cit.*, 27-83.

[18] K. Gies, *op. cit.*, 34. Ich ziehe zetzt diese Mogligkeit vor nach Ueberlegung, und deshalb entschliesse ich mich für diese Mogligkeit. Ich habe das Bewusstsein, dass ich ebensogut die andere wahln kann. . . Je mehr die Motive mich drangen, je mehr emphinde ich dieses Freiheitsbewusstsein.

[19] G. Störring, *Methoden der Psychologie des Hoheren Gefühlslebens* (Berlin-Wien: Urban und Schwarzenberg, 1938), pp. 1431-1450.

[20] N. Ach, *Analyse des Wollens* (Berlin: Urban und Schwarzenberg, 1935), pp. 430 ff. In agreement with Ach is the interpretation of N. Braunshausen, "Le Libre-Arbitre à la Lumière de la Psychologie Expérimentale et de la Science Moderne," *Rev. Sci. Pedag.*, (1946), 8, 75-87. In contrast, a very sound evaluation and criticism of Ach's conclusions are advanced by T. V. Moore, *The Driving Forces of Human Nature and their Adjustment* (New York: Grune & Stratton, 1950), pp. 345-348.

[21] N. Ach, *Ueber die Entstehung des Bewusstseins der Willensfreiheit* (Jena: Gustav Fischer, 1928), p. 92. Cf. also his *Der Wille* (Leipzig: Barth, 1927). A Solé, in a study concerning the effect of the law of probability on psychological processes, arrives at the same conclusion. The subjects were instructed to make freely a series of one hundred choices among two or three colors. The frequencies for the individual subjects, as well as the sumtotal of the frequencies for the entire group, were very close to the frequencies which were predicted on the basis of the law of probability. The results obtained are interpreted as a sign of determination according to the law of probability, even though the subjects were convinced they were making their choices completely freely. Cf. "Ueber die Wirkung des Wahrscheinlichkeitsgesetzes auf Seeliche Vorgange," *Wien Z. Prakt. Psychol.*, 1 (1949), 73-77.

[22] J. Froebes, *Kongr. Exp. Psychol.* (1927), p. 95.

[23] N. Ach, *Verantwortung und Charakter* (1938). Cf. N. Braunshausen, *op. cit.*, p. 80.

[24] J. Reutt, *Badania Psychologiczne nad Wahaniem* (Poznan: Poznankie Towarzystwo Przyjaciol Nauk, 1949). Cf. *Année Psychol.*, (1949), 51, 486-489.

25 Franz Hofmann recently dealt with the new contributions to the problem of the will in his study, *Beitrage zum Problem der Freiheit des Willens unter Berücksichtigung von Erfahrungn mit dem Rorschachschen Psychodiagnostischen Formdeuteversuch* (Zurich: Neue Zürcher Zeitung, 1950). These new contributions are based on the experimental data obtained with the (Rorshach) psychodiagnostic test. He develops his theme in three chapters: (1) the problem of free choice in the history of philosophy, pp. 9-37; (2) the problem of free choice in the new psychology, pp. 38-82; (3) the psychodiagnostic test and free choice, pp. 83-96. It seems to me that Hofmann fell into a serious error in writing the third chapter and in linking it to the two preceding. He was probably led into this mistake by the fact that psychologists speak of *free interpretation* of perceptual forms, when they use the Rorshach psychodiagnostic test. It must be kept in mind that, in this test, even though the response of the subject is a free response to an ambiguous stimulus, it is at the same time *automatic and therefore unconscious.* I think therefore that we cannot use the data of the Rorshach psychodiagnostic test to illustrate positively or negatively the freedom of the will. If Hofmann would have spoken in a broader and more indeterminate manner of freedom, as it is understood by those who identify human freedom with the autonomy of the organism (which we will examine later on), then he would have been more correct. In this latter case, however, he should have written his study in a completely different way.

26 E. R. Guthrie, *The Psychology of Human Conflict* (New York, London: Harper & Bros., 1938), p. 171.

27 P. Janet, *Nevroses et Idées fixes,* 2 vols., 3rd Ed. (Paris: Alcan, 1924), pp. 406 ff. These verifications led Janet to the idea of a "double consciousness" and then to the theory of the "dissociation of personality." This doctrine is the foundation of the Freudian theory of the two zones of the psychic life, the "conscious" and "unconscious." Cf. J. Nuttin, *Psychanalyse et Conception Spiritualiste de l'Homme: Une Théorie Dynamique de la Personalité Normale* (Louvain: Publ. Univ. Louvain; Paris: J. Vrin, 1950), pp. 167, 182 ff.

28 P. Janet, *L'Automatisme Psychologique: Essai de Psychologie Expérimentale sur les Formes Inférieurs de l'Activitè Humaine* (Paris: Alcan, 1930), 10 ed., p. XVIII. These studies on psychological automatism were first published in 1886-1887.

29 P. Janet, *op. cit.,* pp. 444, 452 ff.

30 P. Janet, *op. cit.,* pp. 470-478. For the inferior forms of normal activity, cf. *ibid.,* pp. 460-470.

31 P. Janet, *op. cit.,* pp. 476 ff.

32 P. Janet, *Psychological Healing: An Historical and Clinical Study,* trans. Eden and Cedar Paul, 2 vols. (London: George Allen & Unwin; New York: Macmillan, 1925), pp. 239 ff.

33 R. Dalbiez, *Psychoanalytical Methods and the Doctrine of Freud,* trans. T. F. Lindsay, 2 vols. (New York: Longmans, Green, 1941), p. 295.

[34] According to Karen Horney it is true that, theoretically speaking, the psychoanalyst "refrains from deliberately mobilizing will power in a constructive direction." But it would not be exact to say that "Freud does not recognize at all the role which the patient's will power plays in therapy. He does so indirectly." *New Ways in Psychoanalysis* (New York: Norton, 1939), p. 292. Horney maintains that Otto Rank "rightly criticizes the disregard of this faculty in psychoanalysis. Will power, however, is too formalistic a principle to form the theoretical basis of therapy." *Ibid.*, p. 292, note 7.

[35] O. Rank, *Will Therapy* and *Truth and Reality*, trans. Taft (New York: Knopf, 1945), p. 11.

[36] O. Rank, *op. cit.*, p. 44. Cf. the introduction by J. Taft quoted by Rank, p. XII.

[37] O. Rank, *op. cit.*, p. 91. It has been objected that Rank says nothing really new, because he simply uses the term "will" in place of the Freudian term "wish." Rank answers that "there is hardly an objection that would do Freud as well as myself greater injustice. Freud's psychology is anything but a doctrine of will, which he not only does not recognize but actually denies since he conceives of the individual as ruled by instinctual life (the id) and repressed by the super-ego, a will-less plaything of two impersonal forces. On the contrary, I understand by will a positive guiding organization and integration of self which utilizes creatively, as well as inhibits and controls the instinctual drives." *Ibid.*, p. 111, note.

[38] O. Rank, *Truth and Reality*, pp. 221, 233 ff, 239 ff. While Otto Rank was formulating his "will therapy," Wilhelm Reich was developing his techniques for character analysis, adding in this way a notable contribution to the problem of decision. No matter how numerous might be the determining factors which are involved in the problems of an individual, he himself, simply because he is a living being, always takes a position regarding everything. The first decision of a person to undergo psychotherapy constitutes an act or a sign of intentionality which is really very important. Cf. W. Reich, *Character Analysis* (New York: Orgone Institute Press, 1945).

[39] J. Jacobi, *The Psychology of Jung: An Introduction with Illustrations*, trans. K. W. Bash, Foreword by C. G. Jung, 4th Ed. (New Haven: Yale Univ. Press, 1945), pp. 1-9.

[40] C. G. Jung, *Contributions to Analytical Psychology*, trans. H. G. and C. F. Baynes (London: Kegan Paul, 1928), p. 237.

[41] K. Goldstein, *Human Nature in the Light of Psychopathology* (Cambridge: Harvard Univ. Press, 1940), pp. 113 ff.

[42] K. Goldstein, *op. cit.*, p. 204.

[43] H. Baruk, "Le Probleme de la Volonté: Nouvelles données Psychophysiologiques," *J. Psychol. Normal Path.*, 36 (1939), pp. 401 ff., 421 ff.

[44] H. Baruk, *La Desorganisation de la Personnalité* (Paris: Press Univ. France, 1952), p. 94.

[45] C. R. Rogers, *Counseling and Psychotherapy* (Boston: Houghton

Mifflin, 1942), p. 208. Cf. also his *Client-Centered Therapy: Its Current Practice, Implications, and Theory* (Boston: Houghton Mifflin, 1951), p. 485.

46 C. R. Rogers, *Counseling and Psychotherapy*, pp. 210 ff. Rollo May, in a passage which resembles the position described above, affirms: "We are well aware, of course, that the decision could not be made unless there had been long and patient work on clearing up the unconscious aspects of the conflict. No decision is made de novo; actually therapeutic progress is a constant series of minor decisions, a continuous chain of putting one's intents into practice. . . Most therapists would agree, no doubt, that the most significant signs of progress in therapy—that is, progress defined as psychological growth—are the little decisions the person is able to make here and there. This emerging capacity may be the surest sign that sooner or later he will be able to make crucial and basic decisions independently." Cf. O. H. Mowrer, "Historical and Philosophical Presuppositions for Understanding Therapy," *Psychotherapy: Theory and Research* (New York: Ronald Press, 1953), pp. 32 ff.

47 C. R. Rogers, *op. cit.,* p. 355. Anita J. Faatz arrives at the same conclusions in a study concerning the nature of choice during the "casework" process: the subject acquires more self-perception of his needs and becomes able to make significant and constructive choices by himself. *The Nature of Choice in The Casework Process* (Chapel Hill, N. C.: Univ. North Carolina Press, 1953).

48 C. R. Rogers, *Client-Centered Therapy,* op. cit., p. 510.

49 C. R. Rogers, *op. cit.,* p. 514. Cf. T. W. Richards, *Modern Clinical Psychology* (New York: McGraw-Hill, 1946), pp. 130-215.

50 F. C. Thorne, *Principles of Personality Counseling: An Eclectic Viewpoint,* (Brandon, Vermont, J. of Clinical Psychology Printing Press, 1950), pp. 389-409; and "The Psychology of Control," *J. Clin. Psychol.,* (1949), 374-386.

51 F. C. Thorne, *Principles of Personality Counseling,* p. 392. According to Thorne "the viewpoint of psychic determinism is nihilistic in the sense that if a person is regarded as being an automatism controlled by predetermined and unalterable natural forces, then he is the victim of 'fate,' i.e., factors largely outside his control and which he has no capacity to modify." *Ibid.,* p. 390.

52 F. C. Thorne, "The Psychology of Control," *J. Clin. Psychol.* (1949), 5, 375.

53 I. DeForest, "Significance of Self-Control as Developed during Psycoanalytic treatment," *J. Clin. Psychopathol.* (1947), 8, 611-622.

54 C. R. Rogers, "Significant Aspects of Client-Centered Therapy," *Amer. Psychologist* (1946), 1, 422. The passage quoted can be found also, with very slight modifications, in another study by Rogers: *Dealing with Social Tensions* (New York: Hinds, Hayden & Eldridge, 1948), pp. 29 ff.

55 S. Lipkin, "The Client evaluates Nondirective Psychotherapy," *J. Con-*

sult. Psychol. (1948), 12, 141.

[56] C. R. Rogers, "Client-Centered Therapy," 71.

[57] From the Preface of Carl R. Rogers to Charles A. Curran, *Personality Factors in Counseling* (New York: Grune & Stratton, 1945), p. XX.

[59] F. H. Allen, *Psychotherapy with Children* (New York: Norton, 1942), p. 306.

[60] A. E. Royer, *An Analysis of Counseling Procedures in a Non-Directive Approach*, M. A. Thesis (Columbus: Ohio State University, 1942); V. W. Lewis, "Changing the Behavior of Adolescent Girls," *Arch. Psychol.*, (1943), n. 219, 1-87; W. U. Snyder, "An Investigation of the Nature of Non-Directive Psychotherapy," *J. Gen. Psychol.* (1945), 33, 73-77; V. C. Raimy, 'Self-Reference in Counseling Interviews," *J. Consult. Psychol.* (1949), 12, 153-163.

[61] R. Zavalloni, "Il Processo della Scelta Volontaria in Casi di Psicoterapia Centrata-sul Cliente," *Arch. Psicol. Neurol. Psichiat.* (1954), 15, 104, 120 ff. A more complete study of voluntary choice, with the reproduction of numerous passages of the original clinical material, can be found in the following article by the same author: "The Process of Choice in Therapeutic Counseling," *Antonianum* (1954), 29, 157-208; 269-324.

[62] The major work of Ludwig Binswanger is his *Grundformen und Erkenntnis Menschlichen Daseins* (Zurich: Verlag Max Niehans, 1942). A profound study of this work was made by Danilo Cargnello: "Amore, Amicizia, Aggressività ed Ipseita nella Antropologia Esistenzialista di Ludwig Binswanger," *Riv. Psicol.* (1947), 43, 111-142; (1948), 44, 36-59, 178-199. Concerning the fundamental doctrine of Existential Analysis (Daseinsanalyse) cf. also the following: D. Cargnello, "Antropoanalisi e Psicoanalisi," *Arch. Psicol. Neurol. Psich.* (1949), 10, 406-434; "Frankl e la Logoterapia," *Arch. Psicol. Neurol. Psich.* (1953), 14, 413-419; S. Brambilla, "Il Metodo di Rorschach nell Analisi Fenomenologica Esistenziale," *Arch. Psicol. Neurol. Psich.* (1949), 10, 188-193.

[63] D. Cargnello, "Amore, Amicizia, Aggressività," *loc. cit.*, p. 112.

[64] Silvio Brambilla in his short article, "Daseinsanalyse: Scienza non Filosofia," *Arch. Psicol. Neurol. Psich.* (1953), 14, has examined the reactions and dissensions which arose against the phenomenological trend in psychiatry, and says that "Binswanger, by refusing to draw any conclusions, by avoiding at all cost making a diagnosis, in order to let things speak for themselves, is not a phenomenologist of Husserl's type. Binswanger's method can be derived from Husserl. But actually what Binswanger does is to order the data of phenomenological experience into an empirical discipline." *Ibid.*, p. 2.

[65] L. Binswanger, "La 'Daseinsanalyse' en Psychiatrie," *L'Encephale*, 1 (1951), 110, writes: "La science phenomenologique, la 'Daseinsanalyse', est une science exacte, mais dans un autre sens que l'exactitude des Sciences Naturelles par example. La phenomelogie est la seule methode applicable a l'Anthropologie."

66 D. Cargnello, "Antropologia e Psicanalisi," *Arch. Psicol. Neurol. Psich.* (1949), 10, 406. The same author states as a conclusion to his own study of the Grundformen of Binswanger: *"Daseinsanalyse* prefers to define itself as an *anthropology* rather than as a *psychology,* because it treats man in his totality which uses its own methods and has its own goal of exactness: it is the *science of human phenomena."* "Amore, Amicizia, Aggressività," *loc. cit.,* 197.

67 I. A. Caruso, *Psicoanalisi e Sintesi dell'Esistenza: Intorno ai Rapporti fra l'Analisi Psicologica e i Valori dell'Esistenza,* trans. G. M. Merlo (Torino: Marietti, 1953), p. 140. For a critical evaluation of existentialist psychotherapy, cf. *Ibid.,* pp. 135-144. Caruso points out the positive contribution of the phenomenological trend in psychology and psychiatry, but stresses also some serious deficiencies. To these "partial solutions" he offers a personalistic psychotherapy which develops in two phases, through a *psychological analysis* and an *existential synthesis.*

68 D. Cargnello, "Amore, Amicizia, Aggressività," *loc. cit.,* 178-181.

69 Aligning himself with Charles Baudouin, Igor A. Caruso posits some reservations to Binswanger's idea of existential responsibility. "The nihilism of the psychological age is not overcome by stoic heroism: 'the being-thrown-in-the-world' can have a conscious responsibility within himself only if we have clear ideas of the role of the subject and of the hierarchy of world-values." But Caruso recognizes the need and the usefulness of the reaction which the new phenomenological trend aroused. "In the framework of classical depth psychology man was mainly a being who was rigorously determined. Retrospective analysis of man's motives led to the discovery of the causes; this means that only non-free determination was asserted, and not free motivation." Caruso, *op. cit.,* pp. 11 ff.

70 Man experiences his own singularity as a "being-in-itself." Existence is the main factor of singularity. "The *feeling of freedom* is lived and more or less acutely experienced by the being-in-itself." Cargnello, "Amore, Amicizia, Aggressività," *loc. cit.,* 191. No matter how depressed is man, there is always a portion of his being which feels free. Even an obsessive-compulsive person feels this experience of freedom at the very moment in which he recognizes the absurdity of his strange ideas. *Ibid.,* 190-192.

71 D. Cargnello, "Antropoanalisi e Psicoanalisi," *Arch. Psicol. Neurol. Psich.* (1949), 10, 406-434.

72 D. Cargnello, *Ibid.,* 410.

73 V. E. Frankl, *The Doctor and the Soul: An Introduction to Logotherapy,* trans. Richard and Clara Winston (New York: Alfred A. Knopf, 1957); *Psicoterapia nella Practica Medica* (Firenze: Editrice Universitaria, 1953). For a clear synthesis of Frankl's thought cf. Danilo Cargnello, "Frankl a la Logotherapia," *Arch. Psicol. Neurol. Psich.* (1953), 14, 413-419.

74 V. E. Frankl, *Psicoterapia nella Pratica Medica,* p. 13: "This method has this prerogative: of being a psychotherapy from the spiritual viewpoint.

It seeks to make the subject conscious of his own responsibility and of the spiritual essense of 'being man.' In addition it tries, with the use of existential analysis, to bring to consciousness those spiritual factors which were in the unconscious (while psychoanalysis limits itself to making conscious the *instinctive* unconscious)." Frankl upholds the value of a school "whose supreme norm, whose highest principle, whose noblest imperative culminates and terminates with the invocation of *being conscious* of one's responsibility," p. 15.

75 V. E. Frankl, *The Doctor and the Soul:* "When we look upon human life without the blinkers of preconception, we must conclude that both consciousness and responsibleness play the basic roles in the drama of existence. One might in fact state it as a basic theorem that *being human means being conscious and being responsible.*" p. 5. Cf. also p. 268.

76 V. E. Frankl, *op. cit.* "Inherent human freedom, which obtains in spite of all these constraints, the freedom of mind in spite of nature, has been overlooked. Yet, it is this freedom that truly constitutes the essence of man," p. 23. The same author writes in *Psicoterapia nella Pratica Medica:* "The fundamental human freedom in the face of every fate, the constant possibility of being able to assume an attitude towards destiny as well as towards a task which must be somehow solved, the ever real freedom of acting in this way or that in a given situation, all this must be put in the right perspective by the therapist. In fact in this way, and only in this way can the therapist help his patient to understand what kind of internal and external potentialities he has." P. 172.

77 V. E. Frankl, *The Doctor and the Soul,* op. cit., p. 36.

78 V. E. Frankl, *Ibid.,* p. 88. Concerning the relationship between freedom and destiny, i.e., concerning the influence of biological, psychological, and sociological determinants on human behavior, cf. *Ibid.,* pp. 89-120.

79 It seems to me that we cannot deny to Frankl the merit of having contributed notably to the evocation of a picture of man which is more adequate than that given by the naturalistic trend. But we raise an objection against Frankl's overemphasis on human freedom in its concrete possibilities. Cf. D. Cargnello, *Frankl e la Logoterapia, loc. cit.,* p. 7; I. A. Caruso, *Psicoanalisi e Sintesi dell'Esistenza, op. cit.,* p. 142.

80 H. Baruk, "Le Problème de la Volonté: Nouvelles Données Psychophysiologiques," *J. Psychol. Norm. Path.* (1939), 36, 397-423; "Hypnose, Volonté, et Personnalité Morale," *Press Medic.* (1947), 55, 479-498; "La Psychiatrie synthétique et le Problème de Personnalité Humaine," *Psyche* (1948), n. 15; "Experimental Catatonia and the Problem of Will and Personality," *J. Nerv. Ment. Dis.* (1949), 110, 218-235; *Psychiatrie Morale Experimentale, Individuelle et Sociale: Haines et Réactions de Culpabilité, Tsedek et Volonté, Psychosociologie de la Paix et de la Guerre, Bibliothéque de Psychiatrie* (Paris, Pres Univ. France, 1950), 2nd Ed.; "Les Methódes Scientifiques d'étude de la Conscience Morale en Psychologie et en Psychopathologie Individuelle et Sociale," *Le coupable: est-il un Malade ou Un*

Pecheur? Group Lyonnais d'Études Medicales, Philosophiques et Biologiques, Coll. Convergences (Paris: Spes, 1951), pp. 91-109; *La Desorganisation de la Personnalité* (Paris: Press Univ. France, 1952); "Constatations Objectives du Problème Moral," *Actes du II Congrès International de Criminologie* (Paris: Sorbonne, Septembre, 1950; Paris: Press Univ. France, t. IV, 1953), pp. 457-464. Cf. supra what has been said about the thought of Henri Baruk on the "creative and integrative power of man."

[81] H. Baruk, "Experimental Catatonia and the Problem of will and Personality," *loc. cit.*, 233. In another article Baruk calls psychologists and psychiatrists to the synthetic study of human personality, and reminds them that 'à coté des infrastructures il faut aborder les fonctions superiéures de l'homme qui résident dans la conscience et la volonté" (233). To those who, after the example of Ribot, systematically minimize these functions or eliminate them completely, Baruk says: "Malgré son apparente objectivité, une telle attitude n'est pas réellement scientifique, puisqu'elle élimine systématiquement une partie du problème, et précisément cette partie qui donne à la personnalité humaine sa physionomie spécifique." Cf. *Psychiatrie Morale Experimentale, op. cit.,* p. 148.

[82] H. Baruk, *Ibid.,* p. 5. Contemporary clinical research demonstrates, according to O. Hobart Mowrer, that psychoanalysis has its problem of unrealistic and wishful thinking. Such research shows that in a neurotic conflict it is not the desire which is repressed, but rather consciousness. This concept of neurosis calls attention to individual as well as social responsibility, and the main goal of psychotherapy is that of creating in the patient the feeling of responsibility for his actions. No matter how uncertain is the position of the aforementioned author, moral responsibility seems reconcilable with a scientific vision of human nature, while the great ethical principles of religion are considered as the psychological and social safeguards of man. Cf. O. H. Mowrer, "Some Philosophical Implications in Mental Disorder and its Treatment," *Harvard Educ. Rev.* (1953), 23, 117-127.

[83] H. Baruk, *Psychiatrie Morale Experimentale, Individuelle et Sociale, loc. cit.,* p. XXVIII. Concerning the complexity of the factors of human personality and their intimate relationship, Henri Baruk says that "il est vain de separer le jugement moral et social des instincts et des données biologiques." Cf. "La Psychiatrie Synthétique et le Problème de la Personnalité Humaine," *loc. cit.,* 66.

[84] H. Baruk, "Experimental Catatonia and the Problem of Will and Personality," *loc. cit.,* 233.

CHAPTER FIVE

Empirical Experience of Freedom as "Lived"

The situations and the particular problems which are discussed in the positive studies of man's free activity do not, generally speaking, closely represent the real circumstances of life. This can be said of both the experimental investigations and clinical research. Laboratory studies doubtless have resulted in a notable contribution to the phenomenology of volitional activity. These studies have especially clarified the mechanism of automatic reactions in the individual, but perhaps have never expressed the complexity and depth of meaning of human behavior. The clinical studies present, from this particular point of view, an undeniable superiority over strictly experimental studies. The deficiency of precision in the clinical studies is greatly compensated for by the more integral view that they offer of the problem under consideration. The motivation of human behavior, as it can be deduced from these investigations, is much closer to the experience as it is actually lived. However, even in these studies there is a restrictive factor: the subjects who are examined are always either abnormal or psychically disturbed persons; they therefore do not represent the common condition of mankind.

Because of these limitations—the artificial character of the experimental studies on the one hand, and the non-representative character of the clinical studies on the other—it seemed promising to the present author to look towards empirical experience for an exemplification of human behavior which is less artificial and at the same time more representative. This led to a line of research whose main goal was to become acquainted with numerous concrete cases which would provide a realistic picture of freedom and of its limitations.

The present study of the data of empirical experience consists essentially in an *analysis of personal documents,* developed from deliberately induced introspection. This analysis enables us to define in what way the *feeling and experience of freedom* emerge and develop in the important phase of adolescence (the age of true volitive development); it permits us also to differentiate the *multiple causes of limitation* on free human activity; and, lastly, it enables us to evaluate *coercion and the exercise of freedom* in their pedagogical implications.

1. Analysis of Personal Documents

The material upon which this research is based belongs to a type of "personal documents" obtained in a systematic way. The method of gathering this material is distinct from both the questionnaire method and from the method of the clinical protocol. It is an intermediary form, which could be defined as a particular type of "induced introspection" or, more exactly, as a type of "interpersonal conversation."

The following topic was presented to subjects who were from eleven to twenty years of age: *"Describe a concrete event of your own life in which you had an experience of freedom or an experience of its limitation."* In presenting this topic to the subjects two conditions were respected: (1) the matter of cooperation was kept on a completely voluntary basis — students could refuse to contribute to the experiment if they so wished; (2) anonymity and personal secrecy were guaranteed. With but a few exceptions, these two conditions were met perfectly.

The topic presented for the introspective examination of the subjects in this experiment must not be confused with common scholastic homework or a scholastic test of the essay type. In the case of the latter, the student writes on the assigned topic only because he is obliged to do so; the essay that he is asked to write may interest or annoy him, but he is not free to speak and write on whatever he wishes. In our case, on the contrary, the subject had the option of writing or not writing; he felt free in expressing himself with all sincerity, because he was assured and guaranteed of the secrecy of his response.

The method which was followed in the present experiment presents a notable advantage over the questionnaire method. In fact, while the latter rigidly limits the possibility of expression of an individual to a definite number of questions, in our method the subject confronted a stimulus which enabled him to respond in the most varied ways, according to his various personal circumstances. There was no question here of accumulating answers and reducing them to a statistical formula, but rather of examining the individual documents in order to note the personal characteristics of the subjects. The questionnaire method imposes predetermined categories into which the individual must be inserted; in our method it is the individual himself who presents his own psychological portrait.

These personal documents can be considered in every case as the expression of an interpersonal account: the record of a conference or a conversation between two parties, not carried on orally, but in writing. The subjects, in fact, have the feeling — as the protocols themselves show — that they are confronting the experimenter and are conversing directly with him. The experimenter asks them only one question and "listens" to them in a very remote way.

The subjects, seemingly ignoring such remoteness, attempted to answer the stimulus-questions by describing their personal experiences, experiences which were sometimes pleasant, sometimes sad. It is indeed an intimate world which was thus revealed and the method has enabled us to catch the varying attitudes of the subjects, their personal conflicts, their hidden aspirations in facing the problems of life.

a. Evaluation of Personal Documents

The collection of personal documents was examined from the clinical viewpoint by the author; he left aside quantitative evaluations because they seemed not to lend themselves to statistical analysis. The main point which must be kept in mind while elaborating on this confidential material is the experimental fact that young adults, and to a certain extent, even adolescents, are capable of self-analysis.[1] It is an admitted fact that today there can be no truly human psychology if the data of introspection are not taken into account. We must see how, under what conditions and to what extent, the capacity for self-analysis functions in adolescents and in young men and women.

Introspection presupposes a split in the thinking individual; he becomes a spectator of his own mental life. Even from the beginning of adolescence the individual begins to observe the states of his consciousness almost the moment they are produced, and later to recall them to memory. The introspection of youth, then, presupposes that mental activity is already perceived as a reality, with the same kind of objectivity that external reality has. Interior life is enriched and organized little by little, and the individual acquires the power of reflecting upon himself. The young adult *can* analyze himself and, in fact, enjoys doing so. The introspection of young people tends to be confused with their ways of thinking. But their introspection is a general orientation of their psychic activities rather than a phenomenon of disturbance in their consciousness. We must, therefore, take this into account when we analyze the psychology of adolescence and youth.

Most of the descriptions which psychologists give of introspection seem much more suited to the young than to mature adults. In fact, the analysis of the mental life of adults is distorted by memories of the past, by critical attitudes, and by limitations which are imposed by environment. The introspection of young adults is more ingenuous and therefore more valid. The necessity of utilizing the psychological documentation which is offered to us by young adults is based first of all upon their structure, that is, upon one of the characteristic processes of their psychic activity. Not to take this into consideration would be to deprive ourselves of the most important source of information that we have.

What value can we attribute to the documentation which is furnished us by the introspection of the young? We must keep in mind first of all that this documentation does not always completely reflect the true image of the subject. Maurice Debesse writes: "What these youngsters write, when induced to make use of their self-analysis, is for us—educators and experimenters—a very important and indispensable document for understanding their psyches. However, these documents or protocols do not represent the whole truth."[2] These intimate documents are a direct testimony which must be interpreted, keeping in mind the risks of error that all introspection implies.

There are two kinds of youthful introspection which are completely distinct, according to the method which is used in obtaining the information; the information may be spontaneous or induced by the experimenter. Induced information, which is the form used in this study, depends especially upon the one who attempts to bring it forth from the mind of the subject. Following this method, we attempted to discover, define, and measure psychic phenomena, using both oral and written interrogation. We tried to win the confidence of adolescents and of young adults, to find in their answers some material of interest capable of being interpreted as the manifestation of their youthful psyches. This could be called "inquiry based on introspection" in its proper sense. The response, which closely resembles an intimate diary, is interesting for its content; it is utilized in the same way as the direct testimony of a subject whom we seek to know.

The personal documents used in this research touch upon the third important phase of growth, adolescence and young childhood. The most characteristic and dominant phenomenon of this phase is that the broad receptivity, which was proper to the preceding phases, gives room to a process of interiorization. The young man no longer receives without criticism what the world provides him, as he had in the past. He re-elaborates interiorly what he receives from without. He begins to be himself and is aware of it. Characteristic of this period is the ever more prominent assertion of his personality. A personal evaluation of men, things, and events appears in the adolescent. Of most interest during this important phase of adolescence are not the external manifestations of behavior, but rather the motivation of the interior life, the profound reasons why men act in one way rather than in another.

During the period of developmental growth, interests of a social nature are greatly accentuated. The first symptom of these interests is the child's display (though unconscious) of self-assertion. In the face of conflict, he will insist that his demands prevail. By the time pubescence sets in, his self-assertion has so developed that his home and its restrictive environment often repel him. He is easily irritated by both home and school authority and under the least provocation criticizes his surroundings. If the adolescent is attending a boarding school, this hostile reaction toward authority is often heightened. It matters little whether he is attending the institution of his own accord, for this rebellious attitude seems to be an inevitable phase of adolescence.

This attitude toward authority undergoes a marked degree of change throughout the various phases of growth. During infancy it has a purely affective content. In childhood this tendency takes the form of intellectual self-sufficiency. By adolescence it has become characterized by a strong desire for autonomy, and during this stage, self-assertion takes on a more precise form. The adolescent feels a real need for freedom, and vague though this feeling be (confer the responses below), it is very influential. As one enters his young adult years his feeling of freedom "interiorizes" itself. It becomes an "experience" of freedom and develops into a capacity of conscious self-determination, which constitutes the highest ideal of human personality.

During adolescence one's intellectual and volitional activity reaches a degree of maturity which affords him a greater capacity for forming "value judgments." With the formulation of these "value judgments" comes the adolescent's assertion to his right of freedom. Through the greater part of adolescence this concept of freedom remains vague, though the aspiration toward freedom may become more vocal. Not until one becomes a young adult is this tendency toward freedom actualized in the assertion and defense of his own personality. Once young adulthood is reached, one demands not only the recognition of his own personal freedom but also urges that everyone else's right to freedom be respected.

Agostino Gemelli wisely notes that this response to social interests on the part of the adolescent as well as the young adult is, from the psychological point of view, of great import.[3] Unconsciously the young man "objectivizes" what is more intimate and more natural to him, namely, the tendency to assert his own personality and to seek recognition from his associates. The appeal that the young adult makes for the rights of minorities and the underprivileged classes is nothing more than the projection of his desire for individual freedom.

This tendency toward freedom is revealed to a great extent in young adults who, because of an overly-rigoristic background, find themselves almost always in conflict (whether overt or otherwise) with authority. Under the guise of freedom the young man applauds every act, public or private, which seems to have a revolutionary tone. He is a man who is easily dissatisfied, and often plays the rebel even though his stand in these matters is not clearly defined. This tendency to side frequently with the rebel's cause should engender no alarm, for it is characteristic of an adolescent's normal development. The young man would not be a normal person if this trait were lacking in his psychological profile.

b. Objective Data of Empirical Experience

In order to evaluate the student's concept of freedom, an assignment was given to members of both sexes, ranging in age from eleven to twenty, and of different social, cultural and national backgrounds. They were asked to describe by means of a concrete example an experience which had entailed the use of their freedom or its restriction. As is often the case, the response fell short of the experimenter's expectations. Many educators thought the task beyond the capabilities of their students. But a good number of replies were received and, of these, 173 met the specified requirements. Of the responses, 69 were in Italian, 87 in French, and 17 in English. These data will be indicated with a progressive number, preceded respectively by the letter *I* denoting Italian, *F* French, and *E* English.

Though the educational systems differ among the various countries represented, the subjects can be divided into two groups. The younger set is made up of students attending the last year of grammar school, junior and senior high school — secondary school and the Gymnasium in the European system — (58 subjects); the older students represent the first two years of college — or the Lycaeum — (115 subjects). Conditions of family background are the most varying, of course. This was to be expected since the responses come from individuals of different nationalities. The scholastic environment is sufficiently varied: students from public as well as private schools participated in the experiment. Some were aspirants to the secular professions, others were seminarians preparing for the priesthood.

From the qualitative viewpoint these documents are very interesting, even though not all the subjects understood the true meaning of freedom (contrary to the intention of the experimenter). But perhaps herein lies the real value of these responses: the subjects did not express a psychological concept of freedom as understood by the experimenter, but their own concept of freedom, one which varied according to their age and their grade placement, i.e., according to their personal development. This experiment gave to some of the subjects the opportunity to explore a problem that up to that time they had ignored. Some of the subjects conducted (perhaps for the first time) a true self-analysis. Such is the case of a twenty-year-old in the third year of the Lycaeum. He responded in the following manner:

(*I.* 47) "I confess that this assignment has given me the opportunity to do a little thinking about myself. However, no matter how hard I've tried, I've been unable to recall an incident or something like that in which I had the feeling of freedom or the restriction of it. Perhaps such a reaction will surprise you, for I know that it's hard to imagine that in all my past twenty years I never once found myself in a circumstance in which the operation or violation of my freedom was involved. But this can be easily explained in that I left my family at the age of eleven, to follow what I believed to be my vocation. As a result, the circumstances of my life changed completely. . . . To tell the truth, I can't seem to concentrate on this topic. Something is bothering me. It's a problem that is growing more serious every day; I know I should get some advice, but I can't seem to talk about it to anyone. I am awfully sorry if I haven't been of much help to you."

This response shows clearly that a real dialogue took place between the subject and the author of the experiment. A sudden awakening of the desire of freedom can be detected between the lines, a desire which, if repressed, was at least dormant.

And in the following protocol of a seventeen-year-old student in the second year of college (Lycaeum), the dialogue form shines through. In this case, however, *the condition of freedom* required by the experimenter was not respected. The reaction of the boy indicates a close rapport between himself and the experimenter:

(*I.* 60) "This assignment is, of its very nature, a limitation of freedom. Why? Because we don't get any class time to complete this assignment. No, we have to do it during study time which right now, with finals approaching, is so valuable. We have to work on these papers immediately after lunch. It's hot then, and I'd much rather be taking a nap. Perhaps it was your intention that this assignment be optional; well, here, they forced us to do it. A topic on freedom should at least be free."

Sometimes, the answers to the topic take the confidential form of a letter. Such was the response of a candidate for the priesthood: "I hope that your project will be successful; may it add to the glory of God. Best regards." (*I.* 50.) Most of the subjects took the assignment seriously. They realized that the topic required some laborious thinking. The seminarian just mentioned approached the topic in this manner:

(*I.* 50) "It's not an easy task to speak about freedom; as a matter of fact, I think it's beyond my capacity. But I'll try my best to recall everything that has happened to me regarding the use of my freedom. I may not have much to offer since I am only nineteen. But I'll try my best to help you in your endeavor to find the psychological explanation of the adolescent and to offer him opportune remedies for his particular needs."

Some subjects preferred to remain silent. They feared that they were taking the assignment too lightly and thus might write something that would be misleading. Such was the reaction of a sixteen-year-old student in the fifth year of the Gymnasium. (Equivalent to a senior in high school. *Trans.*)

(*I.* 67) "From the little I've heard it seems that some importance has been attached to this task. And because I'm supposed to give the subject some serious consideration, I'd rather not answer. I feel that it's better to write nothing than to write something asinine. Therefore, since the problem seems so important, I'll refrain from answering. I can't see any reason for leading the experimenter into error."

All responses reveal a great amount of spontaneity and freedom of expression. This was especially so among students from an excessively rigoristic family. Their response was no doubt a reaction to their repressed desire for freedom, a desire quite normal in the adolescent and young adult. For some of the subjects this experiment was a beneficial task. It afforded them their first opportunity to express themselves with complete sincerity. The following response will show what we mean. The student, eighteen years old, is a junior in college (third year of the Lycaeum).

(*I.* 64) "My concept of freedom was something very vague until a couple of years ago, when I started to study philosophy. And the concrete example in my life where I experienced a limitation of freedom is the fact of having been put in this school, where (to speak frankly) freedom is known only as a word, while its essence is completely ignored."

Because of the great variety of these personal documents, which were obtained from normal subjects in the common circumstances of real life, the "model" of this research can be considered sufficiently represented. Without intending to attribute to this material an excessive value, it seems valid to say that it succeeds in achieving the goal that the author had in mind: to present concrete examples of the empirical experience of freedom and of its limitations. If the data which were collected in this investigation do not have the scientific value of a laboratory study, they do have the human significance of clinical research. In fact, they reveal to us in an objective form the experience as it is "lived" by many individuals in one of the most important and striking phenomena of life.

2. Feeling and Experience of Freedom

The protocols reveal, in most of the cases, a vague feeling of freedom — almost a need of the organism to live in the open, in the fresh air under the sun. But this aspect of freedom, even though it is completely natural to man at every moment of his life, reveals a tendency of psychic immaturity which recalls to these subjects an earlier period in their growth. But in this same group there can be noted some better developed manifestations of the feeling of freedom: a desire for a certain personal autonomy, that is, for an increasing independence from external circumstances as well as from the pressures imposed by others. Very rare are the cases in which the true notion of psychological freedom is hinted at, even implicitly. There are, however, some concrete examples that reveal an authentic voluntary decision.

a. Typical Expressions of the Feeling of Freedom

The feeling of freedom is expressed by these adolescents by the feeling of joy experienced in a race in the fresh air, or in the green fields; by the climbing of a mountain, or by a day at the beach. It shows up especially when the subject is in contact with the beauty of nature.

(*I.* 16) "The sun was shining high in the sky and it gave me a feeling of great joy and well-being. Everything invited me to run and to enjoy the happy freedom of that moment."

(*I.* 37) "How wonderful it is when I am on vacation! School is over and there are not many thoughts on my mind. In the morning, when I wake up, I do not have to think about anything. I can go out when and as long as I want, and I can run in the green fields and woods without having to study."

(*I.* 24) "I love nature, flowers, the sun and the fresh air. All this expands my heart, makes me happy, and even a better individual. To live in this way would be a dream."

(*E.* 3) "Once I had a feeling of complete freedom, when I was alone up in the mountains. I felt that I wanted to stay out there forever. I was experiencing a strong feeling of freedom within me. I felt freer than I had ever felt in my life in those small backyards around my home."

A thirteen-year-old boy believes he can have the feeling of freedom when he is in contact with the waves of the sea. Taking his canoe, he tries to find where the water is deep. The agitated sea does not stop him. He writes: "Although presumptuous, I believe I can overcome the sea and test my feeling of complete freedom" (*I.* 34).

After having overcome the roughest, the highest and the most dangerous waves, a strong current takes him farther and farther from the shore; he tries to get back, but the increasingly stronger current does not permit him; only through the help of some sailors who were nearby is he saved. The boy feels himself overcome by the force of the sea and is very much ashamed of what has happened to him.

Various subjects say that they feel free when, alone at home, they are not under the controlling surveillance of their parents and relatives. They feel, then, they can do what they wish, that they can go where they choose. Their feeling of freedom is even more vivid when they go out in the evening without their father or mother as chaperons. Then they feel they have become as free as grownups.

(*I.* 13) "Nobody else is at home: a drop of water breaks the silence. Father and Mother went to Milan. The housekeeper is sick. Finally, I am free."

(*I.* 18) "Only then, when we are not kept under control by the vigilant eyes of our mother, without worrying over her disappointment in seeing us return home late all covered with dust, we experience the feeling of freedom, which is so vivid in us boys. . . . The joy which makes us happy is based mainly on the thought of not having anyone who can prevent us from doing what we like."

(*I.* 21) "My grandfather and I decided to take a walk through the city to visit the principal monuments of Turin. . . . That day I enjoyed an almost absolute freedom, because, wherever I wanted to go, my grandfather always said yes."

(*I.* 4) "The day before yesterday my parents let me alone out of the house for the first time to go to a play rehearsal. I put my jacket on over my sweater and left. I do not know what I would have done because of my joy: I was jumping, running, singing in the street. I went to the rehearsal and I tried to finish as soon as I could so that I could go out to have fun. When the rehearsal was over, I looked at my watch . . . there were 45 more minutes of freedom. A real true pleasure!"

Among the personal documents of the second group there is one which describes with vivid expressions and freshness of feeling the memory of an indelible experience of freedom which the subject felt at the age of six. A girl fifteen years old describes with joy, and probably with a feeling of gratitude towards her mother, her first experience of freedom. But it is evident that there is not and cannot be — at the age to which the remembrance refers — a true experience of freedom. According to the distinctions which will be clarified later on, in this case we are dealing with a desire for freedom in the common sense of autonomy, not in the specific sense of self-determination.

(*F*. 19) "I was only six years old when my mother told me that from tomorrow on I would have to go to school by myself. This was a great event for me. My joy was unlimited. The maid who used to come every day to pick me up and was my guardian angel was not enjoying my sympathy any more in those days. She used to hold my hand too tightly, she dragged me now by the right, now by the left hand. She treated me as if I were a doll. I found this coercion exasperating. Certainly, for her it was a great responsibility, but I believed that I was big enough to take care of myself. Consider, therefore, with what pride I went to school alone for the first time. I believed I was somebody. This freedom which I desired was given me suddenly, without a thousand warnings even though the road was very dangerous. My whole being was filled with happiness. I felt like a bird that is freed from the cage where it was a prisoner."

b. The Awakening of the Social Feeling

Many of the subjects considered the use of freedom on the social plane. Freedom is a personal right which must be respected by men and protected by law. The right of reprisal, if it is ever justified for higher reasons by adults, does not find any justification at all in the mind of a thirteen-year-old boy. In seeing a group of men passing by, who had been taken and condemned by the Germans to the firing squads in reprisal, he is moved by indignation and says loudly without fear, "But this is an injustice; you cannot condemn innocent men to death" (*I*. 41).

These subjects, by means of a concrete example, express the opinion that one's freedom must somehow be subject to social exigencies. We have rights, but also duties: particularly the right that others respect our freedom and the duty of respecting theirs. But this will not be possible — adolescents themselves tell us — if we do not spontaneously give up part of our freedom.

(*I*. 38) "Sometimes when I get up in the morning and I feel happy, I would like to sing. But I cannot do that, because I feel the duty of restricting my freedom for the freedom of others, and in this case for that of my little sister, who must be free to sleep as long as she wishes."

Here is another example of the social feeling of freedom. An entire school must choose a name for its team for the games that it will play against other schools. This problem arises: how can we agree if everyone wants to impose his own will upon the will of others? At last, after long discussions, they succeed in finding a name that satisfies everybody. A twelve-year-old boy makes these comments on their success:

(*I.* 6) "This happened because everyone of us renounced his own initial ideas and limited his own freedom in favor of the freedom of others. Only in this way was it possible for all of us to feel a little freer to agree upon the choice of a satisfactory name. Under that name, then, which no longer was the name proposed by a single individual but which belonged in some measure to each, we went on playing, free and happy until the final tournaments. This small event served to make me understand that it is not always possible to use one's freedom completely without forcing others to renounce their own freedom, and it is therefore necessary to limit ourselves so that all can participate in common life."

An eleven-year-old boy confesses that he does not understand what freedom means. What perplexes him more is the fact that "adults speak of freedom all the time, discuss it and often fight for it, but they never agree" (*I.* 8). The boy mentions a concrete case which happened during the last world war, where this freedom was not respected at all. His Aunt Helen, who was a nurse, did not return home one evening; she had been arrested by the partisans who accused her of being a spy for the Germans. The boy describes the situation in this way:

(*I.* 8) "What sad days we went through during that period! I always have my poor aunt before my eyes. They locked her up in a castle, and I visited her sometimes with my mother and brought her something to eat. She lost weight and was always crying, saying that she hadn't done anything wrong. Thinking that over, I still feel the great pain that I suffered at that time. They kept my poor aunt in prison for a period of forty days, and then they let her go because she was innocent. I understood then how beautiful freedom is, and I think that nobody should deprive anyone else of it who possesses it and is worthy of it."

In some cases, even among subjects from eleven to fourteen years of age, freedom assumes the idea of a conquest or the significance of a true decision in the face of conflicting alternatives, even though such a decision is more intuitive than reflexive. Sometimes it can have the characteristic of a free choice actualized after mature deliberation. A fourteen-year-old boy expresses himself in this way: "Many are not able to find freedom, but we must remember this—nobody will give us freedom. We ourselves must win it" (*I.* 4). An eleven-year-old boy in the first year of his secondary education (Italian system), feels happy about performing an act of human solidarity as the result of a voluntary decision which was both prompt and difficult. When faced with more immediate and personal interests, he preferred to choose higher and more altruistic values. Here is the description of the actual event, which appears to be inspired by a short story of De Amicis.

(*I.* 5) "There is nothing more beautiful than an act of charity which is performed with human understanding. Christmas was near, and I insisted on having an electric train as a present. My mother tried to convince me that the toy was too expensive, and that I was already too big for such toys. She told me there were many people who were suffering and who lacked everything. There was no reason therefore to waste money this way. But I did not let her convince me. I insisted so much that my father, who was tired of being annoyed, gave me the money to buy the train. Overjoyed, I left our apartment immediately to buy it. But on my way downstairs I met the poor widow who lived in the attic. She was going upstairs all sick and tired and bent under the weight of a sack of wood. I then remembered the words of my mother. At once I approached the poor woman, grabbed the sack of wood from her hands, and climbed the stairs without paying any attention to her weak protestations. I entered the attic and set down the bag of wood. On standing up, I noticed her children lying close together in bed, perhaps to keep warm. I did not hesitate for a moment—I handed all the money my father had given me to the poor woman, who in her complete confusion could find no words to thank me. With that money Christmas would be a day of joy for them also. At that moment I felt my heart become lighter and I was filled with a great happiness."

Not only adults, but boys, too, feel they possess a certain inde-

pendence and freedom in their way of thinking and acting. Here is
a description of a twelve-year-old boy's feeling of pride in being
able on his own initiative to make a decision in regard to his future.

(*I*. 19) "A few days ago I had a clear example of that freedom
which makes us boys so proud. One evening at suppertime we were
talking about the studies I would pursue after my secondary education, and about my future. My parents gave me permission to
choose the path I would like to follow. My answer, which expressed my desire to begin studying at an institute of technology,
was favorably received by them. With great satisfaction I became
aware that what I said had been very well thought out. In this way
I had an example of the freedom that each individual possesses. I
must add, however, that I so presented my reasons only because I
knew them well, and that I had made my decision after much
meditation."

A vague idea of freedom, such as that which we indicated above
in the term "feeling of freedom," can also be found in young adults,
but this is certainly not the predominant idea they express. In the
personal documents taken from young adults, the idea of freedom
passes from a purely *"organismic"* conception of freedom to an
existential one. The influence of existential philosophy and literature are often obvious, and in such cases the document usually appears less personal. But it must be pointed out that a true majority
of the documents speak of a concept of freedom understood as a
capacity of voluntary self-determination, such as that described in
the experimental research and clinical studies, analyzed in the
preceding chapter.

c. Various Aspects of the Experience of Freedom

Some subjects manifest this feeling of freedom in a particularly
vivid form when they are in contact with nature, as did those of the
preceding group. But in the following cases the same feeling appears to be much deeper, because the subject does not feel he is a
being lost in the vastness of nature, but rather almost immersed in
and identified with nature itself. In addition, in these cases the subjects pass immediately from the "feeling" of freedom to the "true
experience" of it.

(*E*. 17) "Standing here and admiring the 'freedom' of the impetuous sea, I am enjoying nature. The wind whistling by my ear seems to despise the freedom I enjoy. I feel that this freedom in my contact with nature has nothing in common with the freedom that the city offers. I feel free from the laws and commands of others. Free to take part in that freedom which only nature enjoys."

A young lady writes:

(*F*. 8) "At first sight I found this topic (on freedom) very vague. First of all, in what sense should I take freedom? Is it a question of physical freedom? Of freedom of independence? Or is it a question of the freedom which we acquire when we become masters of ourselves? Whatever the question is, I believe I experienced one day the feeling which can be called freedom. It was at the beach, towards sunset. The wind was very strong. I was alone, almost the only one walking by the surf. I was fighting against the wind. Alone on the deserted beach I challenged the storm, and in spite of it I continued on my way. Along with the feeling of independence caused by the fact that I was alone, that I could go where I wanted, I experienced also the feeling of being victorious over the wind. I felt free."

In the case of an eighteen-year-old girl, the feeling of freedom is almost only a memory of years gone by or a momentary feeling where every care disappears. But reflection and the search for the basis of her own power of acting soon enter into the picture.

(*F*. 23) "I was a member of the 'Little Explorers' and of the 'Girl Guides.' When I recall the days when I was eleven or twelve, I think that I had at that age a better understanding of the feeling of freedom. To run through the thick woods, paying little heed to the thorns, to follow a hard path, to walk across the fields, to sing aloud my own joy of living: all this gave me a joyful feeling of life and a strong impression of freedom. I no longer recall quite clearly my first feelings, but I can analyze those that I experience now when I come in contact with nature. In the thickness of the woods I feel completely free. Every care, both physical and moral, disappears and gives place to a feeling of complete freedom. Then I ask myself if this freedom is based upon something true. Most of the time I understand very well that I depend upon God and must live my life accordingly. In those moments I can reflect and decide with full tranquillity. Every decision to be taken is thought out this way. I am not very self-conscious: I do not know how to analyze myself except with great difficulty. This is what I feel or believe I feel during those moments when I experience my freedom the most."

Another eighteen-year-old girl describes her thrill of being in the open air and her freedom. Again in this case the feeling of freedom reveals an affirmation of her personality. To be free for her does not mean simply to be free in contact with air, water, and wind — in contact with the phenomena of nature in general — but to be free means the conquest of her own personal independence by means of overcoming obstacles. Her first flight in an airplane is like an escape from the bondage of infancy in order to enter the psychological phase of maturity.

(*F.* 78) "For a long time I had a great desire to fly in an airplane with a classmate of mine. We used to buy aviation magazines; we were acquainted with all the new models, with competitions, etc. In short, our greatest desire was that of flying in an airplane at least once; but many obstacles impeded our dream. We were only fourteen years of age and we could not enter an airplane without permission from our parents. My parents would have forbidden me to go on an airplane as soon as I even hinted at the idea. I did not intend to disobey my parents in this because, if an accident had occurred, there would be serious consequences for them and for me. I was timid, as we generally are at the age of fourteen, and I believed I would never have dared to ask the personnel at the airport to grant this wish I craved so greatly. It was also necessary to have a large sum of money to go on an airplane, and, as is normal at fourteen years of age, I did not have enough in my pocket. In addition, the airport was so far away from the city that it was necessary to take a bus and a taxi to get there. And lastly, I needed my parents' permission to go out alone for the afternoon. All these obstacles seem nothing to me now, but at the age of fourteen they were an insurmountable barrier. However, on a Thursday afternoon I had the necessary money and I went to the airport. Since it was very late, no one asked me for my parents' written authorization. Finally I flew in an airplane. At that moment I had a distinct impression of freedom: I had overcome all obstacles both from within and from outside forces."

Some subjects had the feeling of freedom when they went out for the first time after a long illness; after having been freed from the tension provoked by difficult exams; when they felt relieved from monotonous daily work. From the religious point of view, some subjects felt free after a sincere confession, when they had the satisfaction of having been freed from the burden of their own sins (*F.* 77). A seventeen-year-old boy experiences a vivid expression of freedom when, tired of seeing always the same places and meeting the same persons, he can take a trip for a week with one of his friends.

(*E.* 9) "This was not simply a trip to go a long distance and see new places, but to show ourselves what freedom meant, after having been in college for one year. We were annoyed at seeing the same places every day from one vacation to the next. How happy we were to get away from difficult studies, from the ordinary life of school! It was as if the nausea and pains of life did not exist for us. We felt as free as birds."

Protocol *F.* 32 does not present a personal experience of freedom, but a kind of inquiry concerning feelings which prevail among girls in this regard. A nineteen-year-old girl, a member of a youth group, conducted an inquiry on freedom among the young student girls, from fifteen to nineteen years of age. Here are the answers to some of the questions.

First question: Did you ever experience a feeling of complete freedom? If so, under what circumstances? The answers show these percentages: 20% of the girls had experienced it while alone or in contact with nature; 20% during vacation time or during a time of relaxation; 20% when they were not under any control or being chaperoned; 12% after they had overcome some obstacle or had performed a good act.

Second question: Do you believe that you feel freer than your mother did at your age? and why? The results: 50% of the young girls feel freer today because there is greater possibility for higher studies, for trips, contacts, reading, relationship between the two sexes; 18% feel freer because they are not forced to work as their mothers had been, and because they have the possibility of continuing thir studies.

Third question: Do you think that some persons are freer than you are? The answers show these percentages: about 50% of the subjects hold that the freer persons are those who are not under any regulations: parents, superiors, old people, spinsters and unmarried men, unbelievers, orphans; 10% find that persons without any financial worries are freer: old people who have a great deal of money, members of religious orders, individuals who do not have to take care of a family.

Some subjects understand freedom as the affirmation of their own personality, as the expression of their wills against the opinions of others or the impositions of human respect.

(*F*. 57) "We must exercise our own personality at every moment of our lives, and in everything. We must always act on our own, make decisions even in small things, in our official duties of life as well as in ordinary life."

(*F*. 36) "I made an effort; I was happy. It is certain that we have freedom, but freedom is often opposed by our environment, by human respect, etc. What counts is the effort we make to show our freedom."

A seventeen-year-old girl asserts her will by reacting against conversations which are carried out in an anti-religious meeting. She is proud of this assertion of her personality as a real conquest. Facing a group of young people who seem to her to be too free in their morals, she says: "You laugh about what he said; you encourage him to lead a life of vice, and this is simply shameful." And she concludes with this observation: "It was human respect which made them participate in this conversation. Rather than show what they really were, they went along with everything; but they were slaves of human respect" (*F*. 58).

The following is a concrete experience in which a twenty-year-old girl makes complete use of her freedom. She has a flirtatious interest in a boy friend. Her mother, aware of this, does not push her daughter into it, but she does not want to interfere with it either. The girl begins to feel that the use of freedom implies a great responsibility.

(*F*. 44) "A friend of mine came to my house to pick me up for a walk in the open fields. Both of us were very serious. After a long walk, we had a lot of fun in an innocent way. We came back home after three or four hours. There had been no flirting, but there was a tendency towards it. I could have gone further than that very quickly if I did not have a little bit of will power. And if the occasion would present itself once more, I would certainly involve myself more seriously and engage in petting, because there was a real sexual attraction and much sympathy between the two of us. *Conclusion:* I hope that I will never go again with him alone, because I am afraid of myself and fear that I might lose, little by little, my simplicity and innocence. I am glad that I was able to use my freedom, but the next time I will use my freedom by telling him two things: that I consider him a very good friend of mine, and that I do not want to be alone with him in the fields. . . In fact, freedom for me is obedience freely accepted — obedience to duties of one's state, to moral and religious laws in my entire conduct. This will still constitute the use of my freedom."

d. Facing One's Future

Every adolescent will have to face, sooner or later, the problem of his own future. There is a period, during adolescence, in which he finds himself at the crossroad, facing the problem of choice for his future life. Every path presents its difficulties and its attractions. He would like to follow all paths, so that he does not have to be forced to renounce any. Since this is impossible, he prefers to procrastinate for one year, two years . . . but the moment comes when he cannot procrastinate any more. He must choose. The subjects of this experiment had long-standing and good study habits, which heightened their intelligence; but perhaps because of this, they never had the occasion to face life with a true sense of responsibility. But they too, had to choose their future. The responses of the present experiment show that this problem presented itself to their minds with a feeling both of worry and urgency as well. The feeling of anxiety is experienced mainly by those subjects who are not used to choice. An eighteen-year-old boy says: "We did not yet have any particularly acute and critical cases in which freedom to choose was left to us, except for a few personal actions of very little importance. Up to the present time, others had chosen for us" (*F.* 55). The responses show the urgency of this problem and an awareness of a new phase of their life which is about to begin.

(*F.* 24) "Freedom, in some cases, is something which demands much effort, and consequently much will power. The only time in which I can say that I experienced being really free is when I had to choose my future. After having finished my secondary education, I expressed the desire of entering a professional school in order to continue my education and obtain my degree. This is the only proof of freedom that I can quote at the present time, because I cannot say that I was really free in any other case. To say that I was free in other cases would constitute a lie."

(*F.* 43) "At the end of five years of my professional studies, I will obtain my degree in engineering. When I decided for engineering, I was only 16 years of age. At that time, I had the opportunity of exercising my freedom without any coercion. I could end my studies at the age of 16 or continue them. I hesitated for a long time because various circumstances were influencing me both from one side and the other . . . One day I made up my mind: "I will continue my studies." My parents approved my decision. I see that to make that decision entailed a serious responsibility. . . In that moment I was perhaps putting in jeopardy at least part of my future life. . . But, after all that has happened, I think that the decision I took then was good."

(*F.* 65) "I must choose my career. What shall I do? Since I am in my classical studies, the problem of choosing my career has to be faced with decision. I feel free, horribly free. I hesitate. I cannot make up my mind. I think of this, of that, but no decision. I think that I would really be happy if somebody else would choose for me. But it is I who must choose—and upon this choice my entire life will depend."

At the end of secondary education, the subjects are facing the problem of deciding whether to go on for graduate academic studies, or to take up a professional career. Various protocols which were received from the subjects show that the parents, generally speaking, leave their children free to choose the kind of studies they like or the career they prefer. It follows that the true responsibility of choosing falls upon the adolescent, who feels a state of uncertainty and perhaps even becomes emotionally upset because of the responsibility which he has to assume; at the same time, however, he is also proud of being able to decide of his own accord.

(*F.* 83) "My parents, by strange coincidence, proposed that I finish my studies in Brussels (I was living in Antwerp). They even told me that I could be free to choose between being a boarding student or a day student. All of a sudden I became totally free to choose among three possibilities: (a) to stay where I was, i.e. in Antwerp; (b) to be a boarding student in the school at Brussels, under supervision; (c) to be in Brussels as a day student of the school, without any supervision after classes. After considering and weighing the pros and cons, I freely chose the third alternative (day student in Brussels) because this choice seemed to correspond better with my desires. Nothing forced me to choose one alternative rather than another. As a matter of fact, the first alternative offered an easy life in Antwerp, and the third offered a hard life in Brussels (day student means freedom from chaperones and supervisors, but it also means cooking for yourself, etc.). I therefore experienced freedom in that moment because I had to choose among three possibilities or alternatives. I could have decided to stay in Antwerp; I could have decided to be a boarding student; but my freedom gave me what my will really desired."

(*F. 25*) "After I finished my secondary education, I found myself facing the problem of my future course in life. . . What shall I do? After examining various possibilities, I decided to continue my studies in a professional school to become a technical supervisor. I hope to be successful and be able thus to achieve the goal to which I have aspired for the last five years. I certainly was advised and encouraged, but I was free in making my choice. I am very happy; I am not sorry about anything."

Some subjects of the experiment say that they are not worried very much by either the problem of their future or the problem of freedom. But when they were requested to make an analysis of their experiences, these adolescents realized the truly close relationship between these two problems. How will they be able to solve one if they are unable to solve the other? Two girls, one seventeen and the other eighteen years old, perceived the relationship between one's future and one's freedom in very realistic terms. They are free from any kind of coercion, but they feel some kind of limitation on their own freedom. The reason for this is that the circumstances in which they live render their freedom of choice no more than relative.

(*F*. 75) "Before the end of this year I will have chosen what I will do later on. But before I come to that point, I must choose and I am free. Freedom is the power of choosing what I want, what seems to me to be my real vocation. Apparently, I am free; free from the influence of my parents, free from the lack of means, of which I have sufficient. But I feel the limitation of this freedom. It is relative. There is no need of ten alternatives; two incompatible ones are sufficient. On one side I would like to dedicate my entire life to helping boys in a juvenile home who had a difficult adolescence; on the other hand, I would like to have children of my own. So I find myself now in a dilemma: either I dedicate myself entirely to the boys of others, or to children of my own. I would like to do both, but this is impossible. So I must choose one way or the other. But no matter which way I choose, at the present time I feel that I will be unhappy. Perhaps my feelings will change after I have chosen my future life."

(*F*. 71) "To give a satisfactory reply to your topic on freedom, I would like to say something regarding the choice of my future career. This question of one's future career is a simple and very concrete case which should be in the minds of all of us of the same age who are approaching the end of our secondary education. To speak of our future career is a subject where, if we overlook every material consideration, the choice is important and freedom plays a great role. Yes, freedom and choice, together with everything painful, are involved in this problem of our future career. To return to our starting point, the freedom of weighing the pros and cons and the freedom of lengthy consideration is certainly given to us. If by freedom we mean the power of choosing, then we surely have freedom. But I ask myself if man can be considered free when he is influenced by his human temperament and his surrounding environment. When, therefore, can man say that he is free if he is always influenced by some factor or other (such as environment, heredity, reading, etc.)? True, for choosing one's career—selecting one's vocation, if you prefer—we have the possibility of option. But we can still ask: to what extent is this choice the result of my own will? Actually we do not know our own tastes and attitudes; we do not even know the kind of studies we shall pursue in the future. The environment exercises all its influence and the will cannot exercise its independence because the intellect, determined by circumstances, cannot exercise its clarifying function. The intellect does not possess all the necessary resources for a complete knowledge of the matter. Therefore, the will, which is poorly served by its principal helper, the intellect, is, at least partially, a blind force. In the Supreme Being only, the will is adequately served by its illumining power, the intellect."

The personal documents we have just quoted show how difficult a decision it can be when one faces the problem of choosing his studies or his career. But there are cases regarding one's future in which the problem of choice is felt much more strongly than ever: these are the cases where a boy or a girl has to make a decision and choose between two states of life which are profoundly different, e.g., between the religious life and matrimony. Protocols *F.* 51, 52 and 53 describe the feelings of three students, seventeen-year-old girls, who are facing their future life. They reveal to us hidden aspects of the profound and complex motivation of human behavior. The choice which these girls must make is not easy; they have to decide between the vocation of a family of their own and the vocation of a religious call; they must choose one and renounce the other.

(*F.* 51) "I think sometimes of my future. This year's retreat was particularly good. The retreat master aroused great enthusiasm within us. I saw clearly that the religious life is a great good, a more perfect state. I was free to choose; my freedom was complete. My parents would not oppose my future. I was free to choose either the married life—which, if it is well understood, is a great and beautiful life having the function of continuing God's creative work —or the religious life. A conflict arose within me. I would never be able to remain enclosed in a monastery; I would never have the courage; I would never be able to pray all the time! But, all these feelings notwithstanding, this kind of life was attracting me very much. I felt that I was full of love and yearned for an active life. I could yield to these feelings and leave for the missions. But if I did, I would have to give up everything. I would not be able to love a young man and to have my love returned by him, a plain-spoken young man whose ideals would lead to a good life and with whom I could raise a Christian family. I would not be able to have my own children, to have a large family as my pride and joy. The sacrifices of family life did not discourage me. There were seven of us children at home, and my parents had to work hard for us; but we were happy. I could choose! A strange feeling of melancholy caught hold of me. I did not want to think about it any more. But I have chosen: I decided in favor of the greater good. I made a vow to enter the religious life. If I come to understand that I have made a mistake, then I will change. But I hope that I will have the courage to keep my vow and that I will always be able to choose freely the greater good."

(*F.* 52) "Until I was fifteen or sixteen years old, I was not aware of being free. I used my freedom, but without realizing it, and only in cases of little physical, physiological or moral importance. Now I am about to finish my studies in the humanities, and my future life stands before me. I must choose; I am free. I received some advice, but nothing was forced on me. The great responsibility for my own future life and for choosing a vocation rests solely on my shoulders, and this responsibility scares me. I have to choose between two goods. Almost any vocation can be good if we offer ourselves first of all to God, then to those around us, and then to our work. But since the most beautiful of all is the religious life, we must examine first whether or not we have such a vocation. After examining myself from various points of view, I thought I understood that God was calling me. My first impressions were surprise and fear. Then came sadness because I would not be able to be married like my sister. I would not be able to fondle my own children on my lap, children whom I would love so much and would love me so much. But after much thinking and meditating on the subject, my feelings turned to joy and thankfulness to God because of my admiration for this life which will be mine. I, therefore, completely and totally used my own freedom, and when I submitted my decision to those in authority, they approved it. But there was some kind of limitation on this freedom. If I had chosen another kind of life, it would not have been a happy one because my conscience would always be stinging me with regrets. Therefore, in my case, of all the roads available to me at the end of my studies in the humanities, there was only one which constituted the true, correct road. For others, too, there is only one road. This, therefore, is a certain restriction on our freedom."

(*F.* 53) "I was sixteen years old and was already very much concerned with what I would be and what I was going to do later on. I proposed to myself the choice between the married and the religious life. No one imposed his will on me. I was free as I stood facing the two attractive alternatives. Since my freedom gave me the possibility of choosing, the question was: how would I know which of these was the better one? After thinking it over, I reached a decision. Then, for the first time, I felt that freedom is the power to choose which of two goods we believe capable of making us happier. But what obstacles later on to preserve this freedom! My parents oppose my decision. I must wait and obey. Within myself I feel a rebellion rising. I fight to obtain their approval because I wish to regain this freedom at any cost, this freedom which is the most precious gift that God has given to all. When we are seventeen, we must still like children obey the advice of adults who believe, without doubt, that they perform their duty by being strong and inconsiderate. But I feel very deeply that they are wrong; their stubbornness sometimes makes me suffer very intensely."

A strong personality knows how to break the barrier of human frailty and overcome the conflict that everyone feels between the flesh and the spirit, between the human and the divine. To know how to triumph over this conflict means to know how to assert one's personality through self-determination. Two candidates for the priesthood experienced this power of self-determination very deeply in the act of decision with which they chose their own future.

(*I.* 42) "When I chose my vocation I felt completely and truly free. I chose the vocation to the priesthood. I could have refused or accepted this vocation without any actual sin. No force of any kind was determining me to follow it, while, on the other hand, carnal links were keeping me tied up with the world. I assented to this vocation and accepted. In my acceptance I felt really free because I cut as with a sword every link that was yet tying me to the world."

(*I.* 44) "The acceptance of my vocation became more conscious when, at the end of novitiate, I found myself in the situation of having to make a more concrete and conscious choice of my future life. I pondered it at length during that year, examining myself to see if there were other causes determining my will. No! I felt that I alone was supposed to decide. It was a question not only of choosing my future way of life, but of a kind of life which certainly would not be easy. I had to renounce my own will with an act of complete freedom; from now on I will have to obey, to be poor, to be chaste. Certainly it would have been foolish to choose all that under the impulse of a vague and useless feeling. . . That evening (before the day of my complete surrender to God) I understood how much I could do and accomplish with my own will. I could have chosen a life which was going to be—under certain aspects— a little easier, richer perhaps in sense-pleasures. But I felt the strength of saying "yes" to God. That "yes," completely concrete and free, decided my entire life."

3. Various Causes of Limitation of Freedom

There can be both *feelings* and *experience* of the limitations on freedom. These limitations on freedom can be of an external or internal character, of a moral or social nature. They can proceed, in other words, from environment and society, and from circum- stances within the individual himself and from his psychic func- tions. While in the subjects from eleven to fourteen years of age the external limitations prevail by far, in the subjects from fourteen to twenty, on the contrary, the references to internal limitations are seen to be more stressed in the protocols. This is an evident sign of that process of interiorization which begins during childhood but which develops during the late stages of adolescence.

a. Feelings of Limitation on Freedom

Feelings of limitation on freedom are shown in the inability to go skiing because of parental disapproval, in the inability to buy a desired article because of lack of money, or in having to finish homework while other boys are playing. A subject writes: "How furious I was because I could not go out. If I had been alone at home, I would have left my homework unfinished, and I would have followed my impulse to freedom; I would have gone out, but my mother repeatedly insisted that I study, and then I would feel the burden of the lack of freedom" (*I.* 37).

The lack of economic resources is a typical cause of the feelings of limitation on freedom. See, for instance, the example of a boy who stops before a fine display of sporting goods in a downtown store. What strikes him most is an attractive soccer ball. What a joy to be able to buy it!

(*I.* 7) "But how great was my disillusionment when my mother told me, with sadness, she could not afford it because we were too poor. I had to hide my face in order not to show that I was crying. How hard it was for me to accept this decision! I wished that I could have rebelled! I wished that I had the power to be free, to act freely, to satisfy my desire! The beautiful yellow soccer ball was there, behind the thin glass window, and seemed to invite me! But I could not do anything. I couldn't because I was poor, because I was not as rich as many other boys, and therefore I was not free to satisfy my desire."

According to the observations of a twelve-year-old subject, freedom often seems on the verge of being experienced, but seldom does the experience become actualized. The unexpected circumstances which limit freedom are many: an illness, a prohibition, etc. Sometimes trips and picnics that seemed as though they were going to be wonderful end up in tears, curses, swearing, lamentations and complaints. An example of these complaints is the following. During the war, the Germans prohibited the civilians in Italy from traveling from one town to another because of the fear that the civilians would bring help to the partisans. Notwithstanding the prohibition, two boys decided to take a walk and to climb a mountain which was not far from their home. The mountain was in normal times a popular place for picnics. The picnic area was particularly attractive because of the many beautiful pine trees. But here is what happened to the two boys:

(*I.* 20) "We were already on our way towards the winding path which leads to the top of the mountain when we were stopped by a German colonel, who in a very unkind manner told us to go back, without giving us an explanation. Shocked and angry we went back to our house, displeased that we had to give up our picnic, but much more—at least so we thought—over the injustice of men. Why do foreigners have the right to forbid us to move freely in our own country?"

A boy tells us a story from which we can deduce that a limitation of a moral nature was forced upon his freedom. He bought a watch from one of his friends at a low price. But afterwards he found out that the watch had been stolen. Even though he wished very much to keep it, his conscience was bothering him. He decided, therefore, to return the watch and to get his money back.

(*E.* 11) "Even though I felt very unhappy about it, I could not buy the watch. I learned that it had been stolen, and my conscience will not let me buy stolen goods. This was the greatest limitation of freedom that I ever experienced until now."

Another boy tells us with delicate and deep feeling how he was prohibited for social and moral reasons from continuing a friendship with one of his companions. Among his classmates there was one whom he very much respected. He liked him because his friend was sincere, kind and good, and because he shared his own ideas. They went to school together, talked together, played together. They were real friends. But one day this friendship was stopped. His mother called him and told him he could no longer associate with the boy, because a member of his family happened to be involved with the police. "I do not want to see you anymore with him," the mother told him very plainly and frankly. These words pierced the heart of our subject. The thought of being separated from his friend almost froze the blood in his veins; the world became very gloomy for him. He became sick and depressed; going to school was now a torture, while before it was a joy. An emotional state of general dissatisfaction took hold of him so that he could not even eat. It was a torture for him to tell a lie when his classmates asked him what had happened between him and his friend. During vacation time he felt very lonely when he walked by himself in the fields, while before he used to run and play freely with his friend. But now that his friend was gone, the world, once full of light, became a black and miserable place to live in, for he had lost his real and only friend. The subject concludes with this reflection:

(*E.* 5) "From the very beginning of the world, that is, when Adam was put on this earth, he had a friend: Eve. The Creator Himself thought that it was fitting to give man a friend. Our human nature requires friendship, and without it life has no real meaning. This thwarted need is exactly what I experienced."

b. Experience of Limitation on Freedom

Among the adolescents there are some who complain about those unscrupulous professors who enforce the moral and civil education which the students received at home. Some young men complain about school, its curriculum and programs, its schedules. If the programs are too broad and the number of units too many, the poor students are forced to stay up late each night; consequently, they become nervous and lose that peace of mind which is so necessary in order to obtain good results in studies. Many students feel that their freedom is greatly curtailed because they cannot read the books that are on the Index. We could say that the list of things which limit their freedom is endless.

(*F.* 32) "I believe that there was no moment in my life in which I could have said: I am free. But the moments in which I felt a limitation of my freedom are numberless."

(*F.* 47) "A feeling of complete freedom is never felt, because one thing or the other impedes us from reaching our aspirations."

(*F.* 24) "To my mind, freedom is not the most simple thing to obtain, because we always depend somehow upon our parents, who have a duty to know what we are doing."

(*F.* 31) "According to my opinion, one thing is certain: that we never can be completely free. Just when we think that we are free, we are still determined. For example, we believe that we have a day off, completely for ourselves, a free day in which we will be able to do what we like; but then later we realize that we are still forced by circumstances. . . To think freely is the only freedom man enjoys. Nothing, nobody will ever be able to impede a man from reflecting and thinking. This is, in my opinion, the only true freedom that man has; but, by itself, the freedom to think has little value."

(*F.* 26) "My freedom is always reduced to a limitation of freedom. I never had the occasion of feeling my freedom in society. This limitation of my freedom arises from its dependence always or often upon somebody else, as must be the case with so many others. We cannot do what we want, and God knows that we have great ideas! But our parents are there, to restrain and to force us. They must have their reasons. They like—for good reasons, of course—to be heard."

The limitation of freedom which has its origins in the fear of the opinion of others is felt very strongly. This type of social slavery, whose victims are mostly the parents and not the children, impedes, for instance, a young girl from continuing her membership in a club and from participating in any kind of evening meetings. A twenty-year-old boy feels the greatest limitation of his freedom when the choice of his own future was opposed bitterly by his parents and relatives. This was " a very serious limitation of my freedom, because I was fifteen and I was certain of my choice, which later I succeeded in carrying out after many complaints and quarrels" (*I.* 48). An eighteen-year-old boy considers his life in a boarding school almost a continuous restriction of his freedom: "For the last nine years I have been living in this boarding school which is separated from the world. The limitations to my freedom are plenty" (*I.* 61).

But of all limitations of freedom, perhaps the most typical is that which is expressed in the following protocol:

(*I.* 46) "A violation of my freedom happened when I was still a boy and was unable to choose and to will. At that time I was taught to perform something bad, in other words I was taught to do an immoral act. This was for me a true coercion, a real limitation of my freedom. On the part of the individual who taught me that bad thing, it was an irrational act. This bad act which he had taught me proves that my freedom had been violated. Could he really do this at the expense of my freedom?"

In the opinion of a seventeen-year-old girl, "at every hour of the day we feel the limitation of our freedom; our acts are determined by circumstances" (*F.* 64). A nineteen-year-old girl does not feel free in showing her simple and pure affection for a young boy. When she returned to her native town, she felt attracted towards a young Catholic boy who was from a very good family. "From that moment, my mother left me less free to go to see my uncle's family, and I feel sad in not being able to go freely to the town where I was born."

(*F.* 46). Another nineteen-year-old girl thinks that the occasions in which we can show our freedom are very rare. The limitations of freedom are many, especially in the life of a girl who is still studying: her parents keep her home as much as they can, and, if she wants to remain good and serious, she will have to accept such restrictions. The reflections of this young girl are as follows:

(*F*. 42) "All this is swell, in my opinion, but there are certain times in which we feel the need of rest, in which some form of relaxation is needed, in which some form of social activities are needed. I formed a small club with my girl friends, and we also met with some young men who are my girl friends' brothers. And here restriction enters into the picture. My brothers also belong to this club. Notwithstanding our meeting in turn at the house of each member of the club, of course we are supervised. We are forced to engage in some form of 'correct fun.' Do not believe that I, or even my friends, would like to have more than this innocent fun. We understand each other very well, we joke, we laugh together. That's all. Of course, we are not seen on the street together. . . Ah. . . we have to save our reputation. . . People talk easily . . . and all this fun which we have could become known. . . Would we, then, have a chance of getting married? Nothing extraordinary happens among ourselves. But there is a limitation on the part of our parents, because of the famous saying: 'And what would people say?' We ourselves have arrived at the same conclusion."

The invitation to describe a concrete fact of experience of freedom or its limitation was the occasion for an eighteen-year-old girl to reflect seriously on this problem and to express its dramatic aspects. In a passage of profound introspection she brings to light especially the intellectual and physical obstacles which oppose the actualization of a free activity.

(*F*. 30) "I will receive my diploma in the humanities at the end of this school year. A new phase of my studies, therefore, is going to begin. I want to pursue the sort of graduate studies which will permit me to lead an independent life or to be able, later on, to meet the usual financial difficulties of life. Now my parents leave me absolutely free to undertake any kind of studies. I must therefore decide alone on my future. One professor told us that we should decide by Christmas vacation. During Christmas vacation, therefore, I remained in my room, the only place where I feel completely free, and reflected. At the beginning, I felt a very great joy to be free, to be able to decide all alone; I was very happy over not hearing anyone else tell me: 'Do this, do that.' But little by little,

I understood the force was almost overwhelming me. It is the first time that I felt that to be free is perhaps marvellous, but also terrible. At this first stage, I was certain that freedom existed and that, in certain hours of my life, I also possessed it. But the more I reflected on one career, that I liked very much, or on another career which seemed very interesting, the more I understood that freedom did not exist in the way I was taking it. I would have liked to become a teacher of physical education, but I realized that it was more difficult than I believed, and that maybe I was not going to succeed. I would have to combine theory with practice. If each could be taken separately, I might be successful. But to take both together was a problem; I did not feel intellectually fit. I would have liked to enter into aviation, receive a license as a pilot and then become a hostess, but I realized that one's sense of sight has to be good, a requirement I do not meet. So here I found a physical obstacle, etc. Only a few minutes were needed to make me realize that I was not free after all. I felt a terrible disillusionment, because I firmly thought that to be free means to do anything we like, without any restriction. In practice this is not true. Freedom always has some limits. To be free perhaps means to choose, but we must choose within a certain framework, from which we cannot depart. The human being is a limited being, whether we like it or not. A man who is riding a horse through obstacles is not completely free. He depends on his horse and on the obstacles that he meets."

The passage which we just quoted offers a vivid and real picture of the "conditionism" of human freedom. Doubtless our freedom is always limited somewhat; but maybe the dark colors of the picture are magnified; in fact, the description which was given by this girl seems to exclude, or at least minimize excessively, the capability that man has to overcome the obstacles that he might meet on his free path.

Let us see now the response of a seventeen-year-old girl who speaks of limitations in the moral order. With reflections that show a notable psychic maturity, she puts into clear light the distinction between physical and moral liberty.

(*F.* 62) "I had the occasion of using my freedom last year during my vacation. I was in London, England, in the house of some friends of mine where there were no boys. My parents remained in

Belgium. My actions and my behavior were not controlled. I could go out and come back at any time I wanted (at least, so I thought), except that I had to be home at 11 p.m. (by the way, the last movie ended always at about this time). During my outings, while visiting London, I met various boys who wanted to take me to a movie or to a cafe. I felt then that I did not have the moral freedom to follow them. I felt that at my age of seventeen, and as a student, I could not accept their invitation. The most difficult thing was that I had the physical freedom; nothing and nobody impeded me from going out. It was only I who was to judge my actions. I had, however, the courage to go out in the evening and was very happy because of this. As soon as I refused the invitation of the boys, I felt I had escaped a dangerous situation. Once, however, I accepted the invitation to walk with a boy in a city park. It was in the afternoon, and it was because of this that I accepted. Later on I felt (notwithstanding the afternoon hour) that I did not act prudently in this way and I still feel it. I chose the inferior alternative opposing my moral feeling. This was a good lesson, and I believe that I have learned from it what moral and physical freedom are."

There are limitations of freedom which we must suffer even against our own will, and there are limitations which we must know how to impose on ourselves. The limitations which are imposed on us by others are those which coerce our freedom from without and forbid us more or less from acting freely. The voluntary limitations, on the other hand, are those which regulate the more or less prudent use of our own freedom. In order to live in society within the bounds of rational behavior we must know how to use our freedom. This is what can be deduced from the experience of a sixteen-year-old girl who reveals a finesse of analysis which is not too common. The incident which the girl describes would seem insignificant to a superficial observer, but actually it illustrates a particular point which helps one to understand the value of the voluntary limitations of freedom.

(*F.* 4) "Last summer, I was a supervisor in a playground for little girls. I went to pick up the girls every morning; I brought them back to their mothers every evening. I loved these little girls very much, that is, I felt a deep sympathy which changed into a real affectionate love for some of them. It is here that my story begins. I prepared and learned all kinds of plays, stories, songs; I had magnificent projects in my mind for these girls. I was full of enthusiasm, ideas and love for them. I did not foresee the obstacles that were going to be in my way during that week in which I was going to be their supervisor. I believed myself free to do anything at my own pleasure. One morning I arrived at the playground and immediately I called the girls around me. I would have liked to begin to teach them all that I had learned and prepared. But that did not happen. They wanted to play in the same way they were accustomed to each day. I felt that my preparation was useless. I could still have been free to show them everything I had planned; nobody was there to forbid me to do that. But these little girls with their expressive faces and eyes, and with their innocent behavior and their talk, impeded me from going ahead with my plans . . . . Here is another incident, which might seem insignificant and small, but which seems to me to have a particular interest. We were in the open-air theatre near the train depot. I was near a girl whom I loved with a particular affection; I tried, however, never to show this affection. This little girl must have guessed that I loved her. All of a sudden she asked, 'Tell me, Mademoiselle, which one of us do you love most?' I was dying to tell her, 'Certainly you, my dear.' But I answered, 'Little one, why do you ask me such a question? You know that I love everyone equally!' But she insisted over and over again on the same question. I always answered, 'I love you all equally.' I could have answered what I wanted, but I felt something within me which impeded me from it. There was an obstacle within me and I could not overcome it. I might think that I was free, but this little girl was impeding me from calling myself free. I could not tell her what I was thinking because, otherwise, this girl would have gone to the other girls and told them my answer. I had to avoid jealousy at any cost. But the conclusion is this: that all of a sudden my desire to answer truthfully was impeded. I understood then, on that occasion, that my duty consisted in what I did answer. However, it is also equally true that this little story illustrates an obstacle to the use of my freedom on that occasion. The incident is a minor one; but it seemed very important to me for all its insignificance."

4. Coercion and Exercise of Freedom

Some protocols are particularly interesting because the subjects write on the negative effects of the coercion of freedom. These negative effects are the result of both the family and social environment. They show how adolescents, when a reasonable use of their freedom is not granted them, are influenced by this denial, and how it might really cause serious consequences in the formation of their personalities. On the other hand, there are some protocols which permit an evaluation of the kind of influence that prudent exercise of freedom has upon the integral development of the individual's personality.

a. Reactions Against Excessive Rigorism

The reaction of the young people is more vivid when a negative attitude and denials are continuous on the part of their parents; the same thing happens in the relationship between teachers and pupils. The less justified the denials of the teachers seem to be, the stronger is the feeling of rebellion by the pupils. Some subjects, to whom permission for a picnic, a trip, or any kind of amusement with their friends is constantly denied, sadly make the following comments:

(*I.* 22) "I do not know how mad I was when I was confronted with these continuous denials. I thought I also had the right to the freedom that so many other boys were enjoying."

(*I.* 26) "Sometimes, within myself, I felt a rebellion against everything which was coercing my thoughts and my will, such as the imposition of school schedules and programs. I would have preferred to study Latin, and instead I had to apply myself to geography; I would have liked to read Torquato Tasso, and I had to occupy myself with Romulus and Remus. I felt I was a passive element in the hands of others."

(*I.* 35) "I was exasperated, I almost wanted to rebel. Looking out the window, I thought, 'When I grow up, I will do everything in my own way and I will be free to go where I want to, as the others do.' Meanwhile I saw a swallow flying happily and the other boys playing. . . I envied them, as a hungry person envies one who is eating."

It is very difficult for an excessive rigorism to control its subjects convincingly. The youngsters react negatively, and take only that freedom which is denied to them. They do this even though they know from experience that they will be punished for the freedom they exercise.

(*I.* 23) "I loved amusement parks. You cannot imagine my joy. I asked my parents permission to go to them, but my father refused me because I was convalescing from pneumonia. I felt unhappy. However, I thought out all the possible and imaginable ways to go to the town of San Michele. The right moment finally came: Dad was called out by urgent business and Mother went to my grandparents'. I was left in the care of the old maid, Clementina. While she was busy cleaning the house, I jumped over the backyard fence and with a friend of mine I went to the amusement park. How happy we were. . . When the sun was close to setting my friend and I started for home, all tired and dirty. . . When I got home, my Dad met me with a slap on the face, and without a word, he pointed to the stairs. I understood that I had to go to bed immediately. I still once in a while cut out like that, but when I come back home one punishment after another awaits me, each rougher than the last."

Some subjects, after having described some concrete facts of limitation of their freedom, write reflections which are very interesting from the pedagogical viewpoint. An excessive control and coercion have the effect of exasperating them and inducing them to search illicitly for the freedom of which they believe they were unjustly deprived. But this is not the only damaging consequence. Deprived for too long of a moderate exercise of freedom, these youngsters will find themselves suddenly in an occasion where they will have to make full use of their freedom, and then they are unprepared. The reflections which are expressed in the following two passages might seem to be over the heads of the two thirteen-year-old boys, but they reflect a real situation which must be kept in mind by educators.

(*E.* 8) "Some individuals are not very much preoccupied by the limitation of their freedom. They are very willing to let their parents, as their guardians, always keep them away from every danger in life. But what will happen when their mother no longer observes them, when they will be without guidance and must face the turbulent waters of an unscrupulous world? Are their characters strong enough to face the great temptations that they will certainly encounter? I say no! A man won't learn to swim, no matter how hard he studies from a book the required way of moving his body in the water. He must go into the water and undergo that experience."

(*I.* 9) "One afternoon (during my third year of college) a prefect kindly offered to take us out for a walk. That made us quite happy, because he was very good and would let us use our freedom more than usual. Since we were accustomed to a very rigid discipline, we soon took advantage of the prefect's kindness. Anyone under obedience enforced with a stick who has the chance to do what he wants all of a sudden, immediately abuses his freedom, against all the advice of good and kind prefects or superiors. No rule, then, can contain him, not even the voice of conscience or the fear of God. Since he generally obeys because of a fear of punishment, once he is free he fears punishment no longer and does what he darned well pleases. Why should adolescents be trained with a stick instead of with conviction and reasonableness?"

A seventeen-year-old girl expresses her complaints toward parents who did give her many freedoms, but withheld the more important freedom of choosing her studies. Consequently she feels obliged morally to do what she does not like. "I must say that at least most of the responsibility must be laid to my parents for not allowing me to choose my own profession. If I have any children I would not like to repeat the same mistake" (*F.* 37).

Particularly interesting in this respect is the story of a nineteen-year-old boy. He describes how he came to lead a life dangerous to his soul when about fifteen years of age, while in the preceding years he had always been faithful to his duties as a Christian and had felt the inclination to become a priest. It was really the opposition of his parents to his vocation that induced him to lead a morally reprehensible life. Here is the reaction of the young man to the coercion of his own will.

(*I.* 50) "From that time on, I began to grow cold toward my vocation. After that, I erred along the path of my life and fell from one precipice to another . . . in the mud. I was so bad that I became a scandal to my friends. I did not go to Mass on Sunday; my daily Communions became annual ones (and they were bad Communions!). My favorite pastime was card playing. I occupied myself in looking for English soldiers and taking them to the whores, in inciting my friends to do evil, and in spending at the movies the money my mother (sick in bed with shock) had given me to buy her prescriptions. I have written all this very briefly. But my intention is to answer your question and to point out the consequences of the mistake of being forced and coerced in my freedom. In this I do not curse my parents—I love them—but I wish that my experience, objectively considered, could help others. Now, why do so many young boys have to follow a path, perhaps worse than mine, because of the wishes of some other people, be they parents, guardians or leaders of a party? Why should young people not be left free to follow the vocation towards which they are inclined? Why should adolescents be obliged to live in the anguish of uncertainty and then in the torment of remorse because of the mistakes committed perhaps against their will?"

With regard to social and common-life environment, various subjects consider the boarding school—and perhaps even college life and the convent—as a rather abnormal place from the viewpoint of freedom. The life in common necessarily imposes many restrictions and often true coercions to the free activity of the individual. One subject writes: "We do not have, or there is not offered to us, the possibility of exercising our freedom" (*F*. 26). This is not without a negative effect upon the psychic development of youngsters of both sexes. Here is how two girls, one nineteen and the other seventeen, describe their experience of life in a boarding school:

(*F*. 42) "I experienced numerous feelings of freedom after the victories over myself, but these feelings are not too pleasant. The feeling that I have of freedom has certainly atrophied. I have been in a boarding school for six years. It is probably useless to tell you that freedom is experienced by the boarders only outside the boarding school. Inside the boarding school we feel oppressed: rules, silence everywhere, regimentation, etc. And when we are out we believe we have freedom without limits, and we abuse it. . . The memories that I have of having been free concern physical rather than moral aspects."

(*F.* 59) "Oh, certainly, I can think of an event of my life in which I experienced a limitation of my freedom: the fact that I am locked up in a boarding school, among religious persons, from whom we must hide what we think, because, naturally, what we think is not always too good and beautiful. If I could choose, certainly I would not go to Mass every day. Faced by this obligation, I went to Mass out of habit, which changed into indifference and perhaps even into disgust. Doubtless, this is not very Christian. I should profit by this opportunity and try to find a personal delight in attending Mass, but I am forced to think of the mechanical aspect of the duty: to get up in the morning, to be controlled by nuns, to be counted when we go to Mass and Communion, etc., etc. Actually, we are forced to go to Mass and Communion. I detest life in a boarding school. After having been treated in this way, when we enter into the world with all its attractions, only defeat awaits us. If freedom is offered to me all at one time, I will use and abuse it in every way. Here is what the limitation of freedom produces."

This conclusion could not be more exact and more realistic. The passage just quoted reveals, however, some exaggeration, perhaps because it was written during one of her darkest moments. It must be pointed out that the conditions in the boarding school which have been described here, might find, perhaps, some confirmation in other particular boarding schools, too, but such practices are never recommended by the Church.

b. Educational Value of Voluntary Choice

Various protocols give us the opportunity to point out what influence the prudent use and exercise of freedom have upon the integral development of the personality of the individual. Freedom, expressed first by the repetition of voluntary choices in ordinary circumstances and then in important decisions, assumes in this way a primary position in the training process. This is the case, for instance, of an eighteen-year-old girl who had the opportunity to choose the school she wished and the studies she preferred to pursue. For this reason she felt more conscientious and more responsible with regard to her duties. She writes: "This freedom influenced my character a great deal and helped me a lot, because I was free to work and to create a position for myself without being forced by others" (*F.* 35).

The formative value of the daily decisions in which the individual makes *conscious decisions and voluntary choices* is expressed with a notable depth of intuition by two eighteen-year-old college girls.

(*F.* 74) "We are no longer so rigidly controlled by the professor as we were in high school. I can conduct myself as I see fit. For example, I may talk when normally there must be silence, etc. Thus, I am entirely responsible for my own actions. I do not have to obey the rules which are imposed by the professor. He will not be aware of it. Nevertheless, I wish to conform and to observe some kind of discipline. In this way I feel that I am doing what is right. I have consented to these actions, and yet I am free of any strict obligation. I am the only one responsible for my actions, bad or good. But I understand that the best method of conquering myself and my passions, of forming my personality, and accomplishing what the others expect from me at every moment of the day is to lead a good life."

(*F.* 66) "There is nothing extraordinary in my life, and there are no hard decisions to make every day which will change my life. No, nothing of this kind. But freedom asserts itself in a rather peculiar way: getting up! A little thing each day. Perhaps it might seem scrupulous to attribute such a great importance to such a little thing, and to let it have such an influence. . . . However . . . in the morning, my bed is the most sacred and sweetest of all the things in the world to me. I would like to live for hours with this enjoyable feeling of not being completely awake . . . of being there . . . half-asleep . . . half-awake . . . of hearing in this pleasant state of mind the birds singing . . . and to stay there, in my comfortable bed. People pretend that we can and must get used to everything. I am already seventeen, almost eighteen, but I am not yet used to getting out of bed in the morning. Every day, as I am waking up, when I am still half-asleep and half-awake, I hear the bells of the nearby church, and I tell myself that this is the time to get up. Each day is also the beginning of a small conflict within myself. I feel here that my freedom should play its part, and that it depends on me to reinforce it or to limit it, according to what I want to do, that is, whether I want to get up or want to remain undecided. This is so true that when I get up half an hour later than usual, I feel that I am a slave to my body throughout the entire day, that I cannot make a decision. I feel that I am not free, that I have rejected my freedom, and that I have 'said yes to the devil,' as the children say. To have begun my day by rejecting my freedom is sufficient to create in me a strong conflict, and this will last until the next morning. I feel that if I act like this when faced by small things, the rest of my actions will be forced or menaced by something. Nevertheless, I want to lead a respectable life based upon my own freedom."

The passage just quoted permits us to make the following observation: Just as an unconscious habit — be it good or bad — is the effect of automatic responses of the organism, so also a conscious and voluntary habit is the effect of the acts in which the personality of the individual plays its role, that is, the effect of acts of self-determination. The acquisition of constructive habits is only an apparent one if it is not grounded in the wise exercise of freedom. Thus, the *many good habits* which the youngsters acquire in boarding schools, where a regimented system of discipline is in force, are only superficial. Let us consider a typical example in the following passage from a seventeen-year-old girl:

(*F.* 69) "At the boarding school we are forced to attend Mass every day. This becomes a habit. Actually, we do not attend Mass. The most important moments pass sometimes without being noticed. We think of other things, we daydream. But I felt perfectly free when, during my vacation, I got up earlier than usual without being forced. It is hard to get up early in the morning during vacation time, especially in the winter. It is so warm in bed. . . Nevertheless, I went to Mass. I could, if I wanted, have stayed in bed. . . But among the alternatives which I could have chosen, I renounced what momentarily seemed to me a better thing. I chose the hardest thing. . . Because of this I followed the Mass with less distraction than usual."

The following incident, which is described by a seventeen-year-old girl, tells us something of the negative effects that the use of freedom might have upon the behavior of an individual when prudent control and wise direction are lacking.

(*F*. 11) "Last year, during the whole month of June, I remained alone with my brothers who did not pay any attention to me. I was free. Since I do not like to be alone, I often invited a girl friend to my house. Miriam also liked freedom. Thus, one day when she was at my house, both of us went riding on our bicycles. Nobody knew we had left, and nobody knew when we were coming back. These were exciting moments. Free, we raced on our bicycles, and went farther and farther away from our house. Riding along narrow roads in the open country, we met some of our friends. They rode their bicycles with us for a while, and then we stopped, all four of us, to take a breath and to talk more readily. We were at the highest point of a bridge, where it seemed nobody would pass. It was 9:00 P.M., but it was still clear and beautiful—it was June. Neither Miriam nor I thought of putting an end to this moment, in which for the first time, in company with two boys, we did not have to think, 'Will they see us? Will our parents know it?' We were enjoying our moment of freedom. This was our first meeting with the opposite sex, a friendly, pleasant meeting, without any fear of 'What will they say?' Since the sun was already set, and it was getting dark, we had to leave our boy friends. We did so against our wishes. Miriam and I continued to discuss at length, while returning home, the problem of love. This is a tópic which we would not dare to discuss in the presence of our parents, even though it is such a natural problem of life. . . We arrived home at 10:00 P.M. There was nobody home, and we went to bed, dreaming about our happy freedom."

This example can be classified among the most original protocols. The parents are absent for a month; they leave their children home alone. Everyone tries to take care of himself in the best way he can; as a matter of fact, when the girl returned home at 10:00 P.M. —as she says—nobody was at home. The behavior of the parents could be considered excellent from one aspect, and dangerous from another. Excellent, in the sense that, at seventeen years of age, the parents must allow a notable margin of freedom and must show some trust in their children. Dangerous, because the parents seem to be absolutely unaware of the flirtatious tendencies of their sons and daughters, who have to learn everything about love on their own initiative.

To hold the formative value of voluntary choice does not imply that we must admit an absolute freedom in the field of education and training. But if the two terms "education" and "freedom" are interchangeable, they cannot be identified in theory, and must not be confused in practice. Freedom cannot be absolute. The uncontrolled use of freedom and the sudden and full use of a freedom which has not been previously exercised, expose the individual to situations which he is not always able to control and to dominate. Hence there results a negative influence upon the formation of personality.

FOOTNOTES

1 A. Gemelli, *La Psicologia dell'Etá Evolutiva,* 4th Edition, Revised, (Milano: A. Giuffré, 1955) pp. 32-43; M. Debesse, *Comment Etudier les Adolescents. Examen Critique des Confidences Juveniles* (Paris: Press Univ. France, 1948), pp. 33-51.

2 M. Debesse, *op. cit.,* p. 46.

3 A. Gemelli, *op. cit.,* pp. 326-331.

PART TWO
Theoretical Evaluation

CHAPTER SIX

Foundation of Personal Freedom

In the preceding chapters we have analyzed the data of psychological experience with a view to sufficient clarity and completeness. We can now concern ourselves with a theoretical evaluation of this material. But first it might be best to review synthetically and systematically the various elements which have emerged from our analysis thus far. The result should be a synthetic picture, phenomenological in character, drawn according to the principles of interpretation examined in the introduction to this work.

A theoretical evaluation becomes most manageble if we see the various elements of the preceding analysis under two main headings: the "foundation" of personal freedom and its "meaning." The first of these we shall discuss in the present chapter.

In order to define the positive foundation on which human freedom is based we must first clear the field of every obstacle. It is necessary therefore to evaluate the objections which are advanced against the possibility of the existence of man's freedom. Most difficulties encountered here refer substantially to the following three elements: (1) *the testimony of consciousness,* to prove its validity; (2) *the role of motivation in a free act,* to determine its characteristics and limitations; (3) *the value of scientific hypotheses,* to exclude their presumed decisive contribution for or against freedom.

A critical examination of these debated points will permit us not only to eliminate the obstacles against the existence of freedom, but also to evaluate the inconsistency of some false principles on which freedom has been based. Thus we shall be led to examine the concepts of causality and prediction of human actions in order to understand their specific meaning from the psychological viewpoint.

1. The Testimony of Consciousness

The analysis of experimental data offers clear proof of the "feeling" or "consciousness" that men have of freedom.[1] The subjects insist that their choices are, in most cases, true voluntary acts, during which various motives are discussed until, finally, one is adopted as a line of action. What is of greatest importance in this context is the positive demonstration that introspection provides of the intimate connection between the intervention of the "ego," intuitively apprehended, and the alternative which is actually chosen. The difference between the case in which the feeling of freedom is present and those in which it is absent must be sought in the consciousness of the "ego" that resolves and chooses. In other words, it must be sought in the action of the "ego," which determines its own activity, gives its consent to one of the alternatives, chooses it, makes it its own, and identifies it with itself. This is the conscious experience of "free resolution," of "free choice" or self-determination, by which man converts a value into an efficacious motive.[2]

a. Consciousness of Freedom as a Fact of Experience

The different interpretations that psychologists give to experience justify a question which would otherwise seem superfluous: whether the feeling or consciousness of being able to act freely in the process of voluntary choice is the experience of a really free person or is merely an illusion. To face the matter squarely, we must admit that if any experience is real, this one surely is. The conviction that his will is free is a datum of every man's personal experience.

No one, not even the most rigid determinist, can deny that man is conscious of experiencing his own free activity. Every man who enjoys the normal use of his psychic functions is fully convinced that, at least in the normal conditions of life, he can choose his own goals freely, and use the means that he believes most adequate to reach such goals. Every man is convinced that, when he performed an act in a certain manner, he could have decided to perform it differently if he had wished. But many psychologists maintain that they must deny the existence of a true personal freedom and therefore discard this experiential fact as mere illusion. Let us examine the position, for example, of the following authors.

In a recent study on new psychological trends, Francis Schiller holds that "Our conception of consciousness as a complex grouping and a sequence of unconscious nervous processes implies a certain freedom of choice." Where simple reflex movements and habits are concerned, the distribution of forces is able, through well-defined channels, to reach the eventual final step of action. Of the same character, but much more complex and unforeseeable, are also the configurations of the reasoned and projected activity. The same author says, "When the introspective concept of the ego enters this configuration, we get the feeling of free will." [3]

To Rudolf Ekstein's mind, man can be free from external chains and at the same time not feel internally free. This feeling means that man *is* not free, even though society has given him external freedom. Man can feel he is not free because of *internal conditions*. Psychology can find the causes of this interior slavery and help man use the necessary means to regain his internal freedom or his state of psychic health. Psychological laws do not make us either free or slaves; they only help us to understand why we feel we are free or slaves. "Freedom is a feeling, a state of mind. The feeling of freedom has nothing to do with the possibility of describing the cause of such a feeling of freedom. Freedom is not more than the feeling of freedom. Freedom is a psychological term." [4]

A decision which is in harmony with an individual's character seems to merit the reward of a *pleasant feeling* of freedom. It is difficult to analyze phenomenologically the characteristics of freedom which appear in this context. But we can describe them. *Negatively* speaking, we notice the absence of anguish, of irrational doubts and those inhibitions and restrictions which paralyze choice and action. *Positively,* we notice the feelings of well-being, of self-esteem, self-confidence, and internal satisfaction based on the success of our own efforts. As Robert P. Knight rightly observed: "This freedom has nothing whatever to do with free will as a principle governing human behavior, but it is a subjective experience which is itself causally determined." [5]

It is evident that we have the experience of choice — the feeling and the consciousness of free activity. If we were to try to give a scientific explanation of man by comparing him to a machine, we should presuppose that his actions are predetermined by his constitution and by environment. But in reality we are the ones who *choose,* exactly as we are the ones who *know* with certitude the facts and laws of science. It is said to be perfectly sound to reject as an illusion the first type of experience (freedom of choice) and to accept as certain the second (the knowledge of scientific facts and laws). If the scientist accepts the objectivity of human knowledge of the external world as certain, there can be no reason why he should reject the validity of knowledge of his interior world. It is the same man, with the same personal faculties, who sees through his eyes and knows through his consciousness. It is nothing more than prejudice to think that the knowledge of the external world and its laws is more perfect and real than self-knowledge.

b. *Value and Limits of Consciousness of Freedom*

We cannot deny that the testimony of consciousness can be erroneous in many cases. But it cannot be universally wrong, as those contend who consider consciousness of freedom a mere illusion. Such a fallacy would be inconsistent with the principles of the most elementary logic. Agostino Gemelli has written:

> "We cannot forget that the testimony of consciousness which attributes the act to us as our own, is a testimony so strong that no valid objection can be raised against it. If we do not admit the validity of such internal testimony, no other testimony can be held as valid." [6]

This concept is an echo of the assertion of Charles Fox: "Any outside observer who thinks this freedom an illusion must be prepared to explain why the illusion arises only in the latter case." [7] We must therefore hold that "science cannot explain or deny human freedom of the will." [8] Neither can psychologists explain or deny that man is conscious of his own freedom. Simply to affirm freedom as an illusion is not enough. To make this assertion acceptable, one must explain why and how such an illusion came to exist. Rudolf Allers maintains that "proclaiming free decision to be an illusion is quite unsatisfactory: definite proof is needed. There is no such proof, nor has any of these philosophers ever been able to point to such a proof." [9]

In his attempt to defend the determinism of human actions, N. Braunshausen discusses what type of freedom is guaranteed to man by the testimony of his consciousness. Consciousness guarantees, first of all, *physical freedom*. The martyrs of every great humanitarian ideal stand as irrefutable proof that man is capable of suffering the most cruel torments, and even death, to follow the interior voice of duty. This renunciation of the instinct of self-preservation implies also *ethical freedom,* i.e., the power of overcoming the strongest physiological tendencies in favor of a superior ideal. Moreover, man is endowed with *psychological freedom,* i.e. freedom of action, stemming from the personality as a whole. What is not included in the testimony of consciousness is *metaphysical freedom,* which would mean that the human will, under pressure of the demands of duty on one side and physiological instincts on the other, is not influenced by either side, thus remaining the supreme arbiter of its own actions.[10]

It is evident that consciousness cannot guarantee metaphysical freedom as it is conceived by Braunshausen. It is my belief that there is no one—excluding perhaps some defenders of the so-called "freedom of indifference"—who pretends to attribute to man this type of freedom. The freedom of which consciousness is the guarantor is certainly sufficient to satisfy the essential prerequisites of human responsibility.

2. The Role of Motivation in Free Action

The motivational factor is fundamental in human activity. In discussing various authors and psychological schools, we encountered this factor many times, and often with different meanings. Leaving out other differences of less importance, this factor appears under two profoundly different aspects: *conscious motivation* and *unconscious motivation*. The first type we analyzed mainly in the light of "experimental experience"; the second, in the light of "clinical experience." From the analysis of objective data, three main questions emerge which deserve special attention. These concern the meaning, the efficacy, and the origin of motives.

a. The Meaning of Motivation

The human tendency toward consistency in action represents a conscious effort of the mind to identify itself with an object which is known as appetible. For such an attraction to occur, it must be presupposed that this object has a particular value for us. Even though an act of *perception* does not presuppose any kind of conscious preparation, but can be, at least theoretically speaking, a primary conscious process, we cannot conceive a *volitional* act that does not begin in consciousness. Of the conscious contents that precede the volitive act, some appear to be only accidental, while some are inevitably connected with the act. These last constitute the "motives" of volition.[11] Everything that is presented to the mind as a value to be realized by the voluntary act can be considered as a motive for action.

By defining motives as "rational considerations" from which the acts of the will have their origin, we evidently consider them from the conscious viewpoint. This does not imply, however, that motives are always conscious. It is an evident fact—with regard to activity in general and not free activity proper—that motives do not always have a "rational" character. Consequently, a broader application of the meaning of this term is imperative, a meaning-application which takes into consideration also the *unconscious* aspect of motivation. Thus the term "motive" is used more properly to indicate "the sum total of all processes which prepare the act." [12] We could say, therefore, that the goodness of an object, or the evil connected with it, "moves" us to an act of the will. In other words, the good or the evil of an object is the "motive" of that act of the will.

The motive of an internal act of the will may be masked in various ways, so that an empirical description of that act does not seem to contain its motive. An essential characteristic of all human motivation is its complexity. Through the course of psychic development, a great number of elements and components of every kind—cognitive factors, tendencies and divergent affects, concrete circumstances, etc.—join together and form an organic whole, which constitutes the concrete form of an actual motive. A fundamental need is only one of the elements of concrete reality which lead to action.[13] The personal factor plays an important role because the power or the force of a motive depends not only on the quality of the alternative, but also on the tendencies of the subject.

Motives must not be considered separately from the natural place they occupy in the motivation of human behavior. They are not separate entities; they are not independent forces in conflict among themselves while the "ego" remains a mere spectator. On the contrary, motives of action become true reasons of action to the extent that they are assumed by the "ego" itself. They presuppose, therefore, the concept of the "ego" as a determining factor. If we presuppose that an individual enjoys a sufficient integration of his personality, we admit he is free from being forced to follow the "suggestions" of his motives.

Let us consider, for example, the case of a boy who is tormented by his desire for a forbidden piece of candy on the one hand and by his fear of punishment on the other. The candy is near, the punishment far away and uncertain. He takes the candy. In this case it is obvious that the boy gives into the stronger of the two motives. We must keep in mind, however, that it is the active subject who gives in, not one motive succumbing to another. This latter is an unintelligible proposition, which Horace G. Watts characterizes very aptly as the "fallacy of hypostatization."[14]

In a similar situation, another boy may experience the same motives in conflict but not take the candy, because to his mind it would involve doing something in opposition to a moral principle. He does not, then, remain suspended between two motives, giving into the stronger one; but it is he himself who performs this act. As a human being he is dominant over both motives, without being attracted (at least, not decisively attracted) by one or the other, in the sense of an instinctive impulse. Adhering to a more elevated motive, to a principle, he inhibits his inferior motives or impulses. Under this aspect we can call him free. He is not—properly speaking—determined, but he himself determines himself.

The reasons one recognizes for a decision cannot, therefore, constitute the true cause of the decision itself. Behind them there is always the whole personality that acts. What this assertion implies cannot always be analyzed completely and expressed under the form of reasons or of well-defined motives.

b. The Efficacy of Motives in the Volitional Act

While the process of deliberation is going on, ideas and desires in conflict are considered as possible motives of action. When decision is reached, they become actual motives of the voluntary act; with the full emergence of decision, the conflict of motives ceases.

The ending of the conflict does not mean—properly speaking—that an impulse or group of impulses became stronger than their adversaries. When we give consent to one of the two or more motives in conflict, we experience the active interposition of the "ego," through which the issue of the conflict is decided. Hence we do not need a new motive, but only the personal capacity of deciding in favor of one of the existing motives. In this way, the intervention of the "ego" becomes an additional factor over and above the prevailing motive; but the motive for this interposition of the "ego" is identical with that of the desire to which we consent.

This assertion leads to the problem of whether it is really an evident fact that *"a choice proceeds always in the direction of the greatest pleasure"* [15]; or, in more general terms, whether it is true that *"man always obeys the motive or the impulse which, at the moment of decision, is the strongest one."* [16] The problem which was just formulated, if understood exactly, can be answered in the affirmative; but it must be defined with precision.

It is certainly true, as Braunshausen maintains, that the best method of studying such a problem is to consider those states of consciousness where the feeling of freedom is strongest.[17] But I think that Braunshausen makes a serious mistake when he confuses a simple feeling of freedom with the true consciousness of acting freely. And he is patently illogical when he concludes, from the fact that man always acts for a motive, that such acts are always prompted by the strongest motive, as if he were pulled almost irresistibly by its force.

Because man is a rational being we must presuppose that he acts rationally. It is in complete accord with his human nature that a man decide according to the motive that best fits his category of values. To the extent that man is capable of exercising his superior functions, he is also capable of opposing one group of motives to another in order to reach a decision which is in conformity with the goal that he imposes on himself. Even when we are occupied with important tasks, an insignificant detail can attract our attention. The will does not behave in the presence of values like a scale under the action of a series of weights. A minor value can provoke the same decision that a major value does: the *fiat* of decision happens in every case in exactly the same way. *A value must be present: this is the indispensable condition of the volitional act.* Subjectively, major and minor values provoke a conflict. But this does not imply that we are determined always to choose the greatest value.

The problem of motivation is, first of all, an effort to avoid *causalism* (the motives are the *causes* of the act) and *irrationalism* (the motives are actually *invented* to justify a decision already made) at the same time. These two positions are actually harmful to freedom. It is true that motives justify decision, and it is also true that they become motives only because of the decision taken. But if motives justify decision, they do not *cause* it. And it is false to say, as Paul Ricoeur did recently, that "causality is the objective equivalent of an absolutely non-free motivation." [18] At the human level, non-freedom and causalism are not synonyms at all. Carl A. Berndtson is certainly right when he says that "the freedom required by the phenomena of remorse, punishment and responsibility is not that based on non-causality"; but he is wrong when he says that these same phenomena are based "on the causation of choice by the enduring motives or values of the empirical self." [19] Actually, it is the subject himself who is punished and does penance. It is the conscious "ego" of the subject, and not his motives, that determines the choice effectively.

This latter assertion of Berndtson, which expresses the view of many other authors, reveals a surprising confusion between the concept of "causation" and "motivation." A "non-determined" choice is considered as equivalent to a "non-motivated" choice; and consequently a free volition is characterized as an unintelligible caprice, which would have no relation to the character of the agent and could in no way explain the meaning of moral responsibility. The objection would have some value if the process of choice should be unmotivated in order to be free; but such a notion is false.

Many authors accept the theory that ideas are forces which tend toward actualization and therefore we must seek in our motives not merely the goal of our acts, but also the energy through which we tend to actualize them. Our ideas, these authors say, are not only final causes; they are also the efficient causes of our actions. To this we answer that if the motive were an efficient cause the will would follow the idea fatalistically, as a trailer follows the car that pulls it. But can motive really be considered an efficient cause? Obviously not.

Man cannot be bound to a determinism of motives, because he acts from a point of view which dominates them and which permits him to judge them and appraise them. Motives that are in opposition, Louis De Raeymaeker writes, are not simply annulled.[20] No matter how high the value of a particular good may be, this does not contain and does not suppress the value of other goods. No particular good, no matter how considerable it is, can deprive other goods of their values, no matter how small they may be. A particular good is fundamentally incapable of binding us to itself and of leading us away from other goods which by no means cease to be attractive. None of these goods can enslave us. If therefore we choose one good in preference to others, it is because we ourselves have decided to act in this way, viz., to choose one and to sacrifice the others.

Doubtless the superiority of one motive can sometimes appear so overwhelming that it would seem to be irrational not to follow it in our behavior. But this does not prevent us, psychologically speaking, from remaining free to reject it in favor of another. Such a decision, which could be characterized as "unreasonable," does not cease to be rational. In fact, one always makes use of his faculty of reflection because one always bases his behavior on a reason. Certainly the reason is of very minor value in this case, but it still preserves sufficient value to inspire behavior. Because of this, it is by no means impossible for man to sin, to choose deliberately what he knows very well to be a moral evil; if he did not know it, there would be no sin. He who commits a sin does so because he finds a positive value in the reprehensible act, which he decides not to forego. He sacrifices a better good for a lesser one; for that which, in the last analysis, is an evil, but which retains, in a certain sense, a truly real value. It is always man, *as a person,* who acts, giving his preference to one motive or to another. It is not the motive which determines man's activity. *The motive in itself does not have the power to produce any action: it is not a cause, but only a condition.*[21] However, if we are careful enough in distinguishing between "efficient cause" and "final cause," motive can be considered a kind of final cause.[22] In fact the process of a voluntary act is put into effect by the perception of an object which is considered worth acquiring. The good to be attained is the final cause: without the perception of such a good a volitive act would be impossible. But the final cause cannot induce the preferential choice in a determining manner.

This seems clear especially in the case of a choice between two equal alternatives. Of course, if the motives for both alternatives have the same force, a voluntary choice is possible only under the hypothesis that we have the power to resolve the issue of the motives in conflict through the active intervention of the "ego." The "ego-in-action" can tip the scale in favor of one motive which up to then seemed equal to the other, thus adding an additional subjective force to the motive which is preferred. It is important to point out that in the experimental conditions created by Michotte, Prüm and Wells, it was not the "strengthened motive" which determined the choice but rather the choice which strengthened the motive. The intervention of the "ego" was particularly evident when an unpleasant alternative was chosen for a moral reason.[23]

We could agree, in the last analysis, that choice always favors the "good which seems greater" and that "the stronger motive always prevails," but under one condition: that the qualifications "greater" and "stronger" refer to the motive which is actually *adopted* and *strengthened* or reinforced by the active intervention of the "ego." Whenever we express our voluntary choice through a practical judgment like "this is better" or "this must be done," such a judgment presupposes the preferential and active consent of the "ego"; it means, in all cases, that the subject has made a decision. "This is what I want," "This is my choice."

c. The Source of Motivation

A problem which is often the cause of no little confusion remains to be considered. This is the problem of the source of motivation, of the origin of the motives which influence human behavior. In dealing with this we must reconsider the post-hypnotic and unconscious phenomena which were treated in a previous chapter.

Theoretically post-hypnotic phenomena include several important stages that can be summed up as follows: (1) the subject consciously feels the tendency to perform the act; (2) this tendency derives from truly unconscious psychic contents; (3) in some cases the subject surrenders to this tendency, while in other cases he resists it. What is critical is that the tendency—and consequently behavior—has an *unconscious* origin: it proceeds from an unconscious level of experience.[24] Actually, the problem is the same for post-hypnotic suggestion as for unconscious motivation in the Freudian system. In both cases it is a question of unconscious psychic contents at the basis of the representations and tendencies which arise in consciousness.

In reality we are facing an act which has all the characteristics of a free act and is inspired by unconscious impulses. A man has a decision to make; he has before himself a possibility of choice— shall he kill this person or not? One might be tempted to think that there is question here of a free choice, of an act which will be consciously materialized. But, even though the subject is not aware of it, his choice is already determined for him. His conscious will is only an instrument, a slave in the hands of a deep unconscious motive which determines his action.

Now the problem is to determine whether these facts are compatible with man's freedom. Paul Ricoeur believes he has found a solution. He claims that the "unconscious does not think," but that human consciousness never has full control of itself. This amounts to saying that human consciousness attempts to control the thoughts and desires which are hidden within its own depths, without, however, being able to do so. The reason for this failure is that such thoughts and desires are primarily affective and emotional in character, and therefore give rise to an infinite number of problems and offer an infinite number of possibilities. The only thing that consciousness can do about this emotional and affective content is to attempt to give a meaning and a form to it. All the unconscious material described by the psychoanalysts exists within the human consciousness as the raw material of desire, as *hylé* or matter in search of a form or intelligent interpretation, as latent and potential feeling.[25]

With psychoanalysis in mind, Hospers confesses that he is reluctant to characterize as free many actions which he had considered as such in the past. He also affirms that he is forced to consider man as much less free than he had previously believed.[26] We could readily admit that these assertions are substantially true. But the real problem is this: Can human beings in the light of psychiatric knowledge be called free in any respect at all? Hospers answers that if the psychoanalysts had to suggest a criterion for distinguishing the free from the unfree, they would say that "a person's freedom occurs in inverse proportion to his neuroticism; the more he is compelled in his behavior by a *malevolent* unconscious, the less free he is." This is certainly true. But Hospers adds that if we believe a man is free only to the extent that his behavior is *not* unconsciously motivated at all, "if this be our criterion, most of our behavior could not be called free." [27] His stand therefore compels us to define the affective role of unconscious motivation more precisely.

The origin of a need which leads to this or that form of behavior does not intervene as such in the formation of a free act. It is not the conscious or unconscious origin of a need, but rather the felt need itself and its mode of influencing behavior which is of greatest interest here. In a case of free activity, a person takes a position in regard to different elements of value or motive to the extent that these elements are really experienced in a concrete situation. The power of attraction or the value of any motive is a function of the aspirations and impulses as they are felt at the moment of the action. The depth of origin of these aspirations and impulses does not enter directly into the picture either in the evaluation of motives or in the attitude that the subject takes in their regard. "It is to the extent," Nuttin writes, "that they are actually *felt* that the *motives* are to be considered as forces influencing freedom of action." [28]

It is important to realize that both conscious and unconscious motivation are factors which condition human behavior. Besides conscious incentives of the will, it is evident that there can be others which proceed from more obscure areas and activate the true forces which feed man's conduct. But voluntary activity is free only in so far as it is carried out on the basis of conscious motives, of motives which are conceived as the real "reasons" for acting. What G. E. Stout asserts is most pertinent here: "Motives are not mere impulses. They come before consciousness as reasons why I should act in this or that way." [29]

This bears out our contention that *consciousness and will are essential requirements for free action.* If they are rejected on the theoretical level, or if they are nonexistent in practice, it follows necessarily that freedom cannot exist either.

The field of free activity thus appears rather limited, but in spite of this it is no less real. As we have seen in the Freudian system, the examples of unconscious motivation offered as proof that freedom is an illusion do not compel assent. On the other hand, it is certainly true that there are many doubtful cases with respect to freedom. Subconscious conflict can result in external actions and so can become a great obstacle to the practical use of freedom of choice. In reality *a limitation of freedom in the psychological field always implies a limitation of consciousness in respect to the motives of acting.*

Acts which derive from an unconscious source do not present a special problem in the question of freedom.[30] As for all other acts, their character of necessity or freedom depends on the knowledge of the dynamism which urges the individual to perform them. We must know whether or not this dynamism has been elaborated and put into action on the spiritual level of psychic activity. In the problem which concerns us now, all depends on the psychic character of the person. Certainly there would be no room for free activity if the entire motivation of human behavior were reduced to a sublimated form of unconscious sexuality. In this case, man's psychic dynamism would be reduced to a process which excludes a true "personal" elaboration of motives.

But this is not man's real situation. The motivation of a normal personality is made up of many components which form an inextricable knot wherein the conscious and the unconscious (at a psychological level), and the inferior and the superior (at a moral level) are mixed. Thus we return to the problem examined in the preceding section of this chapter: whether man is a complete delusion to himself or not; whether the testimony of consciousness concerning freedom is a total illusion or not. And we have seen that the answer must be negative.

3. The Value of Scientific Hypotheses

Attempts have often been made, during the last few years, to demonstrate the existence of free choice through a presupposed physical and biological indeterminism, and with arguments which are derived from contemporary quantum physics, from Heisenberg's "principle of indetermination." [31] Physics ventured into the field of philosophy when it attempted to discuss the problem of freedom. Psychology, which is without doubt the discipline most interested in the problem of freedom, passed it on to philosophy. Psychology has become more and more behavioristic. At the same time, physics has become more and more indeterministic and free. Physics repudiated causality only because it could not establish the position and the velocity of an electron. Physics accepted freedom from this motive and from this alone.

a. The Indeterminism of Physical and Biological Phenomena

The attempt to establish man's freedom on the basis of the uncertainty and indetermination which seem to reign in nature has not been infrequent.[32] This is the intention for example, of Arthur H. Compton: "It seems that some degree of uncertainty, such as the physicist has recently found, is necessary if such non-physical things as thoughts and motives are to have any relation to the physical world. It is, in short, only because the world in a physical sense is not wholly reliable that it can have any human meaning." [33]

There are many scientists who believe that physical indetermination in some way proves freedom. Their position can be expressed synthetically by these words of Eddington: "If the atom has indeterminacy, surely the human mind will have an equal indeterminacy; for we can scarcely accept a theory which makes out the mind to be more mechantistic than the atom." [34]

Assuming the role of philosophers, these physicists hold that the quantum theory reveals indeterminism; the principle of causality thereby becomes invalid. But has this been proved? The principle of causality is not necessarily invalid because it seems that it cannot be applied to the world of electrons. Russell Wilson writes: "the fact that I cannot know the exact position and velocity of the small body does not mean that it has no determined position and velocity, for the relation of cognition is a unique relation in which the thing is independent of whether it is known or not." [35]

What is called indeterminism may be only the effect of our ignorance concerning the world of nature. But even if indeterminism were proved beyond any doubt, could this annul in any way the principle of causality in the field of the ultimate causes? [36] There is, therefore, *absolutely nothing in the quantum theory and in the principle of indetermination that shows that some physical events are not caused. Therefore, there is no basis in physics for psychological freedom.*[37]

Modern theories in the field of physics have developed in a fashion almost parallel to those in biology. The broad evolution of biological forms seems to presuppose, besides that of autonomy, the principle of indetermination. Psychic differences which are encountered, for example, among individuals having the same genotype clearly illustrate the existence of margins within whose limits we can free ourselves from hereditary determinism. From this biological indeterminism consequences in favor of human freedom can be deduced, parallel to the process which obtained among the physicists. It is said, for example, that "the more man profits from this partial indeterminism . . . the more freedom he gains, a freedom which is *constructive*." It has also been said that freedom is the "result of what is indeterministic at the hereditary roots of the psyche, and of those very particular conditions on which man's consciousness and thought are constructed and by which they function." [38]

b. Statistical Regularities and Human Freedom

The indeterminism which we have noted in physics and biology substituted, at least partially, *statistical* measurement for *exact* measurement. What is the relationship between the statistical study of the natural phenomena and man's free activity? [39] Recently Henry N. Russell tried to explain freedom by means of his theory of "statistical properties." [40] According to his formulation, a statistical property has some remarkable characteristics. (1) It is a creation of man's imagination intended to describe the relationships of the observed phenomena; (2) it is a simplified description of a very complex situation; (3) it is of great theoretical and practical usefulness; (4) it permits us to predict experimental results with sufficient accuracy. All the physical properties which we ordinarily attribute to material bodies are statistical in character. With these premises Russell attempts to confront the problem of behavior and human responsibility.

Russell leaves aside the problem of whether man is also and essentially *something more* than an extremely complex physico-mechanical system; he considers only the consequences of the hypothesis that man is merely a physico-chemical system. According to this hypothesis it would be possible through scientific means to deduce the properties of human beings from the structure of the system. These properties are only statistical properties. Among them the most evident and important property is self-determination. Russell thinks that a mechanical hypothesis of human nature, statistical in character, does not at all imply the denial of the belief in man's responsibility or man's freedom.[41]

A critical examination of the data of experience reveals that statistical regularities do not offer any proof or confirmation that determinism is needed to explain human behavior and, in particular, moral phenomena. Man's freedom is perfectly compatible with the results of statistics. If the will were a capricious power, independent of any influence, acting blindly without any rule and any goal, without any objective basis of evaluation, then we could not expect any regularity in its effects. The constancy of the results in such a case could not be explained. Evidently, this is not the way the human will operates.

A student of natural phenomena does not pretend (and *cannot* pretend) to penetrate the essence of the causes behind the phenomena themselves; he only observes the effects. His techniques will permit him to take an inventory of man's free acts, but not to grasp the essence of this specifically human activity. Freedom is an internal phenomenon which escapes statistical measurement and of which we can be aware only through psychological analysis. The objection against human freedom derived from the external data of scientific experimentation lacks all foundation. It is said that freedom is the possibility of change, and therefore that it should make its appearance in such a manner as to be able to disturb the regularity of nature. This objection confuses a freedom influenced normally by motives of action with the absolute caprice of an unbalanced will. Moreover, from the regularity of ethical phenomena, those who deny freedom draw the conclusion of psycho-physical determinism. They forget that regularity appears only in the sum total of the mass of people, not in single individuals.

If statistical regularities do not permit an adequate study of man's individual activity, still they give us the opportunity to formulate, to a certain extent, some sociological inductions.[42] Regularities found in nature are sufficiently explained through the constant presence of a body of environmental causes that influences the individual. A convincing proof for true social determinism has not yet been offered. It is merely a question of a body of influences, relatively constant, that proceed from the relative stability of the social environment, to which the majority of individuals normally conform. Such a formula leaves human freedom its integral role, and legitimates, though with certain limitations, the so-called "laws" of the sociologists. In other words, it permits us to formulate sociological inductions, but with this twofold condition: (1) that the results be applied only to society in general, not to individuals; (2) that the impossibility of predicting with certainty the behavior of future social and moral phenomena be recognized, keeping in mind the mutability of the environment and any possible personal influences.

c. Human Freedom as a Phenomenon of Divergence

Among all the scientific hypotheses in favor of free human activity, perhaps the most interesting—though just as inadequate as those already evaluated—is that of Ivan D. London.[43] His point of departure is the admission that freedom of the will appears to be a universal datum of experience, even though its acceptance as a respectable theory remains doubtful. He points out quite rightly that the problem is not solved by ignoring it, as is fashionable among psychologists, or by exiling it to the field of metaphysics.[44] In the elaboration of his theory London utilized explicitly or implicitly the contribution of three empirical sources: (1) quantum physics, with the simultaneous demonstration that a law is simply the result of a process, called by Irving Langmuir a process "of convergence or divergence"; (2) the methodology of modern physics, which frankly calls its data and its theories "as if" theories, that is, in terms of one or another type of model; (3) the modern theory of evolution which, by taking into consideration the phenomenon of the changes in nature, can be called "neo-Darwinism." [45]

London's doctrine is the result of Langmuir's *convergence* and *divergence* concepts. It is imperative therefore to define these terms. A satisfactory theory, Langmuir thinks, should render possible the prediction of new experimental results under different conditions. As there are two kinds of physics (classical and quantum) which for twenty-five years seemed irreconcilable, there must be recognized two types of natural phenomena: (1) those in which the behavior of the system can be determined by the behavior of the component parts; (2) those in which a single discontinuous event expands in its effects, so that the behavior of the entire system depends on something that began as a small entity. The phenomena of the first type are called *convergent* because all the fluctuating details of the individual atoms give a result which converges into a definite state. Those of the second type can be called *divergent* phenomena because broader effects are always produced by a small beginning. Classical physics can be applied satisfactorily to the convergent phenomena, which fit the old concepts of cause and effect. The divergent phenomena, conversely, can be understood on the basis of the quantum theory of modern physics.

This distinction between natural phenomena is applied by Langmuir to man's psychic processes also. Evident examples of divergent phenomena in human life are those implied in the mechanism of heredity and of the origin of species. Phenomena of the same type are seen, though less clearly, at a more elevated level of human activity. Even the ideas that develop in the human brain seem to have all the characteristics of divergent phenomena. Frequently in life we have to face situations where we must choose. At times this choice can alter the entire future course of our life. [46] Voluntary choice could then be called a divergent phenomenon. What happens, then, to the principle of causality, to the cause-effect relationship? Langmuir cannot find any justification for the statement that science proves that general causes (convergent phenomena) are predominant over the results of individual actions (divergent phenomena) in human processes. According to him the existence of divergent phenomena almost excludes the possibility of human activity being determined primarily by convergent phenomena. But, notwithstanding the great importance of divergent phenomena in human life, the author reminds us that we still have to cope with causes and effects, that is, with convergent phenomena. After all, we still have to make plans for the future. We can do this by calculating the probabilities, even though we do not believe that definitive results will follow inevitably.[47]

The idea of "divergent phenomena," applied very hesitantly to human behavior by Langmuir, constitutes the basis of Ivan D. London's theory of freedom.[48] To London's mind, the term "divergence" refers essentially to the principle of indetermination, which implies the impossibility of formulating or discerning rational models for certain sequences of phenomena. Free choice must be accepted as a convenient neutral term; we must be on guard against confusing this position with the classical theory, which makes of free will an independent agent. To London's mind, *free will becomes a function of divergence;* it acts "as if" it were a free agent, exactly as divergence makes indetermination act "as if" determinism were prevailing; so for practical reasons free will must not be denied.[49]

Whether or not we are disposed to accept fully the implication of indeterminism, London wrote in a second article on the same subject that man is constituted *as if* he were a free agent.[50] If our world were governed by rigid determinism man could take advantage of its laws for his own welfare. On the other hand, if our world were ruled by chance and abandoned to total chaos, man could still use all the favorable elements which he encounters, and eventually he could concentrate them to his advantage. Man is not tied either to necessity or to chaos.

London suggested a fundamental analogy between the effects of divergence in the evolution of the "species" and the effects of divergence in the development of the "individual." On the basis of this analogy, he says with a sense of certainty, both continuity and discontinuity in the development of an individual can be deduced from the divergences which influence him in varying ways. From this it follows that the will, which acts *as if* it were free, is free in the sense that divergence constantly offers to it the occasion for modifying itself, and even of remaining outside the broad convergences which mark and give consistency to its life.

But we must point out that this admission of free choice does not have any relationship to the problem of whether there is a being who wills freely. Free choice, understood as a function of divergence, by no means implies the existence of an agent. London clarifies his position. The admission of indeterminism is not the admission of free choice in the classical sense, but the admission of a free choice which acts as a function of divergence and which, although it does not operate as an agent, produces the same effects as if it were.[51] Understood as such, human freedom is not something which man manifests as his natural prerogative, but something that must be *acquired;* and once acquired it can still be lost.

In a later study, London holds that the development of human personality—as it occurs in biological evolution—can take irreversible directions. Because of this the divergences can act only in those directions and be diversified only in details.[52] Free choice would then manifest convergence in various of its aspects and would tend to lose its characteristic of freedom. Contrarily, the possibility of separating the response from the original stimulus permits us to expect from an individual a progressive development of individual divergence. The development of personality considered as the joint function of convergence and divergence, according to London, would solve these two contradictory aspects of predetermination and indetermination.

London's theory, though ingenious, appears to be founded on an inconsistent basis. At best it could be considered a phenomenological description, but never a causal explanation of human activity. This theory permits us to recognize in man only the appearance of freedom and certainly not the reality of conscious and voluntary control. The principle of indetermination of quantum physics and Langmuir's consequent theory of convergent and divergent phenomena may be considered the source of physical—even biological —freedom, but cannot be the basis of man's psychological freedom.

4. Causality and Prediction of Human Acts

Psychological freedom implies the existence of the principle of causality. The persistent confusion which exists in this regard depends mostly on the ambiguous use of the word "determined." It can mean "caused" or simply "measured." For the physical and psychological determinists, it means "caused," i.e., something which is explained in terms of physical antecedents. For those who hold the quantum theory, the same term means "measured": the quanta are determined or free simply because we cannot define either their velocity or their position. Now it is evident that man's free activity has nothing to do with the problem of measurement, but only with that of causality. The will is not free merely because it cannot be measured or even because it is uncaused; the will is free because its acts are not simply the product of physical causality and cannot therefore be completely predetermined.

We would not be free to choose what we wish if the principle of causality, and therefore causal determination, were not a real fact. If the principle of indetermination were true, it would not constitute a "facilitation" but a limitation of our freedom.[53] In reality event the most simple human actions could not be actualized under the hypothesis of an indeterministic universe. To say that *I could* have acted differently amounts to saying that *I would have acted differently* if I had decided to do so, and that no one forced me to do what I did. When these conditions are fulfilled, I can say that I acted freely. But this does not mean that my action happened without any causality and that it cannot be explained.[54]

The controversy between the doctrines of freedom and determinism is the result of a misunderstanding. The two terms in question are fully capable of coexisting. Even more—one of them somehow implies the other.[55] It is not a question here of reconciling two opposite terms, but only of understanding their exact meaning.[56]

a. The Double Causality of Human Activity

Man's freedom certainly implies a power and indicates the absence of any interference with the exercise of this power. I have the power of willing one thing or another; if I wish, the act of willing takes place. One of the most surprising characteristics of the will is this: the will appears as a "cause"; it seems certain that the will is the most important "causal factor" of the interior world. Volitive activity organizes mental life through a genuine psychic causality. The action which results from the voluntary choice is not "uncaused" as was erroneously held, for example, by Hartley and Bain.[57] To act freely does not mean, by any means, to act without any cause. In reality it is the sign of a serious misunderstanding of the problem to use the terms "free" and "uncaused" as synonymous.[58] The origin of this confusion must be sought in a restricted and unilateral concept of causality.

At times various authors have maintained that there exists only one kind of causality, physical causality, and that the law of conservation of energy dominates the entire universe. This law therefore eliminates all possibility of acting freely. In fact, in a world in which only physical causality reigns, voluntary choice would be a mechanically undetermined event; and such an event could take place only by adding or subtracting energy to or from the universe. But this would be in contradiction to the law of conservation of energy.

Actually the study of the physical and mental life of man leads us to the conclusion that man is a being in whom the physical and the psychic are united intimately. Because of the presence of these two factors in the human organism, it is logical and natural to suppose that two kinds of causality act in man's conduct: *physical and psychic*. Man himself is the real being who serves as the basis of both kinds of causal activity.[59] In addition to the existence of mechanical energy and physical causality, we must recognize in man a spiritual power of acting and psychic causality, both of which produce in mental life phenomena to which the concept of matter in motion cannot be applied. No objection, therefore, can be raised against freedom on the basis of the law of conservation of energy; this law is applicable only to mechanical energy, while free will is a power of action which is subject to psychic causality. In man "psychic causality" involves intelligence, the notion of goals, the relationship between means and ends, the evaluation of values and consequences in the light of ideals and principles. Volition is the power of choosing among the various means by which a certain type of goal can be reached; it is the power of determination of oneself in favor of one good rather than another. As William Stern rightly affirmed, freedom "is not the lack of causation but causation by the self-determination of the person at a given time." [60]

Thus the paradox—freedom-determinism—is solved. But we must remember that paradox does not mean dilemma; it does not exclude, it even includes, the coexistence of the two terms.[61] We can say with Robert E. Brennan that freedom lies midway between the extremes of determinism and indeterminism; [62] or better, that *freedom is a special type of determinism; to be precise—self determinism.*[63]

The old postulate that all psychic processes or *reactions* are the effects of a necessary cause is replaced by the postulate that all psychic processes or *activities* necessarily have a cause, though at first sight they seem to be a product of chance. How does this cause actually function? After affirming the existence of a psychic causality which explains free human activity, we must now define its mode of acting at the level of concrete experience. Does it follow the same procedures as physical causality, or does it have laws of its own? Supposing that psychic causality follows laws specific to man, what possibility do we have of predicting human behavior at the level of scientific as well as of that of empirical experience?

b. Psychological Laws and the Possibility of Prediction

The special type of determinism which characterizes man's free activity must be distinguished accurately from a state of potentiality in general. Man is truly free not *before* the free action, but at the *actual moment* in which he acts. Consequently, it is inconceivable that we could try to establish the non-existence of freedom through experiments. All our experience demonstrates that it is impossible to deduce determinism from the infallibility of prediction. The possibility of predicting an event tells us only that the event itself will take place; but it does not tell us anything about the way in which it will be realized, whether by a process of purely mechanical causal succession or by the free choice of the means to reach a goal. We can be certain that a man who abstains from liquor will not get drunk at a banquet. The deeper the roots of motivation of the character of an individual, the easier and more certain is the prediction of his behavior. With all this, the virtuous man remains free. He is responsible for his habits, and this is what makes him a person on whom we can rely.

Narciss Ach, after one of his later experiments, held that voluntary choice is determined, and that he could predict it in all cases with one hundred per cent accuracy.[64] Actually, nothing in Ach's experiments shows that his subjects could not have acted in some other way had they so willed. This is evident from the condition that he laid down that the subjects must not know that the experiment aimed at predicting their behavior. Such knowledge would not have altered in any way their psychological constitution, determined by heredity and years of experience, but their behavior would at once have become unpredictable. In the field of psychology, prediction can be extended only to the point of very limited probabilities. Raymond B. Cattell writes: "Whatever the degree of theoretical determinism we are prepared to admit in regard to human behavior, it is certain that in practice, no matter how good our measuring instruments and our understanding of the process at work, the accuracy of our predictions is limited . . . Our laws may always give only statements of probability." [65]

It is known that psychoanalysts in certain cases do succeed in associating the present to the past in such a way as to be able to predict the patient's behavior in satisfactory fashion. But when we deal with the inverse process—the prediction of the future in terms of the present—the limits of psychoanalytic approximation appear quite variable. Freud himself understood this fully. In a study of a case of a woman's homosexuality, he says that to trace the development of the past is relatively easy. But when we want to proceed from the premises discovered during the psychoanalytic treatment, and then venture into the future to follow them to their final conclusions, we no longer have the impression of an inevitable succession of events which could not be determined in a different way from what we would expect from the premises. Freud adds that we can at the same time see another conclusion as possible, a conclusion which we would have been able to understand and explain just as easily. From a knowledge of the premises, therefore, we are not able to foresee the nature of the conclusion.[66] These statements of Freud have been considered by various interpreters as a model of scientific integrity, but they are not held in due respect by the psychoanalysts themselves.

If we could evaluate completely the weight of heredity and the history of the life of a man, his "archetypes," his "secret goals" and all the other concepts of depth psychology, then we could explain, *at least partially,* the present state of this man and even predict his future. Psychoanalysis holds that in this case we could explain his present state entirely and predict his future with exactitude. Such total prediction is actually impossible. A *relative* prediction, however, is possible; and this is sufficient for psychology. We can—at least frequently—predict human behavior with that degree of certitude which is required for a prudent action. This degree of certitude is characterized as "moral certitude" in the broad meaning of the term. It is on this kind of certitude that all social life is based. This limited possibility of prediction is in perfect harmony with the idea of man's freedom. It does not exclude regularity; it even makes the normal rhythm of human conduct possible. It is precisely because we are endowed with freedom that we are able to act rationally (or irrationally) by subduing instinctive and acquired tendencies that militate against the laws of the spirit.

Undoubtedly, as Gordon W. Allport says, there is an urgent need to know the method by which it is possible to reach valid predictions in individual cases.[67] And this should not make psychologists forget how complex the human being is; it should instil respect and caution in dealing with man. Man's power to adhere to a principle to the disadvantage of an impulse makes his behavior foreseeable in part, when we know the principles that are followed. But human behavior is never completely foreseeable, even when we know all the external circumstances and the principles of behavior which have been adopted. Man is always free to adopt higher and more comprehensible principles when his intelligence reveals them to him. Nor does this mean that volition exposes human behavior to mere chance.

Freedom tends to decrease the possibility of prediction; but some free acts are foreseeable. This conclusion is of great importance for human relations.[68] Just as we presume that a rock or a tree which are deeply rooted will not be swept away by a storm, in the same manner we presuppose that the word of an honest man will be kept, no matter how strong the pressure of interests and threats might be. We know that the credibility of a virtuous man does not proceed from the same kind of cause from which the uniformity of a natural force arises; we always count on the trust that this man inspires in us. This leads us to believe that a certain degree of foresight can be taken for granted in man's behaving; this is likewise true in the formal aspects of psychological and social science.

A concept of human freedom, not as indeterminism but as self-determination, makes prediction of human conduct scientifically possible for clinical and social purposes. It makes it possible (albeit in a relative form) by reason of the uniformity of physical events on which psychic life is based, and by reason of man's rationality, which demands from him a coherent way of acting. Freedom, in fact, is not something anarchical or irrational; it is not the absence of causality or motivation. For this reason science can give a rational and valid explanation of the free act in terms of factors and predisposing circumstances. Man's behavior can present a predisposition sufficient to justify the scientific investigation of the causes that are producing it. At the same time it can present a freedom of choice sufficient to make man aware of his own responsibility.

FOOTNOTES

[1] Concerning the experience of free activity under experimental conditions cf. the following statements taken from a study by A. Bovet, "La Conscience du Devoir dans L'Introspection Provoqué: Experience sur la Psychologie de la Pensée," *Arch. Psychol.* (1910), 9, 349 ff. J'ai éprouvé surtout une sorte d'angoisse, d'hésitation, c'est-à-dire un embaras du choix"; "J'ai eu le sentiment qu'il est détestable d'être libre"; 'Comme un sentiment de trop grande liberté, comme quand on voudrait fair quelque chose qui fait plaisir et qu'on sent qu'on ne le fait pas, parcequ'il vaut mieux faire ce qui ne fait pas plaisir. Sentiment du devoir. Ne pas faire ce qu'on veux"; "Sentiment d'angoisse de ne pas chercher librement"; "L'impression que le choix est force," 349 ff. Roters has written a very interesting study on the consciousness of freedom: "Psychologisches zum Bewusstsein der Willensfreiheit," *Arch. Ges. Psychol.* (1932), 86, 191-211.

[2] F. Aveling, *Personality and Will* (Cambridge: Cambridge Univ. Press, 1931), 199 ff.

[3] F. Schiller, "Consciousness Reconsidered," *Arch. Neur. Psychiat.* (1952), 67, 211-212.

[4] R. Ekstein, "Psychological Laws and Human Freedom," *J. Soc. Psychol.* (1947), 25, 189.

[5] R. P. Knight, "Determinism, freedom and Psychotherapy," *Psychiatry* (1946), 9, 256.

[6] A. Gemelli, *La Responsabilità del Delinquente nei suoi Fondamenti*

Biologici e Psicologici (Milano: Giuffrè, 1946), 230. Hadley Cantril writes: "Human beings have the capacity to choose. And the opportunity to exercise this capacity of choice cannot be denied to man without violating his very nature. This is a fact about human beings which cannot be liquidated." "The Qualities of being Human," *American Quarterly* (1954), 6, 12.

7 C. Fox, "The Mind and Its Body," *The Foundations of Psychology* (London: Kegan Paul, 1931), 298.

8 F. S. Taylor, *Concerning Science* (London: MacDonald, 1949), 128.

9 R. Allers, *The Successful Error: A Critical Study of Freudian Psychoanalysis* (New York: Sheed & Ward, 1940), 94.

10 N. Braunshausen, 'Le Libre-Arbitre à la Lumiere de la Psychologie Experimentale de la Science Moderne," *Rev. Sci. Pedag.* (1946), 8, 33-48, 75-96; (1947), 9, 8-23, 38-46; For a more exact treatment of the problem from the philisophical viewpoint, cf. Theodor Steinbuchel, *Die Philosophische Grundlegung der Katholischen Sittenlehre,* in Tillman, F., *Handbuch der Katholischen Sittenlehre,* Band I. (Dusseldorf: L. Schwann, 1938), 357-410.

11 J. Lindworsky, *Experimental Psychology,* trans. H. R. De Silva (New York: Macmillan 1931), 303 ff. Cf. *supra* Chapter Three.

12 E. Meumann, *Intelligenz und Wille* (Leipzig: Quelle u. Meyer, 1925), 215.

13 An interesting treatment of the functional autonomy of motives is Gordon W. Allport's *The Nature of Personality* (Cambridge, Mass.: Addison-Wesley Press, 1950), 190-212. For a critical evaluation of this concept, cf. Joseph Nuttin, *Psychoanalysis and Personality,* trans. George Lamb (New York: Sheed and Ward, 1953), 242 ff.

14 H. G. Wyatt, *The Psychology of Intelligence and Will* (London: Kegan Paul, 1930), 144. Cf. also the short but substantial article of N. Mailloux, "Psychic Determinism, Freedom, and Personality Development," *Canad. J. Psychol.,* (1953), 7, 7 ff.

15 T. Ribot, *The Diseases of the Will,* trans. J. Fitzgerald (New York: Humboldt, 1884), 8.

16 Braushausen, "Le Libre-Arbitre," *op. cit.,* 75.

17 *Ibid.,* 96.

18 P. Ricoeur, *Philosophie de la Volonté: Le Volontaire et l'Involontaire, Philosophie de l'Ésprit* (Paris: Aubier, 1950), 373. Gino Corallo draws, in my opinion, an unconvincing distinction between "self-determinability" and "self-determination." He writes: "If we presuppose such self-determinability, the determination will afterwards be accomplished necessarily by the object or motive." Educazione e Libertà: Presupposti Filosofici per una Pedagogia della Libertà," *Collana Pedagogica "D. Bosco."* First series, Vol. XVI (Torino: S.E.I., 1951), 189. If I understand the ambiguous meaning of the proposed distinction, the author almost attributes a true causal function to the motives of the volitional act.

19 C. A. Berndtson, *The Problem of Free Will in Recent Philosophy*

(Chicago: Univ. of Chicago Press, 1942), 112. The same ambiguous position can be noted, for instance, in Eugen Bleuler, *Textbook of Psychiatry,* trans. A. A. Brill (New York: Macmillan, 1924), 51. He is right when he says that "the much mooted question whether there is a *free will* in the sense that a decision can be reached without any reason does not exist in natural science." But he is wrong when he says that "there is no decision which does not have a complete causal basis in motives as striving. . . *Motives* are a cause even though they are complicated."

20 L. De Raeymaeker, "Le probleme de la Liberté Personelle et le Principe de sa Solution," *Giorn. Metafis.* (1949), 4, 581-590. Agostino Gemelli writes on this point: "Entre le but que nous choissons et notre choix basé sur ces motifs, il n'y a pas de rapport mécanique, nécessaire; tout en nous présentant le choix dans une direction déterminée (un but determiné prend une valeur plus grande), les motifs ne nous obligent pas toutefois à choisir dans cette direction-là." *Le Psychologue* (1951), 77.

21 William Stern defines the relationship between personality and motivation as follows: "Those factors within the person that cause the eventual act of will are called the *motives* of the act of will. It is by means of motives that a particular act is attached to the totality of the person." *General Psychology from the Personalistic Standpoint,* trans. D. Spoerl (New York: Macmillan, 1938), 406.

22 Following a terminology that seems less exact, but which has essentially the same meaning, A. Lehmen writes: "The motives are the *moral cause,* the volition is the *psychic cause.* The free act, then, allows the principle of causality to *subsist* in its total integrity." "Lehrbuch der Philosophie auf Aristotelisch-Scholasticher Grundlage," *Psychologie* (Freiburg: B. Herder, 1902), 440.

23 Honoria M. Wells, in her study of the phenomenology of acts of choice, records this passage: "Subject A sometimes voluntarily strengthened the motive for taking an unpleasant alternative in this manner, even when he had the option of taking a pleasant one." "The Phenomenology of Acts of Choice," *Brit. Psychol. of Monogr. Suppl.* (1927), 11, 75.

24 What Joseph Nuttin writes on this point is of particular interest. *Psychoanalysis and Personality, op. cit.,* 123 ff.

25 P. Ricoeur, *op. cit.,* p. 354. Ricoeur reduces character to "manner" and the unconscious to "matter"—a notable positive contribution to the phenomenology of volitional activity. This interpretation demolishes Freudian causalism according to Alphonse De Waelhens, *Une Philosophie de la Volonté* (1951), 435.

26 J. Hospers, "Meaning and Free Will," *Philos. Phenom. Res.* (1949-1950), 10, 329. "The more of this sort of thing you see, the more you can see what the psychoanalyst means when he talks about *the illusion of free will.* And the more of a psychiatrist you become, the more you are overcome with a sense of what an illusion this precious free will really is." *Ibid.,* 320 ff.

27 *Ibid.*, 329.

28 J. Nuttin, *op. cit.*, 127.

29 G. F. Stout, *A Manual of Psychology*, 4th Ed. revised in collaboration with the author by C. A. Mace (London: Univ. Tutorial Series, 1932), 632. Motivation, understood in this context, is very different from that examined by Gardner Murphy: *Personality: A Biosocial Approach to Origins and Structure* (New York: Harper, 1947), 104. None of these types of motivation, such as "visceral drives," "activity drives," "sensory drives," "emergency drives," and not even "purposivism," satisfy the fundamental conditions of human free activity.

30 Jacques Maritain is very clear on this point: "The fact, revealed by psychoanalysis, that there are unconscious motivations which the subject obeys without knowing them, furnishes in no manner, as some would imagine, an argument against free will, for free will begins with intellectual judgment and consciousness." "The Conquest of Freedom," in Anshen, R.N., *Freedom: Its Meaning* (New York: Harcourt, Brace, 1940), 633.

31 Of the many authors who have treated this problem, cf. G. E. Jaunces, *Modern Physics* (New York: Van Nostrand, 1932); K. F. Herzfeld, "The Quantum Theory of Matter," *Thought* (1936), 11, 566-588; P. Lecky, *Self-Consistency: A Theory of Personality* (New York: Island Press, 1945); O. Miro Quesada, *El Problema de la Libertad* (1945).

32 For more on the contemporary development of the new theories in physics and their philosophical implications, cf. particularly J. Jeans, *The Mysterious Universe* (London: Cambridge Univ. Press, 1930); F. R. Hoere, "Physical Determinism and Free Will," *Irish Eccl. Rec.*, (1934), 43, 27-35; R. Wilson, "The New Physics: Does it Vindicate Free Will?" in *New Schol.* (1937), 11, 332-349; T. Crowley, "Some Philosophical Aspects of Physical Indeterminacy," *Irish Eccl. Rec.* (1948), 70, 785-799.

33 A. H. Compton, *The Freedom of Man* (New Haven: Yale Univ. Press, 1935), p. 69. With regard to the attitude of Arthur H. Compton on this point, Jacques Maritain writes: "The efforts of eminent scientists, like Professor Compton, to link indeterministic theories of modern physics to our natural belief in free will may be highly significant and stimulating to the mind and efficacious in eliminating many prejudices, but I do not think that a strict proof providing this belief with an unshakable intellectual basis can be found in that direction." "The Conquest of Freedom," in Anshen, R.N., *Freedom: Its Meanings* (New York: Harcourt, Brace, 1940), p. 633. Prescinding from Compton's good intentions it seems to me that Maritain is too lenient towards these attempts to prove the freedom of man with arguments derived from indeterministic theories. He gives the impression of believing that these theories, even though they do not give us a *strict positive proof*, can however dissipate many prejudices. To my mind, on the contrary, these theories contribute to increase prejudice and confusion on the problem of freedom for the simple reason that they posit it erroneously.

34 A. S. Eddington, "The Decline of Determinism" (Presidential Address

to the Mathematical Association), *Nature*, Feb. 13, 1932, 240. For the orientation taken by many scientists, cf. for example the following assertions of Oscar Miro Quesada in *El Problema de la Libertad:* "En nombre de la teoría de los quantos y del principio de incertidumbre propio de la física atómica puede aceptarse la libertad del espíritu, porque hay una región de la realidad, el mundo de los átomos, donde tambien reina la espontaneidad," p. 61. And later the same author writes: "Ahora bien, si el principio de la determinación de Newton fué considerado por la Filosofía como uno de los puntos de partida para el tratamiento del problema de la libertad, no es natural que ahora lo sea el principio de indeterminación de Heisenberg?" *Ibid.,* p. 67.

35 R. Wilson, "The New Physics: Does It Vindicate Free Will?" in *New Schol.* (1937), 11, 348.

36 Arthur H. Compton (whom we have criticized before for his theory of physical indeterminism) posits the problem that we have just mentioned in this way: "Does this mean, however, that for the proton the law of causality, that all things happen *with necessity,* is no longer valid? It means at least that no physical experiment can test this principle on an atomic scale. The philosopher may retain the idea of rigid law as applied to *things in themselves* if he desires; but he cannot refer to experiment for its verification." *Op. cit.* (1935), 39. After the publication of the notable experimental work of Albert Michotte on *La Perception de la Causalité* (Louvain: Publ. Univ. Louvain, 1954), 2nd Ed., I think that Compton should modify, at least in part, the formulation of the passage just quoted.

37 The following assertion of Rudolf Allers should be understood in the same way. "The ideas proposed by some physicists, who talk of freedom in nature, because of certain results of modern physics, are absolutely meaningless. One cannot prove freedom by referring to statistical physics and to the law of probability." *The Successful Error: A Critical Study of Freudian Psychoanalysis* (New York: Sheed & Ward, 1940), 112. Cf. also Ernest Cassirer, *Determinismus und Indeterminismus in der Modern Physik* (Goteborg: Boktryckery, 1937), 253 ff.

38 E. Guyenot, "Hérédité et Liberte," *L'Homme devant la Science* (Texte des Conférences et des entretiens organisés par les Rencontres Internationales de Genève; Neuchâtel, Baconnière, 1952), 81-99; 295; 319. Because some people who attended this meeting objected to his conference, Emile Guyenot modified his thought, or at least made it more precise: "Quant è la marge qui résulte de ces discordances, bien entendu elle n'impose pas la notion de liberté. Elle nous montre simplement que le déterminisme heréditaire a des limites. . . Ces limites pourront être comblées par l'éducation, elles pourront être l'occasion d'une démarche libre de notre ésprit qui essaiera de se glisser en quelque sorte par ces fissures et de se modifier lui même" (*Ibid.,* 301). Further on he makes an even clearer affirmation: "C'est par l'esprit que nous évadons du fatum héréditaire." *Ibid.,* p. 314.

39 For interesting studies of the above problem and particularly of the

relationship between moral statistics and determinism, cf. C. Gutberlet, *Die Willensfreiheit und Ihre Gegner*, 2 Aufl. (Fulda: Fuldaer Actiendruck, 1907), 41-120; J. Lottin, "La Statistique Morale et le determinisme," *Rev. Neo-Scol.* (1908), 15, 48-89.

[40] H. N. Russell, *Determinism and Responsibility* (1934), 251 ff.

[41] These remarks of Henry N. Russell clarify his thought: "If an interpretation of the human individual as a purely statistical system is assumed to be possible, then the empirical characteristics of consciousness, memory, reason, self-determination, and responsibility must *ex hypothesi* appear as statistical properties of this system; if freedom and responsibility were statistical properties, we might expect them to have the distinctive ear-marks of such properties." The author concludes that "the mechanistic hypothesis of the nature of man is not an enemy, but an ally, of morals and religion." *Determinism and Responsibility* (1943), 252.

[42] J. Lottin, "Le Statistique Morale et le Determinisme," *Rev. Neo-Scol.* (1908), 15, 87.

[43] I. D. London, "Psychology and Heisenberg's Principle of Indeterminacy," *Psychol. Rev.* (1945), 52, 162-168; "Some Consequences for History and Psychology of Langmuir's Convergence and Divergence of Phenomena," *Psychol. Rev.* (1946), 53, 170-188; "Free Will as a Function of Divergence," *Psychol. Rev.* (1948), 55, 41-47; "The Developing of Personality as a joint Function of Convergence and Divergence," *J. Soc. Psychol.* (1949), 29, 167-187.

[44] I. D. London, "Free Will as a Function of Divergence," *ibid.*, 41.

[45] Concerning the Process of Convergence and Divergence, cf. I. Langmuir, "Science, Common Sense, and Decency," *Science* (1943), 97, 1-7; *Phenomena, Atoms and Molecules: An Attempt to Interpret Phenomena in Terms of Mechanism or Atomic and Molecular Interactions* (New York: Philosophical Library, 1950). Concerning the "principle of Complementarity," cf. N. Bohr, "Causality and Complementarity," *Philos. Sci.* (1937), 4, 289-298; "On the Notions of Causality and Complementarity," *Science* (1950), 111, 51-54.

[46] I. Langmuir, *op. cit.* 6 ff. The theory of Irving Langmuir was followed enthusiastically by many authors. E. Terry Prothro, for instance, writes: "A complete determinism involving the helplessness of man and the consequent futility of psychological action research is unnecessary to a science of culture. . . . With the recognition of divergent phenomena has come the recognition that determinism is not a universal magic." Cf. "Cultural Determinism: A Challenge to Action Research," *J. Soc. Psychol.* (1952), 35, 214.

[47] I. Langmuir, *ibid.*, 9 ff.

[48] I. D. London, *op. cit.*, 168.

[49] I. D. London, "Some Consequences for History and Psychology of Langmuir's Convergence and Divergence of Phenomena," *op. cit.*, 181.

[50] I. D. London, "Free Will as a Function of Divergence," *op. cit.* Re-

calling the theory of E. T. Whittaker, London thinks that "to admit the possibility of new intrusions, that is, to aver that the present is not completely determinable in terms of antecedent conditions, is not the same thing as asserting free-will in the sense of an agent, because then free-will would imply determination of another sort—absolute personal determination. This is the very thing we wish to evidence." *Ibid.*, 44. Cf. E. T. Whittaker, "Chance, Free Will, and Necessity in Scientific Conception of the Universe," *Proc. Psychol. Soc. London* (1943), 55, 459-491.

51 I. D. London, "Free Will as a Function of Divergence," *ibid.*, 43 ff.

52 I. D. London, "The Developing Personality as a Joint Function of Convergence and Divergence," *op. cit.*, 174.

53 Cf. Russell Wilson: "Such an objective indeterminacy, even if admitted, would in no way explain free will, and even if it would *explain* it, it would be no demonstration of the fact, but merely the withdrawal of an objection which was by no means the most difficult of solution." "The New Physics: Does it Vindicate Free Will?" *New Schol.* (1937), 11, 348. R. Wilson is generally correct and exact in studying the relationship between the new physics and free choice, but I do not believe that the presupposed truth of the principle of indeterminacy can make the objection against freedom fall; it seems the opposite to me.

54 P. Nowell-Smith, "Free Will and Moral Responsibility," *Mind* (1948), 57, 46. Patrick Mullahy opposes the very common opinion that volitional activity cannot be free because it has definite causal conditions: "Only because willing—choosing intelligently—has determinate conditions can one be free. Suppose acts of will were not caused, would they not then be subject to change or vagary? What indeed would decide one to act at all? What kind of freedom would this be? . . . Only because events have causes are they subject to control and change." "Will, Choice, and Ends," *Psychiatry* (1949), 12, 384.

55 According to R. E. Hobart, free choice implies determinism and is inconceivable without it. Everything that concerns the absence of determination is free activity, "if and so far as it exists, is no gain to freedom, but sheer loss of it." "Free Will as Involving Determinism and Inconceivable without It," *Mind* (1934), 43, 2. And further on: "Just so far as the volition is undetermined, the self can neither be praised nor blamed for it, since it is not the act of the self." *Ibid.*, 7.

56 On this subject Etienne Gilson writes: "The unsound welcome recently given by some philosophers to the merely *statistical* interpretation of physical law is a safe indication that too many among us are still looking irrationally at the last bulwark of liberty." *The Unity of Philosophical Experience* (New York: Charles Scribner's Sons, 1950), 293. Cf. T. Crowley, "Some Philosophical Aspects of Physical Indeterminacy," *Irish Eccl. Rec.* (1948), 70, 797.

57 P. Priestly writes: "To suppose that the Action A, or its contrary *a*, can equally follow previous circumstances, that are exactly the same, ap-

pears to me the same thing as affirming that one or both of them start up into being without any cause." *Hartley's Theory of the Human Mind, or The Principle of the Association of Ideas, with Essays Relating to the Subject of it,* 2nd Ed. (London: Johonson, 1790), 337. Cf. A. Bain, "Dr. Ward on Free-Will," *Mind* (1880), 5, 116, 119.

[58] In a study of the Freudian system, Joseph F. Donceel writes: "Only man's will, in its deliberate and conscious decisions, escapes the law of psychic determinism. Freud, of course, does not mention this exception." "Second Thoughts of Freud," *Thought* (1949), 24, 469. Donceel seems to think that our free decisions are without a determinate cause. This would evidently be a serious mistake which would have as a consequence the criticism of Freud from a totally erroneous viewpoint.

[59] T. V. Moore, *The Driving Forces of Human Nature and their Adjustment* (New York: Grune & Stratton, 1950), 330 ff. "One of the striking characteristics of the will is that it appears as a cause in mental life and that too as the most important causal factor in the inner world of man." *Ibid.,* 332; "Volitional activity organizes mental life by a genuine causal activity." *Ibid.,* 333.

[60] W. Stern, *General Psychology from the Personalistic Standpoint,* trans. D. Spoerl (New York: 1938), 434. Rudolf Allers has insisted very strongly on the same point in *The Successful Error: A Critical Study of Freudian Psychoanalysis* (New York: Sheed & Ward, 1940), 94. According to Allers, freedom is very different from indetermination or from chance.

[61] It is worthwhile to note this passage of Edward L. Thorndike, in which he maintains the possibility of the coexistence of the freedom-determinism paradox. "They have thought the paradox was a dilemma—that if the ways of nature, including human nature, were invariable and immutable, then no acts of man could change nature—that one must choose between science and freedom. The paradox is not a dilemma. Science does not necessitate fatalism. The uniformity of nature is consistent with changes in nature made by human thought and action, especially as guided by science itself." *Human Nature and Social Order* (New York: Macmillan, 1940), 396. Cf. A. B. Wolf, "On the Content of Welfare," *Amer. Econ. Rev.* (1931), 21, 221 ff.

[62] R. E. Brennan, *Thomistic Psychology* (1941), 221.

[63] According to Charles Fox, a solution of the problem of freedom implies "that freedom and determinism are the very same thing; or that one particular form of determinism guarantees the freedom of the will." *The Mind and Its Body: The Foundations of Psychology* (London: Kegan Paul, 1931), 294. Of these two hypotheses, only the second is exact.

[64] N. Ach, *Analyse des Willens* (Berlin: Urban u. Schwarzenberg, 1935). Cf. The analysis of the thought of Narciss Ach which was made above in Chapter Four. It must be pointed out that the knowledge which we can have of another person does not determine his behavior. Even the Divine Knowledge of human events does not determine them. On the other hand,

no volitional act of man takes place without being motivated in some way. Therefore, the more we know about the concrete situation of a person, the greater is the facility and certainty with which we can predict his behavior.

65 R. B. Cattell, *Personality: A Systematic, Theoretical and Factual Study* (New York: McGraw-Hill, 1950), 662-663. On the nature and limitations of the prediction of human behavior, cf. Gordon W. Allport, *The Nature of Personality: Selected Papers* (Cambridge, Mass.: Addison-Wesley Press, 1950), 63-65.

66 After pointing out the difficulties of passing from the premises to the final conclusions, Freud gives this objective justification of the case: "It is very easy to account for this disturbing state of affairs. Even supposing that we thoroughly know the 'etiological' factors that decide a given result, still we know them only qualitatively, and not in their relative strength. Some of them are so weak as to become suppressed by others, and therefore do not affect the final result. But we never know beforehand which of the determining factors will prove the weaker or the stronger. We only say at the end that those which succeeded must have been the stronger. Hence it is always possible by analysis to recognize the causation with certainty, whereas a prediction of it by synthesis is uncertain." "Psychogenesis of a Case of Homosexuality in a Woman," *Collected Papers* (1950), Vol. II, 226.

67 G. W. Allport, *The Nature of Personality*, 64.

68 Y. R. Simon, "On the Foreseeability of Free Acts," *New Schol.* (1948), 22, 357-370. Regarding the relationship between freedom and prediction of human actions, N. Mailloux writes: "Creativeness and originality, which are the characteristics of free activity, were confused with indeterminacy, freedom came to be synonymous with unpredictability and was discarded from the realm of science. Free behavior, far from being unpredictable, is the most predictable, but not predictable in the same way as behavior which is the result of a deterministic process, or of a repetition compulsion. Confronted with a difficult and problematic situation, the man who is really free is the only one who is entirely reliable, the only one capable of making the right choice and executing it." "Psychic Determinism, Freedom, and Personality Development," *Canad. J. Psychol.* (1953), 7, 8.

CHAPTER SEVEN

The Meaning of Personal Freedom

In the preceding chapter we considered the *foundation* of personal freedom. Let us now examine its *meaning*.

Our analysis of the experimental data shows that the various factors which emerged seem to concur more or less directly in establishing the existence of freedom. It seems opportune now to discover which of these factors plays a more direct part in the concept of freedom and which of them best defines its nature. This will be determined to the extent that it proves possible to establish the prevalence, or even the exclusiveness, of some of these factors. To arrive at the understanding of the meaning of personal freedom, it will be necessary to examine the various points in question and to see which of the following alternatives must be accepted or excluded.

The following questions will be discussed in this chapter: (1) *autonomy and self-determination,* that is, whether human freedom must be considered as a simple phenomenon of autonomy (which all living organisms enjoy in different degree), or a process of self-determination proper to human activity; (2) *completion of action and creative power,* that is, whether freedom must be understood as the conclusion or the final stage of an action or whether it implies the idea of a creative power; (3) *freedom and process of liberation,* that is, whether freedom resolves itself into a process of liberation or whether it presupposes the initial capacity of acting freely; (4) *conditioning of human freedom,* that is, whether man's freedom has an absolute character or admits of various degrees according to the greater or less influence of the factors that condition human activity. *A personalistic synthesis of the data of experience* will follow in order to embrace in an overall view the most characteristic and most essential elements of free human activity.

1. Autonomy and Self-Determination

One of the essential characteristics of living organisms is what may be called their capacity for "autonomy." This means that the organism does not represent simply an inactive point, in which various causal chains operate, but also an entity which, in a broad sense, governs itself. The biological process is not the result of external forces but is dominated principally by specifically biological, internal factors. The organism itself is the cause of its functions because it is endowed with spontaneity. A. Angyal writes:

> "We could say that the organism possesses a certain degree of 'freedom,' if we use the term in the sense of Spinoza and call free that which acts according to its own inherent nature, according to its intrinsic law, and not under the compulsion of exogenous forces." [1]

The freedom of which Angyal speaks is "biological," not "psychological."

The fundamental difference between these two kinds of freedom will become immediately clear if we consider that their essential characteristics are completely opposed to each other. With the process of *liberation*—as we can observe it especially in clinical experience—psychological freedom increases its efficiency. Biological freedom, on the contrary, decreases with the progress of organismic development. In the biological process, as well as in the physical, the result is determined. But it is not restricted to a single possibility; it has a range of possibilities. Moreover, every choice serves to reduce the future possibilities of an autonomous development. The course of life proceeds from a lesser determinism to a greater one; that is, from greater to less biological freedom.

Henry A. G. Murray, in his studies of personality, found that the characteristics of an autonomous character are very strongly pronounced. An autonomous individual resists any form of external influence or coercion, challenges authority and, in case of trouble, looks for freedom elsewhere and fights for independence. Under the title *Autonomy-Freedom,* Murray regroups the various types of action that would constitute the expression of freedom: mobility, breaking the rules, non-conformity, independence, irresponsibility, hatred for social customs and habits, fight for freedom.[2] Truly, there is nothing here which specifically characterizes human freedom. But the power of self-determination seems to be implicit in the description given. In fact, we cannot understand how a simple *organismic autonomy* could be the reason, for example, underlying such a process as the evasion of social customs and habits.

a. The Characteristics of Self-Determination

Two different factors are present in man's behavior. The acts of each individual can be either impulsive or intelligent. Impulse and intelligence exhaust the entire field of human activity. Each has a very different possibility of development: the manifestations of impulse are very limited and uniform, those of intelligence extremely broad and various. The power of acting rationally is volition. As intelligence rises from lower to higher levels, so volition progressively becomes self-determination. In other words, volition continues to increase until it becomes freedom. Therefore it can be said that while impulse is associated with autonomy, intelligence is associated with self-determination.

Another essential criterion for distinguishing the two processes of autonomy and self-determination is the presence or absence of a conscious state in the subject.[3] Self-determination implies the *highest level of consciousness,* the only level on which deliberation and choice can take place. The more freedom man enjoys the more conscious he is of his decision, i.e. the more light he has to illumine his path in life.[4]

Spontaneity, in so far as it is distinct from mechanical movement, characterizes life. This spontaneity can manifest itself in three degrees of activity: *reflexive* activity, *instinctive* or *impulsive* activity, and *pure spontaneity,* which is true initiative. The first two degrees of activity contradistinguish inferior life forms and distinguish them from human life. The third degree emerges in man, but its manifestation includes simultaneously all the others, and rarely exhibits itself in a pure form. True initiative is intelligent, and volition is initiative. Freedom of the will is intelligence in exercise.

Thus we understand the peculiar quality of conscious volition as it manifests itself, for instance, in a moral crisis. The peculiarity of the phenomenon consists in this, that while we feel attracted in one direction, in reality we choose to go in another. The true meaning of this phenomenon escapes us completely if we consider it a mere conflict of impulses and not a conflict of motives present in the consciousness of the individual. What characterizes conscious volition is the ego imposing itself on the impulse, the ego which creates, the ego which acts as a cause. Horace G. Wyatt writes:

> "The whole significance of human behavior is completely missed, as modern psychology persistently misses it, by overlooking this simple truth: man can cause. Man can create his own motive, can move himself to action, in disregard of the motives by impulse." [5]

Common sense has always insisted that we have the "power of self-determination" and that we use it in every voluntary choice.[6] It is interesting to recall here Luther's expression at the Diet of Worms: "Ich kann nicht anders," which is to say, "Since I am what I am, I must do as I do." Actually both the alternatives with which Luther was confronted appear objectively possible. In effect, the decision was for Luther himself a case of determination—a determination in defiance of the threat of death that his enemies held over him. James Ward asks, "Was he free? Not absolutely free certainly, since he was forced to choose, but free in the sense that the decision was made by him and not for him. It was a case of determination, indeed, but it was self-determination. And this, for psychology at any rate, is all that internal freedom means." [7]

The free act is not the mere result of a process which is determined by physiological and environmental factors, but it implies from its very start a process of self-determination. This process presupposes the reality of an ego-in-action, which is indeed the main outcome of all the experimental investigations on voluntary activity.[8] The central fact on which the whole discussion of the problem of free will hinges is precisely this: *the active interposition of the ego*. We know by experience that certain psychic processes are not free (dreams, for instance) exactly in the same way that we know that other processes are free. The non-free processes happen without deliberation and consent, and independently of them. But free processes depend on voluntary deliberation and consent. The data of experience, both clinical and experimental, show that when man is confronted by various motives in conflict, he frequently exercises the power to decide in favor of one of them by an act of self-determination. This power of self-determination precisely constitutes psychological freedom. In short, controlled laboratory experiments confirm the common sense concept of freedom of the will and better illustrate its profound dynamism.[9]

Self-determination may have a two-fold meaning. It may indicate the *freedom of indifference,* which considers the will in an abstract way as pure sovereign power independent of any circumstance, or the *freedom of choice,* which by no means prescinds from the motivation of a concrete personality.

The indetermination which one must introduce into the concept of freedom has nothing in common with that other indetermination which characterizes freedom of indifference—the choice without reason, or will without motives. Freedom of indifference is nonsense; the opposition between freedom and determinism is also nonsense. The true alternative to determinism is not freedom of the will, but indeterminism, which implies chaos, unforeseeability, and denial of the cause-effect relationship in human events. We could say with Igor Caruso [10] that determinism and indeterminism are "two totalitarian positions," neither of which can be applied as such to man's free activity.

Human freedom is not complete indeterminism; it is rather the intentionality of determinism. Both deterministic and indeterministic psychology ignore the real man. Man cannot be identified with animals or with pure spirits. He is spiritualized in his most animal passions; but he is also determined in his highest spiritual functions. He is neither a sublimated animal nor a repressed angel. His animality is not a pure animality. His spirituality is not that of a pure spirit. Therefore self-determination, which constitutes the essence of freedom, cannot but be relative. Only the Absolute Being is capable of absolute self-determination.

b. The Modalities of Self-Determination

Two problems are associated with the modality whereby free choice is actualized; *when* the psychic phenomenon of self-determination occurs, and *how* it occurs. The problem of "when" concerns determination of the moment in which freedom expresses itself; the problem of "how" concerns the definition of the modality by which free activity manifests itself.

As Roland Dalbiez [11] observes, the problem of the moment of freedom, although extremely important, is seldom discussed by psychologists. *When* are we free? Are we free at *the moment* in which we make our choice or *before that moment?* According to one theory, which we may call *presentism,* we are free at the very moment in which we make our choice. At that instant in which we decide, we take sides in a definitive way for one of the alternatives. At this moment indetermination disappears. If we admit this, we must recognize that freedom is reconcilable with some kind of determination.

According to another theory, which can be called *futurism,* we are free not at the moment of choice, but only *before it.* This theory speaks of freedom only in so far as it is related to the future. Such freedom would be equivalent to indetermination. This concept is a dangerous one because the very act of choosing would make freedom disappear.

Thus the problem of the moment of freedom can have two fundamentally opposed solutions. For *presentism,* to be free is to choose; for *futurism* to be free means that we have not yet chosen. Since for us freedom is identified with self-determination, we accept *presentism.*

It is often said that volition takes place when a voluntary choice is preceded by a process of deliberation which implies effort or delay. According to Claparède, "Every . . . voluntary act results from a conflict of tendencies, and the function of the will is precisely to resolve this conflict." [12] Such a conflict is an evident sign of a division in personality. Every act of the will, then, is a reaction of one part of personality. It is the duty of the will to act as a bulwark against such a division and to rebuild the unity of mental activity.

The psychic state, characterized by conflict and therefore by volitional effort, is certainly common. But contrary to what many think, such a state is not essential to voluntary activity. The ordinary experience of freedom occurs without anxiety and often without any trace of hesitation and effort. It is only in the presence of a serious psychic disturbance that we find the kind of freedom conjoined with anxiety which many contemporary authors discuss. The path followed by Maine de Biran and William James, as well as by a certain type of voluntaristic experimental psychologist, follows the exception to the rule. Effort does not tell us what our action is, but only its relative failure in certain cases.[13]

Horace G. Wyatt has investigated the problem of whether the conflict among impulses, besides being frequent, is also a necessary and universal condition of choice. He says that the essential condition of free choice is not the coexistence of various impulses, but the presence in consciousness of various possibilities of action.[14] The lack of conflict, as well as the presence of it, can be favorable to the process of choice. Impulses, in fact, can diverge and converge. Francis Aveling [15] warns against confusing "volition" with "conation" or experience of effort. Effort often accompanies the act of choice, but effort and selection are not the same. Effort is not a function of volition. Every volition implies some effort, but effort does not depend on the intensity of volition; it depends only on physiological factors.

As the most recent psychological research has demonstrated, there can exist authentic acts of voluntary decision which do not entail any effort and are performed even with pleasure and enthusiasm. The feeling of fatigue which is experienced in the exercise of the will, and the feeling of pain and effort which is experienced in making a decision, are signs of a maladjusted and psychologically non-integrated person. This is the conclusion I arrived at in research on the process of voluntary choice in psychotherapeutic counseling.[16] When self-determination is particularly difficult, this means that the individual is either in a permanent state of maladjustment or in a momentary condition of confusion and emotional disturbance. The more a person increases his power of self-perception and self-control, the easier it is for him to perform an act of preferential choice. It follows that for a perfectly integrated and adjusted personality, the selective acts become very natural and can be actualized without any internal effort.

A man who is well-adjusted and integrated experiences the feeling of a deep peace of soul when performing his actions. He is sure and calm in his evaluation of the possible choices. He is decisive, without being impulsive; prudent, without being excessively hesitant in assuming responsibility for his actions. Therefore the theory of volitional effort, in so far as it concerns conscious determination as the modality by which the act of decision is carried out, loses much of its importance. I think it is a mistake to believe that the feeling of internal effort is an element which characterizes the highest type of decisions. Actually, effort is neither essential to voluntary choice, nor does it manifest man's true creative "fiat." Effort is characteristic of a type of decision which is not welcomed by the subject, and therefore the feeling of effort is a sign of an imperfect volitional act.

2. Completion of the Act and Creative Power

Self-determination cannot be reduced to a final act, to a last "fiat," which would suddenly arise in the midst of a difficult situation where a decision has to be taken. The act of self-determination is never, by itself and for itself, without any relationship to previous conscious states. Whatever the chaos of indecision and the abruptness of choice might be, self-determination does not create a new kind of consciousness. Even though self-determination enters suddenly into the picture of indecision, this sudden change springs from a consciousness which wills. The appearance of self-determination does not change things; the will, which existed before the act of self-determination, does not disappear or become null after it. With the act of decision I do not cease to exist as body and spirit, as a rational and a volitive being, and at the same time as a "situated" person. In this sense, voluntary choice can be said to be practically a continuation of the preceding situation, or a completion of the activity. Free decision is not an absolute self-determination, nor is it a spontaneous appearance without any relation to the preceding psychological state of consciousness. It is merely a new element which has its roots in a pre-existing situation.

How does this binding of the new to the old come about? Various authors rightly accentuate the preeminent role of *attention* in this process.[17] The entrance of attention into the picture is very decisive. The study of *attention* as an active characteristic of perception contains the fundamental answer to the problem of the change from hesitation to choice. Attention is not one power among many which consciousness possesses; it is consciousness itself in relation to the reality on which it focuses. The type of determination which is based on more logically connected reasons and that based on feelings less reducible to intellectual maxims both adhere to the deliberate action of the subject. The individual, who sometimes depends on one kind of deliberation and sometimes on the other, regroups the various forces into one value, acts upon the confused elements, and transforms them into distinct values. *Attention* gives a common freedom to the most disparate forms of motivation: that of feeling and that of reason.

Choice appears to be always a *completion* or *maturation* of what attention has already prepared; but choice appears also as a *break* with the past. At the very instant of decision, a twofold manifestation of activity and passivity can still be distinguished: a) the climax of maturation and b) the appearance of a new act. The phenomenon of choice is tied up with the preceding act of deliberation, of which it is the *conclusion;* and at the same time *choice inaugurates* the project of the act to come. If choice does not proceed from deliberation, what is the purpose of deliberation? If choice is not an original act, how can we be certain of the validity of self-reflection? Continuity and discontinuity, completion and origin, represent the two moments of freedom, one of which concerns the role of past deliberation and the other the novelty of the choice. These are two aspects of the problem, whose solution does not consist in their synthesis, but rather in their coexistence. It is in this that the paradox of freedom consists.

a. The Creative Factor in Human Nature

Free decision has its roots in the existential situation, and is conditioned by it. But at the same time it is also an essentially new act and cannot be considered as the mere product or result of the individual's situation. With the selective act another moment of my life begins. It is this latter aspect which interests an ever growing number of psychologists today. The creative factor in human nature (or whatever name may be given to it) represents the most positive conclusion of modern psychology. But such a result admits of notable differences of interpretation, differences similar to those we observed between autonomy and self-determination. I am of the opinion that an adequate explanation of this *creative process* cannot be given on the level of "motor-innervation," as Leonard T. Troland, for instance, tried to do,[18] but only on the level of decisions and free choice; in other words, on the level of true personal freedom.

A characteristic proper to man is his capacity to participate in the creation of attributes of emerging value which enrich his experience. It is this characteristic which makes him really "human" and gives an orientation to his activity. It is because of this characteristic, proper to man, that both the individual and mankind as such seem to follow an ever-ascending path of progress. The biologists point out that, as soon as the systems of organization become more complex and mixed, there is more probability of emergence and versatility. This psychophysical machine which is man has, according to C. J. Herrick,[19] "a certain field of freedom of action." His most evident characteristic consists in the "free and creative factor of mental activity"; his organization is realized by means of "intentional self-determination."

Man's choices have a range and a variety without equal in the scale of organisms. Even for the most objective observer, they are less foreseeable and more surprising, and the most creative (in the broad and improper sense) of any organism. "Man is a contributing party to his own actions and in this sense has free will."[20] The creative factor in man implies freedom of action. This concept has been well expressed by Henry Delacroix: "There is, then, at the roots of the will *the freedom of invention,* the freedom of a creative activity, of a power of Spirit. Freedom is not acted upon, it acts." [21]

In human behavior we must take into consideration the mingling of these three components: (1) cognitive activity, (2) motivation, and (3) executive action. All three must be considered in their dependence on the past and in their creative possibilities for the present.[22] The "present" element generates the flexibility and plasticity of human behavior and gives to it its constructive character. The "past" element is responsible for its continuity or its rigidity.

To the extent that the creative factor of the present prevails on the rigid factor of the past, there is less or greater possibility of acting freely. The cognitive activity in which motivation and behavioral forms are found is the reason for the novel and constructive character of human behavior.

b. Creative Power and Freudian Sublimation

An assertion by Kurt Goldstein [23] led me to examine to what extent we can speak of a creative factor in the Freudian system, and in what way this can be reconciled with the concept of sublimation proper to that system. Goldstein says that: "Freud . . . conceives of culture as a sublimation of repressed drives. This is a complete misapprehension of the creative trend of human nature."

Let us see whether the two concepts of sublimation and creative power are really opposed, or at least so different that we must exclude the latter from the Freudian system. It is difficult to arrive at a clear solution to the problem because so many interpretations of Freud's thought seem equally acceptable. And an examination of his own writings leaves us with the same difficulty.

In the psychoanalytic school "sublimation" is used to indicate a change in the method of satisfying desires. Such satisfaction is not sought according to the nature of the desires, but at a much higher, more socially acceptable level. For example, it is said that a person who becomes disillusioned in love, "sublimates" himself when he (or she) tries to find relief in some form of religious activity, or, generally speaking, in the form of broader social activities. The new activity is somehow a symbol of the satisfaction of the previous desire. This, in general, is sublimation. [24]

But we must note that sublimation covers two essentially different ideas, even though authors at times use the term interchangeably, a cause of considerable confusion. [25]

The first of these ideas is based to some extent on known facts which have been objectively established, and indicates substantially the transformation of a need into an activity of an utterly different nature. Even though certain pathological facts seem at first sight to favor the idea of such a transformation, precise and controlled evidence for its reality, based on direct observations, is not yet at our disposal. The second meaning of the term is associated mainly with the Freudian theory, which considers the higher psychic activities as such, in the last analysis, to be brought into being through sexual activity, and to be nothing but disguised manifestations of this activity. Sublimation is not real, but a disguised manifestation of more basic needs. In this case, it is no longer a question of the activation or stimulation of a pre-existing psychic function by a transformation or "displacement" of one type of psychic energy into another. Here the psychic activity itself is nothing but the creation of, or a form of, the libido. The higher activity is a way of escape created by the libido. In this case the higher activity is ultimately of the same nature as the libido itself. The logical conclusion from this idea is that all man's higher psychic activity is a "substitute" for sexual libido itself. Freud did not explicitly push these ideas to such extreme limits, but we find in his writings statements which can hardly be interpreted in any other sense.

To the extent that this concept represents the authentic thought of Freud, we can say with Kurt Goldstein that it shows a complete misunderstanding of the creative power of human nature. In contrast to Freud's theory, this power appears as the most positive and constructive in the sense that it stimulates the highest activities of man and produces cultural values, not by means of a transformation of sexual needs, but by means of an "actualization" of specific human potentialities. The objective fact of the opposition between two forms of development—that of human civilization and that of a lack of culture among animals—draws our attention to the dynamic factors that determine such a divergence. This forces us logically to reject the Freudian theory. The reason for this rejection is simply that "man is not only an animal." [26]

Let us attempt now to examine the validity of Maryse Choisy's assertion:

> All of psychoanalysis consists in passing from the conformism of the super-ego to the creative elan of the ideal of the ego. [27]

While many psychologists use the term "super-ego" and "ego-ideal" interchangeably, others prefer to give them a differential connotation. The term "super-ego" is used to indicate "the unconscious component" to which the function of censorship is assigned; that is, the admonition of the super-ego not to give in to the demands of the inferior "ego." The term "ego-ideal," on the other hand, is used preferably to indicate the "conscious component" to which the positive function of controlling and directing sexual needs towards constructive goals is assigned.[28]

Maryse Choisy pushes the distinction between the super-ego and the ego-ideal even further. To her mind, the ego-ideal is a central point around which scattered energies are condensed and put in order. In surmounting the impulses from one side, as well as the anachronistic rules of the super-ego and the psychic mechanisms and automatisms from the other, the ego-ideal achieves its own liberty. It is free to the degree that it conceives of itself as it is; or it moves, changes, and transforms itself in order to become what it thinks it is. "The 'ego-ideal' is a creator; the super-ego is a copyist." When we pass from the super-ego to the ego-ideal, "we pass from commandments to norms, from determination by others to auto-determination." [29]

Doubtless the distinction proposed by Choisy is tenable. But there are some reasons for doubting that this distinction actually corresponds to Freud's views, unless we are disposed to admit that the numerous inconsistencies and contradictions which various scholars find in his writings are true. Instilled with mechanistic prejudices concerning the physical universe, Freud attempted to demonstrate that even the psyche is a totality made up of automatisms and psychic mechanisms. But, from the moment that the psychic structure gains its independence from physiology, a passage is opened from matter to spirit. Here we cannot but agree with Choisy:

> "From the moment that he [Freud] recognized a reality proper to the psychic life, from the moment when he discovered by his patient method that man can also free himself from his mechanisms, Freud emerged towards a psychology open on all sides, even towards heaven." [30]

To the extent that Maryse Choisy's distinction between the super-ego and the ego-ideal represents the authentic thought of Freud, we can say that in his theory of human nature there is place for a true creative power, even though perhaps not in the highly accentuated form that we find, for example, in the clinical writings of Rank, Goldstein, and Rogers.

3. Freedom and Process of Liberation

The living subject as such is dedicated totally to the conservation of life. Man as a living subject conserves his tendencies; as a person he accepts them freely and tries to perfect them. He is not submerged in the world in which he is situated but, since he is so situated, man is always in danger of allowing himself to be overcome by the environment and to live for it. He feels, therefore, the need of defending himself against the materialistic element of his situation in order to safeguard his freedom.

The spontaneous movement of life is diametrically opposed to that of the person. As a consequence of this opposition, there is in man a continuous conflict between the *personal principle* and the *vital principle*—not a conflict between two different beings, but within the same being, which feels itself divided within itself. The inferior principle would like to subject the spiritual forces to its service. The person, on the contrary, feels the need of disengaging himself from the vital element by subordinating it to his essential goals.[31]

There is in us initial freedom; but freedom must also be acquired. Freedom is at the same time the *instrument* and the *goal* of moral life. To be free, in the moral sense, means to choose only the good. Thus the problem that every man has to solve is that of acquiring freedom by discovering the moral values and dedicating himself to their realization, and by assuming his own responsibility in the society of which he is a part. Under this aspect, freedom is a *process of liberation,* a tending toward an ideal which can never be realized completely.

This liberating activity may function on three different levels of human experience: (1) *on the spiritual level:* liberation through grace, which finds in the writings of St. Augustine perhaps its most significant expression; (2) *on the existential level:* the urgency and progress of liberation as found in the reflections of Jaspers and Marcel; (3) *on the psychological level:* liberation from the experiences repressed in the unconscious, which the Freudian analytic method elucidated. It is this last method which interests us here in our attempt to define the distinction and the relationship between freedom and liberation.

a. Positive Interpretation of the Freudian System

There is no other psychological theory which draws attention to the concept of liberation as frequently as that of Freud. What is the precise meaning of this term in Freud's writings? In a preceding chapter we examined the psychological determinism of the Freudian system. The result was a negative picture of man's freedom. Many authors have interpreted Freud in this sense, and such really seems to be the interpretation which is more in conformity with his explicit assertions. But some authors believe that it is legitimate to consider Freudian thought in a much more positive manner. The true problem, then, is that of determining whether the assertions of Freud in general and his open denial of free will in particular are elements essential to the analytic method, or whether they are only expressions of a personal sentiment which seems rather inconsistent with the Freudian system itself. This latter point of view is held by two authorities of the psychoanalystic school, Gregory Zilboorg and Maryse Choisy.

According to Zilboorg, the schematic representation of the Freudian system would not seem to contradict, in any way at all, even the most rigid Thomistic tradition.[32] But he recognizes that such a scheme might be totally unacceptable in the face of the major objection against psychoanalysis: the problem of a psychological determinism which definitely rejects belief in human freedom. Zilboorg thinks that

> "To dismiss psychoanalysis despite the fact that so many objections to it which have been raised can be met with comparative ease, to dismiss it without further examination because it seems to be in conflict with the postulate of free will, means to disregard the fact which has been repeatedly stated and demonstrated in these pages, that psychoanalysis is not a philosophy, nor has it ever discussed seriously the question of free will." [33]

Prescinding from the last assertion (which seems to me very debatable), we can easily concede that the will cannot be free unless the organic and biological system (within which the human person is destined to develop) functions without the impediments which are termed neuroses or infirmities. We can even concede that the psychological determinism implied in the Freudian system "never went and never could go beyond the limited frame, the *closed system* of the psychic apparatus," but only on condition that many assertions of Freud be revised.

We agree with Zilboorg that Freud had a deep respect for human reason. He tried continually to free man's reason from the chains of a malfunctioning psychic apparatus. We can note also Freud's desire to assure man the true capacity of decision, which he believes impossible when the psychic apparatus is not fully integrated and harmonized. It could also be said (even though this already implies an evident incongruity) that, if psychoanalysis does not accept explicitly the postulate of free will, "it supports it by its striving to liberate man's reason and will from the frailties which his biological, and therefore psychological, imperfections impose on him in his daily life." [34] But we cannot go along with Zilboorg when he calls our attention to what he believes to be a very significant anecdote. One day, after Freud had been asked whether a man could be considered responsible for his dreams, he answered: "Who else would you like to consider responsible?" This reply does not offer, to my mind, any proof of man's personal freedom. The "responsibility" to which Freud is referring does not present the characteristics of "moral responsibility" as it is implied in free decision, but simply of "imputability," which demands for its existence a healthy psychic apparatus or, as Grasset would put it, a normal psychic neuron.

To Maryse Choisy's mind, superficial critics have complained too quickly of Freudian determinism because the psychological idea "to accept oneself" has been interpreted illogically by them as "resigning oneself." For the Freudian, "to accept" means to resolve by psychological integration a conflict which opposes the subject to himself or to a situation. Acceptance differs from pure and simple adaptation, for it is possible to adapt oneself otherwise than by a psychological integration, notably in a neurotic manner. Acceptance differs from resignation by its positive and constructive attitude. Choisy tries to make this clear:

> "Liberty is born when determinisms are totally integrated. Freudian determinism is the liberty to create by starting out from mechanisms known and accepted." [35]

What is the meaning of freedom in the passage just quoted?

Does it indicate perhaps a conscious activity, a final process of liberation, a free decision? It is by no means evident that this is the meaning. And the doubt becomes even stronger when we read almost immediately afterwards:

> "Thus it is only when the handling of a car has become automatic that the driver can freely find the proper rate of speed to avoid the accident at a dangerous curve."

This is undoubtedly true. But what does this comparison mean if we apply it to free human activity? It seems to me the opposite of what Maryse Choisy intimates. In fact, to the extent that an action becomes automatic, it ceases to be free.

At any rate, Choisy justifies Freud's psychological determinism because by it he attempted to demonstrate the laws which regulate psychic mechanisms. She admonishes us not to let ourselves be deceived because "psychoanalytical treatment always wishes to prove freedom, and sometimes it does arrive at Freedom." [36] Evidently the concept of freedom is here identified with that of liberation. In order that freedom, understood as liberation, may make a positive contribution to our problem, it must lead the neurotic person to act in the same way as a normal man. This presupposes in man a fundamental capacity to choose among different possibilities of action, a personal power of self-determination. For this reason, the following statement of Choisy is evidently improper: "We are not born free; we become free." [37] It is only just to note that Choisy recognizes the deficiency of such a statement. We must point out, however, that in her writings the step she takes from the concept of liberation to that of freedom is illogical.

b. Freedom in the Framework of the Psychoanalytic Process

As we have seen, the problem of freedom in the Freudian system presents two opposite trends of interpretation. One trend claims that psychic determinism does not leave room for freedom. The other holds that, notwithstanding Freud's explicit denials, psychoanalysis leaves the door open to free human activity. This latter position is that held by Zilboorg and Choisy, among others. There is also a third interpretation which lies between these two. It attempts to reconcile psychological determinism and freedom of action in the framework of analytical procedure.

According to Robert H. Jokl,[38] the general idea of psychic determinism is specifically meaningful for psychoanalysis in so far as it is connected with the principle of free association, which, in turn, is technically anchored in the so-called "basic rule." This rule is the acceptance of the principle of causality in the psychic apparatus, which principle is a fundamental presupposition in every psychic event. It is not without good reason that Freud ascribed so decisive an importance to the *basic rule,* since it is quite evident that the central position assigned to free association is the critically distinctive characteristic of classical analytic procedure or, in other words, that which makes analysis analysis.

The fundamental importance of psychic determinism, according to Jokl, is manifested clearly in free associations. He does not believe that problems such as the relative freedom of the will can be linked to them, although it is precisely analysis which guarantees this freedom within the limits of possibility. Jokl thinks that psychic causality (in psychoanalytic procedure) constitutes not only a particular dynamic factor but represents also one of the regulative powers which maintain the preservation of balance between the psychic instances. The ego can be strengthened and can develop sublimations which at first were not apparent in outline, but only if one grants to the ego the time and the freedom to transfer itself. Jokl adds that this freedom is granted to the ego only in the classical and unmodified form of psychoanalysis. Psychic determinism as represented in the psychoanalytic method through the principle of free association leads to a therapeutic impact only where the psychic order is disturbed. Thus psychic causality may be viewed as a means which protects the ego from unwelcome disturbances. Jokl concludes by saying that "classical psychoanalytic procedure, because of its distinctive tendency to use psychic determinism in a special manner, is capable of giving to the ego formation a certain degree of *autochthonous* freedom somewhat like a right to self-determination." [39]

Robert H. Jokl's attempt to reconcile, within the classical analytical procedure, psychic determinism with man's free activity, leaves us perplexed and unsatisfied. Conceivably this reconciliation could assure to the individual a process of liberation, but not a true freedom of choice. What leaves us even more perplexed in Jokl's interpretation is that the "freedom of transforming oneself" is not a power common to all persons, but only a privilege of those who show psychic disturbances. What kind of freedom does Jokl's position assure to man? The "autochthonous freedom" which he speaks of seems to be only a type of that "organismic autonomy" which was mentioned previously. This freedom, since it can exist only where the psychic order is disturbed, has a rather negative function and cannot therefore explain human behavior satisfactorily.

In conclusion, it seems to me that neither Jokl nor Zilboorg and Choisy are convincing. None of them has shown that there is room in the Freudian system for psychological freedom in the proper meaning of the word. For them freedom becomes simply liberation. It could be said that liberation presupposes freedom. But this is an objection against Freudian doctrine and not an element in its favor. It is evident that there cannot be a *true process of liberation if the existence of an initial liberty in man is not presupposed*. Freud— and with him many other psychologists and psychiatrists—insists very strongly on the process of liberation of the patient, but by no means does he presuppose, in fact he even explicitly denies, this indispensable initial freedom. This is an incongruity, or better, a contradiction in the Freudian system.

Maryse Choisy acknowledges this contradiction and believes herself able to solve the question by saying that "Freud corrects Freud." [40] But the "correction" seems to me very partial and imperfect. The psychoanalytic theory partially corrects psychic determinism with its stress on the process of liberation, but by no means does it assure a true personal freedom.[41] Choisy (who is an eminent analyst) speaks of a paradox in the Freudian system: *the paradox of denying the freedom which seems to be essential in the analytic process*.[42] It seems to me that we must speak of contradiction rather than paradox: *the contradiction of admitting a process of liberation without presupposing an initial freedom*. A paradox presupposes the coexistence of elements which seem incompatible. We have noted the paradox of self-determination, which implies the coexistence of determinism and freedom. There would be a paradox in the Freudian system if it would admit freedom and determinism at the same time. But for Freud there is no freedom, there is only liberation.

4. Limitation of Human Freedom

Volition is not an isolated phenomenon. Freedom implies prerequisites: every decision or voluntary choice in fact presupposes the existence of motives.[43] These motives—as we have previously seen—do not really determine human behavior; they merely condition it. Suggestion, unconscious needs, heredity and environment —including among them the physiological constitution and pathological condition of a person—can be considered as elements of its "motivation" in the broad sense of the word. To the extent that they influence man's activity without reaching the conscious level, they constitute what can be called the "conditionism" or the "limitations" of human freedom.[44]

It is superfluous to say that we are speaking here of freedom from the psychological point of view and do not intend to speak of those limitations of freedom that result, for instance, from the lack of the "four political and social freedoms." The lack of some or all of these freedoms constitutes an increase rather than a limitation of psychological freedom. The execution of a choice is not an essential element of the act of self-determination. Therefore those who are deprived of political freedom or are in prison are psychologically free, because they can "decide" to live in liberty. It would be a mistake to confuse the fact of freedom with its concrete imperfect actualization.

a. *Essential Conditions for Free Activity*

Certain conditions are required in order that the free act exist. Such conditions are those which are proper to a person living in a concrete situation. They fall into the following three components of human behavior: *cognitive activity, motivation,* and *executive action.* Motivation belongs with the other two components because it limits them differently in the various circumstances of life; but it presupposes not only their existence, but also and mainly their real efficacy.

The living being is capable of freedom in virtue of cognition and volition. Man's cognitive power limits and defines what he is capable of doing. Volition is therefore limited by the degree of knowledge which is actually present. No one, in fact, can perform a voluntary act if he does not first conceive it in his mind; and no one can act according to a principle if he is not at least capable of understanding it. Some individuals are more capable than others both in understanding and initiating new forms of behavior. Intelligence without volition is impotent; but volition without intelligence is impossible. Horace G. Wyatt is right when he says that "the will is free in proportion as intelligence directs volition." [45]

Intelligence and will thus reveal themselves in their capacity as correlative principles as well as essential conditions of free human activity. It is true that some controversies on the value of these functions seem to give the impression of excessive indulgence towards abstractionism. But it would be unjust and erroneous to say that the Scholastics considered free choice as a power of action which prescinds from concrete reality. They recognize that our will is immersed in a world of feelings, instincts, passions, and sensual and spiritual desires. [46] The will is solicited on all sides; it is weak, yet it loves and desires every type of good. In the process of liberation, the intellect sees that each particular good, since it is particular, is good under one aspect and not under another; it is convenient and at the same time inconvenient for a person who by nature tends toward an infinite good.

Free activity is subjected also to other conditions. One of the values proposed at the very beginning of the act may, in some situations, awaken feelings and images so vivid that the other value is kept outside our consciousness. This is a process which may depend both on the objective character of the stimulus and on the excitability of the experiencing subject. It may also happen that the awakening in the memory of another value encounters an obstacle because either the corresponding experience is not available or because, even though present and available, it is impeded from emerging. All these conditions do not indicate any extraordinary mental effort; in fact, it may happen that under very normal conditions we lose our freedom of choice. These conditions are not necessarily stable; it can happen therefore that—within the limits of a relatively short period of experience—we act freely at one moment and without freedom the next.

We must not forget, as Joseph Nuttin points out in an important study on human behavior, [47] the element of rigidity and predetermination that influences human behavior. The reason for this rigidity and predetermination must be sought in the fact that the three components of behavior (cognitive activity, motivation, and executive action) exist only in their dependence on the past. No behavior, in fact, is completely novel. Some behavioral responses and some perceptions of the outside world are integrated in the subject's dynamic system and are reborn spontaneously within it. The cognitive attitude, as well as the behavioral response, are, so to speak, "prefigured" to a variable degree in the organism that experiences a need, or in the personality that is pursuing a goal. The projects, the goals and the actual needs of a man are likewise already "prefigured" in some way in his antecedent actions and motivations.

The progressive elaborations of present behavior and its prefigurations in past behavior certainly constitute an element of rigidity, an element of *internal determination* of the behavioral process. This demonstrates that, if it be true that man does as he "wishes," it is also true that his motivation is modeled on what he does and on what he has done in the past. If it is true that his knowledge illumines and guides his motivation, it is also true that his motivation and his needs are the measure of his "openness" to the world and of his capacity for cognitive elaboration. Thus human behavior (and that is what it really is) appears as a process concretely situated between the reciprocal influence of the present and of the past, of the organism and of its environment.

b. The Limiting Action of the Unconscious

Jean Rimaud, considering the attitude of psychologists towards moral science, states the problem in clear terms:

> "In truth the ego is at the same time the subject of both the unconscious psychic phenomena and the conscious phenomena. There is a continuity and a reciprocal causality between the two lives, just as there is a constant link between the organic and the psychic. To build a theory of the moral conscience, as our professors of theology did, on the simple consciousness alone, is to give it a foundation which is too narrow. The true debate on liberty is whether the conscious ego is necessarily the product and the always incomplete and illusion-free expression of the unconscious, or whether we have, and to what extent we can build, given our unconscious, a conscious ego for which we will be responsible." [48]

An attempt to give a solution to this problem in the light of objective data was made in the preceding chapter. Keeping in mind the concluding thoughts, we can say that unconscious motivations do not necessarily determine human behavior; they merely condition it. If it is true that unconscious motivation exists and influences our conscious activity to a notable extent there is no proof that it totally eliminates the freedom of our voluntary decisions. In a remarkable study on determinism, Leon Noel rightly points out that "free choice is attenuated by suggestion, sometimes it is completely repressed; but from this one cannot conclude against the reality of its existence." And later the same author affirms: "Freedom is limited, perhaps imperfect; it is subject to numerous conditions, infirmities, and discouragements. Some will exercise it very rarely in its fullness of energy and intensity. However, it exists, and this is enough for us." [49]

The clinical material of psychoanalysis (prescinding from its theoretical conceptions and its pro and con interpretations in this regard) does not force a conclusion against freedom; it even suggests its affirmation. We know by experience that there is within each of us a hibernating beast, an unconscious personality, which can yet become active unless we maintain our system of control. This system of control can in rare instances be destroyed by disease, but it can also break down through our own infidelity to ideals.[50] Roland Dalbiez' statement is correct:

"Though man may be more reasonable than the psychiatrists believe, he is less so than the philosophers think." [51]

But merely because a great percentage of unconscious motivation is at the basis of human behavior, we cannot conclude that man lacks that minimum of freedom which is needed to make him responsible. We cannot confuse diminished responsibility with irresponsibility, nor must we confuse the circumstances which diminish freedom with those that abolish it completely.

Edward Cros, in a very interesting study on freedom and the subconscious, points out that it is man himself who creates his psychic automatism. He acts voluntarily, though indirectly, even when his automatism evokes some unconscious acts and influences conscious ones. Cros does not wish to say that a particular act, performed under the exclusive impulse of a subconscious element, is free; it cannot be free, since intellectual knowledge and will are lacking. But this does not exclude the influence of free will on the formation of the subconscious factor; hence relative responsibility follows even in this case.[52]

c. Constitutional and Environmental Limitations

Man's voluntary control starts from the simple domination of his movements and passes from this first goal to finalities that become always more remote, until the mind establishes its ideals and, through these, disciplines the entire course of life. What these ideals will be for each of us depends on our interests and desires. These latter, in turn, will depend partially on the kind of tendencies which we inherit and partially on the forces of our physical and social environment. James R. Angell warns that though "we may prate as much as we please about the freedom of the will, no one of us is wholly free from the effects of these two great influences." [53]

A simple examination of empirical data reveals the multiple character of the influences and limitations which act upon human life. In the pathological sphere we often encounter such psychic alterations as compulsive ideas, emotional blocks, repressions and prejudices. Psychopathology reveals an ever-increasing number of cases in which the individual is not able to control his actions. Studies on vestibular and neuro-muscular disturbances, and more importantly the experiments on hysteria, permit us to say that the same subject may be free at certain moments and may have lost, totally or partially, his freedom at other moments (e.g., in the state of drunkenness or under the influence of a drug such as opium). In a study on the problem of free choice in relation to physiology and medicine, George Bourguignon arrives at the conclusion that "freedom is conditioned by the integrity of the brain and has some limitations and degrees even in a normal man." [54]

Although not everyone suffers from pathological disturbance, the effects of the cultural and social environment in which one lives are nevertheless of considerable influence. Both in normal and pathological cases, the individual bears the weight of amorality and degeneration which society bears atavistically within itself. But J. Borel admonishes us that we must not attempt to find in society that false inheritance of the tendency to steal and the instinct to crime which was held without hesitation some time ago. He reminds us that "atavism or heredity transmits only general dispositions." [55] An eminent French psychiatrist, P. Grasset, equally reproaches Lombroso for having "made ancestral heredity play an exclusive role, or, at least a very exaggerated one, in the production of this criminal determinism. There are notably two important elements of which he does not take sufficient account, especially in his earlier works: morality and environment. Moral ideas, whether innate (hereditary) or acquired, education, instruction, example, have a very decided influence on the development of the criminal, which it would be childish to deny." [56]

Even though fully conditioned by physiological, psychological or social determinisms, human behavior can remain free because freedom, bound to conscious will, is not situated at the level of the determinism; it exists to a certain extent even in the most unfortunate man. But freedom is not the absurd possibility of doing everything we wish. We must behave as man and it is to biology that we must turn, in the final analysis, to define the concrete conditions of free human activity, to establish the objective bases of the notion of duty. Biology permits us to evaluate the automatism of an insane man and the possibility of choice of a normal man. "The problem of freedom," says P. Chuachard, "is clarified when we appeal to the objective data of biology in order to understand man." [57] This objective data is an essential element, but it is insufficient for an evaluation of human behavior.

It has often been said that the physique and morphology of a person determine his behavior and his character. Even a typologist like Kretschmer does not agree. He says that there is only some "correlation" between the specific physique on the one hand and the "style of life" as it shows through one's character on the other.[58] As for heredity it is commonly accepted by the best geneticists that illnesses are not inherited, but only dispositions to illness. And who today would go along with the founders of genetic determinism, who once asserted that heredity is everything? But we must leave room for environment, understood in the broadest and most comprehensive meaning of the term.

It is evident that identical twins have exactly the same heredity; but one of them might become a criminal genius and the other an eminent criminologist, even though both use the same amount of intelligence to reach their respective eminences. The different careers of the two are evidently not due to heredity. It is the environment which exercises a balancing influence on the development of attitudes and on the formation of habits. On the other hand, it would be equally erroneous to draw the inference that the behavior of a person is absolutely determined by his environment.[59] Experience proves in fact that, no matter how strong the hereditary and environmental influences might be, a person can sometimes act in a completely opposite manner. It is self-determination that intervenes in such a case and has its own way. The reason is that a man is not a mere aggregate of habits, or a machine which reacts in a fixed manner to the forces which act upon it. As long as man retains his system of control, he is always capable of an independent, creative, personal attitude.[60]

The phenomenon which William Stern calls the production of a "permanent setting-of-will" exists for human beings and for them alone.[61] The total specific structure of human personality is expressed very impressively in this behavioral form, "permanent setting-of-will." Certainly the past and the present (viz., heredity, experience and environment) play their part, but the act is something more than the mere product of the convergence of these extrapersonal factors. The act is made free by the additional factor which is revealed in this manifestation of the personality of an individual.

d. Human Conditionism and Transcendence

We ourselves develop our characteristic way of deciding and acting even though there are well-defined factors that influence our decisions. The individual who acts in conformity to the lower level of egoism, or to the more elevated level of altruism, or to the highest level of divinity, thinks in terms of what is good for him. We as rational beings recognize that the level of egoism is the lowest rung on the ladder of goodness. The correspondence of our decisions and activities to the higher levels of goodness expresses an elevating of oneself from the sphere of egoistic individualism. It is a kind of transcendence from ourselves to others, and from others to God.[62]

Men and things influence us in all those various modes—physiological or psychological, conscious or unconscious—that permit our organism to come into contact with the world. These modes of contact act upon us simultaneously and constitute that concrete situation which directly influences our way of acting. In our conduct the spiritual element is always only one component. There is no purely "spiritual" response or reaction to life situations; there is a "human" reaction. The influences of a situation on a subject, as well as his reaction, are spiritual and material at the same time, as is the subject himself. Under such conditions we may say that our activity is free to the extent to which the situation as well as the reaction are actualized as a function of the autonomous personality of the subject.

Man's psychological freedom does not exclude, but presupposes, the broad and complex dynamism of instincts, tendencies, psychophysical dispositions, acquired habits, and hereditary traits. It is at the highest point, where this dynamism emerges into the world of spirit, that freedom of choice is realized, in order to bestow or to refuse a decisive efficacy to the inclinations and to the needs of nature. It follows that freedom—and consequently—personal responsibility also—admits of a multiplicity of degrees of which only God can judge. But we cannot conclude from this that freedom does not exist. On the contrary, if freedom admits a multiplicity of degrees, this means that it does exist.

Freedom corresponds to that spiritual level which man attains by means of a personal elaboration of his potentialities. According to Joseph Nuttin, "freedom is not a static property of a few limited kinds of behavior. On the contrary, all human activity is characterized by a certain degree of freedom, i. e. a *varying degree of spiritual activity*." [63] Because human behavior is always more or less conditioned, it never reaches a degree of absolute freedom. It is precisely because of this character of relativity that human freedom is distinguished from divine freedom. And because of this conditionism, man's freedom leads us to transcend the sphere of the limited and contingent, to inquire after the meaning of unconditioned freedom, and not remain at the mere existential level of a contingent being.

5. Personalistic Synthesis of the Data of Experience

We have seen in the introduction to this present study that human behavior presents two phases, one internal and the other external. The internal phase reveals a "center of intentionality," which is the unifying principle of man's various operations and has its origins in a "subject" who is also a center of cognition, or of consciousness.[64] Consciousness is the activity of a knowledge which is essentially reflexive—the activity of a subject who returns upon himself. In some of our actions we are "actors" and "spectators" at the same time; we think and we know we are thinking. At this point consciousness becomes self-consciousness.

Consciousness does not exist to the same degree in all human activities. The highest degree of consciousness is reached in voluntary activity, which implies a discussion and a value-judgment on the various possibilities of action and the active intervention of the conscious subject to give or refuse his assent. Consciousness is the *conditio sine qua non* of voluntary choice.[65]

a. Phenomenology of Free Activity

When in a preceding chapter we analyzed the experimental research on volitive activity, we saw that an essential element of voluntary choice is the internal perception or the consciousness of the ego as the subject of the action. Although this experience has been interpreted differently by various authors, it indicated in every case the presence of the ego in the most intimate way. The ego, which is the witness of its own activity, appears as an extended body and as a conscious spirit at the same time.

The reflective consciousness that man has of his own self is made up mainly of sensibility; it is awakened and maintained only in the framework of sensory experience. The senses are organic; their action is only a reaction to the stimulus which comes from physical, external reality. For this reason the ego reveals itself as an ego-in-the-world. The ego is understood and affirmed only in its active and passive relationships with the physical environment. Consequently, the link which joins the ego to material reality is a constitutive element of its structure. The ego finds itself necessarily immersed in what is essential to matter, time and space. Thus every consciousness is consciousness of a "situated" ego in relation to some other thing which appears in time and space.

The followers of the existentialist trend in psychology point out rightly that man's behavior is a function of his "situation." No one can see exactly what I see. My point of view differs from any other's; it varies at every moment because I live in time and do not cease to change. But I know that my behavior depends on each situation. I judge it from a point of view which is not identified with it. I escape its limits. I am aware of continuing, of keeping my identity through the moments that succeed in time and through the various situations that change in space. Evidently, some physical changes take place in my organism. Physiologically I am not at all the same individual that I was ten, twenty years ago. Even psychologically I can be very different. But I know that essentially I am the same person. I feel different and identical at the same time: I recognize the essential identity of my personality in all phases of my development and in all expressions of my conscious processes.

The consciousness of oneself does not include cognition only; it identifies itself with the concrete ego which implies also other kinds of activity. In fact, consciousness is the living, real ego, the ego "situated" in the world, which fully and completely as a whole is elevated to the level of consciousness.[66] The consciousness of oneself concerns both the volitive and the cognitive function at the same time. Internal freedom arises at this level of life. Voluntary choice is characterized as an act of free activity in the sense that it is not predetermined by external forces or by internal motives, but is made by a "subject" that acts according to a process of conscious self-determination. This process is undoubtedly an immediate datum of the personal experience of each individual and, as such, it belongs (at least in order of time) first of all to the phenomenological analysis of human experience, and then to philosophical research.

In this experience there are two components: (1) "personality," which activates a series of psychic functions, and (2) the "series" itself of such functions. These two components exist in such a relation between themselves that one is the subject and the other the object of experience. This subject-object relationship can be designated by the terms "I" and "Me"; but it cannot be identified with the dualism of mind and body, nor as the distinction between the "ego" and the "external world," as Wundt does.[67]

Psychology is not called to transcend the relationship of the subject to the object as an immediate datum of experience. On the other hand, the attempt to ignore one of the two terms of the relationship is made in vain, and vain also is the attempt—as James Ward has rightly observed—to avoid the implications of a conscious subject.[68] Personality, even at the level of psychological experience, is not only a group of activities, but a whole, a functional whole, a psychosomatic unity.[69]

We could go even deeper and ask whether there is a "substrate" upon which the various activities of man are based and from which they have their origin. He who would try to define the nature of this psycho-physical unity would find the true "human person" at the roots of the "personality" of the individual.[70] We could say therefore that man's freedom expresses itself through the manifestations of his personality, but it is realized through a "power-substrate" which is proper to his person. But here the psychologist as such comes to a halt in his research and allows the philosopher to carry on.

b. Personalistic Character of Freedom

The concept of *unity* and *totality* must be considered as fundamental in the study of man. His psychosomatic complexity resists any analytical study and any mechanical assimilation. An "integral" theory of personality must treat both the physical and the psychic aspect of the total individual.[71] Psychic functions are in a relation of real dependence on the organic functions. There is no interior act which does not have its physical correlate, no idea without an image, no volition without an emotion. But the organic aspects of human activity are re-elaborated and fused in the personal experience.

The subjective factor in man is the unifying principle of his many activities into a vital synthesis. Among the components of this synthesis, the emotional and affective traits are of vital importance for man's conduct. Emotion must not be considered as a simple concomitant of the dynamic states of the organism. Emotion, as a psychic phenomenon, has an interior content and has its origin in the structure of behavior, implying dynamic and intellectual processes. Emotional experience, as well as the affective states, exercises a great influence on the perceptions and judgments of man.

From this we can understand the impact of affectivity upon human behavior: every tendency which seeks to be satisfied, every activity, is accompanied in us by an affective vibration.

Affectivity joins the ego to the world, makes it aware of the universe. We judge good and evil men and things with our past and our present personality, that is with our entire personality. We never solve the problems of life with the cold clarity of exclusively intellectual principles. In a clash of impulses, such as the decision to choose between good and evil, the factors that play a role in this conflict include our virtues and our vices, our entire ethical background, the preceding decisions of acceptance or refusal of moral values; it involves the whole personality of an individual. Actually, man is always more profound, more unified and more pliable than he seems to be.[72]

The personalistic theory of freedom presented as the conclusion of this study, *implies a synthesis of rationality and intuition,* as well as *a synthesis of the intellective and volitive functions.*

In the complicated situations of life we are asked to solve numerous problems and make many decisions. It is absurd to think that reason can be our guide in all cases. Reason is too slow and too difficult to use. Often we do not have the necessary data or we cannot sufficiently simplify our problem so that we can apply the methods of reason. How, then, are we to behave? As mankind has, by using the capacities that we have: common sense, judgment and experience, and the power of intuition. As the scientist Irving Langmuir puts it, "we underrate the importance of intuition." [73]

Intuition is not a mere feeling; it is a knowledge through contact rather than through vision: a knowledge less precise than rational knowledge, but more immediate and more comprehensive. The data of experience reveal that there are cases in which decisions seem to be taken unconsciously. It is not possible in such cases to ascertain whether a process of deliberation had effectively taken place in the mind of the subject. Perhaps a conscious deliberation was lacking, as it is understood commonly in the case of a "rational" choice; but there can be an act of immediate valuation which is realized in an "intuitive" choice.[74] In such a case the individual does not need to weigh rationally the proper value of each alternative. Deliberation and decision, then, are not phases really distinct from the process of choice. The self-determination of the subject, following an intuitive apprehension of reality, can express a perfectly voluntary and conscious choice, even though this choice might not be rationally elaborated.

An intuitive understanding represents an immediate evaluation of the alternatives of choice. This evaluation might seem less clear and less logical than a deliberate evaluation, but it might in some cases be either the *only* possible or even the *best* possible under the circumstances. It is in this sense that the famous saying should be understood: "The heart has reasons that the mind does not know." Intuitive understanding can be considered a positive factor in the solution of the problem of freedom in so far as it presupposes an immediate evaluation of the motives of action, which is realized together with the "fiat" of the voluntary decision.

Decisions and free choices of a perfectly integrated person are often intuitive in character. The more a person has control over himself, the less is the effort of the deliberative process in regard to the decision to be made. In this sense it could be said, according to the Bergsonian view, that the most perfect choices are those without visible reasons. The perfection of a choice is inversely proportional to the length and difficulty of deliberation. The goal of the various forms of psychotherapy is precisely that of furthering the integrative development of the personality of an individual, of freeing him from psychic tension and therefore of facilitating his acts of decision, the exercise of his freedom.

Freedom, as a property of a rational being, comprises in its actual functioning both reason and will simultaneously. The free act develops from the basis of complex human motivation as the result of these two psychic functions intimately joined in a vital union. The concomitant presence of these two factors in every act of voluntary decision is undeniable. Man acts as the entire subject of the various dimensions of his personality. For this reason we must say that the *capacity of self-determination, of acting freely, belongs properly to man and not to his volitive function alone.* Human freedom is not the mere expression of a voluntary act; it is essentially the property of a person who determines himself in favor of a preferred value. Rudolf Allers is right: "The question of 'freedom of the will' is somewhat one-sided. It is not the will as a psychological function but the whole human person that is free."[75] The free act is the expression most typical of man, and it involves his entire personality.

We cannot accept, therefore, the opinion of Horace G. Wyatt, who maintains that "it is just when the man is not acting as a whole, just when the individual is divided against himself, that the fact of will, the act of volition, is most in evidence." [76] We said above that the characteristic of volition is not effort but initiative, and that the conflict among two or more alternatives is not essential for free decision. Thus we can go on to say that the more man behaves as a perfectly integrated unity, as a totality in complete harmony, the more he is capable of acting freely. This is not to imply that the act of free decision represents or expresses the whole man;[77] we wish only to say that the free act involves the activity of man as a total personality.

FOOTNOTES

[1] A. Angyal, *Foundations for a Science of Personality* (New York: Commonwealth Fund, 1941), p. 33.

[2] H. A. Murray, *Explorations in Personality* (New York: Oxford Univ. Press, 1938), p. 82 and p. 341. For a phenomenology of freedom in a sense identical to that which is described by Henry A. Murray, cf. G. Bally, *Vom Ursprung und von den Grenzen der Freiheit: Eine Deutung des Spiels bei Tier and Mensch* (Basel: Benno Schwabe, 1945). According to Bally, freedom is the possibility of developing the self into various forms. From the viewpoint of the spontaneous and autonomous activity of man, freedom is synonymous with the possibility of achieving the perfection of one's being in a manner always more varying and always less bound to stereotyped forms.

[3] This distinction is not found in those psychologists who reject a clear distinction between involuntary processes and voluntary activity. Among others, it is omitted for example by A. Bain, *The Emotions and the Will*, 3rd Ed., (New York: Appleton, 1888), p. 491.

[4] The following passage of A. D. Sertillanges seems to me to be very significant: "Qui oserait dire que la liberté est d'autant plus grande qu'elle est moins eclairée? Au contraire, plus on a de lumières pour se décider, plus on est libre, et si la lumière va jusqu'à l'évidence parfaite, le choix est fixé par la même dans la plus haute liberté, bien qu'il le soit infailliblement." *La Problème du mal. . .* (1951), p. 70. This assertion is in favor of the paradoxical thesis, upheld by some Scholastics, that to will freely and necessarily at the same time is possible.

[5] H. G. Wyatt, *The Psychology of Intelligence and Will* (London: Kegan Paul, 1930), p. 153. According to Charles Odier, the autonomy at-

tributed to one's developed moral consciousness and to the ego appears completely relative. It would be a mistake to consider such an autonomy as a "given fact" in the case of a neurotic, psychotic or normal person, since this autonomy is considered an "acquired" habit in psychology. *Les Deux Sources, Consciente et Inconsciente, de la Vie Morale — Etre at Penser,* 2nd Ed. (Neuchatel: Baconniere, 1947), pp. 241 ff. Odier is right when he speaks of the relativity of man's autonomy, but he is wrong when he holds that such autonomy is only an acquired element. The autonomy of the normal man, that is, his capacity for self-determination, is acquired and perfected, but essentially it is a "given fact" even though it is only initial and limited.

6 Cf. Albert Dondeine: "C'est précisément ce pouvoir d'autodétermination active que, de tous temps, on a appelé liberté. L'homme est libre pour autant qu'il est capable de se determiner soi même à agir ou ne pas agir, à agir ceci ou cela." "Approches du Mystère de la Liberté," *Rev. Intern. Philos.* (1948), 16, 23-44.

7 J. Ward, *Psychological Principles,* 2nd Ed. (Cambridge: Cambridge Univ. Press, 1920), p. 405.

8 H. Gruender, *Experimental Psychology* (Milwaukee: Bruce, 1932), p. 432; P. Ricoeur, *Philosophie de la Volonté: Le Volontaire et l'Involontaire—Philosophie de l'Esprit—*(Paris: Aubier, 1950), pp. 54-63.

9 Paul Ricoeur synthesizes the elements which constitute the essence of freedom as a capacity or power for decisions: "Decider c'est (1) projecter la possibilité pratique d'une action qui depend de moi, (2) m'imputer moi-même comme l'auteur responsable du project, (3) motiver mon project par des raisons et des mobiles qui 'historialisent' des valeurs susceptibles de legitimer." *Op cit.,* p. 81.

10 I. Caruso, "Pulsion et Liberté," *Psyche* (1949), 4, n. 30-31, 392; cf. R. P. Knight, *Determinism, Freedom, and Psychotherapy, Psychiatry* (1946), 9, 251-262: "That man is free who is conscious of the law that he obeys, who is capable of acting according to standards which he accepts," 25; N. Mailloux, "Psychic Determinism, Freedom, and Personality Development," *Canad. J. Psychol.* (1953), 7, 1-11; "Free activity, corresponding to the most perfect activity of which man is capable, is certainly the one in which less is left to indeterminacy and unpredictability," 8.

11 R. Dalbiez, "Le moment de la Liberté," *Rev. Thom.,* (1948), 48, 180 ff.

12 E. Claparède, "Does the Will Express the Entire Personality?" in *Problems of Personality* (New York: Harcourt, Brace, 1925), p. 40.

13 R. Ricoeur, *op. cit.,* p. 62; A. DeWaelhens, *Une Philosophie de la Volonté* (1951), pp. 420, 432.

14 H. G. Wyatt, *op. cit.,* p. 209.

15 F. Aveling, *Personality and Will* (Cambridge: Cambridge Univ. Press, 1931), pp. 89 ff.

16 R. Zavalloni, "Il Processo della Scelta Volontaria in casi di psico-

terapia centrata-sul-cliente," *Arch. Psicol. Neurol. Psichiat.* (1954), 15, 124 ff.

[17] C. Piat, *La Liberté:* I. *Historique du Probleme au XIX Siecle;* II. *Le Probleme* (Paris: Lethielleux, 1894-1895), I, pp. 251 ff.; J. Laporte, *La Conscience de la Liberte-Bibliotheque de Philosophie Scientifique* (Paris: Flammarion, 1947), pp. 141-160; P. Ricoeur, *Philosophie de la Volonté* (1950), *loc. cit.*, pp. 142 ff, 155 ff.

[18] L. T. Troland, *The Principles of Psychophysiology: A Survey of Modern Scientific Psychology, III, Cerebration and Action* (New York: Van Nostrand, 1932), p. 230

[19] C. J. Herrick, *George Ellet Soghill* (Chicago: Univ. Chicago Press, 1949), pp. 201 ff.

[20] H. Cantril, *The Why of Man's Experience* (New York: Macmillan, 1950), p. 161.

[21] H. Delacroix, *Les Grandes Formes de la Vie Mentale, Nouvelle Enciclopedie Philosophie,* 4th Ed. (Paris: Press Univ. France, 1947), p. 184.

[22] J. Nuttin, *Tâche, Réussite et Échec* (1953), pp. 456-465.

[23] K. Goldstein, *Human Nature in the Light of Psychopathology* (Cambridge: Harvard Univ. Press, 1940), p. 112.

[24] C. L. Musatti, *Trattato di Psicanalisi,* 2 Volumes, (Torino: Einaudi, 1949), Vol. I, pp. 225-229.

[25] For a clear exposition and critical evaluation of the Freudian doctrine on this topic, cf. J. Nuttin, *Psychoanalysis and Personality,* trans. George Lamb (New York: Sheed and Ward, 1953), pp. 45-57; 131-134, etc.

[26] J. H. Vander Veldt and R. P. Odenwald, *Psychiatry and Catholicism* (New York: McGraw-Hill, 1952), pp. 144 ff.

[27] M. Choisy, "Psychoanalysis and Catholicism," *Cross Currents* (1951), 3, 82.

[28] F. Alexander, *The Psychoanalysis of the Total Personality* (New York: Nerv. Ment. Dis. Publ.: 1946).

[29] M. Choisy, *loc. cit.,* 83. Jerome J. Hayden has attempted in a Thomistic context to draw a distinction between the super-ego and the ego-ideal: "La Formation Integrale du Sens Moral," *Psyche* (1949), 4, nn. 30-31, 347.

[30] M. Choisy, *loc. cit.,* 76. Even though Rudolf Allers has published a very profound criticism of the Freudian system, he recognizes "Freud's greatest and most unexpected achievement. He restored the knowledge of the leading role of the mind, the knowledge of the dominating place held by the soul in human nature. To do this was not his intention. He did not know that he was serving the rebirth of a truer conception of man's nature than he himself was ever capable of imagining." *The Successful Error: A Critical Study of Freudian Psychoanalysis* (New York: Sheed & Ward, 1940), pp. 259 ff.

[31] A. Brunner, *La Personne Incarnée: Etude sur la Phenomenologie et la Philosophie Existentialiste* (Paris: Beauchesne, 1947), pp. 191 ff.

[32] G. Zilboorg, *Mind, Medicine and Man* (New York: Harcourt, Brace,

1943), p. 330.

33 G. Zilboorg, *ibid.*, p. 333. It seems to me that Zilboorg's position is unconvincing. The problem of free will is not affected by Freudian determinism: "This question lies outside of psychoanalysis." *Sigmund Freud: His Exploration of the Mind of Man* (New York-London: Scribner's Sons, 1951), p. 112.

34 G. Zilboorg, *Mind, Medicine, and Man*, p. 334.

35 M. Choisy, "Psychoanalysis and Catholicism," *loc. cit.*, 81.

36 M. Choisy, "La Responsabilité Morale dans la Psychoanalyse de Freud," *Psyche* (1951), 6, n. 57-58, 498.

37 M. Choisy, *ibid.*, 499. Viktor E. Frankl has understood this essential point: that man, in order to actualize the supreme presupposition of existential analysis—the recognition and the observance of human and social duties on the part of each individual—needs not only a process of liberation but also a fundamental human capacity to perform a free act. He writes: "Existential analysis aims to bring the person to an understanding of his true life task, for with such understanding he will find it all the easier to cast off his neurosis. This 'freedom from' therefore comes before the 'freedom to,' the 'decision for' the life task." *The Doctor and the Soul: an Introduction to Logotherapy,* trans. Richard and Clara Winston (New York: Alfred A. Knopf, 1955), p. 203.

38 R. H. Jokl, "Psychic Determinism and Preservation of Sublimation in Classical Psychoanalytic Procedure," *Bull. Menniger Clinic* (1950), 14, 211.

39 R. H. Jokl, *ibid.*, 219.

40 M. Choisy, "Psychoanalysis and Catholicism," *loc. cit.*, 75.

41 I do not believe that an isolated passage of Freud, in which he seems to admit free self-determination in man, is sufficient to deny this affirmation. Cf. Freud, *The Ego and the Id* (London: Hogarth Press, 1927), p. 72: "After all, analysis does not set out to abolish the possibility of morbid reactions, but to give the patient's ego freedom to choose one way or the other."

42 M. Choisy, *Psychoanalyse et Catholicisme* (Paris, L'Arche, 1950): "La psychoanalyse est une psychologie génétique. Mais le déterminisme psychanalytique, plus encore que le déterminisme scientifique, se heurte à un paradoxe. Ce paradoxe est dans la négation même de la liberté. Pour nier la liberté il fault au moins la concevoir. Et comment la concevoir sans dépasser saussitot le déterminisme?" P. 66.

43 For a doctrinal exposition similar to the one delineated above, cf. A. Lehmen, *Lehrbuch der Philosophie au Aristotelich-Scholasticher Grundlage. Psychologie* (Freiburg: Herder, 1902), p. 442; for an opposite opinion, cf. N. Braunshausen, "Le Libre Arbitre à la Lumière de la Psychologie Experimentale et de la Science Moderne," *Rev. Sci. Pedag.* (1946), 8, 33-48; 75-96; (1947), 9, 8-23, 38-46; (1947), 87 ff.

44 A synthesis of the limitations on freedom is offered by John Lindworsky, *Theoretical Psychology,* trans. H. R. DeSilva (St. Louis, Mo.:

Herder, 1932), pp. 104-108. Concerning the criteria for knowing practically the limitations in the exercise of freedom, cf. the study of Agostino Gemelli on the responsibility of human actions from the viewpoint of psychology and psychiatry: *La Responsabilita delle Azioni Umane dal Punto di Vista della Psichologia e della Psichiatria-Contribui del Laboratorio di Psicologia,* Serie XII, (Milano: Vita e Pensiero, 1944), 211-273.

[45] H. G. Wyatt, *The Psychology of Intelligence* and Will (London: Kegan Paul, 1930), p. 245.

[46] On the conditionism of human actions, cf. Theodore Muencker, "Die Psychologischen Grundlagen der Katholischen Sittenlehre," in F. Tillmann, *Handbuch der Katholicischen Sittenlehre,* Band II, 4 Aufl., (Dusseldorf: Patmos-Verlag, 1953), pp. 84-128: "Individuelle Einflausse auf Gewissen-sentscheidung" (Charakter und Temperament; Die geschlechtichen Unter-schiede); pp. 234-267: "Ungunstige Einflüsse der Umwelt auf die Gewissen-sentscheidung" (Die Einflusse der Natur Die Einflüsse des sozialen Lebens; Der hemmende Einflüss der Masse).

[47] J. Nuttin, *Tâche, Réussite et Échec,* pp. 463-467.

[48] J. Rimaud, "Psychologists versus Morality," *Cross Currents* (1951), 2, 34. Jean Rimaud espouses a concept of man which is too negative; his idea of concupiscence leads easily to error. Cf. J. C. Ford, *Depth Psychology, Morality and Alcoholism* (Weston, Mass.: Weston College Press, 1951), p. 9, footnote 19.

[49] L. Noel, *Le Determinisme, Academie Royale de Belgique. Classe des Lettres,* etc. *Memoires*—(Bruxelles, Hayez, 1906), p. 347. As it appears from the passage just quoted, Leon Noel correctly posits the problem of freedom. But it seems to me that he does not posit with the same exactness the relationship between freedom and determinism, since he concludes: "La brech faite dans le system deterministe doit nous porter a le croire univer-sellment faux." *Ibid.,* p. 348. If determinism were universally false, there would be no room for freedom.

[50] T. V. Moore, *The Driving Forces of Human Nature and their Adjustment* (New York: Grune & Stratton, 1950), p. 85.

[51] R. Dalbiez, *Psychoanalytical Methods and the Doctrine of Freud,* trans. T. F. Lindsay, 2 Volumes (New York: Longmans, Green, 1941), Vol. II, p. 302. Cf. R. P. Knight, "Determinism, 'Freedom' and Psycho-therapy," *Psychiatry* (1946), 9, 251; J. C. Ford, *Depth Psychology, Morality and Alcoholism* (Weston, Mass.: Weston College Press, 1951), p. 36.

[52] E. Cros, *La Liberté et la Subconscience: Contribution a l'Étude de la Personalité Humaine* (Lausanne: Imprimeries Reunies, 1917), p. 135.

[53] J. R. Angell, *Psychology: An Introductory Study of the Structure and Function of Human Consciousness,* 4th Rev. Ed., (New York: Henry Holt, 1908), p. 437.

[54] G. Bourguignon, "Le Problème du Libre Arbitre au regard de la Physiologie et de la Médicine," *Temoignages Saint-Leger,* (1947), 12, 16. Basing his theory on the data of physiology and medicine, Georges Bour-

guignon says: "Nous en revenons donc à la conception de Claude Bernard, appuyée maintenant sur des expériences précises et nous pouvons dire à sa suite: la liberté morale n'existe qu'en fonction d'un état normal du cervaux." *Ibid.*, 15.

55 J. Borel, *Le Déséquilibre Psychique: Ses Psychoses, sa Morale* (Paris: Press Univ. France, 1947), p. 370. On the meaning of the "hereditary dispositions" of an individual, cf. Agostino Gemelli, *La Personalita del Delinquente nei suoi Fondomenti Biologici e Psicologici,* 2nd Ed. (Milano: Giuffre, 1948), pp. 225 ff.

56 P. Grasset, *The Semi-Insane and the Semi-Responsible (Demifous et Demiresponsable),* trans. S. E. Jelliffe (New York-London: Funk and Wagnalls, 1907), pp. 285-286.

57 P. Chuachard, "Les sens Biologique de la Liberté Humaine," *Scientia* (1953), 88, 225. This author writes, among other things: "L'acte vraiment libre est au fond très rare, mais il n'en reste pas moins que cette acte est possible et que c'est précisément toute la difference entre l'aliéné et le suject normal, celui capable de se maîtriser et celui qui ne l'est pas." *Ibid.*

58 Cf. E. Kretschmer, *Physique and Character,* trans. W. J. H. Sproutt (London: Kegan Paul, Trench & Trubner, 1925).

59 For genetic determinism and its influences on human behavior, cf. the study of Gino Corallo, "L'Eredita Genetica e l'Educazione," *Salesianum* (1951), 13, 51-74. Vladimir M. Bechterev holds "the complete dependence of the development of criminal actions on the totality of factors influencing the person at the moment of the crime." *General Principles of Human Reflexology: An Introduction to the Objective Study of Personality, trans. E. and M. Murphy* (London: Jarrolos, 1933), p. 65. This assertion by Bechterev doubtless contains some truth, especially if among the determinant factors the perverse or deficient will of an individual is included; but this does not permit him to conclude that the crime "is predestined and inevitable."

60 A substantially correct solution to the problem of human freedom can be found in this synthetic passage of Oliver Brachfield, "El Libre Albedrio como Problema Sociologico," *Rev. Intern. Soc.* (1948), 21, 13-38. "Los conceptosclaves en que al problema de la voluntad y del 'libre albedrio' debe ser planteado son: persona, frente a 'individuo'; subjeto, frente al mero 'objeto,' pues ya estos mismos terminos implican la noción de autonomia frente a la 'eteronomia' del determinismo cualquier uno, y condicionismo, frenta a 'determinismo.' " P. 38. We must keep in mind that the term "conditionism," has a negative significance and does not express the positive character of freedom.

61 W. Stern, *General Psychology, from the Personalistic Standpoint,* trans. D. Spoerl (New York: Macmillan, 1938), p. 434.

62 J. H. Vander Veldt and R. P. Odenwald, *Psychiatry and Catholicism* (New York: McGraw-Hill, 1952), p. 10.

63 J. Nuttin, *Psychoanalysis and Personality, op. cit.,* p. 139. Cf. also J.

Maritain, "The Conquest of Freedom," in Anshen, R. N. *Freedom: Its Meaning* (New York: Harcourt, Brace, 1940), p. 163.

[64] For a good analysis of the various meanings that are attributed to the term "consciousness" cf. James G. Miller, *Unconsciousness* (New York: Wiley, 1942) and Harold A. Abramson (Ed.), *Problems of Consciousness, Transactions of the Fourth Conference,* March 29, 30, and 31, 1953 (New York: Josiah Macy, Jr. Foundation, 1954).

[65] To say that consciousness is a *conditio sine qua non* of voluntary choice implies a clear distinction between conscious processes and volitional processes. The second of these two cannot exist without the first, but not vice-versa; in fact, in cases of psychic abnormalities, both the presence of the conscious function as well as the absence of the volitional function can be simultaneous. For those, however, who identify the two processes, "The capacity of voluntary decision is the main subjective characteristic of consciousness." Cf. W. Penfield, "The Cerebral Cortex in Man," *Arch. Neurol. Psychiat.* (1938), 40, 440.

[66] L. De Raeymaeker, "Le Probleme de la Liberté Personelle et le principe de sa solution," *Giorn. Metafis.* (1949), 4, 581-590, 583 ff. For more information on the problem of the ego and on the meaning that it assumes in modern psychology, cf. Gordon W. Allport, *The Nature of Personality* (Cambridge, Mass.: Addison-Wesley Press, 1950), pp. 114-141.

[67] W. Wundt, *Outlines of Psychology,* trans. Charles H. Judd, 2nd Rev. Ed. (Leipzig: 1902), p. 243.

[68] J. Ward, *Psychological Principles,* 2nd Ed. (Cambridge: Cambridge Univ. Press, 1920), p. 39.

[69] The unity of the human organism has been emphasized strongly by Mary W. Calkins, who says: "There is never perception without a somebody who perceives, and there never is thinking unless someone thinks. And this somebody is not an isolated self but a self which is affected from without and which expresses itself in its behavior." *A First Book in Psychology,* 4th Rev. Ed. (New York, Macmillan, 1919), p. 1.

[70] On the distinction between the idea of "Personality" and the philosophical notion of "person," cf. Theodor Steinbuchel. "Die Philosophische Grundlegung der Katholischen Sittenlehre," in Tillman F., *Handbuch der Katholischen Sittenlehre,* Band I (Dusseldorf: L. Schwann, 1938), pp. 337-357; J. H. Vander Veldt and R. P. Odenwald, *op. cit.,* pp. 1-14; G. Canepa, *Il Concetto di Personalita nei suoi Aspetti Filosofici Biologici e Medico-Legali* (Roma: Edizioni dell'Ateneo, 1953), pp. 96-98.

[71] In an excellent study on the concept of personality in "biology," understood in its broader sense as synonymous with the scientific and experimental study of human life, Giacomo Canepa has delineated the four most representative trends on the basis of criteria of prevalence if not of exclusiveness: *morphological, physiological, psychological* and *integral.* This last trend—which is followed by the author of this book—is represented in Italy by the schools of Pende and Gemelli: *Il Concetto di Personalitá. . .* (1953),

pp. 46-88. For the typically integral and unifying approach of these two authors, cf. mainly the following: N. Pende, *Scienza dell'Ortogenesi* (Milano: Vallardi: 1939); *La Scienza Moderna della Persona Umana* (Milano: Garzanti, 1947); A. Gemelli, *La Personalitá del Delinquenti nei suoi Fondamenti Biologici e Psicologici* (Milano: Giuffré, 1946); 2nd Edition, Revised, 1948: *Lo Psicologo di fronte ai Progressi* (1950).

72 The following assertion of Maryse Choisy is very significant on this point: "Tant que nous ne nous decidons pas à étudier le tout-de-l'homme, nos efforts partiels ne nous offrirons que des images faussées toujours par quelue coté." "Le Problème du tout-de-l'Homme," *Psyche* (1951), 6, no. 51, 5.

73 Langmuir, I., *Phenomena, Atoms and Molecules* (New York: Philosophical Library, 1950), p. 10.

74 R. Zavalloni, "Il Processo della Scelta Volontaria in casi di Psicoterapia centrata-sul-cliente," *Arch. Psicol. Neurol. Psichiat.* (1954), 15, 119. The value of intuition in man's decision is well expressed in the following formulation by Hadley Cantril: "Most of the choices we make are not what we could describe as rational, intellectual or logical. In most choice situations we do not reason out a decision to ourselves in any step by step fashion. Rather we exercise what Kallen terms our *ineffable intuition.*" "The Qualities of Being Human," *Amer. Quart.* (1954), 6, 12.

75 R. Allers, *The Psychology of Character,* trans. E. B. Strauss (New York: Sheed & Ward, 1931). The question of "freedom of the will" is somewhat one-sided. It is not the will as a psychological function but the whole human person that is free. Decision is not on the plane on which the will comes into play as a psychologically determined function, but rather on the plane where that internal affirmation, the "act of appropriation" (*Aneignongsakt*) has its place. Freedom to assent or refuse may be called freedom of the will so long as one bears in mind that it then has a different connotation to the one it usually bears in psychology. P. 43.

76 H. G. Wyatt, *The Psychology of Intelligence and Will* (London: Kegan Paul, 1930), p. 139.

77 On the problem of whether the voluntary act expresses the entire personality, cf. E. Claparède, "Does the Will Express the Entire Personality?" in *Problems of Personality* (New York: Harcourt, Brace, 1925), pp. 39-43.

CHAPTER EIGHT

Ethico-Social and Pedagogical Consequences

We have seen, in the preceding chapters, how complex man's personality is and how varied are the factors which influence his behavior. The results of laboratory experiments and research, of typical cases from psychotherapy, and the ordinary cases of daily life have provided the materials for delineating a concrete phenomenology of volitive activity and a personalistic theory of human freedom. What are the practical consequences of this theory?

We shall limit ourselves to a consideration of consequences related to three factors which are closely linked to human behavior: (1) moral life; (2) social life and (3) education of the will. A false education of the will can be the source of an endless number of prejudices and erroneous evaluations. The external and internal factors of human activity can exercise such pressures on the will of an individual that freedom and responsibility may be diminished or even completely eliminated.

Some problems touch on all three of the factors mentioned. Concerning the relationship between *personal freedom* and *moral life,* it is important to consider the limits of moral freedom; to evaluate the role of moral conscience in man's conduct; to investigate the sources of morality; and to define the relationships among science, morality, and psychology. Where the relationship between *personal freedom* and *social sanction* is concerned, it is necessary to establish the criteria for considering an individual responsible (or not responsible) before society. Lastly, in examining the relationship between *personal freedom* and *education of the will,* it seems useful to outline a personalistic orientation, and to see how we may create the proper psychological atmosphere for arriving at the acquisition of freedom and its control.

1.   Personal Freedom and Moral Life

Free activity is opposed to instinctive activity. Free action is always intelligent action, but not necessarily moral action. Psychologically speaking, to be free means the ability to choose among various possibilities of action. Morally speaking, to be free means the ability to choose between good and evil or between conformity and opposition to the moral law. We have, therefore, two clearly distinct conceptions of freedom: *psychological freedom* (or freedom of choice in the fundamental meaning of the word) and *moral freedom*. The latter presupposes the first, but not vice versa. It seems to me that this element is taken for granted in treating the problem of liberty. However, the case is not rare in which these two types of freedom are confused and even identified. Gino Corallo has recently offered a typical example.

The thesis defended by Corallo is that liberty and morality are "coextensive" with one another practically and theoretically.[1] To Corallo's mind, *"freedom is formally specified by morality";* the action is free in so far as it is moral. In other words, it is free in so far as it is dependent on a judgment, actual or at least implicit, of morality.

Corallo's chief argument: the free act is a rational act, not mere spontaneity; it is a motivated act. Now if we prescind from any consideration of moral order, we find ourselves faced with goods of one type only: hedonistic goods—those which correspond to a tendency, which satisfy an appetite of the subject. Our choice in such a hypothesis has a sufficient basis only in the greatest satisfaction that a determined good provides us at a given moment. We shall always choose *necessarily* the good which is quantitatively greater, and therefore *the choice will not be free*. But when we consider the moral order, the deliberative mechanism is interrupted because we find ourselves facing two orders of immeasurably different goods: the "hedonistic" and the "moral." The latter express what the action should be, but formally do not correspond to a present tendency of the subject. In this case the will can freely decide for one or the other of the two orders.[2]

The fundamental intention of Corallo is to remove the freedom of a human act from the determining influence of the object—to remove this freedom from the role of the motives in which the strongest necessarily prevails—and to *interiorize* it as an orientation which the subject gives to himself, as a disposition of the whole person in the moral sense. We can accept Corallo's good intention: every human act, which is conscious and free, expresses an orientation of the whole person towards a definite goal. We cannot deny that the deepest root of freedom is spirituality, i.e., self-consciousness and the capacity of reflection. But we do not believe that the spark which kindles psychological freedom is the referral to the moral evaluation of the action, namely, the tension between hedonistic and moral goods. True, man cannot, in his actions, prescind from moral option. It must be recognized that the necessary presupposition of morality is freedom. But this does not make morality the *ratio formalis* of a free action.

Corallo writes: "He who considers the goods *within* the hedonistic series only, without looking for other goods outside it, has only an illusory consciousness of freedom; while he passes from one hedonistic good to another, he only changes one kind of slavery for another." [3] But if there is no freedom of choice among the various hedonistic goods, we do not understand how there can be any possibility of choice between hedonistic and moral goods. It is not at all evident that moral considerations produce a substantial difference in the selective act. It is not morality as such that breaks through psychological automatism, but the intervention of the subject as the causal factor of self-determination.

a. The Two Sources of Moral Life

To analyze the genesis of moral life—how freedom develops from the stages of indetermination, ambivalence, and automatism—is no easy task. But it is important today to try to define the various conditions that underlie the emergence and the operation of freedom, since psychoanalysis and other forms of psychotherapy have spread so broadly and rapidly. In the theory and in the prac-

tice of these techniques which tend to free man from internal conflicts by raising them to the conscious level, the idea of a twofold
source of man's moral life is implied: the *conscious* and the *unconscious* source. These often develop in different directions, but they
must be brought back to that unity of synthesis which is expressed
in the moral conscience.

In the theory proposed by Charles Odier, who has recently
thrown new light on this problem, these two sources of moral life
correspond to two spheres of human experience: those of *values*
and *functions*.[4] We can speak of values only when the "ego" thinks
and actually takes a step outside the limited sphere of the functions
—the biological, instinctive, and affective needs. The functional
system is subject to determinism—a determinism of biological origin—while the system of values orient the human being towards
finality. But after overcoming to some extent the rigor of primary
or "functional" determinism through his elevation to the level of
values, man must submit himself to the demands of values. Thus
he is subjected to a new system of determination, of a superior
nature, which may be called secondary or moral, or, if you prefer,
"valorial" determinism. At the level of the unconscious functions,
an almost organic, and therefore rigorous, determinism tends to
destroy the autonomy which must reign at the level of values. There
is coincidence between the person and his value. The true value
becomes almost synonymous with liberty. Under this title it implies
the autonomy of the "ego." But this autonomy presupposes that
the "ego" be freed from the hegemony of the functional tendencies.

Two abuses can be found in the effort to detail the prevalence or
submission of personal values to biological functions. Odier desig-
nates them by the terms "psychologism" and "spiritologism."[5]
"Psychologism" accords to psychological processes the power of
resolving all the problems of psychic life, including spiritual and
religious problems. "Spiritologism" falls into the opposite error:
it confuses science with materialism, and it departs from that life
which is realized and revealed in human experience. In other
words, "psychologism" attempts to reduce values to functions;
"spiritologism" attempts to elevate functions to the rank of values.

Our vital energies are elaborated in the intimate regions of the
bodily organs. Thus a causal system, biopsychic in nature, is built

up; it constitutes the first source of determination and corresponds more or less to primary or functional determinism. This implies the sum total of the influences of the body on the spirit in normal functioning. To this system a second source of determination is opposed: secondary or "valorial" determinism. We must add now a third system of determinism (and ignore the influences which are exercised by the external world, which would constitute a fourth system). This third system can be placed between the first and the second and can interfere with their functioning. Its agent is the unconscious superego. Since this system of determinism places itself between body and spirit, natural causality and spiritual causality, it can be called "intercurrent determinism." [6] If we consider the position of the "ego" in relation to each of these three orders of determinism, we must recognize that the most vigorous of the three is without doubt "intercurrent determinism."

Intercurrent determinism represents the deepest determination of human conduct and constitutes the "unconscious source" of moral life (as opposed to the "conscious source"). These two sources of human experience give rise to two systems of morality: (1) the system of unconscious morality and (2) the system of conscious morality.[7] Conscious morality expresses itself in the "moral conscious"; unconscious morality finds its expression in the "superego" of Freudian theory. Let us now consider some fundamental characteristics of these two systems.

Unconscious Morality	Conscious Morality
The role of the specific faculties of man is excluded or strongly inhibited.	The role of the faculties is operative. Conscious morality tends to develop them.
Reason is excluded or intervenes erroneously.	Conscious rationality is one of the characteristics of action.
The motive is unconscious, rationalized by the subject *post factum*: false motivation.	The motive for the action is conscious, known by the subject *ante factum*: true motivation.
The will is replaced by automatism. Voluntary effort is missing.	Effort is at the center of the moral act. The will attempts to actualize it.

Judgment is excluded or is false. Values are discarded to the profit of the functions or confused with them.	Judgment is at the basis of values. Functions are distinct from values and dominated to the advantage of values.
Automatic type of morality, or moral automatism; passive and egocentric morality.	Deliberate and liberating type of morality; active morality, oriented towards altruistic goal.
Automatic repression excludes every feeling or sense of responsibility, both as cause and effect.	Moral repression implies a sense of responsibility, both as a factor in repression and towards the effects of the committed fault.
Unconscious morality manifests the absence or the extreme weakness of the sense of responsibility; it impedes its development.	Conscious morality manifests the presence and the force of the sense of responsibility; it contributes to its development.

No matter from what point of view the problem is viewed, we see immediately that moral and spiritual life are close to the reason of its being or to its specific nature only to the extent in which it is freed from every unconscious and automatic determination. The normal individual, who is able to develop his personality adequately in his constitutional and environmental situation, can accomplish this process of liberation alone.[8] But the neurotic and, to a certain degree, one who is even psychically disturbed, will not be able to accomplish this liberation alone; he will have to look for help from another person through therapeutic counseling.

The *autonomy* attributed to moral conscience and to the ego (when they are well developed), appears irrefutable, because it manifests itself with great clarity at the end of psychotherapeutic treatment. This autonomy, as an acquired or reconquered property, is more evident if we compare it with the initial neurotic heteronomy. Its acquisition requires the previous establishment of bio-psychic unity, or of that state of equilibrium to which every human being, exempt from mental illness or psychic weakness, tends. (In every man the natural sources of energy spring forth freely; but in every man it is also true that unconscious determinism can erupt at any moment, causing him to lose his biopsychic unity and equilibrium.) Once this accidental source of determination has been eliminated, the psychotherapist witnesses a very surprising spectacle: he sees in the individual the solid re-establishment of moral autonomy and freedom of thought as a function of his return to the exercise of moral conscience.

In relation to the two sources of moral life, and in particular to the liberating action of the therapeutic process, another special problem must be taken into consideration. During the course of the psychotherapeutic treatment, there occurs the phenomenon of "catharsis," an emotional release permitting the patient to bring into the open what has been repressed. This phenomenon is not limited to Freudian psychoanalysis; it occurs in every kind of treatment which tends towards depth analysis. Catharsis is the release of blocked emotions, a release which is apparently caused by recalling to memory and by living over again the experience of a personal crisis which was traumatic for the subject. We must now determine whether these phenomena of emotional release are completely different from those that are experinced in daily life or are only more complicated forms of the same phenomena.[9] In daily life such reactions are realized consciously by socially integrated individuals who are responding normally in a framework of socially accepted relationships. In the analytic catharsis, however, we are dealing with an overactive emotion of the unconscious life taking place in the framework of a social structure which is as exceptional as it is artificial. Thus we ask, to what extent can a man be held responsible for actions, gestures, words, and thoughts that he relives in psychotherapy?

In the psychotherapeutic process there is created between patient and therapist a unique relationship which has very little of the character of an ordinary social contact. It is essentially an affective relationship in which the patient, who trusts the therapist, becomes so sure of himself that his deepest instincts can attain a spontaneous equilibrium. There is no question of a hypnotic state here, because the true personality is always present. The patient is conscious of the external phenomena; but at the same time he feels so confident and so strong in this protective atmosphere that he no longer fears the phantasms of his unconscious life, and he now dares to give them complete freedom of expression. We can legitimately ask who, then, is the one who responds? Who is angry? Who is timid or aggressive? In reality it is not the same person who is acting in the therapeutic relationship, but rather a psyche which, at the end, is integrated into a higher personality. Our experiences can be re-lived at different levels of our concrete personality and can be in-tegrated in a different way by each individual. As long as an in-ternal impulse does not have to be adopted as a deliberately chosen attitude, no moral problem arises. But the problem becomes truly delicate from the ethical viewpoint in the case, for example, of a neurotic who is subjected to a type of treatment which can lead him to perform a conscious and deliberate but unjustifiable action.

Man is responsible for those free acts in which his understanding is clear and his will is sufficiently active. What is not under the con-trol of the highest sphere of man's personality cannot give rise to an act which is formally and totally human. A hypnotized subject, for example, may be *forced* to open a window, but all have the impression that he opens the window *freely*. In an analytic cathar-sis a similar situation occurs. It may happen that a conscious im-pulse, activated by the treatment, works in the patient in a more or less determining way, even though he seems to be endowed with freedom of action. In such cases it is difficult and sometimes im-possible to recognize whether we are dealing with a determining impulse (as in the case of hypnosis), or simply with a suggestion which merely appears in the form of a genuine judgement.

In short, the problem is to determine when and under what con-ditions we can trust our subjective consciousness, and to what ex-tent we judge falsely the motives we adduce for our actions. Since one and the same act may signify different things, the problem of catharsis leads us to ask who is the one who is really performing the act, and what is he actually doing? The true personality may remain absent during the psychotherapeutic treatment, not only during the consultation period, but for some time afterwards. The important question is whether or not it is the true personality of the individual that is acting. A truly human and fully responsible act is performed only by a well-integrated person.

b. Relationship Between Moral Science and Psychology

Freedom is the basis of moral science. To be more precise, we must say that the object of moral science is the use or exercise of free acts and not, properly speaking, freedom itself. The moralist is certainly aware of this, since he has always maintained that immaturity, mental deficiency, or emotional confusion can take away from the individual his capacity for decision, because his rational judgment is obscured. The moralist also knows very well that under certain circumstances human behavior becomes more or less rigidly bound to and involved with the deterministic functioning of phantasy and impulses. But if the moralist wishes to offer to men of all times and circumstances the necessary guidance for a better possible use of their rational resources, *he must make use of psychology as an indispensable source of information.*

The intimate and close contact that existed between the psychological and moral disciplines during their initial phases of development has been lost; the legalist conception of morality gradually won out. Obviously, once moral science had become more or less equated with jurisprudence, the tendency to define responsibility in almost exclusively objective terms prevailed. The only subjective condition which has conserved its importance is the intellectual capacity to distinguish between good and evil, that is, the individual's awareness of what he is doing and the consent given to such an action. N. Mailloux writes: "Unfortunately, we must state that the subjective conditions of the individual conscience remained almost entirely foreign to its consideration. It is a fact that casuistry was mainly concerned with the objective determinations of the moral law, with the existence or non-existence of a certain obligation or with its grievousness." [10] What seems to be urgent today, in the light of recent developments in psychology and psychiatry, is *a change in emphasis from a juridical morality to a psychological morality.*

The duty of a psychologist is to determine the influence of the factors that play a role in the consciousness of a person at the moment of deciding a definite line of action and, in the last analysis, to define the degree of his moral responsibility. To arrive at this we must examine these two points: (1) the constitutive element of moral conscience, by which man believes his action to be licit or illicit, in so far as it is in conformity with a norm, be this norm a positive or a natural law; and (2) the criteria for determining one's responsibility for an action, so that this action may be attributed to him as his own and as actively willed by him.[11] Among these criteria, man's intelligence is of first importance, as was emphasized by juridical morality; nor could it be otherwise. In fact, in order for man's acts to be called morally free, his intellectual capacity must reach at least a minimum of mental development so that it permits him to understand the meaning of the primary notion of morality. But we would make a great mistake if, in the examination of man's responsibility, we were to give exclusive or even excessive importance to the degree of intelligence. All the other factors which characterize the complex motivation of human behavior, and which only a dynamic psychology of personality will be able to reveal (at least partially) must also be kept in due proportion.

The recourse to psychology is indispensable principally in those cases in which particular affective disturbances, psychic alterations (attributable to erroneous or insufficient education), various kinds of character distortions, and a great many deviations of moral judgment are found. Recently Jean Rimaud raised his voice strongly against the erroneous separation of moral science from psychology. His objections have certainly a grain of truth, but they also contain excessive and inexact expressions. Surely, it seems inexact to say that "our morality was based on an extremely simple psychology" and that only "clear self-consciousness, a personal moral conscience, liberty and responsibility were its basic premises."[12] That these were not the only premises of traditional moral science is clear when we recall that from the very beginning the moralist posited a clear distinction between acts over which man has complete control and acts over which he does not have such control. The first type proceeds from a deliberate decision and is in conformity with the principles of reason; this is called a *human act.* The second type, called an *act of man,* proceeds from causes and motivations which are not subject to rational influence.

Leaving aside these and other exaggerations and inaccuracies, Rimaud's stand has the merit of having called attention to the problem of the relationship between moral science and psychology. This young discipline certainly disturbed the peace of many moralists because it showed them that human conduct is much more complex and deep-rooted in its motivation than we would imagine at first sight. What is even more important from the moral aspect is the hard-won truth that the explanation of human behavior must be sought, at least in notable part, in the unconscious tendencies from which it springs. Every theory of freedom which ignores the role of these unconscious tendencies is inadequate.

Our deepest impulses move us without our being aware of it. We cannot consciously impede the images entering and acting upon our subconscious, nor can we deprive the imagination of its motivating force. On the other hand, it is true that we do have a genuine control over the impulses of the senses, once they emerge from the depths to the light of consciousness. Sometimes we can control them and sublimate them, by directing their vitality. Rimaud again:

> "And so we see a double series of disconcerting though equally certain facts: a determinism which continues to act in the awakened conscience, and a power to utilize subconscious and unconscious forces when they become conscious. Moralists should join the psychologists in studying this play of determinism and liberty in order to refute both those who exaggerate infraconscious determinism and those who claim we are free as soon as we are awakened and fully conscious. For we cannot give a valid answer to the former who suppress responsibility if we compromise ourselves with the latter who misunderstand it." [13]

To pose the problem of freedom correctly we must put it concretely, that is, in terms of the real, situated, incarnate person, as experience reveals him to us. Then it is no longer a question of knowing when man *is not* fully responsible, but rather when he *is* really so.[14] The opposition to the concept of degrees of responsibility springs from two sources: either the tendency to *exaggerate the efficacy of the will* in the determination of its acts, or the *fear that an attenuated penalty* (attenuated by a judgment of diminished responsibility) will no longer perform its task as a means of *social defense against criminals*. In both cases we must not forget that to judge the responsibility of a person we must take into account the circumstances in which he has performed his acts.[15] The closer the link between moral and psychological science, the closer also to reality will be this judgment of responsibility. In other words the more decisive *the development from a juridical morality to a psychological morality,* the better will be this judgment of responsibility. But if this evolution is to be realized it will be necessary for the moralists to concentrate more on the inner meaning than on the external structure of the act, to dedicate themselves to a deeper and more concrete study of man's personality.

2. Personal Freedom and Social Sanction

In the various attempts to solve the problem of freedom, much confusion has arisen from the equivocal meaning of the term "responsibility." This term has two fundamental meanings, one of which can be considered in a broad sense, and the other in a strict or proper sense. According to Warren's *Dictionary of Psychology,* a responsible person in the first sense is one who "is actively concerned in the production of a certain specific event or condition or affair." In the strict sense, responsible means: "characterizing the social and legal status of the normal human adult, in that he is assumed to be so constituted as to be able to conform to the prescriptions of social customs, moral standards, and government, and is judged deserving of and amenable to punishment if he runs counter to these prescriptions."

These two meanings are more often and more correctly expressed by the term "imputability" in the first case, and by "responsibility" in the second. Gemelli follows this fundamental distinction, which is often ignored by both psychologists and moralists, and defines *imputability,* from the psychological point of view, as the real, objective capacity of a subject to perform the actions which are attributed to him. In other words, according to Gemelli, imputability is "the capacity or power by which the individual is able to act and to will in a way which corresponds to his character, to his personality." Thus, by viewing the action in the framework of the personality of the individual, it is possible to judge whether that action must be imputed to him or not (as his own). In addition to this psychological imputability, there are two other types, ethical and juridical imputability, according to whether we consider the subject's motives or directions of the will ethically or juridically imputable.

In cases of psychosis, psychological imputability remains, while ethical or juridical imputability (that is, *responsibility* in its proper sense) may be diminished or disappear entirely. This responsibility, which *presupposes* psychological imputability but *is not identified with it,* is defined by Gemelli as "the capacity man has of being answerable for his own actions. This capacity depends on a characteristic inherent in our human nature and permits an act that we perform to be retained and judged as really our own. This characteristic is *freedom.*" [16] In short, *an action* is "imputable" to an individual in so far as it is the expression of his personality; *a man,* on the contrary, is "responsible" for an action in so far as this depends on his own free will.

a. Relationship Between Freedom and Responsibility

Everyone recognizes the existence of human responsibility and acts under the presumption that men are responsible beings. It is a fact of common experience that no one considers his actions as the purely mechanical effects of a machine which could not have acted otherwise. If one honestly looks back to his past, he will find certain things for which he must feel sorry; and there are certain things in the life of every man that he not only deplores, but for which he feels responsible. Everyone acts believing in the power of his own initiative. This belief in personal freedom and in the power of initiative evidently implies the power of acting freely. Since man has the power of initiative and can conceive of goals and perceive means to reach one goal rather than another, he is a free and responsible agent.

In the case of conscious and deliberate actions, we attribute to ourselves and to others a special type of responsibility. But would we have the right to do so if these actions could be explained entirely on the basis of a causal series which goes back beyond ourselves? The attempt has often been made to show that praise and blame, reward and punishment, would have reason to exist even though our actions were determined. Hobbes and J. S. Mill, for example, hold that, even prescinding from man's free will, reward and punishment would be equally justified by the goals of reform and defense. If all punishments were necessitated, they would certainly retain the purpose attributed to them by these authors, but they would not have the place they actually have in man's estimation. Such an evaluation of reward and punishment is deficient because it does not take into consideration the existence of moral responsibility.[17]

Fouillée contends that the ideas of good, right, and duty find as good an explanation in a deterministic theory as in the doctrine of freedom. The idea of freedom contains within itself the notion of an active force; the stronger this force is the more elevated it is; it becomes an ever greater source of moral energy. Science and morality find their reconciliation in a determinism which has the idea of freedom as its foundation. Such a system respects causality and conserves the idea of human life as its true means of realization. But we must point out that there is a constant equivocation in Fouillée's thought: he continually confuses the *idea* of freedom with the *fact* of freedom.

Fouillée's theory can be said to be substantially one of "psychological fictionalism." It recalls to our minds the doctrine of Hans Vaihinger on the "indispensable fictions," among which he includes the concept of freedom.[18] What the latter means by his fictionalistic theory of freedom is simply this: that man's conduct is completely predetermined, but that it is expedient, and even imperative for practical purposes to think and act *as if* moral freedom—a pure fiction—were really true. This would have the result of developing, in completely predetermined individuals, the same sense of responsibility *as if* they believed in the freedom of their actions. But so far as responsibility is concerned, it matters little that such individuals have or do not have a fictionalistic concept of freedom, since this reduces their entire activity to a complete determinism.

There is no possible passage from determinism, physical or psychological, to responsibility except through that typically human form of self-determination which constitutes freedom. It would be meaningless to hold a man responsible for his actions if it is not admitted that he can, under the same circumstances, act in a manner totally different if he so wishes. To be able to act differently means to have the capacity of determining oneself freely. The result is a complete correlation between the idea of freedom and the idea of responsibility. To deny freedom is to reduce voluntary action to mechanical determination, and consequently to destroy the foundation of responsibility in its proper sense.

Many penologists and psychologists are opposed to this kind of solution. Alfred Binet, for example, writes that "among the most tenacious errors of the moralists we must point out in the first place that error which subordinates moral responsibility to free choice." He recognizes, on the other hand, that to be responsible for an act we must have willed and executed it freely. "But this freedom is not identical with the free choice of the philosophers; this freedom is simply the power of acting in conformity to our own character." [19]

According to Binet, moral responsibility can be studied from two very different viewpoints, one subjective and the other objective. From the subject's point of view, it is he himself who appreciates the moral value of his own act; it is he who judges and condemns himself. From the objective viewpoint, we take into consideration the emotional reaction that an act produces in other individuals, in the witnesses of the act and in society in general. Freedom, considered under this second aspect, consists properly speaking in the power of being able to act in conformity with one's character. The act, when weighed and reflected upon, is free if it is in perfect accord with the moral personality from which it emanates. The free act is confused with its agent, and the responsibility for this act is not at all compatible with the doctrine of necessity, as it is defended by Stuart Mill.

What is the true meaning of this theory? The identity between "free activity" and "moral personality," held by Binet to be the foundation of responsibility, is reducible in the last analysis to mere feelings: the feelings of sympathy and antipathy inspired by the act can be imputed to the agent. And this would be, according to Binet, "the exact, practical and human solution of this great problem of responsibility." [20] It is not easy to accept such an opinion. In Binet's thought responsibility is simply a function of the impression produced by the individual actions on society. It follows then that if such an impression accidentally changes, the degree of responsibility also changes. In this way we could have a different responsibility for the same act, performed by the same moral personality, if the degree of impressionability of the observer were to change. And more: an act can induce feelings of sympathy in one person and feelings of antipathy in another. Why should an individual be condemned for a sentiment of repulsion which he inspires, if he is so predetermined by his own character that he cannot change? It would be like condemning someone because he has a physical illness which provokes disgust.

Binet's theory is evidently in open contradiction to reality. But to his credit we must point out that he himself recognizes that "sentimental morality is incontestably the worst of the moralities, because it goes from one excess to the other, sometimes weak, sometimes strong, and is based more upon the dramatic character of things than upon their real value."[21] Binet's insistence on the influence of feelings on the concrete determination of responsibility is surely of great importance, but it can never constitute a criterion of evaluation. This criterion must be sought in the personality of the subject, in his conscious ego.

The psychological analysis of the freedom-responsibility relationship recently attempted by O. Hobart Mowrer seems equally unsuccessful. He holds that we can solve the majority of the difficulties by changing our view of the problem; we should look at the problem not *retrospectively* but *prospectively*. In his view, punishment is inflicted not because somebody is "responsible" for an evil act but because he acted in an "irresponsible" manner. The purpose of the punishment is to change the individual and to make him more responsible, better controlled, more intelligent, and more prudent in the future. According to Mowrer, the capacity to change for the better is the only type of freedom which is significant and personally desirable. Therefore legal and psychiatric debates concerning "sanity" and "responsibility" are to be considered useless nonsense. The essential point is that, if the individual has performed a socially deviant act, he has acted in an "irresponsible" manner.[22]

What needs to be established in the evaluation of an individual's act is this fact alone: whether he is or is not sufficiently normal to draw some profit from the punishment, not whether he deserves the punishment; or whether he has developed so many defense mechanisms that the punishment would not have a corrective influence.

What can we say of such a conception? Perhaps against the author's intention, this notion eliminates every concept of freedom and responsibility without resolving anything. One might even draw this extremely illogical conclusion: that a criminal who from well-established habit persists in his asocial conduct should not be punished.

b. The Problem of Medico-Legal Responsibility

Even when voluntary choice becomes conscious and personal, a human being is circumscribed by the limits of his specific organization. Man's behavior has affective connotations. The anomalies of affectivity exercise a restrictive force on liberty concerning which the individual can be partially or even completely aware. This concrete condition of a restrictive force which lies at the root of the problem of moral freedom evidently explains why many authors favor the notion of medico-legal responsibility. Thus we can understand why Grasset attempted to elaborate a neurological argument which would cut short the whole discussion. But this attempt is doomed to failure because, as J. Borel has justly observed, "The organic basis does not explain psychology; the fact of consciousness is not a nerve fiber." [23]

Grasset, in his various neuropsychiatric studies, develops the idea that there are two psychic forces. He divides human activities into *conscious and voluntary,* which is presided over by the *superior psychic force,* and *automatic and unconscious,* under the control of the *inferior psychic* force.[24] The clearest formulation of this hypothesis was made by Janet, as we have seen, even though it had been hinted at many years before him. The superior psychic force is the center of conscious personality, of freedom and responsibility. The inferior is the center of a polygon of psychological mechanisms.

Grasset attempts to demonstrate in his study of the semi-insane and semi-responsible what is meant by "criminal or legal responsibility" from the medical point of view and how this "criminal or legal" responsibility must be taken into consideration and understood by all concerned, no matter what their philosophical or religious opinions might be on the problem of free choice. His reason is that the moral idea of responsibility, in its association with the problem of freedom, is difficult to reconcile with the doctrine of partial responsibility, while the medical idea easily permits such an interpretation.

To Grasset's mind, the cerebral cortex taken as a whole is psychic; the psychic neurons must therefore be localized in the cortex. There are many proofs that certain parts of the cerebrum are necessary for the higher intellectual functions and that lesions in these parts of the cerebrum do not fully suppress one's entire intellectual capacity. In answer to an objection raised against him, Grasset declares that he has never denied that personality is always "one and the same," even though he holds that "the organ of personality—the psychic center—is multiple and divisible." [25]

Taking as his point of departure the viewpoint just enunciated, Grasset formulates a scientific demonstration of the existence of "semi-insanity." He rejects two theories which deny the existence of such a group. The *two-bloc theory* admits only the existence of the irresponsible insane and the perfectly responsible sane. The *single-bloc theory* places all men in the same universal group, and holds that all men are more or less responsible in varying degrees. The entire structure of the *theory of a single bloc* rests on the development of the idea that the existence of many intermediary phases between two states or two phenomena proves their identity. Grasset holds that this idea is false and unscientific.[26] Against the two-bloc theory he attempts to establish the existence of the semi-insane, who cannot be classified either among the insane or among the normal without error or injustice. The semi-insane are distinct from the sane because they are psychically sick; they are distinct from the sane because they still conserve a certain degree of consciousness and reason. The *mentally sick* have lost reason, freedom, consciousness; they are *insane*. The *psychically sick,* on the contrary, have not completely lost their reason and higher functions, but they are disturbed; they are semi-insane. The true problem then, is that of the "diminished responsibility" of the semi-insane. How can we be certain of such diminished responsibility?

According to Grasset, the medical concept of responsibility cannot be based on the philosophical notion of free choice. It is only upon a physiological basis that we can build a theory of medico-legal responsibility which all the experts can and should accept, no matter what their personal philosophical convictions might be. Thus the physician, while still remaining in his own field, may have a notion of responsibility very different from the moral responsibility of the philosophers. What is the physiological basis on which this new idea is founded? Grasset answers that the experts in medicine, no matter to what philosophical school they belong, always admit that the nervous system plays the most indispensable and important role in the performance of every act and in the control of life. The medical expert interests himself in the nervous system alone; his mission is to decide if the condition of the nervous system permits the subject to weigh and to judge diligently the forces and motives which are encountered in every voluntary and deliberate act. In other words, he must decide whether the condition of the nervous system renders the subject responsible or irresponsible. In order that a subject be clinically responsible before society, it is necessary and sufficient that he have a clear idea of what is permitted or prohibited by the law, knowledge which virtually everyone possesses.[27]

Grasset is of the opinion that all physicians should agree on these two principles: (1) they are to decide only on the responsibility of the individual before society; (2) they are to decide only on the integrity or non-integrity of the nerve-centers in relation to the material action of the volitive psyche. From this stems the different functions of the physician and of the magistrate. For the magistrate the problem of responsibility is much more complex; he must take into consideration the individual's intention. Grasset proposes here a distinction between "responsibility" and "culpability," which substantally corresponds to the distinction between "imputability" and "responsibility" defined at the beginning of this chapter. An individual can be responsible—according to Grasset's terminology —for an act of which he is not culpable. Physiological responsibility is a necessary but not sufficient element for the proof of culpability.

This latter assertion is undoubtedly true. And we could also say that the distinction introduced by Grasset between responsibility and culpability dissipates for the moment a major confusion of terms. Unfortunately the use of the term "responsibility" is too far removed from the common meaning of the word and, practically speaking, the confusion which he attempts to resolve still pervades his writings. In addition it must be noted that many points of his theory are debatable. The presupposition that the knowledge of what is permissible or prohibited is a sufficient criterion for the medical idea of responsibility before society is a type of sophism that has no foundation in reality; it ignores completely the affective factor of motivation. Certainly the "idea" of duty alone is not sufficient in itself to establish responsibility even from the medical viewpoint; and even though it were sufficient, this would not be enough to solve the problem of responsbility in the proper meaning of the word, that is, of moral responsibility. Grasset's physiological concept of responsibility indicates a "condition" of culpability, but it offers us no criterion to solve the problem of whether culpability or moral responsibility can exist independently of an individual's freedom.

In Grasset's theory, responsibility is reduced to the idea of normality; it is a function of the normal psychic neurons. This doctrine can be formulated and summed up in the following sentence: "An individual whose psychic neurons are normal is a responsible being." [28] And the author believes that in this manner freedom is completely bypassed. But the problem of freedom returns every time we attempt to define the concept of responsibility. Responsibility, whether it is characterized as "physiological" or "medical" or even criminal, is simply a criterion for establishing the existence of imputability or responsibility in the broad sense. But this is hardly adequate for the definition of responsibility in its proper and common meaning, i.e., of moral responsibility. And the medical idea of responsibility which Grasset proposes seems at least inexact from the physiological viewpoint, because it is based on the hypothesis, by no means established, that every psychic disturbance has an organic or physical basis. The undeniable connection between the psyche and the brain definitely gives a certain force to this viewpoint, but is not sufficient to establish it as an absolute truth. In fact, it cannot be proved that in certain cases of neurosis there is a real disturbance of the psychic processes of the brain; nor is it possible to say whether disturbances of an endocrine nature are the effect rather than the cause of these diseases.

It must be admitted that a physiological basis is an essential condition for exercising freedom and therefore is a condition of responsibility. To establish this physiological basis is the duty of medical science.[29] But this does not mean that, once such a **condi-**

tion has been found, man's responsibility is sufficiently explained before society, to say nothing of an explanation before his own conscience. The criterion for defining the presence or the absence of responsibility, in the proper sense of the term, can be based only on the concrete condition of personal freedom.

3. Personal Freedom and Education of the Will

I believe that the elements which form the basis of my personalistic theory of freedom can and even must be applied also in the field of education of the will. An excessive emphasis on the intellect to the disadvantage of the emotions, and vice versa, can be harmful to the sound development of personality. Only the closest cooperation of the intellect and will with its real contribution of affectivity can give truly efficacious strength to the integral development of personality, which constitutes the essence of will-training. C. Piat wrote in 1894:

> "Contemporary criminologists have thrown into clearer light two truths of great importance: (1) they have demonstrated that the energy of moral will depends intimately on the state of the organism; (2) they have shown experimentally that honesty is linked less to intelligence than to moral sentiments. This is an idea which is not only profound, but also very timely. We are shocked, we are fearful of the progressive march of criminality. But for the last century we have thought it sufficient to illumine the intelligence to become better, for the last century the education of our youth has been exclusively intellectualistic, for the last century we have not been teaching love." [30]

Piat's words, so full of truth and wisdom, emphasized in passionate tones the falsity of the method of education then prevailing. During the last sixty years notable, even excessive progress has been made from the prevalence of intellectualism to the prevalence of love in training our youth. But it would be equally dangerous if education were to become exclusively affective-voluntaristic. The adequate solution of this delicate problem, it seems to me, can be found only in a *personalistic theory of training and education* which would correspond to the personalistic theory of freedom outlined in the preceding chapter.

a. Personalistic Trend in Education

There is a "personalism" in education which represents the synthesis of intellectualism and voluntarism, not as a simple theoretical concept, but on the concrete foundation of personal activity. By *personalism* we mean here the study of man in the real conditions of life, not only with all the limitations which he has from his state of psychosomatic existence, but also with all the possibilities of autonomy that his spiritual nature offers him. Personalism involves the study of human personality as a "whole," in which nothing is more objective than the personality itself as concrete reality, and nothing more abstract than the idea of the independence or of the primacy of man's higher functions.

In a personalistic theory of freedom the act of decision and voluntary choice belongs, properly speaking, to the person and not to the volitive function.[31] It follows then that that training whose essential task is to develop in the individual the control of his conduct will have to aim at the integral formation of his personality, and not at the training of his will alone. The formation of a habit in man's conduct does not depend on the repeated training of his will, but on an attitude which is a function of the entire personality. It excludes, therefore, the training of the will for its own sake; it excludes also that form of training of the will which is based, according to Lindworsky, on reinforcement of motives.[32]

Lindworsky's theory undoubtedly has considerable importance for the training of the will, but it is partial and deficient. It presupposes a standardization of motives which is psychologically and philosophically untenable. Based as it is on the data of experimental psychology alone, it presents a phenomenology of the voluntary act which is not always in accordance with the concrete conditions of life. Even though this theory helps to put the importance of motivation into proper perspective, it does not take into consideration the most fundamental aspect of the problem, that which constitutes the basis of the volitional act and of motivation itself: man's personality. Clinical psychology studies the whole man in his concrete motivation, and clarifies that aspect of the problem not given due importance by Lindworsky.

Motives have a value which is relative to the personal circumstances of an individual. Their value and interest change with the variations in his manner of perceiving them. Even though the preservation of life is the greatest value for every living being, it can lose its attractiveness to such an extent and can have so many dark moments that it can lead a man to suicide. What is essential here is the subjective element in our perception of values. Motives or preferential values are not efficacious in themselves; they may or may not have an effect, depending on the degree of personal development of the individual. As a terrain badly cultivated will render sterile even the best seeds, so also will the values sown on the uncultivated terrain of a personality that is not sufficiently integrated in all its functions remain without fruit. It should be obvious how important is the integral development of personality in the training of the will.

The essential point here consists in knowing how to lay solid foundations on which the trainee himself can later build. It consists in creating those conditions of his personality which will permit him to act according to those ethical principles proper to his rational nature. Progress in training will therefore consist in progress towards the integration of personality. This is obviously based on the presupposition that a well-integrated personality, which is physiologically and psychologically balanced, can act in conformity to the laws of its rational nature and therefore can respect the moral laws of social life. Experience demonstrates that we can predict, with a criterion of very high probability, the effective realization of this hypothesis. Infractions of the norms of rational living are always the effect of the greater or less influence of an unbalanced mind, or of a greater or less disintegration of the personality of an individual. In order to reach the goals of training, then, it is of the greatest importance to develop in youth that psychic harmony which is an evident sign of personality integration.

b. Education Towards the Conquest of Freedom

The final purpose of the training process is to enable the individual to act in conformity with his rational, moral, and social nature. Training, if it is going to be truly human, must be essentially moral. The duty of the educator in the formation of moral conscience is not only to clarify, in the light of moral norms, all sectors of human activity in which the trainee exercises himself, but also to guide him to subordinate every other interest to the moral good. It can be said, therefore, that psychological freedom or freedom of choice is the means, while moral freedom is the goal of the training process.

The notion of freedom, as we have seen, is broader than the simple notion of free choice. Freedom of choice is properly speaking the source and the fount of the world of freedom; it manifests itself, according to the expression of Jacques Maritain, as *initial freedom*. But another freedom beckons us, a liberty for which we must struggle tenaciously, *terminal freedom*. Freedom of choice is not an end in itself; it is a means which must serve to conquer freedom in its autonomous sense; and the dynamism of freedom is required during this true conquest by the essential nature of human personality.[33] This principle has two particularly important applications, one in the social and the other in the spiritual order.

Our social doctrine should be centered primarily on the progressive interior freedom of persons, not on the acquisition of exterior freedom of power and domination, and not simply on the freedom of choice as an end in itself. This conception in reality is neither individualistic nor imperialistic; it can be called "personalistic."[34] Social life, then, will tend to develop from initial freedom to terminal freedom.

The dynamism of freedom in its application to the spiritual life is centered on the conquest of wisdom. Man's freedom of choice is such that it enables him to attain terminal freedom, which can be characterized as the perfect spontaneity of a spiritual nature. Thus the perfect freedom of autonomy coincides with sanctity. The saint is the master of his own life because his total personality is completely united to the Author of life.

The essential problem for both the social and spiritual life is the conquest of freedom. This is also the main goal of education. But how can we reach such a goal? It seems to me that there is no other means but that of *training youth to use rationally their freedom of choice,* that is, to make them capable of actualizing a constant preferential choice of the good. For this reason, it is indispensable to develop in youth the capacity to form judgments, the spirit of initiative, and the sense of responsibility. It is absolutely necessary to instil the habit of making with serene deliberation the small decisions that orient the daily life, if we wish to train youth to make with full freedom and responsibility the critical decisions of life.

If each man is free, each man is also free in a different manner, according to the various potentialities of development of his own psychic functions. We must not forget that freedom of the will is a property or a function of man and, as with any other function, it can increase or decrease with exercise or the lack of it. To instil the habit of making decisions with a sense of responsibility means to favor the exercise of freedom; it means to increase one's capacity of conscious self-determination. "Our choices and our decisions are endowed with a transforming power. In so far as they are authentic they form our being to their image. Freedom molds nature." [35] It is evident, on the other hand, that decisions and choices presuppose deliberation on the value of motives or an intuitive understanding of the various alternatives. The psychological problem of education can be formulated, therefore, in this fashion: *to teach youth the subjectivization or, better, the "personalization" of the motives for action,* according to a real and objective hierarchy of values. A notable characteristic of man is his capacity to arrive at values through his own experience and to attempt to give further meaning to these values through their participation in new situations. Hadley Cantril is right: "A crucial question for education is to devise a method for teaching people how to improve value judgments which in turn will better guarantee a higher quality of experience." [36]

Man's capacity to experience his emergent values is essentially dependent on his capacity for cognitive activity and creative action, on his rational tendency to transcend the contingent values of life. Moral and religious values cannot be eliminated from those possibilities of choice which a wise educator attempts to propose to youth. The philosophical foundation of these values is a philosophy of transcendence. Just as any philosophical system which denies transcendence is essentially weak and inconsistent, so every training process that ignores values derived from the idea of transcendence cannot be anything but a poor, partial and deficient method.[37] In this framework the option for or against God, the last term of transcendence, is free. Depending on what view of human destiny is adopted, the concrete orientation of educational programs will be directed either towards a theory of isolation which ends in satanic pride, or towards a doctrine of communion which culminates in a demand for sanctity. The exaltation of the human person leads, through the conquest of freedom, either to the super-man or to the man of God.

c. *Freedom of Choice and Control of Behavior*

In moral and educational training two important principles emerge from the experimental studies on voluntary choice: (1) in the normal method of procedure one should first of all try to induce the subject to accept the task proposed to him and encourage him to complete it as if it were one of his personal goals; (2) after having induced in the subject a tendency towards a personal affirmation, one should never interfere by imposing tasks which are directly the opposite. The first of these two principles, which expresses the *harmonization* of objective duty with subjective desire, provides a psychological basis for the ethical postulate of "internal freedom."

The experimental and clinical studies on volitive activity which we have analyzed earlier in this study suggest that we should accentuate the distinction between the volitional act in the sense of "choice" and the volitional act in the sense of "voluntary activity" or "control of behavior." Choice is a particular psychic experience and a manifestation of volitional activity. But this does not end with the act of choice; it continues with the control of behavior.[38] It is clear that this control presupposes on man's part the power of self-determination and, as a continued manifestation of his own activity, the capacity of self-control.

An examination of the data of experience induces us to substitute for an abstract concept of freedom all that we believe to be true and concrete in the complex idea of self-control. What, for example, should be the attitude of an educator confronted with a boy who is difficult and lazy, and has no sense of discipline? He should incite and stimulate voluntary determination, courage, loyalty, and the ambition to become a mature person. He should lead the boy from the small decisions that he is capable of making to greater and more courageous decisions. It is through a constant and confident appeal to the sense of responsibility, to moral judgment, and to the courage to be oneself that the educator will be able to free the boy from the heavy burden of conformity and psychic immaturity.

A human being is in part the complex expression of multiple internal and external influences; but he is also, in great measure, what he makes of himself. Besides motivation, emotionality, environment and heredity, there is in the individual the innate capacity of choosing, determining himself along one line of behavior, or of shaping his own destiny. If it is true that the traits, attitudes and characteristics of an individual are not a matter of free choice, it is also true that personal factors can be influenced strongly by the process of self-control. Every method of psychotherapy which tends to bring the individual to the adjustment and integration of his personality, and similarly every method of education which tends essentially to the formation of personality, must presuppose this fundamental capacity in every human being and must attempt to develop it to the highest possible degree. Thus *the realization of an enlightened self-control can be said to be the essential goal of education.*

A person cannot utilize all his capacities unless he is able to control himself. What is controlled is the continuous change which takes place in each individual in the form of desires, impulses, thoughts and habits. Often there is conflict between the ideals of a person and his fundamental needs; it is really here that self-control is necessary if we wish to assure stability and personal adjustment. Because he lives in society, man cannot lead a life based on impulses. He must act in conformity with his rational nature. To abandon himself to his impulses and to indulge in the unbridled conquest of pleasure is the surest road to maladjustment. Whether we like it or not, we are bound to live according to certain principles and laws which our nature has imposed on us; this implies on our part the exercise of self-control.

In a broader sense self-control means ruling over our tendencies and habits in such a way that we are able to reach harmony within ourselves and harmony between our needs and the world in which we live; it means continuity and coherence of conduct. It is therefore the expression of one's character in the true sense of the word. Self-control, when realized in a stable and uniform manner, becomes discipline, and characterizes man's truly rational behavior.

FOOTNOTES

[1] Cf. Gino Corallo, *Educazione e Libertà: Presupposti Filosofici per una Pedagogia della Libertà, Collana Pedagogica "Don Bosco,"* Serie Prima, Vol. XVI (Torino: S.E.I., 1951); *La Pedagogia della Libertà, Collana Pedagogica "Don Bosco,"* Serie Prima, Vol. XVII (Torino: S.E.I., 1951).

[2] It seems to me that Corallo falls into the previously mentioned error of "futurism" when speaking of the moment of freedom. For a critical evaluation of Corallo's ideas on this topic, cf. Vincenzo Miano, "Educazione e Libertà," *Salesianum* (1952), 14, 317-327.

[3] G. Corallo, *Educazione e Libertà, op. cit.,* p. 216.

[4] C. Odier, *Les Deux Sources, Consciente et Inconsciente, de la Vie Morale, Etre et Penser.* 2nd Ed., (Neuchâtel: Baconnière, 1947), p. 57, p. 95.

[5] *Ibid.,* pp. 88 ff., 96ff.

[6] *Ibid.,* pp. 163 ff.

[7] *Ibid.,* pp. 169-274.

[8] By saying that the normal man can "by himself" accomplish the process of liberation, we simply mean to deny the necessity of a special intervention of another person, as, for instance, the work of a therapist; but we do not at all mean to exclude the constructive influence of education and training, and least of all the manifest or hidden contribution of spiritual factors.

[9] A. Snoeck, "Moral Reflections on Psychiatric Aberrations," *Theol. Studies* (1952), 13, 173-189.

[10] N. Mailloux, "Psychic Determinism, Freedom, and Personality Development," *Canad. J. Psychol.* (1953), 7, 5.

[11] Gemelli, *La Personalità del Delinquente nei suoi Fondamenti Biologici e Psicologici* (Milano: Giuffrè, 1948), 2nd Ed., pp. 238 ff. Virgil P. O'Brien attempted to define the degrees of moral responsibility in relationship to the influence of the passions on human actions. He holds that a passion can be present in innumerable degrees of intensity, so that the diminution of the human act which follows can vary from a slight to a total weakening of the normal function. *The Measure of Responsibility in Persons Influenced by Emotion* (Washington, D. C.: Catholic Univ. Amer. Press, 1948), pp. 2, 67.

[12] J. Rimaud, "Psychologists versus Morality," *Cross Currents,* (1951). Cf. the same article under the title: 'Les Psychologues contre la Morale," *Études* (1949), 263, 3-22.

[13] J. Rimaud, "Psychologists versus Morality," *op. cit.,* 32.

[14] Gerald Kelley writes that, even though it is difficult to establish the responsibility of human action in concrete cases, we can be sure that the normal man performs most of his acts with sufficient freedom to deserve praise or blame, and that he is really conscious of his responsibility. Notwithstanding all this, Kelley hopes that the moralists will take into consideration in the near future "the thesis of diminished or even non-existent responsibility of the mentally ill. It offers, it is true, many practical problems, but not the semblance of a denial of the doctrine of free will." "Notes on Moral

Theology," *Cross Currents* (1949), 84.

15 In this sense the following passage of Andre Snoeck must be understood: "We moralists are much impressed by the external structure of the act and less accustomed to look for its inner meaning. And yet, if we wish to plumb more deeply and to surpass a sociological or judicial ethics we shall have to settle down to the study of the concrete personality as it expresses its dynamic complexity." "Moral Reflections on Psychiatric Aberrations," *Theol. Studies* (1952), 13, 189.

16 A. Gemelli, *La Responsabilità nelle Azioni, op. cit.,* p. 228.

17 J. B. Hawkins, "Free Will and Right Action," *Mod. School* (1949), 26, 279. According to the opinion of N. Braunshausen, there are convinced determinists, both jurists and moralists, who demonstrate that personal responsibility can exist under different points of view even under the hypothesis of determinism. Cf. "Le Libre-Arbitre a la Lumière de la Psychologie Experimentale et de la Science Moderne," *Rev. Sci. Pedag.* (1946), 8, 33-48, 75-96; (1947), 9, 8-23, 38-46. Braunshausen's opinion seems to me to be quite unconvincing unless we attribute to the deterministic hypothesis a profoundly different meaning from the one the author seems to imply.

18 Cf. D. C. MacIntosh, "Responsibility, Freedom, and Causality, or the Dilemma of Determinism or Indeterminism," *J. Philos.* (1940), 37, 42-51.

19 A. Binet, "La Responsabilité Morale," *Rev. Philos.* (1888), 26, 217, 219.

20 A. Binet, *op. cit.,* p. 229. Toward the end of the 19th century, the opinion was very common that to have recourse to a doctrine of responsibility based on the freedom of the will was completely superfluous. Cf., for example, Augustin F. Hamon, who defends the idea of social responsibility. "Man is responsible because he lives in society, and for no other cause than this social existence." *The Universal Illusion of Free Will and Criminal Responsibility* (Watford-London: Univ. Press, 1899), p. 136.

21 A. Binet, *op. cit.,* p. 230.

22 O. Mowrer, "Motivation and Neurosis," *Current Theory and Research in Motivation: A Symposium* (Lincoln, Nebraska: Univ. Nebr. Press, 1953), pp. 175-181.

23 J. Borel, *Le Déséquilibre Psychique: Ses Psychoses, sa Morale* (Paris: Press Univ. France), (1947), p. 374.

24 Cf. J. Grasset, "Le Problème Physiopathologique de la Responsabilité," *J. Psychol. Norm. Path.* (1905), 2, 97-114; "Le Psychisme Inferieur et la Responsabilité," *Rev. Philos.* (1905), 7, 381-412; *The Semi-Insane and the Semi-Responsible (Demifous et Demiresponsables),* trans. S. E. Jelliffe (New York-London: Funk and Wagnalls, 1907); "La Responsabilité Attenuée," *Rev. Deux Mondes* (1911), 3, 903-929.

25 J. Grasset, *The Semi-Insane and the Semi-Responsible,* pp. 44, 46.

26 Hippolyte Bernheim had already developed this doctrine of continuous degrees of responsibility, from the most complete form to the least complete. *L'Hypnotisme et la Suggestion dans leurs Rapports avec la Médicine*

Légale, Rapport du Congrès de Moscou (1897), pp. 57, 458.

[27] J. Grasset, *The Semi-Insane and the Semi-Responsible*, pp. 312 ff.

[28] J. Grasset, *ibid.*, p. 325.

[29] This condition has been expressed, with typical clarity of thought, by Claude Bernard: "Personne ne contestera qu'il y ait un déterminisme de la non-liberté morale. Certaines *altérations* de l'organisme cérébral amènent la folie, font disparaître la liberté morale comme l'intelligence et obscurcissent la conscience chez l'aliéné. Puis-qu'il y a un déterminisme de la *non-liberté* morale, il y a nécessairement un déterminisme de la *liberté* morale, c'est-à-dire un ensemble de conditions anatomiques et physico-chimiques qui lui permettent d'esister. . . Le déterminisme, en un mot, loin d'être la négation de la liberté morale, en est au contraire la condition nécessaire comme de toutes autre manifestations vitales." *Leçons sur le Phenomenes de la Vie*, 2 Vols., 2nd Edit. (Paris: Baillière, 1885), Vol. I, p. 61.

[30] C. Piat, *La Liberté: I. Historique du Probleme au XIX Siecle; II. Le Problème* (Paris: Lethielleux, 1894-1895), Vol. I, p. 286. Recently Auguste Brunner has pointed out the deficiency of Sartre's doctrine. He writes: "Dans la système de Sartre l'éducation devrait être purement intellectuelle, une prise de conscience de la direction que se donne la liberté absolue. La vie est la pour dire qu'une telle conscience claire, si utile qu'elle puisse être, ne suffit pas." *La Personne Incarnée: Étude sur la Phénoménologie et la Philosophie Existentialiste* (Paris: Beauchesne, 1947), p. 190.

[31] R. Zavalloni, *Educazione e Personalità* (Milano: Vita e Pensiero, 1955). It is evident that in this personalistic theory the intellect always maintains a function of first importance. For this reason the author of this study could subscribe without any difficulty to the following assertion of Eduard Cros: "Le degré de la perfection d'agir de l'homme dépend, en grand partie, du degré de l'enrichissement de l'intellect." *La Liberté et la Subconscience: Contribution a l'étude de la Personnalité Humaine* (Lausanne: Imprimeries Reunies, 1917), p. 17.

[32] J. Lindworsky, *The Training of the Will*, trans. A. Steiner & E. A. Fitzpatrick (Milwaukee: Bruce, 1955).

[33] J. Maritain, *Some Reflexions on Culture and Liberty* (Chicago: Univ. Chicago Press, 1939), pp. 29 ff. The goal of education is to create the psychological context which permits us the conquest and the rational use of freedom. Cf. in this regard the following assertion of Michel-Marie de la Croix: "Toute oeuvre d'éducation ou rééducation—et nous donnons a ces deus termes toute l'ampleur possible—vise à créer le contexte psychique qui rende possible l'usage minimal ou plénir de la liberté." *Liberté et Structure del'Acte Humain, in Limites de l'Humain* (Et. Carmelitaines, Paris: Desclée, 1953), p. 99.

[34] This personalistic aspect of the conquest of freedom is strongly emphasized in the studies of Emmanuel Mounier, especially in *Personalism*, trans. P. Mairet (New York: Grove Press, 1952).

[35] Michel-Marie, *Liberté et Structure de l'Acte Humain*, p. 100.

36 H. Cantril, *The "Why" of Man's Experience* (New York: Macmillan, 1950), p. 54. José A. De Laburu thinks that "la subjectivación de los 'bienes valores' debe de hacerse necesariamente por vía del raciocinio, y puede reforzarse convenientemente por vía del sentimiento." *El Poder de la Voluntad en la Conducta del Hombre* (Montevideo: Editorial Mosca Hnos., 1947), p. 38. In my opinion the personalization of values should not really be made either by way of reasoning or by way of feeling, but by means of that "comprehensive" relationship which characterizes human relations.

37 One who recognizes spiritual values is in a better position than those who ignore or deny them because he sees both sides of this psychosomatic being which is man. In this regard Karl Stern writes: "Those who believe in the primacy of the spirit are looking at these issues from a vantage point which Freud himself did not have. . . Those among us, however, who 'see both sides' are at an advantage when it comes to the task of integration." "Religion and Psychiatry," *Commonweal* (1948), 49, 32.

38 T. V. Moore, *The Driving Forces of Human Nature and their Adjustment* (New York: Grune & Stratton, 1950), p. 325. Cf. also the following assertion of Patrick Mullahy, "Will, Choice, and Ends," *Psychiatry* (1949), 12: "To understand the function of choice, we must look not to single acts of choice, but to a whole series of such acts extending over months or years. Then choice can be seen to be the means of ordering one's life rationally whereby it is made more significant and more satisfying." P. 383.

Conclusion

The intent of this study was by means of a psychological analysis and theoretical evaluation to contribute to the critical examination of experimental data. My goal was to clarify the nature and the functioning of man's free activity. It is evident that there is an intimate relation between this study and the psychology of personality and human behavior, of which *personal freedom* is a manifestation—surely the most typical and highest behavioral manifestation.

This study confines itself essentially within the framework of psychology understood as scientific research. It covers a period of approximately sixty years. During this relatively short period, psychology as the science of man made great progress. New psychological trends and new philosophical doctrines succeeded one another with the subjective conviction of certitude. It was during this period of scientific research and reflection that the problem of human freedom had its ascendency and eclipse. At the beginning of this sixty-year period the problem of freedom was the main topic of very animated discussions among the followers of opposing schools; freedom suffered a long eclipse when it was submerged under the behavioristic wave, which stressed scientific objectivity alone. The appearance of the clinical method, of the studies on personality and of existential analysis have, during the last twenty years, returned the problem of freedom to the forefront of psychology, the true science of man.

I could not, nor did I intend to give an exhaustive presentation of everything written on the problem of freedom during this sixty-year period. What I had in mind was to offer a sufficiently broad and elaborate picture to permit an examination of the essential points of the issue.

This examination began with an historical survey of the immediate antecedents of the problem of freedom and its present state. During the nineteenth century, when the development of the scientific method had already made its influence felt even in psychology, the problem of freedom was examined according to three distinct methods: (1) *the philosophical method,* which at times presented a more psychological character, at times a more metaphysical one; (2) *the scientific method,* which maintained the illusory character of consciousness on the basis of the deterministic hypothesis, and even applied to human behavior the laws of physical nature; (3) *the moral method,* which admitted freedom according to the formulations of the Kantian neo-critical method, that is, as an ethical postulate, and not as a datum of experience.

In the framework of contemporary psychology the problem of free human activity has been considered according to three different trends: *physiological, experimental,* and *personalistic.* The *physiological viewpoint,* by reducing mental processes to mere nerve connections and by excluding the data of consciousness from human experience, denies implicitly any possibility of acting freely. Nevertheless, there are some attempts, especially on the part of Pavlov, to reconcile determinism with freedom. The *experimental viewpoint* reveals, generally speaking, an agnostic tendency; it maintains that the problem of freedom is not an object of scientific study and so relegates it to philosophy. This agnostic tendency would seem fully justifiable in so far as it concerns the incompetence of the psychologist to solve the problem, but makes a serious mistake when it ignores even the *existence of a psychic phenomenon* which is extremely important in human life. For this reason, the *personalistic viewpoint* represents a more positive and more satisfactory orientation toward the problem of freedom. The clinical method, which belongs to this trend, in its attempts to give an explanation of the whole human personality cannot ignore, even methodologically, what is most typical in man's behavior: his constructive power and his capacity of voluntary control.

If freedom of the will is a typical manifestation of human behavior, it follows that it is indispensable to establish which factors influence and determine it. These factors may be *physiological, psychological* and *volitional.* With regard to the *physiological determinants,* the contribution of experimental research on conditioning and voluntary control as motor-adjustment has been revealed as completely negative. An examination of Thorndike's thought, however, allows us to interpret the "confirming-reaction" in man as reconcilable with the idea of freedom. The analysis of *psychological determinants* is related to post-hypnotic suggestion, auto-suggestion, and psychic determinism in psychoanalysis, and finally to the influence of perceptual activity upon the actions of the subject. These various elements contribute to the definition of the concrete situation in which man's behavior manifests itself, but do not necessarily imply a denial of his free activity.

The picture of the determinants of human behavior would lack an essential element if it excluded those which depend on the volitional function. In opposition to what many psychologists think, some very well-known authors of psychological treatises backed up in this by the results of various experimental investigations, especially those made with the help of factor-analysis—maintain the existence and the real efficacy of the volitional factor in human behavior.

Freedom of the will, phenomenologically speaking, manifests itself by means of a selective process. Even though every statistical model deforms the eminently dynamic character of man's activity, we can from the theoretical viewpoint distinguish the following steps in the selective process: *analysis of motives* for the action, *evaluation of alternatives, determination* of the act, and *actualization of the preferential choice.* The objective study of human behavior, even in its highest expressions or manifestations, permits of only a phenomenological description of volitional activity.

The experience of voluntary activity is the cornerstone of the psychological foundation of human freedom. This experience summarizes in itself all the objective data concerning this problem. Experimental research has brought to light the specific character of the consciousness of acting and the decisive intervention of the ego-in-action. While some experimentalists refrain from drawing direct conclusions concerning freedom, and others make pronouncements in favor of the deterministic hypothesis, a consider-

able group of experimental studies reveals, on the basis of introspective protocols, how vivid is the consciousness of freedom in the
volitional act. The "mental effort" of Janet, the "volitive power"
of Rank, the "constructive and integrative factor" of Jung and
Goldstein—all of these are fundamental elements in a positive
solution to the problem of freedom.

The power of self-determination as an indispensable factor for
man is placed in final focus by psychotherapy, especially by that
psychotherapy which stresses more than any other the constructive
value of the human person: client-centered therapy (Rogers).
Lastly, the trend in existential psychology—whether under the
name of existential analysis (Binswanger), or logotherapy
(Frankl), or synthetic psychiatry (Baruk)—brings a new and decisive contribution to the phenomenology of human freedom.

Laboratory experiments and clinical studies, although limited in
number, have clarified this issue of freedom in a fresh way. It must
be pointed out, however, that these experiments and studies do not
always represent real-life conditions, because the *experiments* are
made under somewhat artificial circumstances and the *clinical
studies* are limited to abnormal or psychically disturbed subjects.
For this reason I have attempted to add a personal, though very
modest, contribution to the study of the problem of freedom by
means of an experiment on freedom "as lived"—that freedom man
experiences as present or absent in real-life conditions. This experiment on freedom permitted us to distinguish between the feeling
and the experience of freedom on the basis of the psychic development of the individual and to evaluate its importance in the education and training of youth.

The analysis of experimental data presented in the first part of
this study is followed in the second part by a theoretical evaluation.
This evaluation touches on two essential points, the *foundation* and
the *meaning* of freedom. In order to understand the profound significance of these two aspects of the problem, one must go beyond
the data of experience, that is, transcend their phenomenological
character. The psychologist as such cannot ignore the psychic
process of conscious and voluntary activity, even though he can
never understand it fully and discover all the answers.

To arrive at a scientifically adequate knowledge of the problem it was indispensable, first of all, to clear the field of the obstacles on the level of consciousness itself. What is the value of the testimony of consciousness? What is the role of motivation in human behavior? What is the meaning of the scientific hypotheses concerning the concept of freedom? None of these points constitutes a truly insurmountable obstacle. On the other hand, none of these elements is sufficient to furnish a valid explanation of freedom itself. Without recourse to a particular kind of causality—the psychic causality of the personal ego—free action would be subjected either to absolute chaos or to the most rigid determinism.

The idea of freedom can be identified essentially with man's power of self-determination in favor of one alternative in preference to others. Freedom in the last analysis is synonymous with self-determination in a typically human sense, which differs completely from the mere spontaneity found in every living being. This power of self-determination has a real, concrete meaning, which is quite at variance with the abstractionism of the so-called freedom of indifference or the role of autonomous faculties. Freedom is limited by the conditionism of actual life. For the idea of absolute freedom we substituted the idea of freedom in "various degrees."

Freedom of action is really not a privilege of a particular psychic function, but a power of the integral man as a conscious subject of experience. And so for the partial theories which stress the role of determined psychic factors, we have substituted the personalistic theory of freedom, which emphasizes the unified and "total" character of the manifestations of the human person.

This theory of freedom, since it takes into consideration the concrete person and the complex and profound motivation of human behavior, has important consequences on moral life, social sanction, education and training. The concept of "gradation" (freedom in degrees) becomes essential for moral responsibility also, which certainly cannot find an adequate explanation on either the social or the medico-legal level.

But what is essential to bear in mind in every evaluation of human behavior is the twofold source of moral life, the conscious and the unconscious. The contribution of depth-psychology on this point cannot be ignored. These considerations draw me to emphasize the need to substitute "psychological morality" for "juridical morality"—a morality which is more adequate in the concrete conditions of every man's personal freedom,—without of course prescinding from the perennial principles of morality.

A personalistic theory of freedom, which is the basis of this study, requires a corresponding personalistic trend in education and training. Only by adjustment and the integral development of the personality shall we be able to obtain that control of behavior which is worthy of a rational being. Only through exercising freedom of choice will the adolescent be able to achieve the true freedom of a mature man. This analysis and evaluation of the data of experience should offer materials of particular interest for educational problems and training programs.

Bibliography

Abramowski, E. "Recherches expérimentales sur la volonté," *J. Psychol. norm. path.* (1914), 10, 491-508.
"Etudes expérimentales sur la volonté," *J. Psychol. norm. path.* (1915), 12, 13-43, 88-118.

Abramson, H. A. (Ed.) "Problems of consciousness" (*Transactions of the Fourth Conference,* March 29, 30 and 31, 1953), New York: Josiah Macy, Jr. Foundation, 1954.

Ach, N. *Über die Willenstätigkeit und das Denken* (Göttingen: Vandenkoek und Ruprecht, 1905).
Über den Willensakt und das Temperament (Leipzig: Quelle und Meyer, 1910).
Über den Willensakt: Eine Replik (Leipzig: Quelle und Meyer, 1911).
Der Wille (Leipzig: Barth, 1927).
Über die Entstehung des Bewusstseins der Willensfreiheit (Jena: Gustav Fischer, 1928).
Analyse des Wollens (Berlin: Urban und Schwarzenburg, 1935).

Adler, A. *The practice and theory of individual psychology* (New York: Harcourt, Brace, 1946).
Religion und Individualpsychologie (Wien: Rolf Passer, 1933).
Understanding human nature (New York: Permabooks, 1949).
What life should mean to you (Boston: Little & Brown, 1931).

Adler, M. *What man has made of man* (New York: Longmans, Green, 1938).

Alexander, F. *The psychoanalysis of the total personality* (New York: Nerv. Ment. Dis. Publ., 1946).
The fundamentals of psychoanalysis (New York: Norton, 1948).

Allen, F. H. *Psychotherapy with children* (New York: Norton, 1942).

Allers, R. *The psychology of character,* trans. E. B. Strauss (New York: Sheed & Ward, 1931).
The new psychologies (New York: Sheed & Ward, 1938).
"Irresistible impulses," *Amer. eccl. Rev.* (1939), 100, 208-219.
The successful error (New York: Sheed & Ward, 1940).

Allport, G. W. "Guidelines for research in international cooperation," *J. soc. Issues* (1947), 3, 21-37.
Personality: A psychological interpretation (New York: Henry Holt & Co., 1937).

The nature of personality: Selected papers (Cambridge, Mass.: Addison-Wesley Press, 1950).
Bemerkungen su dem gegenwärtigen Stand der Theorie der Motivation in den U.S.A.," *Psychol. Beiträge* (1953), 1, 10-28.

Angell, J. R. *Psychology: An introductory study of the structure and function of human consciousness,* 4th rev. ed. (New York: Henry Holt, 1908).
An introduction to psychology (New York: Henry Holt, 1918).

Angyal, A. *Foundations for a science of personality* (New York: Commonwealth Fund, 1941).

Ansbacher, H. L. "Causality and indeterminism according to Alfred Adler and some current American personality theories," *Ind. Psychol. Bull.* (1951), 9, 96-107.

Anshen, R. N. (Ed.) *Freedom: Its meaning* (New York: Harcourt, Brace, 1940).

Arnold, M. *Emotion and personality,* 2 Vols. (New York: Columbia Univ. Press, 1960).

Arnold, M., & Gasson, J. (Eds.) *The human person* (New York: Ronald Press, 1954).

Aveling, F. *The psychological approach to reality* (London: London Univ. Press, 1929).
Personality and will (Cambridge: Cambridge Univ. Press, 1931).

Ayers, S. *Das Problems der Willensfreiheit mit besonderer Berücksichtigung seiner psychologischen Seite* (Stuttgart: Kohlmann, 1905).

Bain, A. "Dr. Ward on free-will," *Mind* (1880), 5, 116-124.
The emotions and the will, 3rd ed. (New York: Appleton, 1888).

Bair, J. H. "Development of voluntary control," *Psychol. Rev.* (1901), 8, 474-510.

Baker, R. R. *The thomistic theory of the passions and their influence on the will* (Notre Dame, Ind.: Edwards Bros., 1941).

Baker, S. J. "The mathematics of the unconscious," *J. clin. exper. Psychopathol.* (1951), 12, 192-212.

Baladi, N. "La liberté et le passé," *Proceedings of the Tenth International Congress of Philosophy* (Amsterdam: North-Holland, 1949), pp. 976-978.

Bally, G. *Vom Ursprung und von den Grenzen der Freiheit* (Basel: Benno Schwabe, 1945).

Barrett, E. B. *Motive-force and motivation-tracks* (London: Longmans, Green, 1911).
"Couéism in theory and practice," *Catholic Mind* (1923), 21, 21-35.

Baruk, H. "Le problème de la volonté: Nouvelles données psychophysiologiques," *J. Psychol. norm. path.* (1939), 36, 397-423.
"Hypophyse, volonté et personnalité morale," *Presse medic.* (1947), 55, 479-498.
"La psychiatrie synthétique et le problème de la personnalité humaine," *Psyché* (1948), n. 15.
"Experimental catatonia and the problem of will and personality," *J. nerv. ment. Dis.* (1949), 110, 218-235.
"Psychiatrie morale expérimentale, individuelle et sociale," *Bibliothèque de psychiatrie,* 2nd ed. (Paris: Press Univ. France, 1950).
"Les méthodes scientiques d'étude de la conscience morale en psychologie et en psychopatologie individuelle et sociale," in "Le coupable

est-il un malade ou un pécheur?" (Groupe Lyonnais d'Études Médicales, Philosophiques et Biologiques, coll. *Convergences*) (Paris: Spes, 1951), pp. 91-109.

La désorganisation de la personalité (Paris: Press. Univ. France, 1952), "Constatations objectives du problème moral," in *Actes du IIe Congrès International de Criminologie* (Paris: Press. Univ. France, 1953), t. IV, pp. 457-464.

"Les méthodes scientifiques d'étude et d'exploration de la conscience morale: Leurs applications criminologiques," *ibid.,* pp. 475-481.

Bayet, A. *La morale scientifique* (Paris: Alcan, 1905).

Bechterev, V. M. *General principles of human reflexology,* trans. E. and M. Murphy (London: Jarrolos, 1933).

Berge, A. "Déterminisme psychologique et responsabilité morale," *Psyché* (1950), 5, n. 43, 370-377.

Bergmann, W. "Hypnose und Willensfreiheit im Lichte der neureren Forschung," *Frankfurter Zeitgemasse Broschüre* (1912), Bd. 31, 129-156.

Bergson, H. *Essai sur les données immédiates de la conscience,* 31e éd. (Paris: Alcan, 1934).

The two sources of morality and religion, trans. R. Audra & C. Brereton (New York: Henry Holt, 1935).

Bernard, C. *Leçons sur les phénomènes de la vie,* 2 Vols., 2nd ed. (Paris: Baillière, 1885).

Berndtson, C. A. *The problem of free will in recent philosophy* (Chicago: Univ. Chicago Press, 1942).

Bernheim, H. "De la peur en thérapeutique," *Bull. gen. Thérap. médic. chirur,* sept. 30, 1886.

De la suggestion, 2e éd. (Paris: Doin, 1888).

"L'hypnotisme et la suggestion dans leurs rapports avec la médicine légale," *Rapport du Congrès de Moscou,* 1897.

Binet, A. "La responsabilité morale," *Rev. philos.* (1888), 26, 217-231.

Alterations of personality, trans. H. G. Baldwin (New York: Appleton, 1896).

L'âme et le corps (Paris: Flammarion, 1905).

Binswanger, L. *Grundformen und Erkenntnis menschlichen Daseins* (Zurich: Verlag Max Niehans, 1942).

"La 'Daseinsanalyse' en psychiatrie," *L'Encephale* (1951), 1, 108-113.

Blake, R. R., & Ramsey, G. V. (Eds.) *Perception: An approach to personality* (New York: Ronald Press, 1951).

Bleuler, E. *Textbook of psychiatry,* trans. A. A. Brill (New York: Macmillan, 1924).

Bloch, M. A. *Les tendences et la vie morale* (Paris: Press. Univ. France, 1948).

Blondel, C. "La volonté: Essai d'interprétation sociologique," *J. Psychol.* (1920), 17, 606-642.

"Les volitions," in Dumas, G. *Nouveau traité de psychologie* (1939), t. VI, pp. 317-397.

Bohr, N. 'Causality and complementarity," *Philos. Sci.* (1937), 4, 289-298.

"On the notions of causality and complementarity," *Science* (1950), 111, 51-54.

Bonnard, L. "De la liberté psychologique aux garanties le la liberté," *Etudes philos.* (1948), 3, 139-142.

Book, W. F., & Norvell, L. "The will to learn: An experimental study of incentive in learning," *Ped. Sem.* (1922), 29, 305-362.

Borel, J. *Le déséquilibre psychique: Ses psychoses, sa morale* (Paris: Press. Univ. France, 1947).

Boring, E. G. *A history of experimental psychology*, 2nd ed. (New York: Appleton-Century-Crofts, 1950).

Boring, E. G., Langfeld, H. S., & Welds, H. P. *Foundations of psychology* New York: Wiley, 1948).

Bourguignon, G. "Le problème du libre arbitre au regard de la physiologie et de la médicine," *Temoignages Saint-Léger* (1947) 12, 3-16.

Boutonier, J. *Les défaillances de la volonté*, 2nd ed. (Paris: Press. Univ. France, 1951).

Bovet, A. "La conscience du devoir dans l'introspection provoquée: Experience sur la psychologie de la pensée," *Arch. Psychol.* (1910), 9, 304-369.

Brachfield, O. "El libre adebrío como problema sociologico," *Rev. Intern. Soc.* (1948), 21, 13-38.

"La psychología adleriana y la sociología," *Rev. intern. Soc.* (1948), 24, 43-58.

"La responsabilité morale dans la psychologie individuelle d'Adler," *Psyché* (1951), n. 59, 554-573.

Brambilla, S. "Il metodo di Rorschach nell'analisi fenomenologica esistenziale," *Arch Psicol. Neurol. Psich.* (1949), 10, 188-193.

"Daseinsanalyse: scienza, non filosofia," *Arch. Psicol. Neurol. Psich.* (1953), 14.

Bramwell, M. J. *Hypnotism: Its history, practice and theory* (Philadelphia: Lippincott, 1930).

Braunshausen, N. "L'étude expérimentale de la volonté," *Arch Belse Sci. educ.* (1935), 1, 102-126.

"Le libre-arbitre à la lumière de la psychologie expérimentale et de la science moderne," *Rev. Sci. pedag.* (1946), 8, 33-48, 75-96; (1947), 9, 8-23, 38-46.

Brenman, M. "Experiments in the hypnotic production of anti-social and self-injurious behavior," *Psychiatry* (1942), 5, 49-61.

Brennan, R. E. *General Psychology* (New York: Macmillan, 1937).

Breuer, J., & Freud, S. *Studies on hysteria*, trans. J. Strachey (New York: Basic Books, 1957).

Bridges, J. W. "An experimental study of decision types and their mental correlates," *Psychol. Monogr.* (1914-17), n. 72, 1-72.

Bridgman, P. W. "Freedom and the individual," in Anshen, R. N. *Freedom: Its meaning* (New York: Harcourt, Brace, 1940), pp. 525-537.

Brill, A. A. "Determinism in psychiatry and psychoanalysis," *Amer. J. Psychiat.* (1938), 95, 597-615.

Basic principles of psychoanalysis (New York: Doubleday, 1949).

Britt, R. E. "Moral limitations in mental disease," *Linacre Quarterly* (October, 1947), pp. 16-25.

Brown, J. S. "Problems presented by the concept of acquired drives," in *Current theory and research in motivation: A symposium* (Lincoln, Nebraska: Univ. Nebr. Press, 1953), pp. 1-21.

Brugger, W. "Die Verleiblichung des Wollens," *Scholastik* (1950), 25, 248-253.

Brunner, A. *La personne incarnée: Etude sur la phénoménologie et la philo-*

sophie existentialiste (Paris: Beauchesne, 1947).

Buchner, E. F. "Volition as a scientific datum," *Psychol. Rev.* (1900), 7, 494-507.

Bussey, G. C. *Typical recent conceptions of freedom* (Greenfield, Mass.: Morey, 1947).

Buytendijk, F. J. J. "La liberté vécue et la liberté morale dans la conscience enfantine," *Rev. philos.* (Janvier-Mars, 1951).

Cafferata, A. "Notas para una teoría escolástica sobre la responsabilidad: Los elementos del acto libre," *Ciencia y Fe* (1950), 6, 33-63.

Calkins, M. W. *An introduction to psychology* (New York: Macmillan, 1908).
A first book in psychology, 4th ed. (New York: Macmillan, 1919).
"Fact and inference in Raymond Wheeler's doctrine of will and self-activity," *Psychol. Rev.* (1921), 28, 356-373.

Cameron, D. E. "The current transition in the conception of science," *Science* (1948), 107, 553-558.

Canepa, G. *Il concetto di personalità nei suoi aspetti filosofici, biologici e medico-legali* (Roma: Edizioni dell'Ateneo, 1953).

Cantin, S. "Henri Bergson et le problème de la liberté," *Laval théol. philos.* (1945), 1, 71-102.

Cantril, H. *The "why" of man's experience* (New York: Macmillan, 1950).
"An inquiry concerning the characteristics of man," *J. abnorm. soc. Psychol.* (1950), 45, 490-503.
"The qualities of being human," *Amer. Quart.* (1954), 6, 3-18.

Cargnello, D. "Amore, amicizia, aggresivita et ipseità nella antropologia esistenzialista di Ludwig Binswanger," *Riv. Psicol.,* (1947), 43, 111-142; (1948), 44, 36-59, 178-199.
"Antropoanalisi e psicoanalisi," *Arch Psicol. Neurol. Psich.* (1949), 10, 406-434.
"Frankl e la logoterapia," *Arch. Psicol. Neurol. Psich.* (1953), 14.

Caruso, I. A. "Pulsion et liberté" *Psyché* (1949), 4, n. 30-31, 392-395.
Psicanalisi e sintesi dell'esistenza, trans. G. M. Merlo (Torino: Marietti, 1953).

Cassirer, E. *Determinismus und Indeterminismus in der modern Psysik* (Goteborg: Boktryckery, 1937).

Cattell, R. B. *Personality* (New York: McGraw-Hill, 1950).

Chauchard, P. *L'influx nerveux et la psychologie* (Paris: Press. Univ. France, 1950).
"Le sens biologique de la liberté humaine," *Scientia* (1953), 88, 225-229.

Child, J. L., & Whiting, W. M. "Effects of goal attainment: Relaxation versus renewed striving," *J. abnorm. soc. Psychol.* (1950), 45, 667-681.

Childress, M. M. "Efficient causality in human actions," *Mod. School* (1951), 28, 191-222.

Choisy, M. "Insecurite, culpabilite, péché: (Aimons-nous la liberté?)," *Psyché* (1949), 3, n. 34, 674-691.
Psychoanalyse et catholicisme (Paris: L'Arche, 1950).
"Psychoanalysis and catholicism" *Cross Currents* (1951), 3, 75-90.
"Le problème du tout-de-l'homme,"*Psyché* (1951), 6, n. 51, 2-5.
"La responsabilité morale dans la psychoanalyse de Freud," *Psyché* (1951), 6, n. 57-58, 497-512.

Chrysostom, B. "The freedom of the will," *Psychol. Rev.* (1895), 2, 157-

158.

Claparède, E. "Does the will express the entire personality?," in *Problems of personality* (New York: Harcourt, Brace, 1925), pp. 39-43.

Compton, A. H. *The freedom of man* (New Haven: Yale Univ. Press, 1935).

Copleston, F. *Arthur Schopenhauer, philosopher of pessimism* (Andover: Burns, Oates & Washbourne, 1946).

Corallo, G. "L'eredità genetica e l'educazione," *Salesianum* (1951), 13, 51-74.

Educazione e libertà (Torino: S.E.I., 1951).

La pedagogia della libertà (Torino: S.E.I., 1951).

Coué, E. *Self mastery through conscious autosuggestion* (New York: American Library Service, 1922).

Cros, E. *La liberté et la subconscience* (Lausanne: Imprimeries Rèunies, 1917).

Crowley, T. "Some philosophical aspects of physical indeterminacy," *Irish eccl. Rec.* (1948), 70, 785-799.

Congar, Y. "Culpabilité, responsabilité et sanctions collectives," *Vie intellect.* (1950), 1, 259-284, 384-407.

Curran, C. A. *Personality factors in counseling* (New York: Grune & Stratton, 1945).

Counseling in catholic life and education (New York: Macmillan, 1952).

Dalbiez, R. *Psychoanalytical methods and the doctrine of Freud,* trans. T. F. Lindsay, 2 Vols. (New York: Longmans, Green, 1941).

"Le moment de la liberté," *Rev. thom.* (1948), 48, 180-190, 447-458.

Dauches, R. D. "Causation and free will," *Philos. Quart.* (1952), 2, 13-30.

Daudin, H. *La Liberté de la volonté: Signification des doctrines classiques* (Paris: Press. Univ. France, 1950).

Davidson, M. *The free will controversy* (London: Watts, 1942).

Debesse, M. *Comment étudier les adolescents* (Paris: Press. Univ. France, 1948).

De Forest, I. "Significance of self-control as developed during psychoanalytic treatment," *J. clin. Psychopathol.* (1947), 8, 611-622.

Delacroix, H. "Les grandes formes de la vie mentales," in *Nouvelle Enciclopedie Philosophique,* 4th ed. (Paris: Press. Univ. France, 1947).

Demos, R. "Human freedom—positive and negative," in Anshen, R. N. *Freedom: Its meaning* (New York: Harcourt, Brace, 1940), pp. 590-611.

Dempsey, P. J. R. *The psychology of Sartre* (Cork: Cork Univ. Press., 1950).

De Munnynck, M. *La conservation de l'énergie et la liberté morale,* 3rd ed. (Paris: Blond, 1904).

"La démonstration métaphysique du libre arbitre," *Rev. néo-scol.* (1913), 20, 13-39; 181-205; 279-294.

De Raeymaeker, L. "Le problème de la liberté personnelle et le principe de sa solution," *Giorn. Metafis.* (1949), 4, 581-590.

Deutsch, L. "From causality to creative freedom," *Ind. Psychol. Bull.* (1951), 9, 132-142.

De Waelhens, A. "Une philosophie de la volonté," *Rev. philos. Louvain* (1951), 49, 415-437.

Dewey, J. *Human nature and conduct: an introduction to social psychology* (New York: Modern Library, 1930).

Diel, P. *Psychologie de la motivation* (Paris: Press. Univ. France, 1948).

Dollard, J., & Miller, N. *Personality and psychotherapy* (New York: Mc-Graw-Hill, 1950).

Donceel, J. "The psychology of the will," in *Mélanges J. Maréchal* (Bruxelles: L'Edition Universelle, 1950), t. II, pp. 223-232.

"Second thoughts on Freud," *Thought* (1949), 24, 466-484.

Dondeine, A. "Approches du mystère de la liberté," *Rev. intern. Philos.* (1948), n. 16, 23-44.

Dreikurs, R. "Causality versus indeterminism," *Indiv. Psychol. Bull.* (1951), 9, 108-117.

Dukes, W. F. "Psychological studies of values," *Psychol. Bull.* (1955), 52, 24-50.

Eddington, A. S. "The decline of determinism," *Nature* (1932).

Einstein, A. "Freedom and science," in Anshen, R. N. *Freedom: Its meaning* (New York: Harcourt, Brace, 1940), pp. 381-383.

Ekstein, R. "Psychological laws and human freedom," *J. soc. Psychol.* (1947), 25, 181-191.

Erickson, M. H. "An experimental investigation of the possible anti-social uses of hypnosis," *Psychiatry* (1939), 2, 391-414.

Faatz, A. J. *The nature of choice in casework process* (Chapel Hill, N. C.: Univ. North Carolina Press, 1953).

Fabro, C. "La dialettica della libertà e l'Assoluto (Per un confronto fra Hegel e Kierkegaard," in *Kierkegaard e Nietzsche* (Milano-Roma: Bocca, 1953), pp. 45-69.

Fellin, J. *Die Willensfreiheit: Zur Bibliographie des Problems* (Graz: Leuschner und Lubensky, 1928).

Feldenkrais, M. *Body and nature behavior* (New York: Intern. Univ. Press, 1949).

Fischil, P. "Das Problem der Willensfreiheit in individual-psychologischer Beleuchtung," *Int. Z. Indiv-Psychol.* (1951), 20, 175-182.

Flugel, J. C. *A hundred years of psychology* (New York: Macmillan, 1933).

Fonsegrive, G. L. *Essai sur le libre arbitre: Sa théorie et son Histoire,* 2nd ed. (Paris: Alcan, 1896).

Ford, J. C. *Depth psychology, morality and alcoholism* (Weston, Mass.: Weston College Press, 1951).

Forest, A. "Le réalisme de la volonté," *Rev. thom.* (1946), 46, 457-476.

Fouillée, A. "Les nouveaux expédiants en faveur du libre arbitre," *Rev. philos.* (1882), 14, 585-617.

"L'homme automate," *Rev. deux Mondes* (1886), 76, 548-571.

"Existence et développement de la volonté," *Rev. philos.,* Juin (1892).

La psychologie des idées-forces (Paris: Alcan, 1893).

La liberté et le déterminisme (Paris: Alcan, 1895).

Fox, C. *The mind and its body: The foundations of psychology* (London: Kegan Paul, 1931).

Frankl, V. E. "Dimensionen des Menschseins," *Jb. Psychol. Psychother.* (1953), 1, 186-194.

The doctor and the soul: an introduction to logotherapy, trans. R. and C. Winston (New York: Knopf, 1955).

Freud, S. *Introductory lectures on psycho-analysis,* trans. Rivière (London: Allen & Unwin, 1921).

The ego and the id, trans. Rivière (London: Hogarth Press, 1957).

The basic writings of Sigmund Freud, trans. A. A. Brill (New York: Modern Library, 1938).

Collected papers, 5 Vols., trans. Rivière (London: Hogarth Press, 1950).

"Psychogenesis of a case of homosexuality in a woman," in *Collected Papers* (1950), t. II, pp. 202-231.

Frink, H. W. *Morbid fears and compulsions* (New York: Moffat, Yard, 1918).

Fromm, E. *Escape from freedom* (New York: Farrar, Rinehart, 1941).

Man for himself (New York: Rinehart, 1947).

Gadelius, B. *Human mentality in the light of psychiatric experience* (Copenhagen: Lewin & Munksgaard, 1933).

Gemelli, A. *Metodi, compiti e limiti della psicologia nello studio e nella prevenzione della delinquenza* (Milano: Vita e Pensiero, 1936).

"Recherches sur le 'délinquant par tendance' dans le Code pénal italien," *Revue de droit pénal et de criminologie* (1939).

"Lo studio del reato come mezzo di indagine nella valutazione del delinquente," *Jus* (1940), 2, 230-267.

"La personalità nelle azioni umane dal punto di vista della psicologia e della psichiatria," *Revista di diritto penitenziario* (1943), 3.

La responsabilità nelle azioni umane dal punto di vista della psicologia e della psichiatria (Contributi del Laboratorio di psicologia, Serie XII) (Milano: Vita e Pensiero, 1944).

La personalità del delinquente nei suoi fondamenti biologici e psicologici, 2nd ed. (Milano: Ginuffrè, 1948).

"A scientific study of the personality of the delinquent," *Penal Reform News* (1949), Newsletter n. 8, January, pp. 2-4.

"La criminologia e il diritto penale," *La scuola positiva* (1951), n. 1-2, p. 32.

La concezione dinamica della personalità nello studio dei delinquenti (Milano: Giuffrè, 1955).

La psicologia dell'età evolutiva, 4th ed. (Milano: Giuffrè, 1955).

Psychoanalysis today, trans. J. S. Chapin & S. Attanasio (New York: Kenedy, 1955).

Gemelli, A., & Zunini, G. *Introduzione alla psicologia,* 2nd ed. (Milano: Vita e Pensiero, 1949).

Gies, K. "Experimentelle Untersuchungen über den Willen mit Berücksichtigung der Entstehung des Bewusstseins der Willensfreiheit," *Arch. ges. Psychol.* (1930), 74, 1-96.

Glover, E. *Freud or Jung?* (New York: Norton, 1950).

Goldstein, K. *Human nature in the light of psychopathology* (Cambridge: Harvard Univ. Press, 1940).

Gomez, P. R. *Libertad humana y estados morbosos del espíritu,* 2 Vols. Medellin: Imp. Universidad, 1934).

Gonseth, F. *Déterminisme et libre arbitre,* 2nd ed. (Neuchâtel: Editions du Griffon, 1947).

Grasset, J. "Le problème physiopathologique de la responsabilité," *J. Psychol. norm. path.* (1905), 2, 97-114.

"Le psychisme inferieur et la responsabilité," *Rev. philos.* (1905), 7, 381-418.

The semi-insane and the semi-responsible, trans. S. E. Jeliffe (New York: Funk & Wagnalls, 1907).

"La responsabilité attenuée," *Rev. deux Mondes* (1911), 3, 903-929.

Gregoire, F. "La collaboration de l'intuition et de l'intelligence," *Rev. intern. Philos.* (1949), 3, n. 10, 392-406.

Gruender, H. *Free will* (St. Louis: Herder, 1916).

Experimental psychology (Milwaukee: Bruce, 1932).

Gurvitch, G. "Les degrés de la liberté humaine," *Cah. intern. Sociol.* (1951), 6, 3-20.

Déterminismes sociaux et liberté humaine (Bibliotheque de sociologie contemporaine) (Paris: Press. Univ. France, 1955).

Gutberlet, C. *Die Willensfreiheit und ihre Gegner,* 2 Vols. (Fulda: Fuldaer Actiendruck, 1907).

Guthrie, E. R. *The psychology of human conflict* (New York: Harper, 1938).

Guthrie, E. R., & Edwards, A. L. *Psychology: A first course in human behavior* (New York: Harper, 1949).

Guyenot, E. "Hérédité et liberté," in *L'homme devant la science* (Neuchâtel: Baconnière, 1952), pp. 81-99; 295; 319.

Hamel, I. A. "A study and analysis of the conditioned reflex," *Psychol. Monogr.* (1919), 27, n. 118, 1-65.

Hamon, A. F. *The universal illusion of free will and criminal responsibility* (Watford-London: Univ. Press, 1899).

Hansen, V. "L'idée de la liberté chez Kierkegaard et Renouvier," in *Proceedings of the Tenth International Congress of Philosophy* (Amsterdam: North-Holland, 1949), pp. 1191-1194.

Harlow, H. F. "Motivation as a factor in new responses," in *Current theory and research in motivation: A symposium* (Lincoln, Neb.: Univ. Nebraska Press, 1953), pp. 24-55.

Harmon, F. L. *Understanding personality* (Milwaukee: Bruce, 1948).

Principles of Psychology (Milwaukee: Bruce, 1951).

Harper, R. *Existentialism: A theory of man* (Cambridge: Cambridge Univ. Press, 1948).

Hartmann, G. W. *Gestalt psychology* (New York: Ronald Press, 1935).

Hawkins, J. B. "Free will and right action," *Mod. School.* (1949), 26, 279-292.

Hayden, J. J. "La formation intégrale du sens moral," *Psyché* (1949), 4, n. 30-31, 335-350.

Heath, E. A. "A scientific basis for freedom," in *Proceedings of the Tenth International Congress of Philosophy* (Amsterdam: North-Holland, 1949), pp. 135 ff.

Hebb, D. O. *The organization of behavior* (New York: Wiley, 1949).

Helson, H. *Theoretical foundations of psychology* (New York: Van Nostrand, 1951).

Herrick, C. J. "Scientific method and human values," *Amer. Scientist* 1946), 34, 239-245.

George Ellet Coghill (Chicago: Univ. Chicago Press, 1949).

Herzfeld, K. F. "The quantum theory of matter," *Thought* (1936), 11, 566-588.

Hilgard, E. R. "Conditioned eyelid reactions to a light stimulus based on the reflex wink to sound," *Psychol. Monogr.* (1931), n. 41, 1-50.
"Human motives and the concept of the self," *Amer. Psychologist* (1949), 4, 374-382.

Hilgard, E. R., & Marquis, D. G. *Conditioning and learning* (New York: Appleton-Century, 1940).

Hoare, F. R. "Physical determinism and free-will," *Irish eccl. Rec.* (1934), 43, 27-35.

Hobart, R. E. "Freewill as involving determinism and inconceivable without it," *Mind* (1934), 43, 1-27.

Hoche, A. *Die Freiheit des Willens vom Standpunkte der Psychopatologie* (Wiesbaden: Bergmann, 1902).

Hofmann, F. *Beitrdge zum Problem der Freiheit des Willens unter Berücksichtigung von Erfahrungen mit dem Rorschachschen psychodiagnostischen Formdeuteversuch* (Zürich: Neue Zurcher Zeitung, 1950).

Hollander, B. *Methods and uses of hypnosis and self-hypnosis* (New York: Macmillan, 1928).

Holmes, E. "Freedom and growth," *Hibbert J.* (1919), 17, 626-641.

Hoop, J. H. *Character and the unconscious* (New York: Harcourt, Brace, 1923).

Horney, K. *New ways in psychoanalysis* (New York: Norton, 1939).
Are you considering psychoanalysis? (New York: Norton, 1946).

Hospers, J. "Meaning and free will," *Philos. phenom. Res.* (1940-50), n. 10, 307-330.

Howe, E. G. *Motives and mechanism of the mind* (London: Lancet, 1931).

Hudgins, C. V. "Conditioning and the voluntary control of the pupillary light reflex," *J. gen Psychol.* (1933), 8, 3-51.

Hull, C. L. *Hypnosis and suggestibility* (New York: Appleton-Century-Crofts, 1933).
Principles of behavior (New York: Appleton-Century-Crofts, 1943).

Humphrey, G. "The effect of sequences of indifferent stimuli on a reaction of the conditioned response type," *J. abnorm. soc. Psychol.* (1927), 22, 194-212.

Hunt, J. McV. (Ed.) *Personality and the behavior disorders*, 2 Vols. (New York: Ronald Press, 1944).

Hunter, W. S. "An experiment on the disinhibition of voluntary responses," *J. exper. Psychol.* (1938), 22, 419-428.

Hunter, W. S., & Hudgins, C. V. "Voluntary activity from the standpoint of behaviorism," *J. gen. Psychol.* (1934), 10, 198-204.

Huntley, C. W., "Judgments of self based upon records of expressive behavior," *J. abnorm. soc. Psychol.* (1940), 35, 398-427.

Husson, L. *L'intellectualisme de Bergson* (Paris: Press. Univ. France, 1947).

Irwin, F. W. "The concept of volition in experimental psychology," in Clarke, F. P., & Nahm, M. C. *Philosophical essays in honor of Edgar Arthur Singer, Jr.* (Philadelphia: Univ. Penna. Press, 1942), pp. 115-137.
"Motivation," in Helson, H. *Theoretical foundations of psychology* (New York: Van Nostrand, 1951), pp. 200-253.

Jacobi, J. *The psychology of Jung,* trans. K. W. Bash, 4th ed. (New Haven: Yale Univ. Press, 1945).

James, W. *"The dilemma of determinism," "The will to believe,"* and other essays in popular philosophy (New York: Longmans, Green, 1916).

Essays in pragmatism (New York: Hafner Publ., 1948).

Psychology (New York: World Publishing, 1948).

Janet, P. *Psychological healing: An historical and clinical study,* trans. Eden & Cedar Paul, 2 Vols. (London: George Allen & Unwin; New York: Macmillan, 1925).

L'automatisme psychologique (Paris: Alcan, 1930).

Jaunges, G. E. M. *Modern physics* (New York: Van Nostrand, 1932).

Jeans, J. *The mysterious universe* (London: Cambridge Univ. Press, 1930).

Jerome, J. "Psychologie aristotélicienne et psychologie contemporaine de la volonté," *Vie spirit.* (1953), Suppl. n. 27, 446-468.

Joel, K. *Der freie Wille* (München: Bruckmann, 1908).

Jokl, R. H. "Psychic determinism and preservation of sublimation in classical psychoanalytic procedure," *Bull. Menniger Clinic* (1950), 14, 207-219.

Jung, C. G. *Contributions to analytical psychology,* trans. H. G. & C. F. Baynes (London: Kegan Paul, 1928).

Psychological factors determining human behavior (Cambridge: Harvard Univ. Press, 1936).

Psychology and religion, 6th printing (New Haven: Yale Univ. Press, 1946).

Kantor, J. R. *Principles of psychology* (New York: Knopf, 1924).

Karpf, F. B. *The psychology and psychotherapy of Otto Rank* (New York: Philosophical Library, 1953).

Katz, W. G. "Responsibility and freedom: a difficulty in relating christianity and law," *J. legal Educ.* (1952), pp. 269 ff.

Kelley, G. *"Notes on moral theology,"* Cross Currents (1949), 80-89; *Theol. Studies* (1949), 10, 67-117.

Kinberg, O. "Motive, choice, will," *Theoria* (1948), 14, 209-237.

Klein, G. S. "The personal world through perception," in Blake, R. R. & Ramsey, G. V., *Perception: An approach to personality* (New York: Ronald Press, 1951), pp. 68-88.

Klubertanz, G. P. "The psychologists and the nature of man," in *Proc. Amer. Cath. philos. Ass.* (1951), 55, 66-88.

Kluckhohn, C. *Mirror for man* (New York: Whittlesey, 1949).

Klug, I. *Willensfreiheit und Personlichkeit* (Paderborn: Schöningh, 1932).

Knight, R. P. "Determinism, 'freedom and psychotherapy," *Psychiatry* (1946), 9, 251-262.

Knox, H. V. *The will to be free:A critique of deterministic theory* (London: Constable, 1928).

Konczewska, H. *Contingence, liberté et personnalité humaine* (Paris: Vrin, 1937).

Kretschmer, E. *Physique and character,* trans. W. J. H. Sproutt (London: Kegan Paul, 1925).

Kucera, E. "Experimentelle Beiträge zur Charakterristik der Willenshandlung," *Arch ges. Psychol.* (1930), 77, 223-248.

Kunh, H. *Freedom forgotten and remembered* (Chapel Hill: Univ. North Carolina Press, 1943).

Külpe, O. "Die Lehre vom Willen in der neuren Psychologie," *Philos. Studien* (1889), 5, 178-244; 381-446.

Laburu, J. A., de, *El poder de la voluntad en la conducta del hombre* (Montevideo: Editorial Mosca Hnos., 1947).

Ladd, J. "Free will and voluntary action," *Phil. phenom. Res.* (1952), 12, 392-405.

Lagache, D. *L'unité de la psychologie* (Paris: Press. Univ. France, 1949).

Lalande, A. *Vocabulaire technique et critique de la philosophie,* 6th ed., (Paris: Press. Univ. France, 1951).

Langmuir, I. "Science, common sense and decency," *Science* (1943), 97, 1-7.
Phenomena, atoms and molecules (New York: Island Press, 1945).

Leclère, A. "La loi de préformation et prédetermination en psychologie," *Année psychol.* (1912), 18, 145-207.

Lee, R. S. *Freud and christianity* (New York: A. A. Wyn, 1949).

Lehmen, A. *Lehrbuch der philosophie auf Aristotelisch-scholasticher Grundlage: Psychologie* (Freiburg: Herder, 1902).

Lewin, K. "Das Problem der Willensmessung und das Grundgesetz der Association," *Psychol. Forsch.* (1922), 1, 191-302; 2, 65-140.
Vorsatz, Wille und Bedürfnis (Berlin: Springer, 1926).
"Die Entwiklung der experimentellen Willens und Affektpsychologie und die Psychoterapie," *Arch. Psychiat.* (1928), 85, 515-537.
A dynamic theory of personality, trans. D. K. Adams & K. E. Zener (New York: McGraw-Hill, 1935).

Lewis, G. *Le problème de l'inconscient et le cartésianisme* (Paris: Press. Univ. France, 1950).

Lewis, H. B. "The meaning of liberty," *Rev. intern. Philos.* (1948), n. 6, 14-22.

Lewis, V. W. "Changing the behavior of adolescent girls," *Arch. Psychol.* 1943), n. 219, 1-87.
L'humanisme et la grace (Paris: Pierre Horay, 1950).
Limites de l'humain (Etudes Carmélitaines), (Paris: Desclée de Brouwer, 1953).

Lindworsky, J. *Der Wille: Seine Erforschung und seine Beherrschung nach den Ergebnissen der experimentellen Forschung,* 3 Vols. (Leipzig: Barth, 1923).
Experimental psychology, trans. H. R. de Silva (New York: Macmillan, 1931).
Theoretical psychology, trans. H. R. de Silva (St. Louis: Herder, 1932).
Zur jüngsten experimentellen Willensuntersuchung," Arch ges. Psychol. (1932), 86, 533-538.
The training of the will, trans. A. Steiner & E. A. Fitzpatrick (Milwaukee: Bruce, 1929).

Lipkin, S. "The client evaluates nondirective psychotherapy," *J. consult. Psychol.* (1948), 12, 137-145.

London, I. D. "Psychology and Heisenberg's principle of indeterminacy," *Psychol. Rev.* (1945), 52, 162-168.
"Some consequences for history and psychology of Langmuir's convergence and divergence of phenomena," *Psychol. Rev.* (1946), 53, 170-188.
"Free-will as a function of divergence," *Psychol. Rev.* (1948), 55, 4-47.
"The developing personality as a joint function of convergence and divergence," *J. soc. Psychol.* (1949), 29, 167-187.

Lopez Ibor, J. J. *La responsabilidad penal del enfermo mental* (Madrid:

Cosmo, 1951).

Lottin, J. "La statistique morale et le déterminisme," *Rev. néo-scol.* (1908), 15, 48-89.

Louttit, C. M. "The nature of clinical psychology," in *Psychol. Bull.* (1939), 36, 361-389.

Lowrey, L. G. "Psychic determinism and responsibility," *Psychiat. Quart.* (1953), 27, 543-562.

Lüderitz, H. *Beitrag zur experimentellen Untersuchungen des Wahlvorganges* (Göttingen: Akad Buchs, 1929).

Luria, A. R. *The nature of human conflicts* (New York: Liveright, 1932).

Macintosh, D. C. "Responsibility, freedom, and causality, or the dilemma of determinism or indeterminism," *J. Philos.* (1940), 37, 42-51.

MacKinnon, D. W., & Maslow, A. H. "Personality," in Helson, H. *Theoretical foundations of psychology* (New York: Van Nostrand, 1951), pp. 602-655.

MacLeod, R. B. "The phenomenological approach to social psychology," *Psychol. Rev.* (1947), 54, 193-210.

MacMurray, J. "Freedom in the personal nexus," in Anshen, R. N. *Freedom: Its meaning* (New York: Harcourt, Brace, 1940), pp. 507-524.

Mailloux, N. "Psychic determinism, freedom, and personality development," *Canad. J. Psychol.* (1953), 7, 1-11.

Manasee, E. M. "Conversion and liberation: A comparison of Augustine and Kierkegaard," *Rev. Relig.* (1943), pp. 361-383.

Marache, T. J. "Bergson and free will," *Personalist* (1939), 20, 21-28.

Marc, A. *Psychologie réflexive, I. La connaissance, II. La volonté et l'esprit* (Paris: Desclée de Brouwer, 1949).

Maritain, J. *Some reflextions on culture and liberty* (Chicago: Univ. Chicago Press, 1939).

Freedom in the modern world, trans. O'Sullivan (New York: Scribner's Sons, 1936).

"The conquest of freedom," in Anshen, R. N. *Freedom: Its meaning* (New York: Harcourt, Brace, 1940), pp. 631-649.

La philosophie bergsonienne: Etudes critiques, 3rd ed. (Paris: P. Téqui, 1948).

Martin, A. H. "An experimental study of the factors and types of voluntary choice," *Arch. Psychol.* (1922), n. 51, 1-115.

Maslow, A. H. "A theory of human motivation," *Psychol. Rev.* (1943), 50, 514-539; 541-558.

May, R. "Historical and philosophical presuppositions for understanding therapy," in Mowrer, O. H. *Psychotherapy: Theory and research* (New York: Ronald Press, 1953), pp. 9-43.

May, R., Angel, E., & Ellenberger, H. F. (Eds.) *Existence* (New York: Basic Books, 1958).

McCarthy, R. C. *Safeguarding mental health*, 9th printing (Milwaukee: Bruce, 1949).

McClelland, D. C. *Personality* (New York: William Sloane Assoc., 1951).

McClelland, D. C., & al. *The achievement motive* (New York: Appleton-Century-Crofts, 1953).

McDonald, M. F. *Psychological foundations* (New York: Roosevelt Books, 1933).

McDonough, R. "The empirical study of character," *Stud. Psychol. Psychiat.*

(1929), 2, n. 4.

McDougall, W. *An outline of psychology* (New York: Scribner's, 1923).
"Fundamentals of psychology," *Psyché,* (1924), 5, 13-32.
Body and mind, 6th ed. (London: Methuen, 1933).

Menninger, K. *Love against hate* (New York: Harcourt, Brace, 1942).

Mercier, D. "La liberté d'indifférence et le déterminisme psychologique," *Rev. néo-scol.* (1904), 11, 5-17.

Mercier, L. J. A. "Freedom of the will and psychology," *New Scholast.* (1944), 18, 252-261.

Messer, A. *Das Problem der Willensfreiheit,* 3 Vols. (Göttingen: Vandenhoek und Ruprecht, 1922).

Meumann, E. *Intelligenz und Wille: G. Störung* (Leipzig: Quelle und Meyer, 1925).

Miano, V. "Educazione e libertà," *Salesianum* (1952), 14, 317-327.

Michotte, A. "A propos de la 'méthode d'introspection' dans la psychologie expérimentale," *Rev. néo-scol.* (1907), 14, 507-532.
"Note complémentaire," *Arch. Psychol.* (1910), 10, 300-320.
"Note à propos des contributions récentes a la psychologie de la volonté," *Ann. Inst. Sup. Philos.* (1912), 1, 665-705.
La perception de la causalité, 2nd ed. (Louvain: Publ. Univ. Louvain, 1954).

Michotte, A., & Prüm, E. "Etude expérimentale sur le choix volontaire et ses antécédentes immediates," *Arch. Psychol.* (1910), 10, 119-299.

Miller, J. G. *Unconsciousness* (New York: Wiley, 1942).

Miller, N. E. "Experimental studies of conflict," in Hunt, J. McV. *Personality and the behavior disorders* (New York: Ronald Press, 1944), v. 1, pp. 431-465.

Miller, N. E. & Dollard, J. *Social learning and imitation* (New Haven: Yale Univ. Press, 1941).

Miro Quesada, O. *El problema de la libertad y la sciencia* (Lima: Miranda, 1945).

Misiak, H., & Staudt, V. M. *Catholics in psychology* (New York: McGraw-Hill, 1954).

Mitscherlich, A. *Freiheit und Unfreiheit in der Krankheit* (Hamburg: Claasen und Goverts Verlag, 1948).

Montpellier, G. de, "A propos de l'objet de la psychologie expérimentale," *Rev. néosc. Philos.,* (1935), 38, 324-328.
"Psychologie et dualisme," *Rev. néosc. Philos.* (1938), 41, 534-543.
"Qu'es-ce que le comportement?" *Rev. philos. Louvain* (1947), 45, 45-59.
Conduites intelligentes et psychisme chez l'animal et chez l'homme (Paris, J. Vrin, 1949).

Moore, T. V. *Cognitive psychology* (Chicago: Lippincott, 1939).
The driving forces of human nature and their adjustment (New York: Grune & Stratton, 1950).

Morand, J. S. *Hypnotisme et suggestion* (Paris: Garner, 1889).

Morgan, C. L. *An introduction to comparative psychology* (New York: Scribner's, 1901).

Morris, C. "The mechanism of freedom," in Anshen, R. H. *Freedom: Its meaning* (New York: Harcourt, Brace, 1940), pp. 579-589.

Morrison, H. C. *Basic principles in education* (Boston: Houghton Mifflin, 1934).

Mottier, G. *Déterminisme et liberté* (Neuchâtel: Baconnière, 1948).

Mounier, E. *Personalism,* trans. F. Mairet (New York: Grove Press, 1952).

Mowrer, O. H. *Learning theory and personality dynamics* (New York: Ronald Press, 1950).

(Ed.) *Psychotherapy:Theory and research* (New York: Ronald Press, 1953).

"Some philosophical implications in mental disorder and its treatment," *Harvard educ. Rev.* (1953), 23, 117-127.

"Motivation and neurosis," in *Current theory and research in motivation* (Lincoln, Neb.: Univ. Nebr. Press, 1953), pp. 162-185.

The crisis in psychiatry and religion (New York: Van Nostrand, 1961).

Muffelmann, L. *Das problem der Willensfreiheit in der neuesten deutschen Philosophie* (Leipzig: Barth, 1902).

Muencker, T. "Die psychologischen Grundlagen der katholischen Sittenlehre," in F. Tillman, *Handbuch der Katholischen Sittenlehre,* Band. II, 4 vols. (Dusseldorf: Patmos-Verlag, 1953).

Mullahy, P. "Will, choice, and ends," *Psychiatry* (1949), 12, 379-386.

Murchison, C. (Ed.) *Psychologies of 1930* (Worcester, Mass.: Clark Univ. Press, 1930).

Murphy, G. *Personality: A biosocial approach to origins and structure* (New York: Harper, 1947).

Historical introduction to modern psychology, rev. ed. (New York: Harcourt, Brace, 1949).

An introduction to psychology (New York: Harper, 1951).

Murray, H. A. *Explorations in personality* (New York: Oxford Univ. Press, 1938).

Musatti, C. L. "Libertà e servitu dello spirito," *Riv. Psicol.* (1947), 48, 29-42.

Trattato di psicoanalisi, 2 Vols. (Torino: Einaudi, 1949).

Nabert, J. *L'expérience intérieure de la liberté* (Paris: Alcan, 1928).

Neuer, A. "Courage and discouragement," *Int. J. Indiv. Psychol.* (1936), 2, 30-50.

Neufeld, I. "Psychological implication of the causality-finality scheme," *Ind. Psychol. Bull.* (1951), 9, 127-132.

Newcomb, T. M. "Motivation in social behavior," in *Current theory and research in motivation* (Lincoln, Nebr.: Univ. Nebr. Press, 1953).

Noel, L. "La conscience de l'acte libre et les objections de M. Fouillée," *Rev. néo-scol.* (1899), 6, 137-143.

La conscience du libre arbitre (Paris: Lathielleux, 1899).

Le déterminisme (Bruxelles: Hayez, 1906).

Nowell-Smith, P. "Freewill and moral responsibility," *Mind* (1948), 57, 45-61.

Nuttin, J. "Liberté et psychologie du comportement," in *Proceedings of the Tenth International Congress of Philosophy* (Amsterdam: North-Holland, 1949), pp. 915-917.

Psychoanalysis and personality, trans. G. Lamb (New York: Sheed & ward, 1953).

Tâche, réussite et échec: théorie de la conduite humaine (Louvain: Publ. Univ. Louvain, 1953).

O'Brien, P. V. *Emotions and morals* (New York: Grune & Stratton, 1950).

The measure of responsibility in persons influenced by emotions (Washington, D. C.: Cath. Univ. Press, 1948).

Odier, C. *Les deux sources, consciente et inconsciente, de la vie morale,* 2nd ed. (Neuchâtel: Baconnière, 1947).

Oppenheimer, O. "The nature of motivation," *J. soc. Psychol.* (1947), 26, 213-224.

Osequeda, R. "El problema de la libertad y personalidad en la temática bergsoniana," *Univ. San Carlos* (1948), n. 12-13, 7-80.

Pace, E. A. "The problem of freedom," *New Schol.* (1936), 10, 207-225.

Paulsen, P. "Die Rolle des Willens in der Reue," *Arch. relig. Psychol. Seelenführung* (1930), 5, 91-99.

Pavlov, I. P. *Conditioned reflexes* (London: Oxford Univ. Press, 1930).
"The reply of a physiologist to psychologists," *Psychol. Rev.* (1932), 39, 91-127.

Peak, H. "An evaluation of the concept of reflex and voluntary action," *Psychol. Rev.* (1933), 40, 71-89.
"Reflex and voluntary reactions of the eyelid," *J. gen. Psychol.* (1933), 8, 130-156.

Pende, N. *Scienza dell'ortogenesi* (Milano: Vallardi, 1939).
La scienza moderna della persona umana (Milano: Garzanti, 1947).

Penfield, W. "The cerebral cortex in man," *Arch. Neurol. Psychiat.* (1938), 40, 417-442.

Perez, O. B. "El determinativo funcional de la voluntad: El 'instinctus naturae' y el 'imperium rationis'," *Pensamiento* (1951), 7, 295-319.

Perrin, F. A. C. "The psychology of motivation," *Psychol. Rev.* (1923), 30, 176-191.

Piat, C. *La liberté. I. Historique du problème au XIXe siècle. II. Le problème* (Paris: Lethielleux, 1894-95).
"Ou en est la question du libre arbitre?" *Ann. Philos. chrét.* (1896), 34, 457-472.

Postman, L. "The experimental analysis of motivational factors in perception," in *Current theory and research in motivation* (Lincoln, Nebr.: Univ. Nebr. Press, 1953), pp. 59-108.

Pradines, M. *Traité de psychologie générale. III. Le genie humain: ses instruments,* 2nd ed. (Paris: Press. Univ. France, 1948).

Prautsch, K. *Beitrage zur experimentellen Untersuchung der Motivationsgesetze des Willensvorganges bei Normalen und Schwarchinnigen (debilen Hilfsschulkindern)* (Leipzig: Ballin und Topfer, 1931).

Priestley, J. *Hartley's theory of the human mind,* 2nd ed. (London: Johnson, 1790).

Prothro, E. T. "Cultural determinism: A challenge to action research," *J. soc. Psychol.* (1952), 35, 205-215.
Psychoanalyse et conscience morale (Centre d'Etudes Laennec) (Paris: Lethielleux, 1950).

Rabl, C. R. H. *Das Problem der Willensfreiheit unter medizenischen und naturwissenchaftlichen Gesichtspunkten* (Munich: Oldenbourg, 1933).

Raimy, V. C. "Self-reference in counseling interviews," *J. consult. Psychol.* (1949), 12, 153-163.

Rank, O. *Will therapy,* and *Truth and reality,* trans. Taft (New York: Knopf, 1945).

Reich, W. *Character analysis* (New York: Orgone Institute Press, 1945).

Reiner, H. *Freiheit, Wollen und Aktivitat* (Halle: Niemeyer, 1927).
"Die Freiheit des menschlichen Wollens," *Philos Leben* (1931), 7, 243-

251; 303-311.

Reisman, D. "Authority and liberty in the structure of Freud's thought," *Psychiatry* (1950), 13, 167-187.

Reutt, J. *Badania psychologiczne nad wahaniem* (Poznam: Poznanskie Towarzystwo Przyjaciól Nauk, 1949). Cfr. *Année psychol.* (1949), 51, 486-489.

Reymert, M. L. (Ed.) *Feelings and emotions: Wittemberg symposium* (New York: McGraw-Hill, 1928).
Feelings and emotions: Mooseheart symposium (New York: McGraw-Hill, 1950).

Ribot, E. *The disease of the will*, trans. J. Fitzgerald (New York: Humboldt, 1884).
The diseases of personality, trans. J. Fitzgerald (New York: Humboldt, 1887).

Richards, T. W. *Modern clinical psychology* (New York: McGraw-Hill, 1946).

Richardson, C. A. "The measurement of conative factors in children and their influence," *Brit. J. Psychol.* (1928-29), 19, 405-412.

Rickaby, I. *Free-will and four English philosophers: Hobbes, Locke, Hume, and Mill* (London: Burns & Oates, 1906).

Ricoeur, P. *Philosophie de la volonté: Le volontaire et l'involuntaire* (Paris: Aubier, 1950).

Rimaud, J. "Les psychologues contre la morale," *Etudes* (1949), 263, 3-22.
"Psychologists versus morality," *Cross Currents* (1951), 2, 26-38.

Robinson, G. C. *The patient as person* (New York: Commonwealth Fund, 1946).

Rogers, C. R. *Counseling and psychotherapy* (Boston: Houghton Mifflin, 1942).
"Significant aspects of client-centered therapy," *Amer. Psychologist* (1946), 1, 415-422.
"Some observations on the organization of personality," *Amer. Psychologist* (1947), 2, 358-368.
"Some implications of client-centered counseling for college personnel work," *Educ. psychol. Meas.* (1948), 8, 540-549.
Dealing with social tensions (New York: Hinds, Hayden & Eldrodge, 1948).
Client-centered therapy (Boston: Houghton Mifflin, 1951).
"Perceptual reorganization in client-centered therapy," in Blake, R. R., & Ramsey, G. V. *Perception: An approach to personality* (New York: Ronald Press, 1951), pp. 307-327.
On becoming a person (Boston: Houghton, Mifflin, 1961).

Rohracher, H. *Theories des Willens auf experimenteller Grundlage* (Leipzig: Barth, 1938).

Rosanoff, A. J. *Manual of psychiatry and mental hygiene*, 7th ed. (New York: Wiley, 1938).

Roters, W. "Psychologisches zum Bewusstsein der Willensfreiheit," *Arch ges. Psychol.* (1932), 86, 191-211.

Rotthaus, E. "Über die Freiheit und Unfreiheit des menschlichen Willens," *Jb. Psychol. Psychother.* (1954), 2, 169-174.

Rousset, S. "Justice objective et justice subjective," in *Limites de l'humain* (Paris: Desclée de Brouwer, 1953), pp. 201-211.

Royer, A. E. *An analysis of counseling procedures in a non-directive approach*, M. A. thesis (Columbus: Ohio State Univ., 1942).

Russel, B. *Our knowledge of the external world* (New York: Norton, 1929). *An inquiry into meaning and truth* (New York: Norton, 1940).

Russell, H. N. *Fate and freedom* (New Haven: Yale Univ. Press, 1927).

Rowland, L. W. "Will hypnotized persons try to harm themselves or others?" *J. abnorm. soc. Psychol.* (1939), 34, 114-117.

Saleilles, L. *L'individualization de la peine* (Paris: Alcan, 1898).

Salter, A. *Conditioned reflex therapy* (New York: Creative Age Press, 1949).

Salzi, P. "Liberté psychologique et vie collective," *Psyché* (1947), 2, 1414-1422.

Sassen, G. von, "Causality versus iendeterminism," *Indiv. Psychol. Bull.* 1951), 9, 122-126.

Satow, L. *Hypnotism and suggestion,* trans. B. Miall (New York: Dodd-Mead, 1923).

Sheldon, W. H. *The varieties of temperament* (New York: Harper, 1942).

Schilder, P., & Kauder, O. "Hypnosis," *Nerv. ment. Dis. Monogr. Ser.* (1927), n. 46.

Schiller, F. "Consciousness reconsidered," *Arch. Neur. Psychiat.* (1952), 67, 199-227.

Schlosberg, H. "A study of the conditioned patellar reflext," *J.exper. Psychol.* (1928), 11, 468-494.

Schneider, L. "Some psychiatric views on 'freedom' and the theory of social system," *Psychiatry* (1949), 12, 251-264.

Schneck, J. M. "A military offense induced by hypnosis," *J. nerv. ment. Dis.* (1947), 106, 186-189.

Schroeder, H. H. *The psychology of conduct* (Chicago: Row, Peterson, 1911).

Schuetz, A. "Choosing among projects of action," *Philos. phenom. Res.* (1951), 12, 161-172.

Schuster, M. H. *The philosophy of law and freedom* (Boston: Christopher Publishing House, 1948).

Secrétan, C. "Evolution en liberté," *Rev. philos.* août (1885). *La civilisation et la croyance* (Paris: Alcan, 1887).

Seguin, C. A. *Introduction to psychosomatic medicine* (New York: Inter. Univ. Press, 1950).

Sherif, M., & Cantril, H. *The psychology of ego-involvements* (New York: Wiley, 1947).

Simon, Y. R. "On the foreseeability of free acts," *(New Schol.* (1948), 22, 357-370.

Simonart, P. C. "The imputability of the mental patient," *Linacre Quarterly,* October (1947), 8-15.

Simoenit, M. "Die mit Bewusstsein der Freiheit erfolgende Einstellung und Beeinflussung des Bewusstseins als Kern des Willenserlebnisses: Seine phönomenalen Merkmade," *Arch ges. Psychol.* (1937), 98, 286-296.

Skawran, P. "Experimentelle Untersuchungen über den Willen bei Wahlhandlungen," *Arch. ges Psychol.* (1927), 58, 95-162.

Skinner, B. F. "The concept of the reflex in the description of behavior," *J. gen. Psychol.* (1931), 5, 427-458. *The behavior of organisms* (New York: Appleton-Century, 1938).

Science and human behavior (New York: Macmillan, 1953).

Smith, G. "Intelligence and liberty," *New Schol.* (1941), 15, 1-17.

Snoeck, A. "Moral reflections on psychiatric abreaction," *Theol. Studies* (1952), 13, 173-189.

Spearman, C. E. *The abilities of man* (London: Macmillan, 1927).

"A new method for investigating the springs of action," in Reymert, M. L. *Feelings and emotions: Wittenberg symposium* (New York: McGraw-Hill, 1928), pp. 39-48.

" 'G' and after: A school to end schools," in Murchison, C. *Psychologies of 1930* (Worcester, Mass.: Clark Univ. Press, 1930).

Steinbüchel, T. "Die philosophische Grundlegung der katholischen Sittenlehre," in Tillman, F. *Handbuch der katholischen Sittenlehre,* Band I (Düsseldorf: L. Schwann, 1938).

Stellar, E. "The physiology of motivation," *Psychol. Rev.* (1954), 61, 5-22.

Stengel, L., & Rutkowski, D. "Die Frage der Willensfreiheit vom standpunkt der Kulturbiologie," *Biologie* (1940), 9, 213-221.

Stern, K. "Religion and psychiatry," *Commonweal* (1948), 49, 30-33.

Stern, W. *Kritische Grundlegung der Ethik als positive Wissenshaft* (Berlin: Dümmler, 1897).

Meine Auffassung der Willensfreiheit (Paris: Alcan, 1901).

General psychology from the personalistic standpoint, trans. D. Spoerl (New York: Macmillan, 1938).

Stewart, B. "Some determinants of social change," *J. soc. Psychol.* (1951), 33, 33-49.

Störring, G. *Methoden der Psychologie des höheren Gefühlslebens* (Berlin-Wien: Urban und Schwarzenberg, 1938).

Stout, G. F. "Voluntary action," *Mind* (1886), 5, 354-366.

Mind and matter (New York: Macmillan, 1931).

A manual of psychology, 4th ed. (London: Univ. Tutorial Series, 1932).

Sully, J. *The human mind: A textbook of psychology,* 2 Vols. (New York: Appleton, 1892).

Taube, M. *Causation, freedom and determinism* (London: Allen and Unwin, 1946).

Taylor, F. S. *Concerning science* (London: Macdonald, 1949).

Tegen, E. *Moderne Willenstheorien,* 2 Vols. (Uppsala: Ludequist, 1924-28).

Tesson, E. "Description de la conscience morale et incidences psychiatriques," in *Psychanalyse et conscience morale* (Paris: Lethielleux, 1950), pp. 6-31.

Thorndike, E. L. "A pragmatic substitute for free will," in *Essays philosophical and psychological in honor of William James,* New York: Longmans, Green, 1908), pp. 587-610.

Human learning (New York: Appleton-Century, 1931).

An experimental study of rewards (New York: Columbia Univ. Press, 1933).

The psychology of wants, interests and attitudes (New York: Appleton-Century, 1935).

Human nature and the social order (New York: Macmillan, 1940).

Man and his works (The William James Lectures, 1942-1943) (Cambridge, Mass.: Harvard Univ. Press, 1943).

Thorne, F. C. "The psychology of control," *J. clin. Psychol.* (1949), 5, 374-386.

Principles of personality counseling (Brandon, Vermont: J. clin. Psychol., 1950).

Thorpe, L. P. *Psychological foundations of personality,* 2nd ed. (New York: McGraw-Hill, 1938).

Tillmann, F. (Ed.) *Handbuch der katholischen Sittenlehre,* 1-5 Band (Düsseldorf: Druck und Verlag L. Schwann, 1934-53).

Titchener, E. B. *An outline of psychology* (New York: Macmillan, 1923).
A textbook of psychology (New York: Macmillan, 1924).
A primer of psychology, rev. ed. (New York: Macmillan, 1925).

Troland, L. T. *The principles of psychophysiology: A survey of modern scientific psychology. III. Cerebration and action* (New York: Van Nostrand, 1932).

Troude, R. "Aspects sociologiques de la théorie de la culpabilité," in *Le coupable est-il un malade ou un pécheur* (coll. "Convergences") (Paris: Spes, 1951), pp. 43-62.

Trouet, S. "Der Willensakt bei Wahlhandlungen: Eine experimentelle Untersuchung," *Arch. ges. Psychol.* (1923), 45, 157-202.

Vander Veldt, J., & Odenwald, R. P. *Psychiatry and catholicism,* 2nd ed. (New York: McGraw-Hill, 1957).

Varon, E. J. "The development of Alfred Binet's psychology," *Psychol. Monogr.* (1935), n. 207, 1-129.

Virieux, R. A. "La philosophie de la liberté de Charles Secrétan et le portique," in *La liberté* (Neuchâtel: Baconnière, 1949), pp. 408-411.

Wahl, J. "Freedom and existence in some recent philosophies," *Philos. phenom. Res.* (1947-48), 8, 538-556.
"Le problème du choix, l'existence et la transcendence dans la philosophie de Jaspers," in *Etudes Kierkegaardiennes,* 2nd ed. (Paris: J. Vrin, 1949).

Walsh, J. J. *Psychotherapy,* rev. ed. (New York: Appleton, 1923).

Walz, H. H. "Man's freedom in existentialism and in christianity," *Cross Currents* (1951), 5, 56-67.

Ward, J. *Psychological principles,* 2nd ed. (Cambridge: Cambridge Univ. Press, 1920).

Watkins, J. G. "Anti-social compulsions induced under hypnotic trance," *J. abnorm. soc. Psychol.* (1947), 42, 256-259.

Watson, J. B. *Behaviorism,* rev. ed. (New York: Norton, 1930).

Webb, E. "Character and intelligence," *Brit. Psychol. Monogr. Suppl.* (1915), 1, 1-83.

Weiss, P. *Man's freedom* (New Haven: Yale Univ. Press, 1950).

Wells, H. M. "The phenomenology of acts of choice," *Brit. Psychol. Monogr. Suppl.* (1927), 11, 1-155.

Wells, W. R. "Experiments in the hypnotic production of crimes," *J. Psychol.* (1941), 11, 63-102.

Weitzenhoffer, A. M. "A note on the persistence of hypnotic suggestion," *J. abnorm. soc. Psychol.* (1950), 45, 160-162.
Hypnotism: An objective study in suggestibility (New York: Wiley, 1953).
"The production of anti-social acts under hypnosis," *J. abnorm. soc. Psychol.* (1949), 44, 388-397.

Wheeler, R. H. "An experimental investigation of the process of choosing," *Univ. Oregon Publ.* (1920), 1, n. 2.

White, L. A. *The Science of culture* (New York: Farrar, Straus, 1949).

"Man's control over civilization," *Sci. Mo.* (1948), 66, n. 3.

Whitnet, W. R. "Accomplishments and future of the physical sciences," *Science* (1936), 84, 211-272.

Whittaker, E. T. "Chance, freewill, and necessity in scientific conceptions of the universe," *Proc. Phys. Soc. London* (1943), 55, 459-491.

Williams, G. "Freedom of choice in the pre-determined future," *Philos. phenom. Res.* (1951), 12, 130-134.

Wilson, R. "The new physics: Does it vindicate free will?" *New Schol.* (1937), 11, 332-349.

Wolff, A. B. "On the content of welfare," *Amer. econ. Rev.* (1931), 21,

Wolff, W. *What is psychology?* (New York: Grune & Stratton, 1947). 207-221.

Values and personality (New York: Grune & Stratton, 1950).

Woodworth, R. S. *Contemporary schools of psychology,* rev. ed. (New York: Ronald Press, 1948).

Writing, H. F., & English, H. B. "Fatigue test and incentives,"*J. exper. Psychol.* (1925), 8, 33-49.

Wundt, W. *Outlines of psychology,* trans. C. H. Judd, 2nd rev. ed. (Leipzig, 1902).

Wyatt, H. G. *The psychology of intelligence and will* (London: Kegan Paul, 1930).

Young, P. T. *Motivation of behavior* (New York: Wiley, 1948).

"Food-seeking drive, affective process, and learning," *Psychol. Rev.* (1949), 56, 98-121.

Zavalloni, R. "Novi aspectus phaenomenologiae perceptionis," *Antonianum* (1954), 29, 63-88.

"The process of choice in therapeutic counseling," *Antonianum* (1954), 29, 157-208; 269-324.

"Il processo della scelta volontaria in casi di 'psicoterapia centrata-sul-cliente'," *Arch. Psicol. Neurol Psichiat.* (1954), 15, 99-126.

"Studying human conduct and personality," *Antonianum* (1955), 45-62.

Educazione e personalità (Milano: Vita e Pensiero, 1955).

Zilboorg, G. *Mind, medicine, and man* (New York: Harcourt, Brace, 1955).

Sigmund Freud: His exploration of the mind of man (New York: Scribner's, 1951).

Index